Music and Politics

This book is not about music or politics. It is about the 'and' that binds them together. How do these fields intersect, and what theories and approaches can help us understand their interactions? How have the relationships between music and politics changed over time and across cultures, and are the familiar tools we use in dealing with them fit for purpose? This book overhauls our understanding of how these fields interact, offering a rigorous reappraisal of key concepts such as power, protest, resistance, subversion, propaganda and ideology. It explores and evaluates a wide range of perspectives from contemporary political theory, engaging with an array of musical cultures and practices from medieval chant to rap. In addition, it discusses current ways in which the relationships between music and politics are being reconfigured and reconceptualized. Where else can you find Donald Trump, Kendrick Lamar and Beethoven under one cover?

JAMES GARRATT is Senior Lecturer in Music at the University of Manchester. His publications include *Music, Culture and Social Reform in the Age of Wagner* (Cambridge, 2010) and *Palestrina and the German Romantic Imagination: Interpreting Historicism in Nineteenth-Century Music* (Cambridge, 2002).

Music and Politics

A Critical Introduction

JAMES GARRATT

University of Manchester

CAMBRIDGE
UNIVERSITY PRESS

CAMBRIDGE
UNIVERSITY PRESS

University Printing House, Cambridge CB2 8BS, United Kingdom

One Liberty Plaza, 20th Floor, New York, NY 10006, USA

477 Williamstown Road, Port Melbourne, VIC 3207, Australia

314–321, 3rd Floor, Plot 3, Splendor Forum, Jasola District Centre, New Delhi – 110025, India

79 Anson Road, #06–04/06, Singapore 079906

Cambridge University Press is part of the University of Cambridge.

It furthers the University's mission by disseminating knowledge in the pursuit of education, learning, and research at the highest international levels of excellence.

www.cambridge.org
Information on this title: www.cambridge.org/9781107032415
DOI: 10.1017/9781139505963

© James Garratt 2019

First published 2019

Printed and bound in Great Britain by Clays Ltd, Elcograf S.p.A.

A catalogue record for this publication is available from the British Library.

Library of Congress Cataloging-in-Publication Data
Names: Garratt, James, 1974- author.
Title: Music and politics : a critical introduction / James Garratt.
Description: Cambridge, United Kingdom ; New York, NY :
   Cambridge University Press, 2019. | Includes bibliographical references and index.
Identifiers: LCCN 2018029280 | ISBN 9781107032415 (hardback : alk. paper) |
   ISBN 9781107681088 (pbk. : alk. paper)
Subjects: LCSH: Music–Political aspects.
Classification: LCC ML3916 .G366 2019 | DDC 780/.032–dc23
   LC record available at https://lccn.loc.gov/2018029280

ISBN 978-1-107-03241-5 Hardback
ISBN 978-1-107-68108-8 Paperback

For Lucy, Lydia and Emiliana

Contents

Figures

Boxes

Preface

This book is not about music or politics. It is about the 'and' that binds them together, in ways that include yet go beyond the concept of political music. How do these fields intersect and exercise effects on each other? What theories and approaches can help us understand these multiple interactions and the functions they serve? How have these interactions and functions changed over time and across cultures, and are the familiar conceptual tools we use in dealing with them fit for purpose? And in an era often characterized as post-political – or at least one in which confidence in progress and the future has leached away – how are the relationships between music and politics being reconfigured and reconceptualized?

It may seem unnecessary to pose these questions, given the extensive literature that already exists on music and politics. But much research approaches the intersection of these fields narrowly, focusing on either a restricted sphere of music or a limited dimension of politics. Most studies address just one aspect of the political – be it power, protest, resistance or identity – while those that offer a more comprehensive approach tend to focus on just one musical culture, genre or repertory. This is hardly surprising, given that some of the most influential theorists of the present (such as Jacques Rancière) define politics in wilfully narrow terms, and given the still dominant historicist, culturally bound model of knowledge animating music studies. This is not the place to trot out clichés about blind men and elephants, but there is a real need to survey the area from a macro level and to remap it in the light of current theory and practice.

In exploring the 'and' of music and politics, I have three aims. The first is to understand the processes shaping how these two fields intersect. How do they act on each other as causal powers? How can music acquire political agency, and what are its capacities and limitations as a political force? Is it right to conceptualize music and politics as two distinct spheres, and under what conditions can music function politically simply by doing what it does as music? My second aim is to reappraise the concepts that are most often used to stitch together music and politics: protest, resistance, propaganda, subversion, ideology and so on. Are these conceptual tools – most of which had their heyday in the fascist period or the Cold War – still useful, or do they constrict our field of vision and chain us to the politics of yesteryear? Is our continued recourse to them motivated by nostalgia for a time when change seemed possible and when music seemed to have a more meaningful role? The third aim is to explore the interactions between music and politics in a different sense, bringing together insights and approaches from the wide range of disciplines that engage with the interface between these fields. At a time when relationships between the various disciplines within music studies can be fractious, it is worth stressing that neither historical musicology, nor popular music studies nor ethnomusicology has all the answers (or even poses all the questions). A significant amount of the most interesting current work on music and politics stems from outside music studies entirely, whether from the disciplines of cultural studies, sociology, political science, political theory, anthropology, psychology, behavioural science, history, language and area studies, geography and so on. I have fed voraciously on the insights they have to offer, and I hope that this book will be of use to researchers and students working in these fields and help to increase interdisciplinary dialogue.

Methodologically, this book offers a combination of theoretical discussion, conceptual analysis and empirical engagement with cultures, texts and practices that exemplify (or problematize) the broader issues. Given that its whole thrust resists any single strategy for explaining how music and politics interrelate, I have avoided leaning too heavily on any particular theorist or body of discourse (in some ways it would have been easier to write a Marxist introduction to music and politics, or one oriented around Adorno, Foucault or Rancière, but such an approach would have provided too limited a set of resources for dealing with the multiple musico-political interactions we will encounter). My original plan was to have a series of historically oriented chapters, mapping particular political concepts onto the periods of Western music history in which they reached their high point (so propaganda would have been examined through the lens of the Third Reich, while the protest chapter would have focused entirely on the 1960s, and so on). The concepts and material, however, fought against being constrained by such a narrowly historical approach. One reason for this is that political concepts – most notably freedom, democracy, community and equality – are transhistorical in thrust, striving beyond the conditions of a particular present while also looking sideways and backward (it is their future-oriented quality that gives them the effect of universality). Another is that exemplary intersections between music and politics, by their nature, exercise effects that go beyond their original contexts; protest music of the 1960s continues to shape perceptions of such music today, just as the music of the French Revolution provided a model for revolutionary music throughout the nineteenth century. Accordingly, each chapter examines not only key historical moments colouring particular musico-political concepts but also the present state of play, scrutinizing current developments in theory and practice.

Writing about music and politics can sometimes feel like a no-win game, given that every reader is likely to be irked by both inclusions and omissions. Although I have cast my net pretty wide, the majority of examples and case studies are drawn from Western music or from cultures whose music and politics have been informed by Western practices. I have had to be selective in the genres, composers and theorists examined (which regrettably meant omitting any discussion of jazz and leaving out seemingly indispensable figures such as Hans Werner Henze and Jean-Luc Nancy). The exponential expansion of the political field since the 1970s has also necessitated omissions; while social movements are explored in Chapter 6 and identity in Chapter 7, it has been possible to explore only a small fraction of contemporary forms of movement activism and identity politics. More mundanely, I made the choice at an early stage to omit examples from scores as well as links to online recordings, although almost all the music discussed is available on YouTube. Moving from sins of omission to those of commission, it is a fair bet that no one has picked up this book out of an interest in my political views, and I have tried to bear that in mind when writing. Complete neutrality is impossible, however, given the entirely different ways in which those on the left and right understand key terms such as neoliberalism.

Originally, I had intended not to include any acknowledgements in this book (reader, they count toward the word limit!). But it would be churlish not to show my gratitude to Victoria Cooper, who instigated this project, her successor Katharina Brett and all the other staff at Cambridge University Press (including Eilidh Burrett, Fleur Jones and Sophie Taylor) who nudged me along and showed much kindness and patience along the way. I am grateful to Lisa Sinclair, Saritha Srinivasan and Stephanie Sakson for ably and amiably steering the book through the production process. I would also like to thank Simone Schulz and the Bildarchiv Foto Marburg for permission to reproduce Heinrich Olivier's *Die heilige Allianz*; Sperans of the band Laibach for permission to use the photo 'Einkauf'; and Nick Stewart for kindly allowing me to use his photo as the cover illustration.

I remember here Mark Fisher and Kenneth Gloag, both of whom died –
far too young – while I was completing the book. I often thought of them
while writing, and very much doubt that I would have undertaken it
without their inspiration.

Although this is my shortest book to date, my wife Sinéad and
I managed to have three lovely daughters over the course of its gestation.
So it is dedicated to Lucy, Lydia and Emiliana, on the understanding that
they don't delay the next book by so long.

1 | Music and Politics

Key Concepts and Issues

Utøya, Norway, 22 July 2011. Anders Behring Breivik, self-styled commander of the Knights Templar Europe, yells 'You're going to die today, Marxists' as he shoots down teenagers at a summer camp organized by the youth wing of the Norwegian Labour Party.[1] Earlier that day he had car-bombed government buildings in Oslo. Justifying his killing of seventy-seven people to the police who apprehended him, Breivik claimed to be defending Norway and Europe from multiculturalism, Marxism and Islamicization, describing his attacks as 'an expression of love for my own people and country'.[2] In a manifesto released to coincide with the atrocities, Breivik explains the crucial role that music played in developing and reinforcing his extreme right-wing militancy. As well as listing songs which inspired him, he emphasizes the importance of music as an aid to self-indoctrination and motivational control.[3] Dedicating a section of the manifesto to the theme 'How to Sustain Your High Morale and Motivation for Years through Music', Breivik describes how the 'ritual' of listening to his iPod during extended solitary walks helped to nourish his beliefs and morale.[4] In addition, he explains the functions which music would serve during the different phases of his planned terrorist operation, specifying the tracks suitable for accompanying combat situations and even his anticipated martyrdom. Perhaps surprisingly, there's no mention of skinhead bands, Black Metal or for that matter Wagner; instead, Breivik cites film and computer game soundtracks which have little or no clear connection to his ideology. Recommending a track from *Lord of the Rings* as 'very inspiring' and capable of generating 'a type of passionate rage within you', Breivik notes that during the attack, 'I will put my iPod on max volume as a tool to suppress fear if needed. I might just put *Lux Aeterna* by Clint Mansell on repeat as it is an incredibly powerful song.'[5] While it is not clear whether Brevik stuck to his planned use of music, he had an iPod bud in his ear when police finally cornered him.

Kiev, Ukraine, 7 December 2013. Student Markiyan Matsekh and a handful of other demonstrators smuggle a piano into downtown Kiev, setting it down next to a phalanx of riot police protecting the office of the Ukrainian president. Matsekh then plays a musical selection including

Figure 1.1 'The Piano Player', Euromaidan uprising in Kiev, 2013,
photograph by Oleh Matsekh, Markiyan Matsekh and Andrew Meakovski.

Frédéric Chopin's Waltz in C-Sharp Minor, Op. 64 No. 2, Ukrainian folk
tunes and the Queen song 'We Are the Champions'; some of the riot
officers sing along and move their heads in time to the music.[6] Within
forty-eight hours, a photograph of the event goes viral on social media,
inspiring T-shirts and numerous copycat protests (see Figure 1.1). Painted
in the blue and yellow of the Ukrainian flag, and sporting the twelve-star
emblem of the European Union, Matsekh's piano gestured defiantly at
President Viktor Yanukovych's decision to ally with Russia and halt
Ukrainian integration within the EU. But this protest had a more immediate stimulus, countering the government's brutal suppression of earlier
demonstrations and the stigmatization of protesters as extremists. For
Matsekh, the 'innocence of the piano' served to convey the peaceful spirit
of the opposition movement and to defuse tensions between protesters and
police: 'I painted and rolled the piano in front of the riot police to
demonstrate the spirit of the revolution ... that we are actually trying to
change the situation in a peaceful way.'[7] If Matsekh's aims seem straightforward, his protest was represented in quite different ways by the media.
Some commentators treated it as a piece of performance art, while others

ignored the sonic and performative dimensions of the event, focusing solely on the photograph it generated.[8] Indeed, the power of the image led to the protest being forced into default media narratives and misread. One tendency was to view it through a universalizing lens as a clash between freedom and repression; another was to depoliticize the protest by reading it as a plea for peace or by drawing on clichéd notions of music as a healing, unifying force.

Altiplano Prison, Mexico, 11 July 2015. At around 8:55 pm, billionaire drug lord Joaquín Guzmán, aka 'El Chapo' ('Shorty'), escapes from a maximum security jail through a specially constructed mile-long tunnel. Within hours of his escape, dozens of newly written narcocorridos, or drug ballads, celebrating his feat have begun to circulate on the internet.[9] In spite of Guzmán's extreme wealth and power, these narcocorridos stress his humble origins and treat him as a Robin Hood figure: a larger-than-life outlaw who had beaten the federales and foiled the attempts of the United States to extradite him. In a few nonchalant sentences, for example, Lupillo Rivera, one of the best-known exponents of the genre, highlighted Guzmán's ingenuity and bravado, the power of his cartel, the impotence of Mexico's politicians and the eagerness with which his people await his return.[10] On one level, the elevation of a drug trafficker as a bandit-hero reflects the traditions of the corrido genre, celebrating the wily underdog at the expense of the authorities.[11] But on another, it points to the role music has played in helping to entrench the cartels within Mexico's poorest regions. The portrayal of Guzmán as a folk hero in these jailbreak ballads evokes a world in which people have come to accept the power wielded by the cartels. A similar tone of acquiescence was projected a few months earlier in a carefully stage-managed protest march following his arrest, with banners reading 'El Chapo is the defender and protector of the community' and 'We love Chapo and respect him more than any law'.[12] Just as these protesters were paid for by Guzmán's cartel, the singers and bands who honour cartel chiefs through narcocorridos are often commissioned by the traffickers themselves. While these ballads may seem to offer little more than macho bluster, they contribute significantly to what the theorist John P. Sullivan describes as social environment modification; by disseminating and normalizing the values of the cartels, they help to weaken still further state authority and the rule of law.[13]

Moscow, Russia, 21 February 2012. Five members of the punk band Pussy Riot, dressed in brightly coloured clothes and balaclavas, burst into the sanctuary of Christ the Saviour Cathedral and perform their song 'Punk Prayer – Mother of God, Chase Putin Away!' in front of outraged worshippers. Later that day a video of the performance is released on YouTube, triggering the detention, trial and conviction of three of the band for 'hooliganism motivated by religious hatred'.[14] Their arrest and lengthy prison sentences generate widespread condemnation in the West, with celebrities such as Madonna, Elton John and Paul McCartney lining up to support their fellow musicians in the name of freedom of expression.[15] But as the media clamoured to denounce Putin's Russia, little attention was given to the group's aims or ideas, while key details of the protest were distorted or passed over. As with Matsekh's piano protest, the media squeezed Pussy Riot into a narrative of individual freedom versus state oppression, presenting the band as wide-eyed liberals taking on an evil despot.[16] But the members of the band were in no sense naive young rockers who stumbled into trouble with the authorities as a result of their Westernized values. Although feted by mainstream media (the London *Times* gave Pussy Riot the accolade International People of the Year), the group aligned itself with radical anti-capitalist and anarchist standpoints.[17] And rather than being a punk band, or having any connection to the Russian punk scene, Pussy Riot was an activist collective for whom music was just one vehicle for political promotion. Even the grainily authentic YouTube video of the live performance in the cathedral is not quite what it first seemed. The group managed to record only around twelve seconds of the song in the cathedral (the refrain 'Shit, shit, holy shit') before being ejected by security guards, and the video versions splice this footage together with a performance in a different venue; far from documenting a live protest event, the video itself was the protest.[18]

These case studies illustrate just a few of the ways in which the spheres of music and politics intersect in our contemporary world. To speak of spheres may suggest that, as in a Venn diagram, music and politics are separate fields with a thin, clearly defined area of overlap – 'political music' – shared between them. A couple of the examples discussed above could be made to fit into this rigid conception of political music and shoe-horned into its familiar categories, such as protest music (Pussy Riot's 'Punk Prayer') and propaganda (Guzmán's narcocorridos). Yet in general the two fields interact more complexly and fluidly than the Venn diagram suggests, and the concept of political music in the conventional sense does not adequately account for their interactions. Breivik's 'passionate rage' was sustained not by music which mirrored his far-right politics but by seemingly innocuous soundtracks; similarly, Matsekh serenaded riot police with a Chopin waltz rather than songs with a clear political message. As these cases attest, the potential for musical texts and materials to function politically goes well beyond the confines of our conventional notion of political music. The reverse is true too, since if music can temporarily acquire politicality, politics can temporarily acquire musicality: how else can we conceptualize Pussy Riot's twelve-second engagement with punk rock?

The 'and' conjoining music and politics is thus not a fixed boundary or a narrow funnel linking two separate entities. Equally, though, it is not helpful to read the 'and' as a sign of identity (even if it is possible for some forms of music to seem to be political in an unmediated way). While music and politics intermingle across each other's terrain, we need to resist the urge to treat them from the start as one densely entangled whole. To move toward understanding how they interrelate, it makes sense to turn to the most prominent theorist of the 'and', Gilles Deleuze: 'AND is neither one thing nor the other, it's always in-between, between two things; it's the borderline, there's always a border, a line of flight or flow ... And yet it's along this line of flight that things come to pass, becomings evolve, revolutions take shape.'[19] Here, the 'and' – the myriad kinds of interaction linking the one and the other – is a transformative force of becoming, continually triggering change within the fields it conjoins. Rather than being stable objects, the fields of 'music' and 'politics' are mutating and expanding constantly as a result of their evolving exchanges. And rather than being locked into fixed modes of interaction, music and politics can come together in contingent, temporary alliances.[20] As well as seeking to understand the multiple forms of mediation linking these fields, we need to recognize how new technologies and media have redefined the ways in which they interact (making it possible for a lone extremist to radicalize himself through his iPod and for narcocorridos to be disseminated within minutes of the event that inspired them).

This chapter provides a preliminary map of the ways in which the fields of music and politics relate to one another, introducing and analyzing some of the key concepts and issues that can help us understand how they interact. But before going any further, we need to pin down what we mean by 'politics', not to impose a particular view or eliminate areas from discussion, but rather to make sure that we do justice to all sides of the concept.

1.1   Politics and the Political

Definitions of politics – what it encompasses and what is excluded from it – invariably reflect the context and political standpoint of the definer. Indeed, as the philosopher Slavoj Žižek notes, 'every neutralization of some partial content as "non-political" is a political gesture *par excellence*'.[21] From the perspective of contemporary Western liberal democracy (see Box 1.1), politics may seem to comprise a narrow sphere of human activity: the management of public affairs through states, governments and political parties. From this standpoint, as the political scientist Andrew Heywood puts it, 'politics is what takes place within a polity, a system of social organization centred on the machinery of government'.[22] Since this perspective treats most institutions and practices within a state as non-political, it tends to define politics negatively through what is perceived to fall outside its purview (this approach is at work in phrases such as 'governments shouldn't meddle with the economy', 'the state shouldn't interfere with healthcare', 'politics and religion don't mix' and so on). From this standpoint, the relationship between politics and music might seem no less narrow, revolving around national anthems, the use of music on state occasions, party campaign music, but not much else.

A wider view of politics, however, is suggested by the original derivation of the word from the ancient Greek *politeia*, which encompasses not only the organization and running of the state (*polis*) but public civic life in general. Thus for Aristotle, writing in the fourth century BCE, the collective pursuit of self-perfection and the good life is what defines the political and makes the human being a political animal.[23] This broader conception of politics nonetheless marks out some spheres of human activity as non-political: Aristotle famously differentiated between the ethical and political life (*bios*) of man and natural or bare life (*zoē*), excluding the latter from the *polis* and confining it to the domestic sphere.[24] Some kind of distinction between the public and private domains has been present within political theory ever since, marking out the institutions of the state (the government, the police and justice system and so on) from private, non-political areas of life. Just where the boundary between them is drawn is a fundamental marker of different political systems; a communist, for instance, would place the economy firmly in the public realm, while for a liberal it lies predominantly in the private sphere. Contemporary political scientists tend to insert a third term, civil society, into the public-private equation, using this to accommodate institutions and activities which are not part of the state apparatus yet are public in the broader sense.[25] While civil society includes the spheres of religion and education, it also draws in political institutions that are not part of the state, such as trade unions and social change organizations. From this perspective, the sphere of politics – and therefore also political music – naturally extends beyond government and party politics, encompassing social movements and public forms of artistic activism.

Box 1.1 Liberalism, Liberal Democracy, Neoliberalism

The word **liberal** is often used today, particularly in the United States, as a collective term for left-wing progressive and radical ideas. For much of its history, however, **liberalism** has occupied the centre ground within Western democratic politics: on one level, through centrist parties such as the UK Liberal Party (1859–1988), the Liberal Party of Canada (1861–), and the Liberal Party of Australia (1945–), and on another, through the extent to which the core principles and language of liberalism have become common denominators defining mainstream political discourse. This is reflected in the use of the term **liberal democracy** to characterize a form of government in which individual rights and freedoms, safeguarded by the rule of law, are upheld by a freely elected parliament of representatives.

While liberalism has varied substantially since its emergence in the mid-eighteenth century, it has consistently approached politics from an individualist perspective, elevating the liberty, autonomy and rights of the individual over the claims of society. **Classical liberalism** of the eighteenth and nineteenth centuries assigned a limited role to the state, conceiving its task as being to safeguard individual rights (religious liberty, freedom of speech, freedom of association) and to protect life and property. This minimalist conception of the state also characterizes the **economic liberalism** of the period, which conceived the capitalist system as a natural order that should be left to follow its own devices (**laissez-faire**) unimpeded by government regulation or interference.

Liberalism's view of the rights of the individual as universal and its impulse to extend individual freedom gives it a meliorist or reformist dimension which has often been at odds with the idea of the limited state. In the twentieth century, **social liberalism** gave the state a larger role in order to extend equal rights to groups previously denied them, sometimes employing forms of intervention (e.g. affirmative action/positive discrimination) wholly at odds with classical liberalism. Social liberalism also abandoned laissez-faire economics, giving the state a greater role in regulating the economy and in redistributing wealth.

Following the fall of Communism in Eastern Europe (1989–92), the American historian Francis Fukuyama famously proclaimed the global triumph of the 'liberal idea' and, with it, the end of the ideological struggles which had characterized the twentieth century.[26] In retrospect, it is clear that this point marked not the end of ideology but the ascendancy of a new one. The liberal idea Fukuyama had in mind was not simply liberal democracy as a form of government but a virulent new strain of economic liberalism epitomized by the policies of the Reagan era in the United States and by Thatcherism in the United Kingdom. These policies centred on facilitating global free trade, curbing government regulation, shrinking state expenditure, enhancing labour market flexibility and so on. But rather than being restricted to the economic sphere, **neoliberalism** made all aspects of government subject to market principles,

Box 1.1 (*cont.*)

rigidly applying them to the public sector (health care, education and even the prison system) and stripping away welfare benefits as disincentives to market participation. Across Europe and North America, neoliberal policies and the idea that market principles should serve as the benchmark for all state operations were adopted by both left- and right-wing parties. Indeed, the consensus around neoliberalism was so entrenched that even following the global financial crisis of 2007–11, it remained largely unchallenged within the political mainstream. Extraordinarily, the 'solution' to the crisis adopted by some governments – most notably the Conservative-Liberal Democrat coalition in the United Kingdom – was more of the same neoliberal medicine.

The notion that, as Margaret Thatcher repeatedly put it, 'there is no alterative' to the neoliberal order remains hard to shake. One reason for this is the widespread cynicism that the neoliberal consensus has engendered in public attitudes toward parliamentary politics. Another is the extent to which the values of the neoliberal politicoeconomic regime have become naturalized through being mirrored and reinforced across contemporary culture. Citizens have been reduced to consumers and in the process had their political agency constricted (the UK riots of summer 2011 – in which a protest against police brutality and racism degenerated into the looting of designer labels – are emblematic of both developments, demonstrating not only the rioters' alienation and political impotence but their conformity to the values of consumer culture).[27] This acquiescence is also apparent in the aggressively competitive form of individualism which has spread beyond the workplace to pervade every aspect of life, stifling solidarity as well as attempts to construct alternatives to the status quo. In a provocative recent interpretation, the American historian Mark Lilla has identified this hyper-individualism as a symptom of a broader mindset complementary to neoliberalism: **libertarianism**. For Lilla, this mentality is a dogmatic offshoot of liberalism, taking the latter's baseline principles of freedom, the primacy of the individual, disinterested tolerance and distrust of the state and asserting them rigidly and unreflectively in every situation.[28] While this combination of neoliberal policies and libertarian principles retain their grip, it is left to forces outside mainstream social and political cultures to imagine alternative worlds.

Much political philosophy from Plato's *Republic* (c. 380 BCE) to the present has approached politics as the construction of an ideal state, a harmonious, ordered community in which conflict and contestation have melted away. But some radical thinkers have inverted this picture, rejecting such an 'idyll of consensus', identifying politics with dissent and locating it anywhere but the state.[29] The British anarchist philosopher Simon

Critchley, for example, maintains that authentic politics must be conducted at a distance from government, elevating protest activism as ethically and democratically superior to parliamentary politics under liberal democracy: 'Politics, I argue, cannot be confined to the activity of government that maintains order, pacification and security while constantly aiming at consensus. On the contrary, politics is the manifestation of dissensus, the cultivation of anarchic multiplicity that calls into question the authority and legitimacy of the state.'[30] Another contemporary proponent of this kind of revisionist definition of politics is the French philosopher Jacques Rancière, who characterizes the political field as the struggle between what he terms 'politics' and the 'police order'. Under police, Rancière provocatively includes all the forces which maintain a given order of domination – government, justice system, social security and so on – reserving politics for the elements antagonistic to and excluded by that order. Politics thus challenges an existing 'distribution of the sensible' (*partage du sensible*) – Rancière's term for the order governing participation in the public realm – by giving voice to those hitherto denied a place in it:

The police is thus first an order of bodies that defines the allocation of ways of doing, ways of being, and ways of saying, and sees that those bodies are assigned by name to a particular place and task; it is an order of the visible and the sayable that sees that a particular activity is visible and another is not, that this speech is understood as discourse and another as noise ... Political activity is whatever shifts a body from the place assigned to it or changes a place's destination. It makes visible what had no business being seen, and makes heard a discourse where once there was only place for noise; it makes understood as discourse what was once only heard as noise.[31]

Rancière's distinction reflects a long-standing tradition of defining politics in opposition to the political (a pairing even more confusing in French political theory, which opposes *la politique* and *le politique*).[32] This antithesis is more than just a theoretical conceit, since commentators have used it as a means to challenge exclusionary conceptions of politics and intervene directly in political life. The originator of this opposition was the German right-wing theorist Carl Schmitt, who employed it – shortly before Adolf Hitler's ascent to power – to critique liberal democracy by driving a wedge between the political and the official sphere of politics. Rejecting narrow conceptions of the political, Schmitt argues that it is an all-pervading dimension of human existence; this dimension is characterized by 'the most intense and extreme antagonism', which he refers to as the 'friend–enemy' antithesis.[33] Schmitt's opposition of politics and the political resurfaced following the end of the

Cold War, when for left-wing European thinkers it provided a means to envisage a politics beyond the liberal-democratic consensus. Thus for the post-Marxist theorist Chantal Mouffe, Schmitt's antithesis offers a tool for reconfiguring contemporary democracy in order to facilitate dissent:

> By 'the political', I refer to the dimension of antagonism that is inherent in human relations, antagonism that can take many forms and emerge in different types of social relations. 'Politics', on the other side, indicates the ensemble of practices, discourses and institutions which seek to establish a certain order and organize human coexistence in conditions that are always potentially conflictual because they are affected by the dimension of 'the political'.[34]

Schmitt's and Mouffe's view of the political as inherent in all social relations chimes with the massively expanded conception of politics currently operative in arts and humanities disciplines (including musicology). Over the last half-century, the concept of the political has extended well beyond the state to encompass all aspects of life, a development evident in the various conceptions of biopolitics and 'everyday politics' championed by theorists from Michel Foucault onward.[35] This expansion is also clear from the ever-growing lexicon of concepts which theorists use to locate and characterize the various different modes of politicality and interfaces between culture and politics.[36] All this raises the question of whether everything is political, making it illusory to distinguish between political and non-political cultural products and practices, including music (this issue is addressed at the end of this chapter). Two cautions from the Marxist theorist Fredric Jameson are worth bearing in mind at this point. While it may seem common sense to begin by narrowing down the political into something easily manageable, such an operation risks severely constraining subsequent analyses: 'we are, after all, fragmented beings, living in a host of separate reality compartments simultaneously; in *each one of those* a certain kind of politics is possible.'[37] This notion of multiple coexisting realities will prove invaluable in helping us understand the conjunctions between music and politics. No less important is another caveat from Jameson concerning the expansion of the political field: that recent scholarship, in liberally uncovering politicality across culture, has tended 'in the very heat of this interpretive discovery to assign to overtly political practices or texts a lower level of interest'.[38] In order to be political, music does not need to be connected to the spheres of life customarily fenced off as politics; yet this acknowledgement should not lead us to neglect the more traditional territory of political music.

Although the discussion so far has focused on the scope of politics and the political, it has also touched on some of the concepts and categories crucial to understanding the field. Power looms large here, as in Mouffe's view of the political as a conflictual terrain of power and resistance. In addition, we have encountered the idea of politics as the safeguarding of an ordered society, and the alternative view that politics is all about dissent. Another central theme is that of identity and difference, encapsulated in Schmitt's and Mouffe's elevation of antagonism as the crux of the political. Aristotle's conception of politics as the collective pursuit of the good life hints at a host of other concepts which we need to take into account: politics and freedom, community, democracy, equality, social justice and so on. In addition to acknowledging these multiple dimensions, we need to bear in mind the dynamic character which they lend to politics (the ideals of freedom, community, democracy, equality and social justice are what political theorists refer to as 'momentum concepts', impelling us onward and upward yet remaining forever out of reach).[39] As Aristotle's idea of collective self-perfection suggests, politics – where it rises above mere management – is a forward-moving process envisaging change and a better future; for the French political philosopher Alain Badiou, 'the essence of politics is not the plurality of opinions. It is the prescription of a possibility in rupture with what exists.'[40] This combination of prescription, change and hope for the future surely takes us to the heart of politics and can also serve as a preliminary definition of a concept fundamental to understanding the field: political ideology. An ideology is not simply a set of political ideas and principles but a vision of a social order, a lens which simultaneously brings contemporary reality into focus and corrects its defects (the wider connotations and uses of ideology are explored in Chapter 3).

1.2 Musical Messages, Noises and Affects

Music too has always been a conceptually contested terrain, and probing its limits can help us to understand what it has to offer politics. At its extremes, music as political expression morphs into speech or into brute, disruptive noise. While talking and singing have become increasingly compartmentalized within the West in modernity, the middle ground of rhetorically heightened, ritualized speech retains its potency.[41] This zone is occupied not only by preachers and orators – think of the emotive energy, vocal range and rhythmic control of Martin Luther King Jr's 'I Have a Dream' speech – but also by chanting crowds.[42] Even the most banal unpitched rhythmic chant ('Yes we can!' or 'No ifs, no buts, no education cuts!') does more than simply transmit a message, gaining rhetorical force and collective significance through its musical dimension. Such chanting can serve not only to generate solidarity but to choreograph a protest event; during the Egyptian revolution of 2011, rhythmic chanting in Cairo's Tahrir Square – in particular of the word 'silmiyya' (peaceful) – served to control the speed of the protesters' marching and to build intensity during violent confrontations.[43] Similarly, the Occupy Wall Street protesters used chanting and other forms of rhythmic speech in order to maintain a sonic presence, mark out territory and intimidate the authorities.[44] The most notable example used in New York and by the broader Occupy movement was the 'human microphone', the amplification of a speaker's words through crowd repetition, which served initially as a means to evade a ban on electronic sound equipment.[45] For the sociologist Rossana Reguillo, participating in the human microphone promoted a heightened form of listening in which the speaker's words were reproduced bodily, internalized and distilled into ideas.[46]

As James Deaville demonstrates, the mainstream US media exploited the vivid and varied soundscape of the Occupy protest in order to portray it as a shambolic circus.[47] This media standpoint neatly illustrates Rancière's view of the dominant order as determining those forms of expression heard as discourse and those dismissed as noise. If political activity in general aims at a permanent transformation in what is recognized as discourse, some forms of popular protest are more fleeting, offering only a noisy shock to the system: a howl of rage or scorn directed against the powers that be. In a striking metaphor, Badiou characterizes the initial, pre-political phase of activism as an 'interruption of ordinary social listening', a strategic deafness to all the laws and logics of the established order which serve to 'impossibilize' politics.[48]

One example of such activism, the phenomenon of rough music, or charivari, can be found in various forms throughout history and across the globe. The range of practices which can be yoked under this term is very wide, but typically rough music is a raucous, cacophonous form of street protest – produced by banging pots and pans, whistling and screeching or whatever musical instruments are available – directed at authority figures or those who have offended against social mores. Documented medieval examples abound, sometimes involving a carnivalesque suspension and inversion of normal social hierarchies, for example elaborate parodies of royal and civic processional rituals.[49] In Britain and North America, rough music persisted into the twentieth century, while parallels can still be found in the Caribbean and in Latin America (for example the *cacerolazo*, or stew-pot, protests in Argentina and Chile in the 1970s and 1980s).[50] Perhaps the most interesting modern-day examples are from Haiti, where the practice of *bat tenèb* (beating back the darkness) serves momentarily to amplify the voices of slum women, internally displaced people and other groups pushing at the margins of power.[51] Describing a *tenèb* outside the presidential palace in Port-au-Prince, Gage Averill explains how it provides an anonymous and relatively risk-free vehicle for protest:

Car horns were joined by pedestrians clattering sticks along metal fences, by people blowing into conch shells and over bottles, by young boys banging on hub caps, and by the sound of *kola* merchants drumming on their bottles with spoons ... Because so many people were involved over such a distance and because no laws were being broken, the authorities could do nothing ... *Tenèb*s are not music per se, although musical instruments are often used. Rather they constitute a collective performance of sound-as-power and a demonstration of the ability of popular forces to coordinate large numbers of people successfully.[52]

These examples from music's borderlands with speech and noise give us two important steers for understanding its political uses and functions. First, they encourage a focus on music's materiality, its affective dimension and its capacity to organize time and space: here we encounter music as a physical force, choreographing protest and annexing territory, translating political ideals into vividly felt experience, and generating emotional solidarity through collective participation. Second, they usefully direct us away from an exclusive or overstated emphasis on language and verbal content. This is crucial since many of the default assumptions about the functions, workings and effects of political art are oriented around literary models and verbal communication; as a result, they offer a narrow and misleading view of what music can do for politics.

Language and Verbal Content

A preoccupation with verbal content not only erects a wall between it and music's other properties but can lead to the political efficacy of music being exaggerated. This tends to occur when music with words is approached from the standpoint of what Rancière terms the mimetic or pedagogical model of political art: the view not only that it communicates a transparent message but that this message exercises a direct effect on the listener's behaviour. For Rancière, the linear logic of 'cause and effect, intention and consequence' underpinning this perspective is not only implausible but centuries out of date, having been refuted by Jean-Jacques Rousseau in the mid-eighteenth century.[53] If Rancière seems to be attacking a straw horse, consider the moral panics which have ebbed and flowed in the media over violent or misogynistic rap lyrics. While it would be rash to deny the possibility of a mediated relationship between lyrics and the attitudes and behaviours of some listeners exposed to them, critics of gangsta rap have gone further, claiming lyrics have a direct influence through cognitive transmission.[54] Scholars in communication research and media studies have long rejected the 'magic bullet' or transmission model of the effects of language and media, not least because it tackles social problems backward, projecting them onto their supposed causes.[55] Similarly, sociologists have countered this model on the grounds that it isolates textual messages from the social contexts conditioning their production and reception; as Peter J. Martin notes, 'the "message" model seems to imply . . . that both the active "sender" and passive "receiver" are individuals, isolated from any actual social context of music use, and to assume that the "message" is both unambiguous and effective in producing an appropriate reaction in the "receiver"'.[56] Yet this kind of logic continues to be found not only in relation to rap lyrics but in discussions of the dangers posed by other forms of music. Consider, for example, the assumption of German government agencies and media that so-called *Rechtsrock* serves as a 'gateway drug' into right-wing extremism.[57] A warning leaflet issued by the state government of Saxony is typical, stating that 'the danger is that the song texts will manipulate the political world-views of young listeners in particular and that over time they will embrace the extreme right-wing stances conveyed by them.'[58]

From the standpoint of this language-oriented effects model, the musical component of a song is more or less incidental, serving merely to 'sugar the pill' of the verbal message. More broadly and pervasively, this marginalization of music is typical of conceptions of political art conceived around verbal communication. A surprisingly large number of political leaders and theorists have treated music as an unwelcome distraction, considering it to be the antithesis of transparent communication and rational debate; perhaps the classic example in modernity is Georges Danton, who attempted in 1794 to have political singing banned from the National Convention of revolutionary France:

The halls and the bar of the Convention [i.e. the area from which visiting deputations could address the parliamentarians] are meant to hear the solemn and serious expression of the citizens' wishes; none may allow himself to express these wishes with sideshow singing . . . Here, we must coolly, calmly, and with dignity sustain the great interests of the Fatherland, discuss them, sound the charge against tyrants, point out and strike down traitors, and raise the alarm against impostors.

I acknowledge the civic-mindedness of the petitioners; but I request that hence-forth we hear nothing at the bar but reason in prose.[59]

If today Danton's view that music has no place in a parliamentary session seems like common sense, this reflects a more deep-seated assumption that politics is a verbal matter: a world oriented around speeches, debating points, laws and manifestos. But as seen earlier, this narrow understanding of the political field is itself grounded in the politics of exclusion, aiming to detach rational governance by the elite from the irrational passions of the mob (Danton's attempts to sever the politics of the head from that of the body soon resulted in him experiencing a similar fate).

On occasion, music has contributed directly to the densely verbal world of parliamentary debates and disquisitions. One of the odder genres born during the French Revolution (cradle for so much that characterizes political music in modernity) was the *constitution en vaudeville*, which made use of well-known melodies to disseminate, critique and present alternatives to the articles of the revolutionary constitutions of 1791–3; one of these sung constitutions, produced by the ultra-royalist François March-ant, runs to 160 pages.[60] This genre is an interesting by-product of the birth of mass politics, aiming to communicate and engage with sections of the population whose previous involvement in state affairs would have been negligible. But as even the leading modern expert on the genre concedes, 'to sing the articles of a constitution seems to us today an absurd undertaking'; there are some things that music does very well, and conveying complex verbal information is not one of them.[61] In some other ways, too, music proves a defective medium for political work. As David Hesmondhalgh stresses, music is not much help in verifying facts or assessing the truth of one position over another; neither is it capable of elucidating particular views or belief systems.[62]

All of which need not lead us to concede 'the unpalatable truth', as Mark Carroll puts it, that for music, 'any ideological engagement (actual or perceived) depends primarily on the use of texts, whether in the form of libretti, lyrics, titles, manifestos or explanatory commentaries.'[63] Carroll's perspective assumes that ideology is something outside music (in Marcello Sorce Keller's words, a 'garb' which it puts on) and that ideologies are verbal constructs, making words more or less essential to political communication.[64] This view of the primacy of language in politics has recently been challenged by the American philosopher Crispin Sartwell, who argues instead that ideologies are multimedia systems:

Political ideologies and constitutions are aesthetic systems of which texts form a portion, in the precise sense that political systems appear in different media, none of which is fundamental and all of which are related ... A politics is an aesthetic environment, whatever else it may be. Political systems are no more centrally textual than they are centrally systems of imagery, architecture, music, styles of embodiment and movement, clothing and fibers, furnishings and graphic arts.[65]

While Sartwell's phrasing is particularly provocative, he is just one in a long line of theorists to reject the seemingly self-evident notion that ideologies revolve around ideas. In a crucial essay from the late 1960s – 'Ideology and Ideological State Apparatuses (Notes towards an Investigation)' – the Marxist theorist Louis Althusser stressed the 'material existence' of ideologies, that is, how they manifest themselves in human actions, practices, rituals and institutions.[66] Much subsequent ideological analysis has focused on developing what Jameson describes as a 'hermeneutic of practices', probing how symbolic gestures and behaviours produce and reproduce ideologies; this approach shifts attention away from a narrow focus on explicitly political texts, positing that 'all forms of social practice and cultural production can therefore be considered ideological in some larger sense.'[67] Although there are dangers in treating ideology as all-encompassing (see Section 3.4), the expansion of ideological analysis to encompass symbolic practices is indispensable for work on music and politics. This does not simply entail reading the signifying practices within musical texts or activities as if they were verbal artefacts, or translating musical gestures and processes into conceptual content. It also involves, as Sartwell argues, giving due attention to the aesthetic and affective dimensions of ideology, a move which places music's particular strengths front and centre.

Box 1.2 Marxism, Socialism and Communism

As with most -isms, it is not helpful to think of Marxism as a single, cohesive doctrine. Rather, it serves as an umbrella term for a range of discourses that take the political and economic methods and theories developed by Karl Marx and Friedrich Engels ('classical Marxism') as their point of departure. There is no essence of Marxism to which all these discourses can be boiled down, although theorists and activists who identify themselves as Marxists normally embrace ideas and approaches drawn from the categories presented below.

1. At the heart of Marxist analysis is the **critique of capitalism and capitalist society**. Marx and Engels cast the socioeconomic structure or mode of production as the dominant influence within a society, shaping social relations and all the spheres of life (see Boxes 3.1 and 3.2). For Marx and Engels, the capitalist mode of production exploits workers, treating them and their products

Box 1.2 (*cont.*)

as commodities in the process of generating surplus value for the owners of the means of production. It also alienates and dehumanizes them, estranging workers from the products of their labour and blocking their capacity to realize fully their abilities and powers.

2. Marxism's vitality derives from its **positive ideas and values** as well as its negative critique.[68] Although Marx and Engels were reluctant to draw up blueprints for the future (fearing comparisons with 'utopian socialists' such as Henri de Saint-Simon and Charles Fourier), describing how life would be better under communism was essential to their project.[69] Marxism presents an ideal of emancipation in which society is reorganized in order to enable individuals to realize their essential human capacities and powers. Crucial to fostering this holistic development is eliminating the division of labour and actualizing each individual's social essence. Marx envisages labour under communism as a self-activity in which the worker, like a musician in an orchestra (the analogy is Marx's) gains satisfaction from fulfilling labour and shared ownership over the product.

3. Getting from '1' to '2' is the driving force behind Marx and Engels's **historical materialism and theory of historical change**. Material development drives history by generating contradictions between the productive forces and the existing social structure (see Box 3.1); for Marx and Engels, as G. A. Cohen puts it, 'history is, fundamentally, the growth of human productive power, and forms of society rise and fall according as they enable and promote, or prevent and discourage, that growth.'[70] This perspective has often been equated with historical determinism – that is, the idea that history's course is predetermined and controlled by forces beyond human agency – and there are plenty of passages in their writings which suggest this viewpoint (e.g. paragraph two of box 3.1, page 69). Marx and Engels, however, stressed the role of human agency within these structures: 'Men make their own history, but they do not make it just as they please; they do not make it under circumstances chosen by themselves.'[71]

Marx and Engels's sequence of modes of production includes two future phases: a transitional **socialist** mode of production and the subsequent attainment of **communism** proper or 'full communism'. They present a ten-point plan for the socialist reconstruction of society in the *Communist Manifesto*, including measures that became programmatic for socialist governments in reality (including progressive taxation, public ownership and free education for all).[72] Full communism – common ownership of property – would emerge gradually alongside the elimination of divisions of labour, class, race and religion, while individuals' capacity for self-governance would enable the apparatus of the state to 'wither away'. As the latter aspiration implies, the attainment of full communism requires a transformation not merely within society but within individuals: the willingness, in Badiou's phrase, to 'live for an Idea'.[73]

Affect

Music's affective side – its capacity to stimulate bodily sensation and influence emotion, mood and motivation – has dominated discussions of its political efficacy since the time of Plato. The politics of musical affect, however, has been theorized in widely contrasting ways. One model, common in antiquity and recently reinvigorated, conceives affects as 'pre-verbal intensities' working under the radar of conscious perception, stimulating action or modifying behaviour through their direct impact on the body.[74] Similar views of affect can be found throughout Western music history, associated with two very different constructs, both of which have generated extensive literatures: on the one hand, music's elemental power to pacify and heal and, on the other, the idea of it as an intoxicating, irrational force undermining the equilibrium of the individual and society (these two constructions are combined in a passage from Plato's *Laws*, which describes how in the healing rituals of the Corybantes, 'the music of the *pipes* bewitches the frenzied Bacchic reveller', inducing 'a feeling of calm and peace').[75] Both these constructions treat music as a kind of magical power or mood-altering drug, capable of exercising transformative effects through its impact on the body.[76] As well as functioning below the threshold of consciousness and cognition, music's Dionysiac powers of intoxication work at a sub-personal level, serving temporarily, as Friedrich Nietzsche put it, to 'cause subjectivity to vanish to the point of complete self-forgetting'.[77]

From the standpoint of this model of affect, music's capacity to work subconsciously and to strip away individual autonomy gives it a dangerous political potency, fuelling abhorrent forms of collective behaviour. Whether decrying the horrors of the French Revolution or the Third Reich (or, for that matter, the effects of jazz or rock and roll) commentators have repeatedly represented such bodily musical experience as a dehumanizing force, dragging rational beings down to the level of animals. In a description of music's effect on the mob from the period of the French Revolution, for example, the playwright and philosopher Friedrich Schiller claimed that

on all faces there usually appears an expression of sensuality, verging on something brutish, and intoxicated eyes swim, the open mouth is all desire, a voluptuous trembling seizes the entire body, breathing is quick and faint, in short, all the symptoms of inebriation appear – clear proof that the senses are feasting, but that the spirit or the principle of human freedom is falling prey to the violence of the sensuous impression.[78]

Commentators more sympathetic toward music's affective dimension have viewed its political effectiveness in different terms. For the young Nietzsche – reflecting on the power of Beethoven's 'Ode to Joy' by reimagining it as a kind of psychedelic trance music – its suspension of individual freedom functions as a shock community effect, renewing 'the bond between human beings' and breaking down social boundaries and hierarchies.[79] Similarly, ethnomusicologists working on trance states have emphasized music's role in dissolving the boundaries between self and other; the latter is central to Judith O. Becker's definition of trancing as 'a bodily event, characterized by strong emotion, intense focus, [and] the loss of the strong sense of self'.[80] A parallel emphasis on the positive political dimensions of purely affective experience can be found in recent discussions of rave culture. For Sarah Thornton, the experience of rave music and dance serves to suspend rationality and create a collective state of consciousness: 'The constant pulse of the bass blocks thoughts, affects emotions and enters the body. Like a drug, rhythms can lull one into another state.'[81] A more explicitly political take on rave is given by Jeremy Gilbert and Ewan Pearson, who evoke the dance floor as a liberatory communitarian space in which individual egos and identities are dissolved into 'ecstatic collectivity'.[82]

The view of affect outlined above – conceiving bodily response as working independently and ahead of conscious perception and language – has gained a strong traction across the humanities in recent years, serving as a corrective to the perceived 'linguistic imperialism' of semiotics and discourse theory.[83] But by polarizing affect and discourse, and treating affect as pre-discursive, this model may seem to limit its application to visceral shocks and moments of sensory overload like those described above.[84] Such jolts to the system, as the leading theorist of this model, Brian Massumi, acknowledges, do not stray beyond the proto-political, offering only 'the first stirrings of the political, flush with the felt intensities of life'.[85] Even in relation to the experience of music, where the idea of a primary physiological response is more plausible than for verbal media, affect only rarely works in isolation: our responses to sonic stimuli are mediated, shaped and framed by discourses, considered in the broadest sense as assemblages of meaning which organize and make intelligible the world around us.

A second model of affect, therefore, stresses the fluid boundary and constant interchange between it and discourse. Rather than casting affect and cognition as separate systems, and treating political discourses as 'sensually inert', this model acknowledges what Jeremy Gilbert describes as 'linguistic, non-linguistic, affective and sensuous dimensions' of such discourses.[86] This perspective accords with current research in neuroscience, which contends that 'complex cognitive-emotional behaviours have their basis in dynamic coalitions of networks of brain areas, none of which should be conceptualized as specifically affective or cognitive'.[87] While the godfather of affect theory the philosopher Baruch Spinoza considered that any effect on the body has a parallel effect in the mind, more recent theorists have stressed the mixed messages which cognitive and bodily information can convey.[88] For Britta Timm Knudsen and Carsten Stage, 'the body can be affected in complex ways depending on how experiences interact with, are challenged by or intertwined with discourses: sometimes affects simply reproduce or strengthen discourses, sometimes they open possibilities for future changes, and sometimes they motivate discursive crisis.'[89]

Box 1.3 The Affective Dimension of Political Songs

Friedrich Hecker, leader of an abortive republican revolution in Baden, Germany in 1848, and later a Yankee colonel in the American Civil War, reflects on the power of political song to recruit:

> Not every man is capable of being enthused through intellectual arguments, since for most it is the sensual dimension – in the noblest sense of the word – which is dominant. Feeling, emotion and the imagination are the guides which lead him to that hallowed place from which human rights, the dignity of man and liberty can be seen clearly.
>
> On learning a political song for the first time, he sings it with irrepressible joy in the rapture or fervour of the moment, but in those quiet times in which a man contemplates himself or is absorbed in dreams, and while walking here and there, the song re-echoes in his soul. The ideas which it unfolds are clear and vivid, both appealing in themselves and serving to awaken further thoughts. That which was acquired unconsciously or through sensory attraction then gains a nucleus, a form and an enduring existence: the song becomes his lodestar and he becomes politicized ...
>
> Through the mellow tones of song, through its fierce chords, through its passion and fury ideas surge up and down and are inscribed on the depths on the heart. The greatest truths, the deepest ideas of political thought – as if by a process of distillation – attain an unalloyed clarity, becoming the purest gold of the human heart and the inalienable property of the individual. (Friedrich Hecker, 'Das politische Lied' [The Political Song] (1848), preface to Karl Heinrich Schnauffer, *Neue Lieder für das Teutsche Volk*, Rheinfelden, 1848)

Affect, Manipulation and Political Advertising

One of the reasons why affect theory came to prominence in the humanities was to explain what might be termed the politics of affective manipulation.[90] In the contemporary world of 'post-truth' politics, rousing rhetoric and emotional persuasion have increasingly trumped rational arguments; in this climate, music's capacity to provoke visceral reactions and trigger affective resonances makes it an indispensable if volatile tool. Political activists have long been aware of the importance of positive emotions for political mobilization and the role that music can play in instilling them. The nineteenth-century German radical Friedrich Hecker, for example, stressed the importance of 'the sensual dimension' in recruiting for political causes, highlighting how the 'irrepressible joy' generated through political song served as the basis for the process of politicizing individuals (see Box 1.3). It is not hard to find examples of modern political advertising in which music performs a similar function. Consider the campaign ad 'America' from Bernie Sanders's 2016 run for the Democratic presidential nomination, in which a succession of folksy images of everyday American life is combined with the 1968 Simon and Garfunkel song of the same name.[91] Although it presents an artless demeanour, the ad is carefully calculated to press the right affective buttons; the visuals are cut to fit the beat of the song, crescendoing into the climactic refrain 'They've all come to look for America', which is reinforced by surging waves of cheering and applause. Numerous media commentaries have stressed the ad's capacity to generate not only positive emotions but also bodily responses, describing how it produces 'goose bumps', 'chills' and 'a sense of euphoria and ecstasy'.[92] Its success therefore stems not only from cognitive association (the link it constructs between Sanders and the innocent optimism of 1968) but from affect (prompting viewers to experience pleasure and a hopeful sensibility themselves). As a result, viewers of all political persuasions reported responding positively to the ad.[93]

Crucial to the impact of this and other political ads communicating positive messages (the classic example is 'I like Ike' from 1952) is making the viewer share the feeling of elation and belonging that goes with being part of a winning team.[94] Negative campaign ads aim at precisely the opposite, using music to make the viewer feel anxious, alienated and disaffected. In the United States, attack ads are so embedded in the political landscape that commercial music agencies offer package deals on scary soundtracks. The firm Music Cult, for example, sells a package of

'18 ominous and dark instrumental underscores perfect for that Political Negative Attack Ad', identifying its subgenre as 'dark, sinister, brooding, ominous music'.[95] A similar product is available from Firstcom Music, with tracks entitled 'Can You Trust?', 'Unfit to Win' and 'He's a Sneaky One'.[96] On one level, such music relies on negative cognitive associations for its effect, using stock devices and colours (grim ostinatos, ticking clocks and tolling bells) familiar from thrillers and horror movies. But on another, it makes use of low frequencies and thudding repeated notes to impact physically on the viewer, working below the level of consciousness to generate sensations of agitation and anxiety (one example of these techniques in practice is Mitt Romney's 2012 campaign ad 'Believe in America').[97]

If these examples suggest it is straightforward to manipulate affective responses for political ends, there are plenty of campaign ads that prove the opposite. Some fail by underestimating the extent to which music can shape viewers' cognitive and emotional responses. One example is the too-clever-by-half 'Morning Again' from Marco Rubio's abortive 2016 run for the Republican presidential nomination, a reworking of the classic feel-good ad 'Morning in America' from Ronald Reagan's 1984 campaign. Borrowing both visual and verbal elements from its model, the Rubio ad offers a bleak inversion of them with the aim of conveying the need for change.[98] Rather than following suit, however, the music simply replicates the Copland-esque 'American pastoral' idiom and mood of the Reagan original. What is striking in this example is how the music's affective poignancy and style – few classical idioms are so freighted with ideological associations as this one – have the effect of significantly softening the ad's negative thrust.

If here music serves to neutralize the impact of other stimuli, it can also counter a desired political message by overwhelming the viewer with contradictory signifiers and affects. A striking example is the commercial 'Cool' (2012), produced by the Republican campaign organization American Crossroads, which set out to dissuade young voters from backing Barack's Obama's re-election by portraying him as an ineffectual celebrity.[99] The approach used in the ad is simple, presenting a montage of images of Obama goofing around on chat shows to a soundtrack of R&B, before abruptly cutting the music, switching to black and white, and serving up a sequence of downbeat images and stats to illustrate how he failed to tackle young people's problems during his first term. While middle-aged Republicans responded favourably to the ad, it failed to resonate with its target audience and arguably strengthened Obama's reputation; as one YouTube viewer noted, 'Seriously, I cannot be the only one who thinks Obama is one *cool* guy after this ad.'[100] The problem is partly visual (the colourful neon slogans such as 'biggest celebrity in the world' and 'one cool president' catch the attention more than the monochrome, wordy economic factoids that follow them). But music and sound are largely responsible for undermining the ad's aims. Not only does the easy-going R&B soundtrack define and dominate the mood (throwing into parentheses the ad's preachy middle section), but the abrupt interruption of its beat serves to irritate the viewer rather than capture attention or sympathy. The mixed messages the ad sends out are further confused by the samples superimposed on the main soundtrack: chants of 'four more years' and deep moans of 'oh yeah' from Yello's eponymous 1985 single.[101] Small wonder that Donald Trump dismissed it as 'a terrible ad by the Republicans . . . when I first saw it, I thought the Democrats put it out.'[102] As 'Cool' and 'Morning Again' illustrate, music is far from being a simple tool for transmitting and implanting messages and affects. Rather, its signifying and affective power, like all forms of power, can have consequences wholly unintended by those wielding it.

1.3   Agency and Causation

Exploring music's political power requires that we probe the difficult issues of agency and causation. In general, political agency is the idea that individuals and groups have the power to 'be the change you want to see in the world' (a T-shirt slogan often misattributed to Gandhi). As this phrase neatly illustrates, political agency is both the capacity to act politically and the process of exercising that capacity; the freedom to effect change and the activity of interacting with others to bring it about.[103] When defined like this, the centrality of agency for probing music's relationship to politics is immediately obvious. Understanding agency is crucial to grasping not only music's capacity to intervene in politics but its power to construct identities and model collectivities; as Barry Shank argues in a recent discussion, 'music is one of the central cultural processes through which the abstract concept of the polis comes into bodily experience', enabling it 'to consolidate an entirely new sense of the self and its relation to others' and to prefigure 'the emergence of a political community yet to come'.[104] The idea that music can function as a political actor, just like a human agent, is at the root of many key assumptions about its political efficacy, yet this notion is as problematic as it is useful.

The difficulties lie in pinning down precisely who or what invests music with political agency and in how we can grasp the nature of its effects without resorting to crudely mechanistic models of causation.

Broadly speaking, there are three ways to approach the question of how music is able to exercise political agency, centring on (1) intentionality, (2) materiality and (3) aesthetic experience. The first and most familiar model assumes that musical practices and texts convey the political ideologies and aims of their creators or performers; as with agentic conceptions of power, it treats music as a tool wielded to produce political effects, or as a vehicle for realizing the goals of particular individuals and institutions. This view of political agency animates the pedagogic model of political art encountered earlier: the notion that music can be invested with a transparent message that impacts on the recipient's attitudes or behaviour. But we should avoid simply equating the intentional model of political agency with didactic modes of presentation or with narrowly functional forms of political music. The idea that art conveys the intentions of its creators, after all, is also at work in attempts to decode the concealed politics lurking beneath the surface of Western classical works: think of the cottage industry of commentators dedicated to revealing the secret dissidence supposedly animating Shostakovich's symphonies (see Section 6.2). We should also avoid assuming that the category of intentionality applies only to the initial instigators of a musical work or practice; the act of appropriation, too, can imbue works or practices with political agency. Consider, for example, the EU's cooption of Beethoven's 'Ode to Joy' as the emblem of pan-European nationalism, or the use of this music by Ian Smith's white minority government in Rhodesia to represent itself as the last outpost of European civilization.[105] The concept of 'reception' may well seem too passive to encompass such agentic efforts to harness pre-existing music to new political ends.

The second model – that of material agency – contends that musical sounds and objects are not just vessels into which political intentionality can be poured, but rather can acquire their own agency, distinct from the human agencies involved in their production. At first glance, the notion that agency can be exercised by nonhuman actants may seem to owe more to science fiction than political theory. Yet in an age in which the global political agenda is increasingly being dictated by dwindling natural resources, the idea that material objects can exercise an impact on our lives is pressingly real. One of the most provocative advocates of material agency, the political theorist Jane Bennett, argues that rather than treating material objects as passive and inert, we should recognize their 'vitality' and 'thing-power': 'the capacity of things ... not only to impede or block the will and designs of humans but also to act as quasi agents or forces with trajectories, propensities, or tendencies of their own'.[106] Bennett goes on to argue that man-made objects such as artworks can also 'manifest traces of independence or aliveness' irreducible to the intentions of their creators or the responses they provoke.[107] These ideas seem particularly relevant to music, since they help us to grasp the sheer unpredictability that attends attempts to harness it to political ends: the excess or gremlin in the machine that lies beyond the control of human actors.

The idea that material objects can have their own autonomous political agency necessitates a series of manoeuvres, not least detaching agency from intentionality. Rather than viewing agency in terms of aims that generate actions, champions of material agency have shifted the emphasis to efficacy: the capacity of objects to trigger effects and generate change. But given that efficacy is normally conceived in relation to a desired result, or as movement toward an intended goal – reinserting intentionality into the equation – this refocusing in turn requires a further manoeuvre. Bennett's solution is to remove goal-directedness from agency while retaining a sense of motion: movement away from the present and toward an undefined future. In fleshing out this approach, she draws on Jacques Derrida's concept of messianicity as an alternative to goal-directedness governed by intention, that is, the idea that material objects possess an 'open-ended *promissory* quality', an unspecified and insatiable straining toward a future plenitude.[108] This conception of movement toward an unreachable future perfect resonates not only with the definition of politics I presented earlier in this chapter but with the political significance imputed to autonomous art within both romanticism and modernism; for the philosopher Theodor W. Adorno – in a maxim misremembered from Stendhal – art offers a *promesse du bonheur*, an endless striving toward a future world of happiness.[109]

If this second model finds political agency within art's materiality, a third model locates it in the experience of art. In this model, music's sonic configurations and affective power enable it to be heard and felt by listeners in ways that confer political agency on it. This conception smartly sidesteps the issues of intentionality and nonhuman agency, making agency something projected into the music (yet ascribed to its force). The most fully developed example of this third model is Shank's theorization of what he describes as the 'political agency of musical beauty'. As his use of the word 'beauty' suggests, the agency experienced by the listener is stimulated by music's sonic structures rather than just its visceral and affective power:

Wherever we find musical beauty, it results from an attentive (even when not fully conscious) engagement with sound – the flow of rhythms, the assonance of harmonies, the resolution of pitch-based tensions, the surprising splashes of color, tone, timbre, even the disturbing clashes of chaos, dissonance, and silence, all of the coordinated violence shaped by the ludic synchronization of sound.[110]

If music's beauty and agency are something 'found' by the listener, Shank nonetheless discerns agentic properties within music itself, describing the 'luring, inclining, yearning quality of musical sound' as the basis of its political agency.[111] Similarly, from the other end of the telescope, Bennett's conception of material agency – while challenging us to rethink the nature of the interaction between objects and people – also ultimately treats agency as a distributed property shared by both. In a discussion apposite to music, Bennett describes the double sense of the word 'enchantment', which evokes human fascination in material objects as well as their capacity to place humans in their thrall: 'the figure of enchantment points in two directions: the first toward the humans who *feel* enchanted and whose agentic capacities may be thereby strengthened, and the second toward the agency of the things that *produce* (helpful, harmful) effects in human and other bodies.'[112]

Considered together, these models can help us understand how music is able to exercise agency productively in the political field. At this point, we need to recognize that some – perhaps most – of the music normally labelled 'political music' does not involve this combination of agency and efficacy, thematizing politics rather than aiming at political effects. Much political music, in short, is fundamentally unpolitical, being music about politics or music around politics. If that seems like an oxymoron, consider the host of 'political' pieces which are more bystanders than active participants: music which uses politics as a backdrop or draws on political elements simply to be topical or fit in with a particular genre. Consider, for example, the output of the Viennese composer Johann Strauss I during the revolutionary year 1848, in which a composition celebrating revolutionary ideals (the *Freiheits-Marsch*, Op. 226) was swiftly followed by one honouring the leader of the counter-revolutionary forces (the *Radetzky-Marsch*, Op. 228).[113] Rather than suggesting cynicism or a change of heart, these pieces simply point to how such genres cultivated popularity by responding to current events. In addition to music aiming at topicality, there is a form of politicality that might be characterized as 'intra-musical' rather than interventive: politics that works within rather than through culture. Think of the trope of rock rebellion, epitomized by the Beatles' song 'Revolution' (the original version, included in the *White Album*), in

which John Lennon responded to the upheavals of 1968 with a noncom-
mittal 'you can count me out – in'; this is music that takes up a studiedly
ambivalent relationship to contemporary radicalism, exploiting the frisson
of the political for cultural ends.[114] While the music in these examples may
later have acquired political agency, its creators and initial recipients did
not invest it with agency in the senses described above. In contrast, it is not
hard to find examples of music which have no political connotations yet
nonetheless come to exercise political agency. Earlier, we saw how Breivik's
self-radicalization was sustained by testosterone-packed but politically
neutral film and game soundtracks. Similarly, in discussing the functions
of music in the UK riots and protests of 2010–11, Marie Thompson and
Ian Biddle draw attention to the absence of songs with explicitly political
content; the mobilizing capacity of the music lay not in its message or
symbolic content but in its affective construction of collectivity.[115]

Claims about music's agency and efficacy need to be paired with a
plausible conception of causation if they are to be convincing. What kinds
of explanations might be used to justify the idea that music can influence
the political views or behaviour of individuals, let alone mobilize groups,
construct communities or help constitute a new politics? During the
Second World War, the American folk singer Woody Guthrie famously
placed the hyperbolic message 'this machine kills fascists' on his guitar;
political music has always thrived on the notion that a well-chosen chord
can set boots quaking in the corridors of power. In reality, strong
causation – aptly characterized by Timothy Morton as 'clunk causality' –
is seldom at issue in music's relationship with politics, even in cases where
cause and effect might initially seem relatively clear-cut.[116] Recall, for
example, the use of music in the Bernie Sanders campaign ad 'America'.
Music's affective efficacy may seem indisputable in this case; yet even here,
there is no simple causal link between it and a political effect. For a start,
the intense positive emotional and physical response that the ad elicits
owes as much to the visuals (happy, demographically diverse faces) and
sound (ecstatic cheering and applause) as to the Simon and Garfunkel
song; at most, music functions as one causal factor among others. Even if
we take it as read that the music helps generate positive responses, this
does not necessarily translate into straightforward political effects. Viewers
and listeners are not simply submissive recipients, bovinely accepting
whatever is thrust in their direction, but rather active political agents
capable of blocking or reversing the effects intended. While even Republican voters responded positively to 'America', a large proportion of them
reported that they viewed Sanders less rather than more favourably after

watching it; pollsters also stressed the limited capacity of the ad to mobilize supporters or win over unaligned voters: 'They can sway a decent number of voters for about a week after they view it. So the right placement of an ad like this could swing a primary a percentage point or two, but measuring the effect is incredibly difficult.'[117]

Given the difficulty of gauging music's political effects, it may seem preferable to ditch strong forms of causation in favour of weaker alternatives. An example of this approach can be found in the work of the art theorists Mieke Bal and Miguel Hernánder-Navarro, who argue that art's agency lies not in attempting to force a political agenda but in presenting persuasive new ways of viewing the world:

> Without dictating its politics, as propaganda would, art opens up the possible visibility of situations, issues, events, and people and leaves it to its viewers or readers to enact that visibility; to answer its call by seeing. Art is neither didactic nor apodictic but only proposes possibilities. In other words, art proposes, the audience disposes. Thus, art exercises its agency on a level that is itself invisible.[118]

Although Bal and Hernánder-Navarro's polarization of art and propaganda is problematic, the view of art's political agency presented here is attractive, acknowledging the agency of the recipient and offering two distinct models of artistic causation. On the one hand, they present a propositional view of art's efficacy, highlighting how art can serve to model rather than mandate possibilities for change (this kind of modelling is sometimes referred to as exemplar causality).[119] On the other hand, they ground this propositional efficacy in another kind of causation, highlighting art's capacity to transform how its recipients see the world. While both these models are useful, they may seem too tame to accommodate the more interventive and manipulative ways in which art muscles in on politics: paintings or novels that straddle the supposed divide between art and propaganda – think of Harriet Beecher Stowe's antislavery novel *Uncle Tom's Cabin* (1852) or Pablo Picasso's anti-fascist painting *Guernica* (1937), for example – and music in its roles as street fighter, huckster, pusher, enforcer and so on. We need to be able to allow for more emphatic forms of agency while acknowledging the complex, indirect ways in which music's effects manifest themselves.

Some commentators, suspicious of the concept of causation or equating it with the clunky mechanistic model, entirely reject attempts to grasp the connections between art and politics in causal terms. Given that this is the position of arguably the most important contemporary theorist of the relationship between these fields – Rancière – a closer look is clearly needed.

Earlier, we saw that for Rancière, politics centres on disrupting and refashioning the 'distribution of the sensible', empowering those denied visibility and voice so as to create something more closely approximating a community of equals. This task of redrawing social spaces and identities, and reconfiguring what is visible and audible, gives politics its own aesthetic dimension (Rancière is at pains to differentiate this 'aesthetics of politics' from the fascist aestheticization of politics, explored in Section 7.2). Rancière regards art, like politics, as a form of dissent from the given 'natural' order, assigning artistic practices and works the capacity 'to intervene in the distribution of the sensible and its reconfiguration'.[120] Just as politics has an aesthetic aspect, so he regards art as possessing a politics specific to it: 'if there is a politics of aesthetics, it lies in the practices and modes of visibility of art that re-configure the fabric of sensory experience.'[121]

Although Rancière assigns the spheres of politics and art/aesthetics common concerns, he precludes them from talking directly to one another; like Schiller, whom he frequently cites and discusses, Rancière's conception of the politics of aesthetics is grounded in the view of art and politics as autonomous systems. Whatever political efficacy art possesses is not exercised through intervening directly in the field of politics, since there can be no direct traffic from the one to the other.[122] Although Rancière frequently draws on the language of causation in discussing the relationship between art and politics, he explicitly excludes direct cause and effect: 'This politics of aesthetics ... operates under the conditions prescribed by an original disjunction. It produces effects, but it does so on the basis of an original effect that implies the suspension of any direct cause-effect relationship.'[123] Rancière even rules out the weaker, propositional model of art's efficacy outlined above, arguing that 'political art cannot work in the simple form of a meaningful spectacle that would lead to an "awareness" of the state of the world.'[124]

Rancière devoted an essay, 'The Paradoxes of Political Art', to working through the implications of this position. From his perspective, the principal paradox of political art is that it exists at all: as Gerald Raunig notes, Rancière perpetuates the romantic-modernist opposition between 'content-focused "political" art and formalistic "autonomous" art', proscribing the former and investing all the dissensual energies of the aesthetic into the latter.[125] Locking art's politicality into its autonomy has the benefit, arguably, of making politics an inseparable part of what art is and does. But the political value of Rancière's autonomous art seems 'locked in' in another sense, unable to actualize the efficacy he claims for it without surmounting a host of obstacles. While his political theory is all about tearing down walls, these kinds of spatial metaphors work in the opposite direction in his essay on political art; art cannot 'leave the spaces reserved for it' or move beyond its 'borders'; the 'rupture' of aesthetics results in a 'paradoxical form of efficacy' centring on 'disconnection'.[126] In his most revealing statement on how art achieves political effects, however, Rancière employs a more plastic metaphor, in which the fields of art and politics seem able to interpenetrate one another while remaining autonomous:

Art does not become critical or political by 'moving beyond itself', or 'departing from itself', and intervening in the 'real world'. There is no 'real world' that functions as the outside of art. Instead, there is a multiplicity of folds in the sensory fabric of the common, folds in which outside and inside take on a multiplicity of shifting forms, in which the topography of what is 'in' and what is 'out' is continually criss-crossed and displaced by the aesthetics of politics and the politics of aesthetics.[127]

This suggestive metaphor does not resolve matters, but it does point toward two further models of causation that can help us understand how art produces political effects. While Rancière rules out direct causation, the conception he expresses metaphorically has much in common with the view of causality as mediation presented by the cultural theorist Lawrence Grossberg and with the idea of emergent causality formulated by the political theorist William E. Connolly. For Grossberg, all causality is medi- ated, in that the 'trajectories of effectivity' (for example, the 'ands' linking music and politics) are always 'interrupted, intersected, magnified or dimin- ished, transformed, bent, blocked, inflected, redirected, etc. by other prac- tices and events'.[128] Movement from one fold of reality to another is thus an unpredictable, non-linear process of becoming. Similarly, Connolly uses the concept of emergent causality to explain how seemingly autonomous systems act on one another. Inspired by the outlandish causal relationships in the ancient Greek poet Hesiod's *Theogony*, emergent causality stresses the mysterious, unknowable dimensions of a stimulus's effects:

Emergent causality is *causal* . . . in that a movement in one force-field helps to induce changes in others. But it is also *emergent* in that: first, some of the turbulence introduced into the second field is not always knowable in detail in itself before it arrives darkly through the effects that emerge; second, the new forces may become *infused* to some degree into the very organisation of the emergent phenomenon so that the causal factor is not entirely separate from the latter field; third, some of these forces also continue to impinge from the outside on the emerging formation; fourth, the new infusions and impingements may trigger novel capacities of *self-organization* or *autopoiesis* within one of the two systems that had not been spurred into motion before; and fifth, a series of resonances may now roll back and forth across two partially separated and partially conjoined force-fields.[129]

As is apparent from Connolly's fifth category, he moves beyond the idea of causation as one-way traffic, highlighting not just how one system can stimulate motion in another but how resonances and vibrations can echo between both fields. As Connolly stresses, the use of language like 'resonances' and 'vibrations' is more than simply metaphorical: it is indispensable in seeking to get a hold on forms of causality that go beyond the direct or mechanical modes.[130]

While mediated and emergent causality helps us understand how art and politics can fold themselves into each other, a more straightforward idea is at work in Rancière's conception of how art produces political effects: art does politics simply by doing what it does as art. In arguing that art's autonomy and capacity for subversion are two sides of the same coin, Rancière claims that 'the arts only ever lend to projects of domination or emancipation what they are able to lend to them, that is to say, quite simply, what they have in common with them: bodily positions and movements, functions of speech, the parcelling out of the visible and the invisible.'[131] From this perspective, music's contribution to furthering political projects consists simply of exercising the powers inherent to it, producing subjectivities and constructing communities through its own resources. Music and politics becomes music as politics.

Hearing Freedom, Imagining Community

It is not hard to think of examples of how music might exercise political effects simply by being itself. Music's seemingly inherent politicality has led to it being idealized in many cultures as a symbol, prefiguration and catalyst of as yet unrealized forms of human freedom and social harmony.[132] The ubiquity of such ideas is evident from the host of political metaphors derived from musical practices, as well as from the Western habit of listening metaphorically to genres such as the concerto.[133] The idea that the concerto embodies the tensions between individual autonomy and social cooperation may well seem trite, particularly in this vague, generic formulation. But the point of this trope, as Slavoj Žižek recognized in applying it *in nuce* to a range of composers from Mozart to Bartók, is that each work negotiates the balance between these elements differently, striving yet failing to achieve the ideal relationship between the individual and the collective.[134] Of more practical resonance, perhaps, is the idea that the symphony orchestra exemplifies and enacts what Paul Bekker describes as 'the unification of all individualities into a free community', a perspective that has been around in one form or another since the mid-nineteenth century.[135] This trope has recently been reinvigorated, partly as a result of the potent symbolism of the West-Eastern Divan Orchestra, described by its co-founder Daniel Barenboim as a 'utopian republic'.[136] But although this and similar ventures undoubtedly help promote dialogue and social harmony, their political effects are unlikely to match the extravagant claims made for them.[137]

Another staple of social aesthetics is the idea of the choir or orchestra as a model community: an egalitarian social union in which individuals find expression and fulfilment by pooling their varied strengths. One of the earliest examples of this trope can be found in a paean to the democratizing force of choral singing by the Swiss composer and educationalist Hans Georg Nägeli:

> Take masses of people, take them by the hundreds, the thousands, bring them into human interaction, an interaction where each individual expresses his personality freely and actively through emotions and words, where he receives harmonious impressions from all the others, where he becomes aware in the most intuitive and diverse ways of his human autonomy and solidarity, where he receives and shares enlightenment, where he imparts and inhales love simultaneously with every breath: could this be possible through anything other than *choral singing*?[138]

On one level, this trope points to a politics particular to art/aesthetics, locating music's community effect within the fold of its autonomy. At this level, music functions as a kind of experimental social space or alternative reality, symbolizing emancipation and empowerment, prefiguring an emergent political community and anticipating a better life to come. Yet for Nägeli and others invoking such tropes, music does more than offer a metaphorical politics at one remove from the real thing: choirs do not just model egalitarian community, but instantiate it concretely in the present, helping embed a new subjectivity and sensibility.

The idea that everyday music-making can possess its own politicality and efficacy (dissolving the boundary between Rancière's politics of aesthetics and his aesthetics of politics) raises some important issues. Practically every collective musical activity and experience can function on some level as a political act, but this is not the same as claiming that this capacity is intrinsic to it. Any inherent politicality possessed by a musical practice must surely be of very low definition, acquiring specificity and ideological colouration through discursive framing and other mediating factors. Thus while in cultures the world over, collective singing carries the connotation of togetherness, it does not come prepackaged as an emblem of egalitarianism or emancipation. Indeed, one of the reasons music is so open to ideological misuse is that its politics can resemble a hazy, free-floating potentiality, easily moulded to suit any agenda. As an agent of social cohesion, music can serve not only as an emblem of egalitarian community but as a distracting smokescreen or a signal that individual freedom is being eroded. Thus the social anthropologist Claude Lévi-Strauss, while acknowledging music's potential as an experimental political space, contends that its politics serves to generate 'the comforting illusion that contradictions can be overcome and differences resolved'.[139] Similarly, in explaining how music is susceptible to ideological exploitation, Adorno highlights the 'use made of music by politicians and other authorities who regard it as a cohesive social force, as something capable of creating the illusion of immediate community within a reified and alienated society'.[140]

1.4   Is All Music Political?

And so we return to the 'and' with which we started. Broadly speaking, aesthetic theorists, musicologists and other commentators have taken three positions on the question of whether all music is political. The first vigorously segregates political music from music as an autonomous art, treating the former as a marginal, sub-artistic phenomenon. The second similarly regards political music as antithetical to art yet claims that autonomous art offers a deeper form of political engagement as well as better art. In contrast, the third position affirms the proposition that all music is political, rejecting the polarization of political and non-political art as misguided or tendentious. Needless to say, the position that particular commentators take on this issue is shaped by whether they define the political in narrow or broad terms. Anyone who regards politics as limited to the sphere of public governance is unlikely to argue that all music is political, while those adhering to the paradigms of biopolitics or everyday politics are more or less obliged to adopt this stance.

The first of these standpoints – the idea of political music as something distinct to (and distinctly inferior to) music as autonomous art – has its origins in the aesthetic upheavals of the late eighteenth century; until relatively recently it remained the dominant position within Western aesthetic theory and musicology. The conception of art's autonomy formulated by Immanuel Kant and fleshed out by Friedrich Schiller was nothing if not political, constructing a parallel between the liberal paradigm of individual freedom and the autonomy, self-sufficiency, inner purposefulness and intrinsic dignity of art.[141] Yet this analogy precluded direct artistic intervention in politics: Kant fences off political rhetoric from free poetry, while Schiller argued that art's freedom requires it to 'forsake reality and lift itself above the needs of the present'.[142] Such oppositions were swiftly taken up within the discourses of art music, with figures like Nägeli rigidly distinguishing between pure and applied (*angewandte*) art, and consigning political music to the latter camp; its inferior status is confirmed by Nägeli's remark that 'the absence of genius will matter least' in applied music.[143] The dismissal of political art as sub-aesthetic was cemented by the philosopher Georg Wilhelm Friedrich Hegel, whose 1820s lectures on aesthetics drove a wedge between 'service' art (*dienende Kunst*) and free or autonomous art; this opposition was sufficiently pervasive that even the young Karl Marx dismissed socialist engaged literature as non-art.[144]

The fierce aesthetic debates within and around twentieth-century Marxism helped perpetuate this antithesis (see Chapter 3), and in the 1970s and 1980s it was rigorously affirmed by the dominant musicologist of the period, Carl Dahlhaus.[145] Today, few musical commentators would give credence either to this kind of binary thinking or to the emphatic conception of art's autonomy driving it. Yet some of the prejudices bound up with this opposition continue to persist, as is evident from the composer Ned Rorem's quip that 'the more an artwork succeeds as politics, the more it fails as art'.[146] Rorem's perspective stems from the (Cold War era) misconception that politics in art always and everywhere amounts to propaganda and indoctrination. But the principal problem with his stance is that it presents politicality and 'artness' as two entirely separate ingredients within the artwork, taking for granted that cultivating one will squeeze out the other. While there are certainly cases where the politics in a work seems like an afterthought or an optional extra, in most cases it is inseparable from the work's artistic premises. As the art critic Mieke Bal puts it, in terms no less trenchant than Rorem's,

> it is not as if there is art, some of which happens to be political. Political art is art because it is political; it is art by virtue of its political 'nature'. Neither art nor the political are defined by subject matter. They are domains of agency, where acting becomes possible and can have effects. In the case of political art, that agency is one and the same; it 'works' as art because it works politically.[147]

In exploring Rancière, we have already encountered the second standpoint outlined above: that autonomous art is more politically effective than art which cultivates closer relationships with politics. This claim becomes even more counterintuitive when applied to art that is autonomous in a further, more particular sense: abstract painting, say, or pure instrumental music. One influential proponent of this standpoint is the philosopher Lydia Goehr, who contends that 'it is by aspiring towards a purely aesthetic state that works [of music] have played their social or political role. Less successfully, if at all, have they played this role by functioning as merely social entities with explicit or tendentious content.'[148] Rejecting as crude the view of autonomous and political art as antitheses, Goehr argues that music's separation from society engenders a capacity to engage critically with it: 'one may say that music's *freedom from* external constraint gives music a *freedom to* express itself in, with, and on its own terms, which in turn gives it a *freedom to* express or reflect upon society at a critical distance.'[149] Although Goehr does not give a detailed account of music's political capacities or how it discharges them, she describes in Adornian terms its capacity to be 'resistantly social through its purely musical form'; elsewhere, she argues that music's political role is to 'help bring about a better world' by critiquing the status quo and offering an alternative vision.[150]

Even if we accept these claims for now (we will probe similar perspectives in detail at a later stage) they do not justify elevating autonomous music as more politically effective than other forms of political music. Goehr's move recalls some of the logics seen earlier in exploring competing definitions of the political (such as Rancière's restriction of politics to dissensus); choosing to concentrate on just one aspect of politics does not make the rest go away, and no single form of music can deliver the multiplicity of political functions and effects discussed over the course of this book. Another objection which could be levelled at both Goehr and Rancière is that, aside from the historical association with freedom discussed above, music's autonomy is no guarantee of politicality; as Badiou argues in relation to contemporary activist art, the claim that autonomy is 'by itself of a political nature' does not provide a credible means to compensate for the 'real weakness of the relationship between art and politics today'.[151] Perhaps most importantly, it is by no means clear that the idea of aesthetic autonomy is even necessary for assigning to music the political capacities which Goehr and Rancière describe. Some kind of baseline conception of music's autonomy as a social practice – art as a distinct fold within the fabric of common experience – is needed to sustain the idea that it can offer an emancipatory social space or model community.[152] Yet as Nägeli's invocation of the democratizing force of 'applied music' attests, the more emphatic idea of aesthetic autonomy can be dispensed with here.

The third standpoint presented above is a variation on the idea that everything is political. While the latter is a foundational assumption within contemporary humanities disciplines, the ubiquity it ascribes to politics may seem to drain the concept of its explanatory value; for Jean Baudrillard, 'when everything is political, nothing is political any more, the word itself is meaningless.'[153] Perhaps 'meaningless' is too strong, yet as seen earlier, the idea that all artistic texts and practices are political means that in some or most cases, such politicality is of very low definition. We need to acknowledge that while all music is fair game for political analysis, the latter is not always a particularly productive exercise. As Crispin Sartwell argues, most artworks were not regarded as political by their initial producers and receivers, and 'we should take with some seriousness their demand to be considered as something other than political statements.'[154] Genre conventions are important here too, since some genres do not arouse expectations of political engagement and seldom deliver it; while boy bands and string quartets can be grist to the mill of some forms of politicized interpretation, the serious politics is surely going on somewhere else.

In terms that echo Rancière, Mouffe has argued that 'one cannot make a distinction between political art and non-political art, because every form of artistic practice either contributes to the reproduction of the given common sense – and in that sense is political – or contributes to the deconstruction or critique of it. Every form of art has a political dimension.'[155] Framed like this, and when applied – as here – to contemporary avant-garde art, it is hard to disagree with this standpoint; one advantage of Mouffe's formulation is that it enables contingent, temporary overlaps between art and the political, rather than cementing them into a fixed relationship, as the notion that 'all art is political' seems to do. Yet rather than simply dissolving the distinction between political and non-political art, it is perhaps better to replace it with two alternative pairs of coordinates, recognizing the multiple folds of reality – Jameson's 'separate reality compartments' – in which the political is located. The first makes a distinction between intra-musical politics (politics within rather than through culture) and direct interventions in the political field. The second distinguishes between art and music that is explicitly defined by its politics (whether interventive or intra-musical) and that which contains – or possibly conceals – more sedimented forms of politicality. These distinctions will become important in the next two chapters as we explore the relationships between music, power and ideology.

2 | Power and Counterpower

There are strange, subterranean parallels between how music works and the mechanisms of power itself. Or perhaps better, there are striking similarities between Western constructions of the effects of music and the ways in which power has been theorized. Like politics, the concept of power is broad and multifaceted – some would say 'pliable and empty' – and we will encounter several competing views of it over the course of this and the next two chapters.[1] Political science has traditionally concentrated on 'power over' or power as domination, just as commentators exploring music's powers have often focused on its capacity to manipulate and domineer (Oscar Wilde was talking about the rule of the mob when he spoke of 'the despot who tyrannizes over the soul and body alike', but the description fits music pretty aptly too). Domination is our starting point too, extending from musical violence and social control (this chapter) to more understated ways in which music can serve the interests of a dominant order (Chapter 3), then music as propaganda, promotion and affirmation (Chapter 4). As well as exploring competing theories and practices of power, we need to begin to address resistance to it, since much recent theory has treated these concepts as inseparable. The most important theorist to explore power and resistance in tandem was Foucault, and the final portion of the chapter is given over to exploring his ideas and their impact on subsequent political theory and activism.

2.1 Power, Hegemony and Violence

Some of the categories and distinctions which theorists have used to demystify the dynamics of power resonate provocatively with music. One typology particularly popular among contemporary activists, derived from the work of the political theorists Steven Lukes and John Gaventa, distinguishes between three forms of power: visible, hidden and invisible.[2] Visible power is exercised openly through institutions, structures, policies and processes, enabling the dominant figure or group to maintain control. The parallel here is with instances where music is wielded palpably as a symbol of power (military marching bands give the most obvious example) or where music's use for political effects is concrete and transparent (think of the roster of singers and bands marshalled by Hillary Clinton in support of her 2016 presidential bid).[3] Hidden power, conversely, is exercised behind closed doors, controlling the agenda and determining which voices are heard (it can also be the power of the puppeteer behind the throne, the *poder oculto* of guerrilla factions or drug cartels in states undergoing paramilitary or criminal insurgency).[4] Music too can exercise such hidden power, working inconspicuously on the body and psyche, as seen earlier in the subliminal use of very low frequencies in political campaign ads. The third category, invisible power, is even more insidious, controlling how individuals view their place and role, and defining the limits of what they consider to be possible and impossible. This kind of power works at the level of values, beliefs and cultural practices, being internalized by the dominated and convincing them that 'there is no alternative' to the status quo. With invisible power, we leave the field of political music in the narrow sense, since a much wider array of musical practices, texts, institutions and discourses can serve to reproduce such values and ideologies, and thus help the dominant order to maintain its hegemonic position.

Box 2.1 Hegemony

In political science, the term 'hegemony' indicates a form of power secured by the possession of superior strength rather than through the direct use of force. Thus in the nineteenth century, Britain maintained a global empire more through the threat than the practice of military intervention; similarly today, the United States maintains its global dominance by possessing an overwhelming proportion of the world's nuclear and military resources (and as a result of its 'soft power' hegemony, attained through the global diffusion of its cultural symbols and practices).[5]

As above, hegemonic power is normally theorized in terms that distinguish it from the actual exercise of violence. Terry Eagleton, for example, characterizes hegemony as the 'range of practical strategies by which a dominant power elicits consent to its rule from those it subjugates'; similarly, Michèle Barrett describes hegemony as 'the *organization of consent* – the processes through which subordinated forms of consciousness are constructed without recourse to violence or coercion'.[6] These definitions take as their point of departure the work of the key theorist of hegemony, the Italian Marxist Antonio Gramsci. In his *Quaderni del*

Box 2.1 (*cont.*)

carcere (Prison Notebooks, 1929–35) Gramsci draws a distinction between the consensual 'ethico-political' realm of civil society and the coercive apparatus of the state:

> These two levels correspond on the one hand to the function of 'hegemony' which the dominant group exercises throughout society and on the other hand to that of 'direct domination' or command exercised through the State and 'juridical' government . . . These comprise:
>
> 1. The 'spontaneous' consent given by the great masses of the population to the general direction imposed on social life by the dominant fundamental group; this consent is 'historically' caused by the prestige (and consequent confidence) which the dominant group enjoys because of its position and function in the world of production.
>
> 2. The apparatus of state coercive power which 'legally' enforces discipline on those groups who do not 'consent' either actively or passively. This apparatus is, however, constituted for the whole of society in anticipation of moments of crisis of command and direction when spontaneous consent has failed.[7]

This problematic opposition between the violence of the state and the consensual principles of hegemonic power requires careful handling, since it serves a particular function in Gramsci's writings: that of enabling him to envisage, in terms resembling those of Marx and Engels, the withering away of the state as an ethico-political society emerges in its place.[8] Within present-day politics, as Gramsci notes, these two levels are messily intertwined, making the distinction between them 'merely methodological'; Gramsci famously described hegemonic power as being safeguarded 'by the armour of coercion', arguing that 'the "normal" exercise of hegemony in what became the classic terrain of the parliamentary regime is characterized by the combination of force and consent variously balancing one another, without force exceeding consent too much.'[9]

Gramsci uses the term **cultural hegemony** to indicate how, through cultural and intellectual work to win over hearts and minds, a particular group is able to secure discursive domination and thus the consent of the masses. He draws on this concept to explain not only the dominance of the ruling class, but also how the other classes can challenge it. Here, we encounter two further senses of the term: hegemony in Vladimir Lenin's sense of moral and intellectual leadership, and Gramsci's own highly influential view of hegemony as alliance building and the construction of a new 'collective will'. For Gramsci, the leaders of a class faction or 'historical bloc' must construct a position appealing to class groups beyond itself in order to generate a **counter-hegemonic alliance**; rather than being purely a marriage of convenience, these allied groups are cemented by a

---

Box 2.1 (*cont.*)

shared standpoint, which they can plausibly claim represents the interests of society as a whole:

> From this one can deduce the importance of the 'cultural aspect' also in practical (collective) activity. An historical act can only be performed by 'collective man', and this presupposes the attainment of a 'cultural-social' unity through which a multiplicity of dispersed wills, with heterogeneous aims, are welded together with a single aim, on the basis of an equal and common conception of the world, both general and particular, operating in transitory bursts (in emotional ways) or permanently (where the intellectual base is so well rooted, assimilated and experienced that it becomes passion).[10]

The idea that multiple oppositional groups can be drawn into a counter-hegemonic alliance has proved crucial for post-Marxist theory. For Mouffe and Ernesto Laclau, for example, Gramsci's theories point to how the diverse interest groups and social movements characteristic of contemporary left-wing activism might be articulated into a common radical-democratic project.[11] Other radical theorists, such as the anarchist philosopher Richard J. F. Day, have countered this model of social change by arguing that it locks activists into a state-oriented, binary view of politics; for Day, the only way to break out of the logic of neoliberalism is to act '*non*-hegemonically rather than *counter*-hegemonically'.[12] In contrast, **post-hegemonic** theorists such as Scott Lash have argued that the concept of hegemonic power is itself now superseded.[13]

Another relevant taxonomy is Joseph Nye's distinction between hard power and soft power (or as he puts it, 'when one country gets other countries to want what it wants').[14] Music, like power, has the capacity of being able to operate across the whole spectrum, from violence and coercion (hard power) to manipulation, persuasion, coaxing and nudging (soft power).[15] Before exploring the different ways in which music can aid or participate in power as domination, we need to justify the inclusion of violence within the spectrum of political power. Even though the hard/soft power opposition has become a cliché, this inclusion may seem unwarranted given that some of the most influential theorists of the last century, such as Hannah Arendt, categorically exclude violence from the political domain. For Arendt, the tendency to elide categories such as power, authority, domination and violence – that is, to emphasize their shared functions at the expense of their very different modus operandi – results in a dangerous 'blindness to the realities they correspond to'.[16] Arendt's point is that viewing violence as a form of power erases the idea of politics as the exercise of legitimate, collectively sanctioned authority. Instead of treating violence – to quote Carl von Clausewitz – as a 'political instrument, a continuation and development of political discourse by other means', she presents it as antithetical to political power, even if the two often appear in combination, and even if power may be justified in extreme circumstances in turning to violence for its self-preservation.[17]

Other theorists, such as Žižek, reject the idea that power and violence can be neatly segregated:

there is no Power without violence. Power always has to rely on an obscene stain of violence; political space is never 'pure', but always involves some kind of reliance on 'pre-political' violence. Of course, the relationship between political power and pre-political violence is one of mutual implication: not only is violence the necessary supplement of power, (political) power itself is always-already at the root of every apparently 'non-political' relationship of violence.[18]

Žižek takes this view further in his book *Violence: Six Sideways Reflections* (2008), where he provocatively inverts Arendt's perspective by presenting political systems and discourses as inherently violent (he includes within this category 'not only physical violence, but also the more subtle forms of coercion that sustain relations of domination and exploitation, including the threat of violence').[19] Drawing on a distinction similar to that between visible and invisible power, Žižek contrasts 'subjective' violence (those visible actions which we register as departures from a supposed non-violent norm) and 'objective' violence (the steady, constant, invisible backdrop of violence underpinning political power).[20] His argument is that the immediacy of subjective violence in the media age, whether physical (e.g. terrorism) or ideological (e.g. hate speech), coupled with liberal outrage that 'something must be done', detracts attention from the objective violence undergirding liberal democracies, 'the self-propelling metaphysical dance of capital that runs the show', spewing out 'excluded and dispensable individuals from the homeless to the unemployed'.[21] According to Žižek, the systemic violence of global capitalism is paralleled by a symbolic violence, through which hegemonic discourses and cultural practices naturalize and legitimate relations of domination. While Žižek is by no means the first thinker to redefine violence as a structural phenomenon, his analysis of its proximity to political power is acutely relevant in the post-9/11 world. Within both Islamic fundamentalism and what Žižek provocatively terms 'democratic fundamentalism', politics as violence has become normalized, while the shabby euphemisms of illegitimate violence (pre-emptive strike, collateral damage, extraordinary rendition) have become part of everyday political discourse.[22]

2.2   Weaponizing and Controlling Music

The inclusion of violence within the spectrum of music's powers is similarly contentious, going against the centuries-old Western tradition of viewing it as a pacifying, healing medium. Yet music's potency as a weapon and as a vehicle for torture has been a perennial theme in literature and art since ancient times.[23] The most familiar example of music being deployed as a weapon is the biblical story of Joshua's trumpets (or ram's horns) flattening the walls of Jericho. While scientists regard the destruction of buildings as being well beyond the capacities even of modern sonic technology, human beings are more susceptible to such musical violence.[24] If noise is a wolf-like 'weapon of death', as the French economist Jacques Attali rather dramatically puts it, music is its house-trained cousin: normally docile – offering at most a symbolic simulacrum of violence – but quite capable of atavistic reversion when power demands it.[25]

When used as a weapon on the battlefield or in a siege situation, sheer volume is paramount, serving to disorient and incapacitate opponents, or to shock and awe them into flight or submission. Perhaps the best-known modern example of music being deployed as a weapon is Operation Just Cause (1989), in which US Navy SEALs bombarded the papal nuncio's residence in Panama City with rock music in order to flush out the Panamanian dictator Manuel Noriega. Rather than functioning simply as brute noise, the songs chosen by individual SEALs aimed to send what the military described as a 'musical message' to Noriega: the eclectic playlist included 'Wanted Dead or Alive' (Bon Jovi), 'Nowhere to Run' (Martha and the Vandellas), 'I'm Gonna Tear Your Playhouse Down' (by Earl Randle, recorded by Paul Young) and 'Prisoners of Rock 'n' Roll' (Neil Young).[26] The introduction of the long-range acoustic device (LRAD) in 2003 has made the combat use of noise more practicable and efficient, serving not only to disorient opponents but to cause them acute physical distress (leading soldiers to dub it 'the poo sound').[27] Capable of transmitting messages, 'deterrent tones' or music at volumes up to 151 dB, the LRAD was apparently used during the 2004 siege of Fallujah, with US soldiers blitzing the Iraqis with songs by Metallica.[28] As the Panama and Fallujah playlists suggest, the subjective violence of oppressive sound functions in combination with music's symbolic violence, hammering home the cultural as well as military dominance of the United States.

Box 2.2 Attali on Music, Violence and Power

The French economist and theorist reflects on the relationship of music and noise to violence:

> Noise is a weapon and music, primordially, is the formation, domestication, and ritualization of that weapon as a simulacrum of ritual murder ...
>
> Since it is a threat of death, noise is a concern of power; when power founds its legitimacy on the fear it inspires, on its capacity to create social order, on its univocal monopoly of violence, it monopolizes noise. Thus in most cultures, the theme of noise, its audition and endowment with form, lies at the origin of the religious idea. Before the world there was Chaos, the void and background noise. In the Old Testament, man does not hear noise until after the original sin, and the first noises he hears are the footsteps of God.
>
> Music, then, constitutes communication with this primordial, threatening noise – *prayer*. In addition, it has the explicit function of *reassuring*: the whole of traditional musicology analyzes music as the organization of controlled panic, the transformation of anxiety into joy, and of dissonance into harmony ...
>
> The game of music thus resembles the game of power: monopolize the right to violence; provoke anxiety and then provide a feeling of security; provoke disorder and then propose order; create a problem in order to solve it.
>
> Music, then, rebounds in the field of sound like an echo of the sacrificial channelization of violence: dissonances are eliminated from it to keep noise from spreading. It mimics, in this way, in the space of sound, the ritualization of murder.
>
> Music responds to the terror of noise, recreating differences between sounds and repressing the tragic dimension of lasting dissonance – just as sacrifice responds to the terror of violence. Music has been, from its origin, a simulacrum of the monopolization of the power to kill, a simulacrum of ritual murder. A necessary attribute of power, it has the same form power has: something emitted from the singular centre of an imposed, purely syntactic discourse, a discourse capable of making its audience conscious of a commonality – but also of turning its audience against it. (Attali, *Noise*, 24, 27–8)

The use of music as a means of torturing or degrading political prisoners also relies predominantly on excessive volume for its effects. As a form of 'no touch torture', music serves as a surrogate for the kind of techniques prohibited by the UN Universal Declaration of Human Rights (1948) and

the Convention against Torture (1984).[29] In Iraq, US psychological operations personnel used heavy metal music to soften up detainees prior to
questioning; Sergeant Mark Hadsell notes that 'these people haven't heard
heavy metal. They can't take it. If you play it for 24 hours, your brain and
body start to slide, your train of thought slows down and your will is
broken. That's when we come in and talk to them.'[30] In Chapter 1, we saw
how trancing and rave can have the effect of suspending an individual's
sense of self, merging him or her into an ecstatic collective consciousness.
Musical torture, as Suzanne Cusick argues, similarly blocks out thought
and dislocates victims' sense of the passing of time, yet erodes subjectivity
in a very different way, plunging them into a dehumanizing 'dark ecstasy'
in which they are 'utterly at the mercy of a merciless, ubiquitous Power'.[31]

Not all forms of musical torture or cruel, inhuman and degrading treatment rely on extended exposure to ear-splitting rock or metal. Forced
military-style drill to music and coerced singing can serve as ways to intimidate, humiliate and 're-educate' prisoners.[32] These methods have changed
little since they were formalized in the concentration camps of the Third
Reich; a prisoner at the Nazi camp in Sachsenhausen recalled that singing to
order was a daily occurrence and that 'anyone who did not know the song
was beaten. Anyone who sang too softly was beaten. Anyone who sang too
loud was beaten. The SS men lashed out wildly.'[33] Another technique of
humiliation is the use of so-called futility music to convince captors that
resistance to interrogation is pointless. Notoriously, the US military made use
of endless repetitions of Barney the Purple Dinosaur's song 'I love you, you
love me' to wear down intransigent Iraqi detainees.[34] Other forms of musical
torture are considerably subtler. The anxiety provoked by the constant,
unseen presence of power – 'Big Brother is watching you' – is paralleled by
the effect on political prisoners of subliminal acousmatic music: the disorien-
tation caused by not knowing the source of musical sounds or indeed
whether they are real or imagined. Anabela Duarte has investigated the
sophisticated use of music to unnerve political prisoners in Portugal in the
final months of the authoritarian Estado Novo regime (1933–74); here,
barely audible recordings of serenades and *fados*, made to sound as if they
were coming from outside the prison, were used to aggravate the prisoners'
sense of hopelessness by triggering memories of happier times.[35]

Music and Social Control

Next down the scale of power-as-domination is music's use as a form of
non-violent social control (though we should heed Bruce Johnson and

Martin Cloonan's observation that 'imposed music will always tend to constitute a form of violence to a greater or lesser degree, and in any society').[36] The use of music from loudspeakers to quell the chants of protesters, hasten their dispersal and recapture public space is part of the tool-kit of governments worldwide. Often the symbolic violence of patriotic songs and other music associated with the dominant order is wielded for this function; in 2003, for example, the US Army at Fort Benning, Georgia, played 'The Army Song' and 'God Bless the USA' to drown out a demonstration against the School of the Americas, a military training programme linked to human rights abuses in Latin America.[37] Media savvy police chiefs are increasingly turning to alternative playlists, employing pop music to distract protesters and to make light of their concerns. In 2015, police in the Philippines played tracks by Katy Perry, David Guetta, Dolly Parton and the Bee Gees to disperse anti-globalization demonstrators at the Asia-Pacific Economic Cooperation summit, a move which succeeded both in controlling the protest and in trivializing media accounts of it.[38] The use of music as a form of pest control extends well beyond repelling activists. Across the English-speaking world, classical and easy listening music has been played in railways stations, shopping malls and other public places to deter youths from loitering and thus reduce incidents of vandalism and other forms of criminality. Known as the 'Manilow method' following an experiment in Sydney in 2006, the use of music as a deterrent has proved highly successful in reducing crime rates in some circumstances; British Transport Police reported a decrease in robberies by 33 per cent, staff assaults by 25 per cent and vandalism by 37 per cent following the introduction of piped classical music to the London Underground.[39]

These and similar forms of social control through music run the risk of having discriminatory and anti-democratic outcomes; Johnson and Cloonan point out that the kind of music used to drive away loitering teenagers from malls is precisely the same as that used to attract affluent middle-aged customers, suggesting the construction of a civic soundscape that welcomes only those who 'fit the ideology of citizen as paying consumer'.[40] For other commentators, however, the benefits that accrue from social regulation through music outweigh any possible ethical or political objections. An article by the American legal scholar Bennett Capers is a case in point, championing the use of piped music across the New York subway system:

What I am suggesting is using music in a way that is neither elitist nor exclusionary. To be clear, I am not suggesting using music to repel certain groups, but rather a music to bind people together, a music that fosters a sense of community . . . The advantage of such an approach is that it would serve to unify, not divide, to create a sense of togetherness as a component of crime reduction.[41]

Capers's vision of a society brought together and disciplined through music may seem to owe more to Platonist pipe dreams than contemporary reality, since it ignores the power relations and exclusionary dimension present in all top-down attempts to manufacture collectivity. It also surely exaggerates music's capacity to act as a social solvent, since it is hard to see how any music (whether national songs, classic pop hits or sports anthems) could command equal levels of identification and enjoyment from all who are exposed to it, particularly when that music is imposed and unavoidable.

For millennia, theorists advocating social control through (and over) music have drawn on similar arguments about community and the public good. Within the Western tradition, most of these theories point back directly or indirectly to Plato, whose *Republic* and *Laws* offer what Stephen Halliwell describes as an 'ultra conservative' and 'authoritarian' take on the issue.[42] The seriousness with which Plato approaches music stems from his adherence to the transmission model of its effects discussed earlier: the idea that there is a transparent link between music's imitative or representational capacity and the emotions and behaviours it triggers in the listener. In the *Laws* he describes music as an 'education in virtue', contrasting the 'controlled and restrained style of music' with the 'undisciplined style' and contending that 'one environment is invariably a good influence, the other a bad'.[43] An extended passage in the *Laws* gives a context for Plato's views on the relation between musical and social order, describing how the growth of lawlessness and disregard for authority within Athenian music had led to a breakdown in control in other spheres of life: 'Music proved to be the starting point of everyone's conviction that he was an authority on everything, and of a general disregard for the law.'[44] The view that disorder in music can insinuate itself into other forms of private and public life, and thus threaten the stability of the state itself, is behind Plato's impulse to police it:

'Those in charge of the city must devote themselves to ensuring that this principle is not destroyed without their noticing it, and to guarding it above all else, the principle, I mean, that no innovations shall be made in gymnastics and music beyond what is laid down, but that what is laid down shall be preserved as closely as possible . . . People should beware of change to new forms of music, for they are risking change in the whole [constitution and fabric of the state]. Styles of music are nowhere altered without change in the greatest laws of the city . . .

'It seems then', I said, 'that it is here, in music, that the guardians must build their guard-house.'[45]

The policing which Plato proposes for music in his ideal republic takes several forms. One is the formulation of a series of exemplary laws to direct the positive uses to which music is put. Another is the rigorous pre-censorship of texts for composition ('no one should be allowed to show his work to any private person without first submitting it to the appointed assessor and to the Guardians of the Laws, and getting their approval').[46] Best known, however, is Plato's decision to exclude altogether from his republic those genres, modes, instruments and metres which he considers incapable of having a beneficial effect on character (see Box 2.3).[47]

Box 2.3 Plato on Controlling Music's Effect on Behaviour

Socrates and Glaucon debate the place of music in an ideal city-state governed by an elite class of guardian philosophers:

> 'Which then are the mourning modes? You're musical. You tell me.'
> 'The Mixolydian', he said. 'The Syntonolydian. That sort of thing.'
> 'Should these be banned, then?' I asked. 'After all, they are no use even to women – if we want them to be good women – let alone to men.'
> 'They certainly should.'
> 'Drunkenness is also something quite unsuitable for our guardians. And so are luxury and laziness.'
> 'Of course they are.'
> 'Which of the modes, then, are appropriate to luxury and parties?'
> 'There are some Ionian modes', he said, 'and again Lydian, which are called relaxed.'
> 'Will these be any use to men of a warlike disposition?'
> 'No', he said. 'So it looks as if that leaves you with the Dorian and Phrygian.'
> 'I don't know about modes', I said. 'Leave me the mode which can most fittingly imitate the voice and accents of a brave man in time of war, or in any externally imposed crisis. When things go wrong, and he faces death and wounds, or encounters some other danger, in all these situations he holds out to the end in a disciplined and steadfast manner. Plus another mode for someone engaged in some peaceful, voluntary, freely chosen activity ... These two modes, then: one for adversity and one for freely chosen activity, the modes which will best imitate the voices of the prudent and of the brave in failure and success. Leave me those.'
> 'Leave you, in other words, with precisely the two I suggested just now', he said.
> 'That means we shan't want an enormous range of strings, and every possible mode, in our songs and melodies.'

Box 2.3 (*cont.*)

'No, I think not', he said ...

'Ye dogs!' I said. 'Without meaning to, we have purged the city we said was too luxurious.'

'That was sensible of us', he said.

'Come on, then', I said. 'Let's purge the rest of it. Our next concern after mode will be rhythm. We should not pursue complexity, nor do we want all kinds of metres. We should see what are the rhythms of a self-disciplined and courageous life, and after looking at those, make the metre and melody conform to the speech of someone like that.' (Plato, *Republic* (c. 380 BC), in *Greek and Roman Aesthetics*, ed. and trans. Oleg V. Bychkov and Anne Sheppard (Cambridge, 2010), 47–8)

2.3   Music Censorship

Plato's proposals seem modest and reasonable compared with some of the methods used in modern times to control music. In one form or another, music censorship – defined as an instrument of power through which music is suppressed or regulated by state or civic authorities, public institutions or the media – is a pervasive dimension of musical production and consumption the world over.[48] The most extreme form of musical censorship is killing musicians, a method resorted to all too frequently by the authoritarian regimes of the twentieth and twenty-first centuries. Perhaps the best-known example is the Chilean poet, folk singer and Communist activist Víctor Jara, a prominent supporter of the leftist president Salvador Allende, who was tortured and killed by the Pinochet regime following its assumption of power in 1973. Although accounts of his final hours vary, most stress that Jara's hands were mutilated by soldiers as a mocking punishment (he was a guitarist).[49] Similarly, in July 2011 the Syrian poet and folk singer Ibrahim Kashoush, 'the nightingale of the revolution', had his throat cut and vocal chords torn out after leading a crowd of demonstrators singing his song 'Yalla Erhal Ya Bashar' (It's time to leave, [President] Bashar).[50] The country currently most dangerous for musicians is probably Mexico, where dozens of narcocorrido singers have been killed or otherwise silenced following performances which offended the cartels. One of the best known was Valentín Elizalde, an affiliate of Guzmán's Sinaloa cartel, who was gunned down in 2006 following a performance of a song which antagonized the rival Gulf cartel (Elizalde's killers released video footage of his autopsy as a warning to other narcocorrido performers).[51] Even bands unconnected to the narcocorrido scene risk being silenced if they perform in venues associated with cartels; in 2013, seventeen members of the group Kombo Kolombia were kidnapped, shot and thrown down a well as punishment for singing at the wrong bar.[52]

Another form of censorship, the suppression or prohibition of entire musical genres, is generally associated with totalitarian or religious fundamentalist regimes. Some Communist countries in Eastern Europe and parts of the USSR attempted to ban Western pop music well into the 1980s, believing it to be a vehicle for spreading Western values; in 1983 the Soviet leader Yurii Andropov proscribed Western pop as a 'dangerous ideological pollution among Soviet youth', leading to the seizure of imported pop records and disbanding of scores of rock groups.[53] Restrictions on pop music have been even tighter in the Islamic Republic of Iran, and although they were eased following Mohammad Khatami's election as president in 1997, his successor Mahmoud Ahmadinejad imposed a broadcast ban on all forms of Western music.[54] The most drastic recent controls on music were those imposed by the Taliban movement while it held power in Afghanistan from 1996 to 2001. Soon after taking control of Kabul, the Taliban imposed a total ban on private as well as public music-making and musical consumption, alongside bans on pictures and photographic images, beard shaving, pigeon-keeping and kite-flying:

To prevent music. To be broadcasted by the public information resources. In shops, hotels, vehicles and rickshaws cassettes and music are prohibited. This matter should be monitored within five days. If any music cassette is found in a shop, the shopkeeper should be imprisoned and the shop locked . . . If a cassette is found in a vehicle, the vehicle and the driver will be imprisoned . . .

To prevent music and dances in wedding parties . . . In the case of violation the head of the family will be arrested and punished.

To prevent the playing of music drums: First the prohibition of this action to be announced to the people. If anybody does this then the religious elders can decide about it.[55]

In the eyes of the Western media, the prohibition of music was emblematic of the Taliban's denial of basic human rights; as the ethnomusicologist John Baily comments, 'the disembowelled audiocassette, nailed to a tree or post, tape waving in the breeze, became the icon of Taliban rule.'[56] But as the wording of these edicts suggests, the ban on music was slightly less sweeping than media reports initially indicated, focusing in practice on Western music and on the use of musical instruments. Indeed, since the Taliban did not regard singing as a form of music, its own unaccompanied religious singing remained permitted.[57] As Baily stresses, the musical restrictions imposed by the Taliban, although extreme, were not without precedent. However puzzling the impulse to silence music may seem from a Western perspective, music in the Afghanistan region has been under some form of control throughout history, just as it has in many other areas of the globe.[58]

The impulse to ban particular musical genres, musicians and songs is not limited to authoritarian regimes, and it cannot be assumed that such censorship always amounts to an abuse of power. Consider, for example, the on/off attempts by several Mexican states to prohibit public performances of nar-cocorridos, a move which could help reverse the glamorization of the cartels and the normalization of criminal violence.[59] More contentiously, several Latin American countries have banned public broadcasts of reggaeton (a genre fusing Spanish hip hop and Jamaican dancehall, associated with sexually explicit lyrics and the raunchy *perreo* dance style). Justifying the crackdown in Cuba, the president of the official state Music Institute, Orlando Vistel Columbié, condemned 'aggressive, sexually obscene lyrics' that degrade women by representing them as 'grotesque sexual objects'.[60]

Cuba's censorship of lyrics demeaning to women brings to mind recent cases in which student unions in the United Kingdom have banned songs on similar grounds. The most prominent example is Robin Thicke's 2013 track 'Blurred Lines', banned by twenty student unions for its supposedly 'creepy', 'rapey' lyrics, in particular the chorus 'I hate these blurred lines, I know you want it.'[61] Although the lyrics are more ambiguous than these comments suggest, the fate of Thicke's cheesy summer hit is less interesting than the language used to justify censoring it: in particular, the idea that universities should be 'safe spaces' in which 'zero tolerance' is shown to material that crosses (or pushes) the boundaries.[62] The ban on Thicke's song is symptomatic of how the liberal ideal of freedom of expression – at one time, threatened primarily by social conservatism – is increasingly being curbed in the name of other seemingly liberal values. Crucial here is the rise of tolerance – more accurately, intolerance toward perceived intolerance – as the dominant social value within contemporary politics and society. As the political scientist Wendy Brown observes, there is something strange and disquieting about 'the uncritical embrace of tolerance' across the political spectrum within liberal democracies.[63] Rather than simply being an abstract virtue, tolerance for Brown is a mode of governmentality, serving to regulate behaviour not through force of law but through public discourse and custom. As such, tolerance is part of the matrix of invisible power through which governments and civic authorities (and for that matter, student union officials) stitch together isolated individuals into viable communities. In a recent polemical piece, the journalist

Brendan O'Neill draws a similar conclusion, highlighting how the impulse to censor artists and others who offend against the shibboleth of tolerance is a form of social control:

What the right and the left share in common is a devotion to the cult of 'You Can't Say That!' This is the stifling culture of conformism that is threatening free, open and edgy debate in 21st-century Britain. It isn't enforced by the state; rather it speaks to what John Stuart Mill called 'the despotism of custom', where the parameters of acceptable thought are policed, and policed thoroughly, by informal, non-state actors. Today, that dirty job is done by Twittermobs and Change.org uprisings . . . They seek to destroy offensive ideas, and to secure the borders around acceptable thinking.[64]

This kind of unofficial censorship – enforced by public opinion, the media or the art world itself – is more common in liberal democracies than direct state control. Perhaps the best-known example of state censorship of a classical composer, Israel's 'ban' on performances of the music of Richard Wagner, is a case in point: rather than being officially banned, Wagner's exclusion has never been more than an informal convention.[65] In some cases, unofficial censorship stems from arts organizations seeking to avoid being associated with artists who are politically controversial (often for reasons wholly unconnected with their music). In 2015, for example, the management of the Toronto Symphony Orchestra cancelled concert appearances by the Ukrainian pianist Valentina Lisitsa after 'aggressive lobbying' made them aware of her provocative, pro-Russia remarks on social media.[66]

Whether the word 'censorship' is appropriate in such cases may seem a moot point, given that some definitions restrict the concept to deliberate, organized interventions by government agencies; one frequently quoted example from 1988 defines it as 'the systematic control of the content of any communications medium, or of several or all of the media, by means of constitutional, judicial, administrative, financial or purely physical measures imposed directly by, or with the connivance of, the ruling power or a ruling elite'.[67] But while a state-oriented conception of censorship may have sufficed during the Cold War, more recent perspectives stress the broad diffusion and invisible workings of power. The singer-songwriter Damon Albarn of the rock band Blur comments perceptively that 'true censorship is something that we are not really aware of on a day-to-day basis; it's something that's inherent in the system . . . a sort of covert censorship going on everywhere.'[68] Although we should avoid treating the concept too elastically (not all forms of musical regulation and selection can usefully be seen as censorship), it is important to include self-censorship, that is, where musicians steer clear of sensitive areas or genres to avoid falling foul of those in authority. Banning Eyre's 2001 investigation of how censorship worked in Zimbabwe, for example, found no evidence of direct government intervention; rather, a climate of fear led musicians, DJs and the recording industry to avoid material that might offend the Mugabe regime and its supporters.[69] Similarly, the Tanzanian rapper Josiah George (Mjusi Kafir) describes how sustained harassment drove musicians to abandon political and social commentary in favour of more anodyne themes: 'It's not only we musicians who are hindered by such intimidations, no. The media falls in the same trap. I am very sure no such critical song is going to be played by local radio and TV stations here. So, as a musician I ask myself why I should compose such a song at all.'[70] Aside from killing musicians, power's most efficient means of censoring opponents is to intimidate them into silence.

2.4   Resistance, Micropolitics and Constituent Power

To understand power, we need to understand resistance to it. The ease with which power can stifle resistance, evident in practice in the examples from Africa cited above, is paralleled problematically within much theoretical work, which can make domination appear unassailable; the classic example is the output of Foucault, who was largely responsible for catapulting the term 'resistance' to prominence in the 1970s. Since that time, resistance has been firmly entrenched within the vocabularies of political activists and theorists as the dominant way of conceptualizing oppositional activity. In its popular usage, the term has come to encompass not only activism that challenges power but virtually any kind of subversive or nonconformist behaviour, covering everything from revolutions and sit-ins to hairstyles and body piercings.[71] But in spite of its ubiquity, the concept of resistance makes for a problematic antithesis to power as domination. By definition, resistance is principally reactive and negative, being tied to domination in a relationship of dependency and subordination. The sense that resistance is inadequate to the tasks that have been assigned to it – a view that I will return to below – is one reason why some recent activists and theorists have had recourse to the concept of 'counterpower' instead.[72]

Anarcho-Punk and Subcultural Resistance

Before exploring how Foucault theorized the relationship between power and resistance, it will be useful to look at some of the strengths and limitations of resistance in practice. Some of the most striking examples of musical resistance are from the anarcho-punk scene of the late 1970s and early 1980s. Aiming to reinvigorate punk as an oppositional force, British bands like Crass offered a lacerating critique not only of authority but of what they saw as the posturing and charlatanism of earlier punk rock (the lyrics of Crass repeatedly berate the Clash for selling out, while the cover art for their single 'Bloody Revolutions' presents the Sex Pistols as establishment stooges). Crass's anarchist, anti-capitalist agenda shaped not just their lyrics but their approach to music-making and record production. Committed to values antithetical to those of the music industry – summed up in the slogan 'DIY not EMI' – Crass shunned the limelight, kept gig and record prices low and produced their recordings themselves (this DIY aesthetic is encapsulated in the band's trademark stencilled posters and flyers).[73] If Crass, perhaps more than any other British rock band, epitomize the politics of resistance, this is in part because their music was embedded in a broader commitment to anarchist ethics and activism. But it also points to the extent to which negativity – the angry refusal and indictment of power – outweighs the positive agenda in their songs. This is clearest in the band's magnum opus, the 34-minute song/album 'Yes Sir, I will' (1983), in which fragments of an anarchist manifesto are submerged within a densely worded assault on the media, creeping authoritarianism, police brutality, the politics of fear, nuclear weapons, war, inequality, the 'nouveau wankers' of contemporary punk, as well as attempts to censor Crass: 'They've tried to ban our records saying that we're a threat to decent society. Fuck them. I hope we are.'

In his *Cultural Resistance Reader*, the cultural theorist Stephen Duncombe reflects on the positive and negative dimensions of punk as a form of resistance to the dominant order:

Punk was a great tool for articulating the problems of my world, and providing a supportive culture where I could develop that critique, but punk in itself did nothing to affect the root causes of the things – racism, sexism, and class inequality – I was so angry about. Punk had no strategic plan; it had no plan at all ... The culture of resistance that my friends and I had built became a safe place to hide. Fortified by our righteous sense of superiority ... boundaries between 'us' and 'them' clearly demarcated by dyed hair and leather jackets, we closed off the world.[74]

Duncombe's experience of punk opens up broader questions about the relationship between music, subcultures and political resistance. Commentators have often assumed that the music of protest and resistance is tightly bound to political activism, in effect, that music has the relationship of a 'superstructure' to the base of social movements or other oppositional groupings.[75] This presumed link has led to entire genres being construed (and marketed) as subversive; a clear example is the reception of rock, since until relatively recently, even cultural theorists took for granted 'rock's inextricable tie to resistance, refusal, alienation, marginality, etc.'[76] In practice, the closeness of the connection between oppositional music and activist groups varies widely. While some forms of protest music and musical resistance are messily entwined with political activism (e.g. Crass), most are connected only tangentially, if at all, to social change movements (this is also the case with much contemporary art music, which offers what the composer-theorist Federico Reuben describes as an 'imaginary musical radicalism' detached from the kind of activist collectives in which the historical avant garde was embedded).[77]

The assumption that oppositional music is tightly bound to activism is not entirely the result of myth-making on the part of musicians and critics, even though both camps benefit from stressing the subversive credentials of their preferred music. Rather, it reflects a widespread tendency to treat subcultures and more narrowly artistic groupings as if they were activist social movements. While subcultures such as punk, as the cultural theorist T. V. Reed argues, have the potential to develop into interventive political forces as a result of their alternative or oppositional character, their orientation and raison d'être is not primarily political.[78] And while some or all of the participants in a fan community may share a particular oppositional outlook, there is no reason to expect that this will lead to collective action; Bradford Martin sums up the matter succinctly in noting that 'there are limits on what level of political activism can be reasonably expected from a group of people whose identity is shaped by shared musical preferences'.[79]

If the superstructural assumption can lead to the ties between oppositional music and other forms of activism being exaggerated, it can also result in music being sidelined: treated as at best a useful add-on and at worst a distraction from 'real' political activity. One charge frequently levelled at oppositional music – and cultural resistance in general – is that it is incapable of having a political effect outside the cultural fold; Duncombe's frustration at punk for failing to redress the injustices it thematized is a case in point. More broadly, Joe Wood argues that 'the problem with "culture as politics" is that it isn't (and almost never produces) the sort of action that not only challenges, but changes political structures.'[80] One way to rebut such objections would be to argue that it is unrealistic to expect music, or any other form of cultural expression, to deliver the kind of instant, transparent effect associated with squeezing a gun trigger or pressing the nuclear button; a variant version of this argument might stress how reductive it is to apply the late-capitalist logic of direct, quantifiable impact to music's political efficacy. Another response would be to question the idea that 'culture as politics' is walled off from the 'real' political field, as well as the notion that the only meaningful political actions are those that achieve structural change. Even if these arguments convince, musical resistance can still seem a peripheral form of opposition, gazing inward rather than intervening in other folds of reality. As Duncombe's critique of punk highlights, it is a moot point whether such cultural separatism offers an experimental space for developing tools for resistance or whether it simply channels discontent in a direction unthreatening to the dominant order.[81]

Foucault, Power and Resistance

Another reason why musical resistance is sometimes dismissed as a kind of political shadow boxing is its sheer flaky unreliability: this week's angry protest song is next week's commodified hit, catchy jingle or right-wing anthem. The ease with which oppositional music can be coopted (that is, neutralized through appropriation) or put to work in the service of antithetical ideologies is symptomatic of resistance's broader entanglement with power. Indeed, it can be argued that even the most important twentieth-century theorist of resistance, Foucault, does not offer a convincing account of how it might succeed in challenging an established order or bringing about radical change. My equivocal phrasing here stems from the palpable gap between Foucault's theories and their representation by later commentators, who have argued that his conception of resistance offers an endless series of challenges to power without the possibility of overcoming it; as Gerald Raunig notes, 'the reception of Foucault accordingly tends to produce images of an impasse, a padded cell, an inescapable totality.'[82] Given Foucault's continuing influence – thirty years after his death – on how theorists and activists approach the relationship between power and resistance, we need to understand his approach and the challenges it generated.

Box 2.4 Foucault on Power and Resistance

The French philosopher responds to a question from Rancière about how his view of power relates to Marxist models.

It seems to me that power *is* 'always already there', that one is never 'outside' it, that there are no 'margins' for those who break with the system to gambol in. But this does not entail the necessity of accepting an inescapable form of domination or an absolute privilege on the side of

Box 2.4 (*cont.*)

the law. To say that one can never be 'outside' power does not mean that one is trapped and condemned to defeat no matter what.

I would suggest rather (but these are hypotheses which will need exploring): (i) that power is co-extensive with the social body; there are no spaces of primal liberty between the meshes of its network; (ii) that relations of power are interwoven with other kinds of relations (production, kinship, family, sexuality) for which they play at once a conditioning and a conditioned role; (iii) that these relations don't take the sole form of prohibition and punishment, but are of multiple forms; (iv) that their interconnections delineate general conditions of domination, and this domination is organised into a more-or-less coherent and unitary strategic form; that dispersed, heteromorphous, localised procedures of power are adapted, reinforced and transformed by these global strategies, all this being accompanied by numerous phenomena of inertia, displacement and resistance; hence one should not assume a massive and primal condition of domination, a binary structure with 'dominators' on one side and 'dominated' on the other, but rather a multiform production of relations of domination which are partially susceptible of integration into overall strategies; (v) that power relations do indeed 'serve', but not at all because they are 'in the service of' an economic interest taken as primary, rather because they are capable of being utilised in strategies; (vi) that there are no relations of power without resistances; the latter are all the more real and effective because they are formed right at the point where relations of power are exercised; resistance to power does not have to come from elsewhere to be real, nor is it inexorably frustrated through being the compatriot of power. It exists all the more by being in the same place as power; hence, like power, resistance is multiple and can be integrated in global strategies. (Michel Foucault, 'Pouvoirs et stratégies (entretien avec J. Rancière)' (1977), translated as 'Power and Strategies', in *Power/Knowledge: Selected Interviews and Other Writings 1972–1977*, ed. Colin Gordon (New York, 1980), 141–2)

In an interview with Rancière from 1977, Foucault gave a useful summary of the key hypotheses underpinning his conceptions of power and resistance (see Box 2.4). Significant here is his rejection of centralized, top-down models of how power operates; instead, he stresses that power is everywhere, interwoven with all social relations, leaving 'no spaces of primal liberty' or '"margins" for those who break with the system to gambol in'. At first glance, particularly for those familiar with Foucault's earlier text *Discipline and*

Punish (*Surveiller et punir*, 1975), this claim suggests a dystopia of domination from which resistance has been wholly expunged. But Foucault goes on to reject conceptions of power grounded in a 'massive and primal condition of domination', stressing instead its diffuse, dispersed and localized nature (although power's emergence 'from below' does not preclude it being integrated within a larger system or overall strategy).

Resistance, as is evident from the last point in the extract, is crucial to Foucault's conception of what he here terms 'relations of power', being embedded within them and a precondition for their existence. The idea that power and resistance are mutually dependent, suspended in a relation of continual give and take, receives an aphoristic formulation in Foucault's best-known discussion of this topic: 'Where there is power, there is resistance, and yet, or rather consequently, this resistance is never in a position of exteriority in relation to power.'[83] Maintaining this position requires Foucault to redefine both power and resistance, a manoeuvre which he does not always carry out consistently or unambiguously. His clearest definition of power is from a 1984 interview in which he differentiates between power relations and states of domination (elsewhere, he sometimes uses the capitalized 'Power' to indicate the latter):

When one speaks of power, people immediately think of a political structure, a government, a dominant social class, the master and the slave, and so on. I am not thinking of this at all when I speak of relations of power. I mean that in human relationships ... power is always present: I mean a relationship in which one person tries to control the conduct of the other. So I am speaking of relations that exist at different levels, in different forms; these power relations are mobile, they can be modified, they are not fixed once and for all.[84]

Power relations for Foucault are fluid matrixes which include not only actions but reactions to them; this is what he means by arguing that resistance is built into power, or is 'inscribed in the latter as an irreducible opposite'.[85] This makes the possibility of resistance a prerequisite for the exercise of power, an idea that limits power relationships to instances where both parties have some degree of freedom of action; for Foucault, such relationships require 'that "the other" (the one over whom power is exercised) is recognized and maintained to the very end as a subject who acts; and that, faced with a relationship of power, a whole field of responses, reactions, results, and possible inventions may open up'.[86] The exercise of power consists therefore in marshalling such interactions into sequences and limiting the field of actions (including resistances) that can be taken by others, without wholly and continually impeding their freedom. Power only becomes domination when power relations become 'blocked, frozen' and 'perpetually asymmetrical'; in places, Foucault sets such stringent conditions on domination that it serves as a purely abstract category, since in practice some form of resistant action is always possible:

Even when the power relation is completely out of balance, when it can truly be claimed that one side has 'total power' over the other, a power can be exercised over the other only insofar as the other still has the option of killing himself, of leaping out the window, or of killing the other person. This means that in power relations there is necessarily the possibility of resistance because if there were no possibility of resistance (of violent resistance, flight, deception, strategies capable of reversing the situation), there would be no power relations at all.[87]

So far, tellingly, we have encountered Foucault's conception of resistance only as an element that enables power to function, rather than as a countervailing force. Problematically, Foucault's resistance seems inspired in part by the role of the concept in electronics; just as in an electrical circuit, Foucault's resistances serve as necessary blockages, working ultimately to facilitate the functioning of power networks: 'points of resistance . . . play the role of adversary, target, support, or handle in power relations. These points of resistance are present everywhere in the power network. Hence there is no single locus of great Refusal, no soul of revolt, source of all rebellions, or pure law of the revolutionary.'[88] While Foucault's writings give greater attention to power than to resistance, there is no sense in which resistance is the lesser or passive element; rather, he argues that 'resistance comes first, and resistance remains superior to the forces of the process; power relations are obliged to change with the resistance. So I think that *resistance* is the main word, *the key word*, in this dynamic.'[89] While the placing of resistance at the heart of power relations may seem to neutralize its disruptive potential, it also emphasizes that power – no less than resistance itself – is fragile and unstable. Foucault's work rejects the large-scale antagonisms of Marxist theory in favour of distributed, localized conceptions of power and resistance. But if he was convinced that the age of fundamental ruptures was in the past, he nonetheless emphasizes that it is possible for micro-resistances – just like power actions – to cohere into an irresistible force for change: 'the swarm of points of resistance traverses social stratifications and individual unities. And it is doubtless the strategic codification of these points of resistance that makes a revolution possible, somewhat similar to the way in which the state relies on the institutional integration of power relationships.'[90]

This is thin gruel for Foucault's critics, who argue that his model of resistance is too bound up with power to generate radical change. The anarchist theorist John Holloway is typical in complaining that the complex world of power relations which Foucault presents is akin to 'the richness of a still photograph or a painting': 'in Foucault's analysis, there are a whole host of resistances which are integral to power, but there is no possibility of emancipation. The only possibility is an endlessly shifting constellation of power-and-resistance.'[91] Similarly, Žižek argues that Foucault's resistance is locked into the 'eternal game Power plays with itself', restricted to a narrow set of actions and incapable of game-changing moves: 'Power and Resistance are effectively caught in a deadly mutual embrace.'[92] Such critiques do not entirely do justice to the subtlety of Foucault's analysis, since they strip away his careful redefinitions of power and resistance. On one level, they oversimplify Foucault's conception of power by replacing it with a view of power as domination: this serves to reduce any relationship between power and resistance to one of cooption and neutralization. On another, they fault him for the failure to accommodate a fundamental antagonism between power and resistance, even though his model is specifically designed to supersede such binary oppositions. If Foucault's theorization of resistance does not lend itself to modelling revolutionary upheaval, it is because its ambition was to account for how resistance functions at the micro level: 'Are there no great radical ruptures, massive binary divisions, then? Occasionally, yes. But more often one is dealing with mobile and transitory points of resistance, producing cleavages in a society that shift about, producing unities and effective regroupings.'[93]

Power after Foucault

Foucault's theorization of power continues to impact on political theory. One decisive aspect of his influence lies in the expansion of the political to include every aspect of life; if power is everywhere, shaping all social relationships and interactions, then politics is no less ubiquitous. Another key dimension of Foucault's impact lies in his reaction against power-as-domination and the narrow agency-centred standpoint that it fosters: the idea of power as a tool wielded intentionally by individual agents to serve their own ends. In places, Foucault's formulations go to the opposite extreme, treating power as a structural force working within every individual and leaving practically no room for independent action: 'In thinking of the mechanisms of power, I am thinking rather of its capillary form of existence, the point where power reaches into the very grain of individuals, touches their bodies and inserts itself into their actions and attitudes, their discourses, learning processes and everyday lives.'[94] As critics of Foucault's conceptions of resistance have observed, the idea that power inserts itself into the bodies and minds of individuals makes it hard to see how they could exercise agency independently of it; thus for Michèle Barrett, 'we are all already regulated, already participants in networks of power', making 'notions such as the "free individual", on whom power descends from above, completely meaningless'.[95]

For many theorists of power post-Foucault, this eclipse of individual agency is a strength of his conception, enabling an understanding of how power functions in modern 'societies of control'.[96] Champions of post-hegemonic power, such as Scott Lash, argue that the idea of power as something external and centralized, securing consent through discourse and ideology, is wholly superseded in the contemporary world; instead, a networked, micro power 'grasps us in our very being' as a 'virtual, generative force', working subconsciously and affectively on the individual.[97] The best-known advocates of this new paradigm of power are the philosopher-activists Michael Hardt and Antonio Negri. Like Foucault, they use the term 'biopower' to convey how power manifests itself in every aspect of daily life, organizing minds and bodies and encompassing all social relations:

Biopower is a form of power that regulates social life from its interior, following it, interpreting, absorbing it and rearticulating it. Power can achieve an effective command over the entire life of the population only when it becomes an integral, vital function that every individual embraces and reactivates of his or her own accord.[98]

For Hardt and Negri, as for Lash, the 'mediatization of life' has facilitated the process through which individuals have become complicit in the actions of power, subjugating them to the hidden rules and algorithms of the internet age.[99] The idea that individuals have come to embrace their own exploitation has recently been taken a stage further by another theorist building on Foucault's paradigm of power, the philosopher Byung-Chul Han. For Han, neoliberal capitalism thrives as a result of its highly efficient model of subjugation, relying on the auto-exploitation of 'achievement-subjects' as they pursue the goals of efficiency, self-optimization and quantifiable success.[100] The 'smart power' of the neoliberal regime works through 'the freedom of *Can*' rather than the coercion of should, instilling dependency on its values and reward systems; as a result, individuals blame failure on their own inadequacies rather than on the defects of the system, inhibiting resistance and fostering depression.[101] For Han, the internet and especially social media serve as 'digital panoptica' for ensuring conformity with neoliberal values, relying on the willing collaboration of individuals for their effects; rather than clunkily imposing compliance, 'the digital Big Brother *outsources* operations to inmates.'[102]

Micro-Resistance, Infrapolitics and Constituent Power

It is as a theorist of 'everyday' or micro-resistance that Foucault has had the most impact on activists and new social movements. The terms 'everyday resistance' and 'infrapolitics' were coined by the anthropologist James C. Scott to describe small, dispersed acts that go unnoticed by the authorities or whose politicality is not recognized.[103] At this level, questions of the effectiveness of resistance need to be finely calibrated, since micro-resistance could encompass anything from a minority group's struggle for rights to an individual's quest to live out alternative values. For its champions, such everyday resistance may be measured by nothing more concrete than its capacity to instil hope; as Deleuze argues, 'if you believe in the world you precipitate events, however inconspicuous, that elude control ... Our ability to resist control, or our submission to it, has to be assessed at the level of our every move.'[104] Foucault's ideas and language reached their zenith of popularity among theorists and activists in the 1990s, chiming with a world in which the binary oppositions of the Cold War had fragmented into a multiplicity of more localized resistances. But their origins coincide with those of anarcho-punk and its encouragement to individuals to ground resistance in their own imaginations and behaviours: as Crass expressed it, 'anarchy is a personal choice, an act of commitment, a decision in your own head to pursue a life that is ENTIRELY your own, free of restriction, free of fear, free of intimidation. OK, so you won't change the world tomorrow by becoming an anarchist today, but it's a start.'[105]

As can be seen even from these brief quotations from Deleuze and Crass, resistance needs to be combined with other political ingredients in order to inspire and engineer change: a vision of emancipation, a new model and practice of social organization, an alliance of like-minded individuals or groups, leverage over existing power-holders or the means to displace them, and so on. If the term 'counterpower' makes sense as an alternative to resistance, it is as an umbrella that accommodates these other dimensions of radical change (elements of this more comprehensive view are present in Foucault's conception of resistance, leading Hardt and Negri to argue that the term 'does not really capture what he has in mind').[106] Crucial to counterpower is what Foucault described as power's productive dimension: in this context, its capacity to generate new subjectivities and practices of freedom.

Theorists building on Foucault's work have explored this productive dimension using the concepts of 'power-to' (Holloway) and creative or constituent power (Negri).[107] For Negri, constituent power – the collective formation of new social and political configurations – is one of three interwoven elements essential to counterpower and to the revolutionary 'machine': 'we must think of resistance, insurrection and constituent power as an indivisible process, in which these three are melded into a full counter-power and ultimately a new, alternative formation of society.'[108] Rather than conceiving these three elements sequentially (i.e. as the before, during and after phases of revolution), Negri presents constituent power as a generative energy or potential that anticipates, models and helps bring about revolutionary change: 'the paradigm of constituent power is that of a force that bursts apart, breaks, interrupts, unhinges any preexisting equilibrium and any possible continuity.'[109] As the fluid embodiment of the democratic aspirations of a collective, constituent power generates an 'overflowing constitutive activity', modelling new forms of social organization outside state institutions and the existing mechanisms of politics. [110] In their 2012 response to the Arab Spring and the Occupy movements, Hardt and Negri invoke constituent power as an intense externalization of a new collective sensibility:

The common sense that dwells in the hearts and heads of the subjects who conduct the struggles and imagine a new society has a prescriptive value and the power to generate, animate, and regulate new forms of life. Declaring their independence from the ancien régime, they root themselves in a new ontological condition and establish the circumstances under which more equal, common, and sustainable relations can grow. This constituent power is deeply embedded in the struggles.[111]

Collective music-making, like other forms of participatory art, has an immediate relevance to the creative, world-making dimension of constituent power evoked by Negri and others working with the concept.[112] As seen earlier, music's capacity to prefigure new forms of social organization enables it to function as a kind of political laboratory: an experimental space in which the hierarchies and power flows of the outside world are temporarily suspended. From the perspective of this view of counterpower, music's contribution to resistance lies not necessarily in its activist commitments but in what Anja Kanngieser describes as the 'composition of new relations and modes of interaction between people, environments and worlds'.[113] While Kanngieser links this task of social and political recomposition to the artistic avant-garde, everyday musical practices can also contribute to the process of reconfiguring the social fabric, anticipating new subjectivities and helping draw them forth from participants and listeners.[114]

Hardt and Negri's conception of counterpower as a triadic machine – the interaction of constituent power, resistance (in the sense of 'isolated, individual acts') and insurrection ('a collective gesture of revolt') – can help us understand the multiple roles played by music in recent popular uprisings.[115] Given that Hardt and Negri elevate the Arab Spring and the Occupy movements as epitomes of this triad in action, it makes sense to look more closely at an example drawn from one of these movements: how music, more specifically mass singing, helped to bring down Hosni Mubarak's regime during the Egyptian revolution of 2011. During the eighteen-day occupation of Tahrir Square, a clinching role was played by Ultras football fans (Ultras Ahlawy and Ultras White Knights), associated respectively with Cairo's Al-Ahly club and Giza's Al-Zamalek club. As well as leading violent confrontations with the police and security forces, the Ultras dominated the space sonically through their chanting and singing; for some observers, they took a more significant part in the revolution than any formal political faction.[116] Although Hardt and Negri do not fully explain how the components in their triad interact, the resistance–insurrection–constituent power model helps explain how the Ultras became politicized so rapidly and took such a leading role in the revolution.

From their emergence in 2007 until the outbreak of the revolution, the Ultras groups had not been politically oriented. But their systematic repression by the police from 2008 onward stimulated acts of low-level resistance, fuelling a broader sense of injustice as well as hostility toward the Ministry of Interior. Regularly involved in clashes with the police, the different Ultras groups were to come together under the slogan 'A.C.A.B.' ('all cops are bastards').[117] At this stage, the anti-authoritarian dimension of the Ultra groups had yet to coalesce into a revolutionary threat to the regime. What triggered this rapid transformation – and the insurrectionary moment – was a symbolic event which served to underscore that the police and Mubarak's regime were one and the same and that the Ultras tried-and-tested tactics were uniquely suited to undermining them.

The demonstrations that broke out on National Police Day in 2011, and in particular the brutal treatment of protesters by the police, politicized individual Ultras and put their experience of thwarting police tactics to revolutionary use. Alongside their combat skills, it was their extraordinary synchronized chanting, honed weekly on the football terraces, which enabled the Ultras to impose their dominance on spaces like Tahrir Square. As well as serving as a form of 'sound-based territorialization', the Ultras' singing functioned as a redistribution of the sensible, giving voice to hitherto marginalized young working-class men.[118] Rather than simply drowning out the noise of existing power, the synchronized singing and gestures of the Ultras modelled a disciplined yet decentralized form of social organization, prefiguring and helping to constitute – if not fully realize – a new, post-revolutionary politics.

3 | History, Ideology and the Politics of Context

Up to this point, the focus has been on how music acquires political agency and exercises effects in the political field, whether as an instrument of power or counterpower. In this chapter, attention shifts to how politics affects music: how it functions as a structural pressure on musical institutions and discourses, and how it inscribes musical texts, practices, materials and forms with unconscious politicality. This may seem merely a complicated version of the axiom that all music is shaped by its political contexts. But like many ideas we take for granted, the assumption that music reflects its contexts raises difficult issues, and the concepts of structure and what Jameson describes as the 'political unconscious' can help bring them into focus.[1] Two issues are crucial here. First, what claims are we making in elevating political contexts as causal powers, and how exactly does music absorb and encode their politicality? How is it possible for a political system to imprint itself on musical practices and forms in ways that seem to short-circuit the agency of composers, performers and listeners? Second, is music's latent political dimension limited to reproducing the hegemonic beliefs and values within a particular political context? If so, does that mean that even overtly oppositional music is on some level conditioned by the ideology it opposes? By far the most substantial theoretical discourse devoted to these issues stems from Marxist and post-Marxist thought, and much of this chapter is given over to exploring how the key concepts of structure and ideology have been theorized within the Marxist tradition. This body of theory remains an indispensable resource for thinking about how music relates to its political contexts. But we also need to explore how its historicizing approach – epitomized by the zeal to uncover hidden layers of ideology within musical texts – risks neutralizing any positive political value they may have for the present.

3.1 Context and Causal Power

Musicologists, like their colleagues in other humanities disciplines, rely heavily on political contextualization in interpreting the meanings and functions of texts and practices. The boom time for such politico-contextual approaches was probably the 1990s, coinciding with a period of intense scepticism toward Marxist historiography and other supposedly deterministic or totalizing methods. As a result, musicologists tend to be wary of language suggesting mechanical cause–effect relationships, describing music euphemistically as being 'situated' or 'located' within contexts rather than being produced or determined by them.[2] There is more of course to contextualization than just lining up musical and sociopolitical practices alongside each other. Its primary function is to make cultural acts and artefacts comprehensible, by understanding them in relation to the conventions of discourse particular to their world; as the historian William Sewell Jr explains, 'we cannot know what an act or utterance means and what its consequences might be without knowing the semantics, the technologies, the conventions – in brief, the logics – that characterize the world in which the action takes place.'[3] The idea that texts and acts operate within the parameters set by particular discourses already nudges us toward causation: contextualization as an explanatory mechanism, a means of elucidating the complex relationships that cause things to come into being and condition the way they are.[4]

Political contextualization is not just a synchronic manoeuvre, clustering music with chronologically proximate ideas, issues and institutions. It also permeates diachronic approaches to music history, carving up time into chunks bookended by cataclysmic political events (1789, 1848, 1914 and so on) or regulated by other political rationales (such as the 'long nineteenth century' and the 'short twentieth century'). While musicologists continue to draw on explanatory frames designed around political history, few today invest them with the kind of structural or causal power that they had for earlier generations of scholars. Consider, for example, how the Marxist philosopher and critic Walter Benjamin mapped the revolutionary ruptures of political history onto artistic development:

It is a truism that political tendencies are implicit in every work of art, every artistic epoch – since, after all, they are historical configurations of consciousness. But just as deeper rock strata emerge only where the rock is fissured, the deep formation of "political tendency" likewise reveals itself only in the fissures of art history (and works of art) . . . In every new technical revolution the political tendency is transformed, as if by its own volition, from a concealed element of art into a manifest one.[5]

The idea that artistic phases march in lockstep with political tendencies, and that such politico-artistic contexts are carved in stone, points to some fundamental difficulties with political contextualism. One problem is that it can erect and reify arbitrary boundaries, locking texts and practices into a box constructed by the musicologist. The danger here is that musicologists sometimes treat these self-erected boundaries as givens, chiding others for applying supposedly acontextual or anachronistic perspectives to their chunk of musical culture. But are chronologically or geographically proximate elements necessarily more pertinent as context than ones from further afield? As the philosopher Ernst Bloch argued, a key aspect of the experience of modernity is the non-contemporaneity of the contemporaneous (and the contemporaneity of the non-contemporaneous): 'not all people exist in the same Now. They do so only externally, by virtue of the fact that they may all be seen today. But that does not mean that they are living at the same time with others.'[6] This raises the broader issue of where one should draw the line in reconstructing a context: what counts as contextually relevant, to coin a phrase, is always a matter of context. Another problem is choosing the right context to reconstruct. (Should we locate Richard Wagner within the culture of early socialism or the pre-history of fascism? 'Both', you may well say, yet is it realistic to expect contextual work to exhaust all possibilities?) And how do we adjudicate between competing, contradictory contexts, or accommodate multiple overlapping micro and macro contexts? As the historian Martin Jay observes, contexts may not fit together neatly like Russian nesting dolls, but rather produce 'an overdetermined effect irreducible to any one dominant contextual influence'.[7]

The nature of the relationship between text and political context raises other crucial issues. Often, we talk of musical works, practices and cultures as 'reflecting', 'mirroring' or 'echoing' a political stimulus, making music seem like a passive receptacle into which politicality is inserted. This kind of language is symptomatic of a broader tendency to treat music as the junior partner in its relationship with political contexts. In a recent critique of late twentieth-century ethnomusicology, Barry Shank draws attention to how the discipline enforced the dogma that music could merely reproduce already existing identities, values and social relations, a standpoint that 'frustrates any effort to think about the political force of music'.[8] The idea of political context as an all-powerful determining factor, and of artistic texts as 'haplessly and hopelessly entangled in fine-meshed filaments of power', has been summed up and skewered by the literary historian Rita Felski in an article entitled 'Context Stinks!' Like Shank, Felski critiques the idea that 'the macrolevel of sociohistorical context holds the cards, calls the tune, and specifies the rules of the game; the individual text, as a microunit encased within a larger whole, can only react or respond to these preestablished conditions.'[9] At its extremes, the consequence of this overinflated view of the power of context is that texts, authors and readers are stripped entirely of political agency, being unable to evade the machinic determinacy of this subterranean politics:

> In such scenarios, texts are munificently awarded supermanlike powers with the one hand, only to have them immediately whisked away with the other. A novel is charged and found guilty of manufacturing docile bourgeois subjects but this jaw-dropping achievement – how remarkable, if true! – turns out to be the mere reflex of systems of power steering the action behind the scenes, occult forces that fully determine without themselves being determined.[10]

The problem being diagnosed here is not simply one of inflating structure at the expense of agency. Rather, the text–context dichotomy always risks privileging one side of the equation, whether through assigning excessive causal power to political contexts or through treating the latter merely as a colourful but dispensable backdrop. While political contextualization aims at probing the dialogue between music and politics, the danger – as Georgina Born and David Hesmondhalgh observe – is that we lose 'any sense of the dialectical relationship between acts of musical communication on the one hand and political, economic, and cultural power-relations on the other'.[11]

Box 3.1 Marx's Materialist View of History

From the mid-1840s on, Marx and Engels argue that penetrating the 'real ground of history' requires an approach that 'does not explain practice from the idea but explains the formation of ideas from material practice'.[12] Historical materialism, stressing the primacy of the economic structure, emerges through the critique of Hegel's idealist conception of history; this oppositional context in part explains the one-sided relationship between base and superstructure found in some of their writings.

Marx's best-known exposition of the materialist view of history, from the Preface to *A Critique of Political Economy* (1859), is actually intended as a summary of his mid-1840s standpoint. Three key aspects of historical materialism are presented here: (1) the emphasis on the economic structure as determining (*bestimmen*) and conditioning (*bedingen*) social consciousness and the political superstructure, (2) the role of contradictions within the economic structure in triggering social revolution and (3) the progressive development of history – or the 'prehistory' of communism – through successive modes of production:

> In the social production of their life, men enter into definite relations that are indispensable and independent of their will, relations of production which correspond to a definite stage of development of their material productive forces. The sum total of these relations of production

Box 3.1 (*cont.*)

constitutes the economic structure of society, the real foundation, on which rises a legal and political superstructure and to which correspond definite forms of social consciousness.

The mode of production of material life conditions the social, political, and intellectual life process in general. It is not the consciousness of men that determines their being, but, on the contrary, their social being that determines their consciousness. At a certain stage of their development, the material productive forces of society come in conflict with the existing relations of production, or – what is but a legal expression for the same thing – with the property relations within which they have been at work hitherto. From forms of development of the productive forces these relations turn into their fetters. Then begins an epoch of social revolution. With the change of the economic foundations the entire immense superstructure is more or less rapidly transformed. In considering such transformations a distinction should always be made between the material transformation of the economic conditions of production, which can be determined with the precision of natural science, and the legal, political, religious, aesthetic, or philosophic – in short, ideological forms in which men become conscious of this conflict and fight it out. Just as our opinion of an individual is not based on what he thinks of himself, so can we not judge of such a period of transformation by its own consciousness; on the contrary, this consciousness must be explained rather from the contradictions of material life, from the existing conflict between the social productive forces and the relations of production.

No social order ever perishes before all the productive forces for which there is room in it have developed; and new, higher relations of production never appear before the material conditions of their existence have matured in the womb of the old society itself. Therefore mankind always sets itself only such tasks as it can solve; since, looking at the matter more closely, it will always be found that the task itself arises only when the material conditions for its solution already exist or are at least in the process of formation.

In broad outlines Asiatic, ancient, feudal, and modern bourgeois modes of production can be designated as progressive epochs in the economic formation of society. The bourgeois relations of production are the last antagonistic form of the social process of production – antagonistic not in the sense of individual antagonism, but of one arising from the social conditions of life of the individuals; at the same time the productive forces developing in the womb of bourgeois society create the material conditions for the solution of that antagonism. This social formation brings, therefore, the prehistory of human society to a close. (Marx, Preface to *A Critique of Political Economy* (1859), in McLellan (ed.), *Selected Writings*, 425–6)

3.2   Regime Change: The Politics of Periodization

The term 'metapolitics' is sometimes used to designate the politics of politics, that is, a form of political discourse that probes and challenges the most basic assumptions of the field.[13] Similarly, 'meta-contextualism' indicates a level of abstraction one step above ordinary contextualization: a focus on overarching contexts, on the merits of different types of contextual work or on how the tools and approaches we bring to context are themselves always context-dependent. These two meta-concepts come together in exploring the politics of music-historical periodization, that is, the process of mapping the shifting relationships between music and politics by carving up music history into a sequence of epochs or regimes.

This section examines three periodizing constructions or emplotments of music history: one from the beginnings of Marxist music historiography (Hanns Eisler) and two more recent post-Marxist examples (Jacques Attali and Jacques Rancière). Each of these periodizations divides the course of Western music history, or a sizable chunk of it, into three or four phases: large-scale musico-aesthetico-political 'contexts' within which music's politicality is activated and conceptualized in different ways. As the scare quotes here signal, the kind of expansive periodizing concepts encountered in these schemes – categories such as 'modernity', the 'age of feudalism', the 'bourgeois era' and so on – have a different function to the smaller-scale contexts which musicologists normally handle, and do not promise the same type or degree of cohesion. Contexts, like discursive frameworks, are in general localized assemblages of meaning, marking out the repertory of political concepts and practices available at a given point in time and space. But the meta-contexts discussed in this section are larger and looser constructions, drawing together under one concept cultures and historical phases that in other respects may be fundamentally different.

Eisler and Marxist Music Histories

While Marxist approaches have been applied to literary history since the late nineteenth century, it was only in the late 1920s that musical commentators followed suit. The pioneering figure here was arguably not Adorno (whose first important Marxist interpretation of music, 'Zur gesellschaftlichen Lage der Musik' [On the Social Situation of Music] dates from 1932) but rather the composer Hanns Eisler. Arguing that 'as good as nothing' had hitherto been written on music from the standpoint of historical materialism, Eisler published a series of Marxist representations of music history from 1927 onward.[14] Most of these grew out of contributions to Marxist discussion groups or workers' education societies, serving the dual function of disseminating the method of historical materialism and laying a foundation for a revolutionary art of the proletariat. While Eisler did not set out in detail the theories underpinning his view of music history, his starting point was that non-Marxist approaches to music history were in terminal crisis.[15] Arguing that musicologists 'often falsify history in the interests of the bourgeoisie', Eisler highlighted the ideological character of concepts such as autonomous art and absolute music, rejecting historical constructions conceived around them.[16] This standpoint precluded purely musical accounts of stylistic or generic development, instead making changes in social function the engine driving music-historical narratives: 'history teaches us that each new musical style arises not from a new aesthetic standpoint ... but rather the change in the material is conditioned inevitably by a historically necessary change in the function of music in society.'[17]

Most of Eisler's discussions of the relationship between social and musical processes are presented through potted periodizations, a format aimed at making a political point rather than at sophisticated historical analysis. These periodizations outline the social functions of music under the feudal and capitalist modes of production before envisaging its future under socialism. The briefest example is a 1929 fragment on radio music:

(i) Music under feudalism, court music-making, exclusively served the musical needs of a tiny elite: music as a privilege.

(ii) Music in bourgeois society: the producer sells music just like any other commodity. Democracy in music amounts to music being the privilege of the property-owning classes.

(iii) Radio embodies art's potentiality in a new society. Here too technology has made possible and anticipated a social development. Radio music: privilege extended to all.[18]

This fragment packs in several Marxist explanatory mechanisms. It charts the progressive democratization of music through successive modes of production, taking it as read that developments in the economic base impact on superstructural elements such as music (see Box 3.2). In addition, it sketches how conflicts within the base (technological revolution destabilizing the existing relations of production) trigger the emergence of new forms of society and new possibilities for art. Eisler presents a similar, if vaguer, linking of socioeconomic crisis and artistic change in the article

'Über moderne Musik' (1927), which again gives a compressed overview of three historical phases:

The highpoint of music as a communal art was in the 16th, 17th and 18th centuries. At that time music, as an important part of the liturgy, was truly in the service of the community.

The crisis of feudalism and ultimately the [French] Revolution brought a tremendous upsurge to music too, and in the 19th century, in the age of Beethoven, music became increasingly the expression of the private feelings of the individual.

While Beethoven still expressed the *revolutionary* individual, in the following period, as Heine put it, 'From my great sorrows I make little songs.' In the age of Romanticism the role of music was to express the private experience of the individual or at most his personal 'worldview'. Examples of the latter: the songs of Schumann, the philosophical operas of Wagner, the symphonic works of Strauss and Mahler.

With the crisis of the bourgeoisie, with the general crisis of capitalism comes also the new crisis in music, ushering in the chapter 'modern music' ... The proletariat will have to create a new music via the *knowledge* and *artistic materials of the bourgeoisie.*[19]

These miniature narratives read history backward in order to convey a present-minded message: in the first example, that radio offers the possibility of extending the privilege of music to all; and in the second, that the musical culture of the bourgeoisie is exhausted and that the proletariat must appropriate its materials to create a new music of its own. Typically, the message is withheld until after the narrative, making it appear a necessary outcome of historical development.

Box 3.2 Base and Superstructure

The idea that the cultural and ideological superstructure (*Überbau*) is determined by the socioeconomic base (*Basis* or *Grundlage*) is fundamental to Marx and Engels's historical materialism. But the meanings of this metaphor and of the key concepts of 'base', 'superstructure' and 'determination' are neither consistent nor straightforward in their writings; the task of refining these concepts has been central to subsequent developments in Marxist theory.[20]

As seen in Box 3.1, Marx and Engels divide the base within a society into two spheres: the **forces of production** (labour, skills, raw materials and the technological means of labour) and the **relations of production** (the social relationships sustaining a particular socioeconomic formation, including relations of ownership and class relations). Together, the productive forces and relations of production constitute the **mode of production** within a given epoch. Rather than restricting their analyses to the kind of small-scale contexts described earlier, Marx and Engels's modes of production are meta-contexts,

Box 3.2 (*cont.*)

carving out the history of production into key stages; in constructing these epochs, they map materialist categories onto Hegel's phased conception of the course of universal history (thus Hegel's 'oriental despotism' becomes the 'Asiatic mode of production').[21]

For some Marxist theorists, the social dimension of the economic base (the relations of production) has explanatory primacy over the technological dimension (the productive forces): Althusser, for example, described the relations of production as 'the real stage-directors of history'.[22] Others, such as Alex Callinicos, have given priority to the technological side, arguing that the developmental level of the productive forces 'sets limits to what is socially possible in a sense that is not true in reverse for the production relations'.[23] In contrast, Jameson presents the relations of production and the productive forces as balancing, mutually correcting perspectives, the one safeguarding against technological determinism and the other against an overemphasis on human agency.[24]

Jameson is surely right to view these two aspects of the mode of production as functioning, for Marx and Engels, as complementary mechanisms and modes of historical explanation. Yet in their texts, the relationship between the productive forces and the relations of production is in general asymmetrical, with the former having the upper hand. Indeed, the imbalance between these dimensions – and the contradictions that it generates – is essential to Marx and Engels's theory of historical change. In the 1859 Preface, for example, Marx describes how developments in the productive forces clash with the existing relations of production, triggering social revolution. More specifically, he argues that the progress of the forces of production will enable the antagonisms characterizing the capitalist mode of production to be overcome (Marx's puzzling phrase 'social productive forces' refers to the cooperative labour characteristic of industrialized capitalism, glossed in *Capital* as 'the creation of a new power, namely, the collective power of masses').[25]

The concept of an ideological superstructure – reflecting and reinforcing the existing relations of production – was part of Marx and Engels's historical materialism from the start. Initially, the pairing base and superstructure was just one of a series of metaphors (earth and heaven, body and mind, and so on) they employed to underscore the primacy of material activity and relations over the production of ideas.[26] From the *German Ideology* onward, the concept of superstructure serves two distinct functions, encompassing the spheres of society that most directly maintain the existing relations of production (legal and political structures) and also those discourses that more obliquely serve to legitimize and safeguard the power and interests of the dominant class ('morality, religion, metaphysics, and all the rest of ideology', including education, the arts and the media).[27] According to Marx and Engels, it is through the latter that

Box 3.2 (*cont.*)

the dominated come to internalize ideas that perpetuate the interests of the dominant (we will return to this idea later in exploring the concept of **ideology**).

The base/superstructure distinction has frequently been criticized for reducing the superstructural elements – including the arts – to being mere effects or reflections of the economic structure. In some texts, Marx and Engels appear to strip these elements of any autonomy, even arguing that they 'no longer retain the semblance of independence. They have no history, no development [of their own].'[28] This forcible annexation is intended only to counter the idea that the artistic and intellectual spheres are wholly separate from the base. But the effect of the base–superstructure metaphor is to embed a unidirectional model of how the arts relate to the forces and relations of production (the superstructure of a building rises from its foundations, after all, not vice versa), locking the cultural sphere within a predetermined, externally controlled trajectory. This impression of one-way traffic was reinforced by attempts by later Marxists to transform the base–superstructure metaphor into a rigid system.

Some of Marx and Engels's best-known discussions of the relationship between base and superstructure, including the 1859 Preface, may seem to confirm the popular view of Marxism as a more or less crude form of **economic determinism**. Engels was later to acknowledge that such summary presentations of their theories tended to 'lay more stress on the economic side than is due to it'.[29] The functions assigned to the ideological superstructure, however, demand that it has the capacity to exercise a reciprocal effect on the base, and from the *German Ideology* onward, Marx and Engels set up the relationship between the base and superstructure as paralleling that between the forces and relations of production. In the case of both pairings, one element appears firmly in the driving seat, yet the workings of the whole require what Jameson describes as a 'back and forth' dynamic.[30] Marx and Engels state this explicitly in the *German Ideology*, arguing that the whole point of depicting the totality of the base and superstructural elements was to show 'the reciprocal action of these various sides on one another'.[31] Similar phrases regularly occur in their later writings, which also stress the historically variable nature of the relationship between base and superstructure: 'if material production itself is not conceived in its *specific historical* form, it is impossible to understand what is specific in the intellectual production corresponding to it and the reciprocal influence of one on the other.'[32]

The most important discussions of this interaction come from Engels's final decade. In a series of letters from the early 1890s, Engels repudiated the view that the superstructural elements were incapable of exercising effects on the economic base, arguing that this misconception stemmed from 'the ordinary, undialectical conception of cause and effect as rigidly opposite poles, quite

Box 3.2 (*cont.*)

regardless of any interaction ... An historical element, once it is ushered into the world by other, ultimately economic causes, will react in its turn, and may exert a reciprocal influence on its environment and even upon its own causes.'[33] Engels now emphasizes the 'relative independence' of the superstructural elements, arguing that it would not be possible for them to disrupt and be disrupted by the economic base were they not relatively autonomous systems.[34] This emphasis on reciprocal effects, or what became known as **dialectical determinism**, was not intended to challenge the fundamental view that 'in the last instance' economic factors have primacy: 'The economic situation is the basis, but the various elements of the superstructure ... also exercise their influence upon the course of historical struggles and in many cases preponderate in determining their *form*. There is an interaction of all these elements in which, amid all the endless host of accidents (that is, of things and events whose inner connection is so remote or so impossible of proof that we can regard it as non-existent, as negligible) the economic movement finally asserts itself as necessary ... We make our history ourselves, but, in the first place, under very definite assumptions and conditions. Among these the economic ones are ultimately decisive.'[35]

Here, Engels makes two emphases that were to prove crucial for subsequent Marxist aesthetic theory. While retaining the base/superstructure distinction, he stresses the causal efficacy of the superstructural elements: politics, culture and the other spheres of the superstructure act reciprocally on each other and on the economic base. In addition, he (re)defines the concept of determination to make it less mechanistic and thus to open up space for a plurality of determinations and for human agency. Rather than directly determining human actions or superstructural events, the economic structure generates the 'assumptions and conditions' under which 'we make our history ourselves'. The twentieth-century Marxist theorist Ernest Mandel usefully describes this view of determination as **parametric determinism**, since it stresses that human actions are not 'mechanistically determined' but rather operate 'within a given set of parameters'.[36] For the philosopher Alasdair MacIntyre, the Hegelian terminology of 'determination' and 'correspondence' is apt to mislead, since Marx and Engels's economic structure simply serves as 'a framework within which superstructures arise'; similarly, the cultural materialist Raymond Williams argues that 'we have to revalue "determination" towards the setting of limits and the exertion of pressure, and away from a predicted, prefigured and controlled content.'[37] Some conception of pressure and of constraint, however, is crucial to determination and to the relation between base and superstructure; the whole point of the concepts, for Marx and Engels, is to convey humanity's unfreedom and subservience to material conditions prior to the liberation of communism.

Such potted narratives may seem to confirm the view that Eisler's takes on music history are crudely 'reductionist'.[38] Similarly, his contextualizations of individual compositions sometimes verge on caricatures of Marxist approaches, as in this gloss on Mozart's *Le nozze di Figaro*: 'The content of this piece is the protest of the bourgeoisie against the privileges of the nobility. The ending admittedly is still reconciliatory; yet eight years later the revolutionary bourgeoisie stormed the Bastille. "Figaro" was a step towards this Bastille.'[39] Several of his longer texts from the 1930s, however, offer subtler and more expansive historical overviews, and also incorporate reflections on Marxist methodology. Although Eisler summed up his method as being 'to see how the general social and economic conditions are reflected in music', he was keen to avoid unidirectional causal explanations, which he derided as 'vulgar sociologism'.[40] Instead, he stressed the dialectical relationship between socioeconomic structures and musical materials: 'a particular social situation leads to a particular musical technique which, when actualized in practice, helps in turn to make that particular social situation possible.'[41] Rejecting mechanical attempts to link composers and works with their social and economic contexts, Eisler argues that the value of dialectical materialism lies in its capacity to illuminate coexisting and contradictory historical forces. In discussing Mozart, for example, he rejects as undialectical the habit of labelling him a 'rococo' composer, arguing instead that 'in Mozart's works you find the latest manifestation of feudalism – rococo – coexisting with a completely new feeling and expression of the uprising [*sic*] bourgeoisie.'[42]

Eisler's most sustained music-historical periodization is presented in the 1931 essay 'Die Erbauer einer neuen Musikkultur' (The Builders of a New Musical Culture). Here, Eisler explores not only the interrelation between music and successive socioeconomic structures but also music's shifting political functions in different modes of production. He argues, for example, that in the Middle Ages church music served the interests of the ruling class and 'made feudalism possible and stabilized it time and time again'; by 'stirring up and strengthening a state of remorseful penitence in churchgoers', music exercised a 'disciplinary function' over the dominated classes.[43] Eisler's explanation of how the contradictions within feudalism reached crisis point draws directly on Marx; for both, the quest for political emancipation (and, by extension, the autonomy of art) on the part of the bourgeoisie was dictated by an economic idea of freedom, swiftly shrinking back into the latter once political dominance was secured. Accordingly, music is 'refunctioned' (*umfunktioniert*, a term borrowed from Eisler's friend and collaborator Berthold Brecht) in the late eighteenth century so as to serve as a vehicle for bourgeois liberal aspirations; Eisler endorses the liberal view of Beethoven's music as embodying freedom, while stressing the subsequent retreat of the bourgeoisie into economic self-interest and of music into a commodity:

While in revolutionary periods revolutionary bourgeois music mirrored the great revolutionary individual in his existing struggle against feudalism, it came by the middle of the 19th century to mirror the disillusioned, property-owning petty-bourgeois. Great emotions became poorer, smaller, more intimate. And the 'Ça ira' of the sans-culottes, the revolutionary energy of the 'Eroica', turned into the Schumann song 'Ich grolle nicht'.[44]

For Eisler, the rise and fall of the concert and of absolute music mirror the trajectory of capitalism itself. Thus the rise of the concert in the eighteenth century went hand in hand with 'the great progress of the struggling bourgeois class as it fought for private property, the free production of goods, and freedom of enterprise against feudalism'.[45] Eisler argues that this form of music became regressive over the course of the nineteenth century in line with the development of capitalism and that both entered a phase of crisis at the same time. Part of the purpose of this and similar narratives was to set out which aspects of bourgeois musical culture were worth preserving; Eisler echoes the long-established line that the proletariat was 'the only class which will fervently take up the heritage of great bourgeois music, following the collapse and decay of the musical culture of the bourgeoisie which we are experiencing at present'.[46] Another rationale was to stress that what he regarded as the chaotic, rudderless condition of contemporary composition would persist until a new social formation triggered a further refunctioning of music: 'new musical techniques cannot emerge through a revolution in musical materials, but can only emerge through a societal revolution in which a new class takes power and in which art also has a new social function.'[47]

Post-Marxist Historiography

Many of the features of Eisler's periodizations persist in later Marxist readings of music history.[48] From the late 1960s up to the present, however, key elements within the Marxist theory of history have been rejected or reworked by successive phases of post-Marxist thinkers. Before exploring how the periodizations of Attali and Rancière reflect these developments, it will be useful to outline more broadly how post-Marxist conceptions of history diverge from the ideas and methods seen earlier.

For Eisler, historical materialism offered a rigorously scientific method, definitively superseding other methodologies.[49] Post-Marxists in contrast reject Marxism's claim to offer unique access to the '"absolute truths" of History'.[50] Similarly, while Eisler embraced Marx and Engels's teleological view of history, with its unstoppable progress through modes of production toward full communism, post-Marxists treat such grand narratives with scepticism; stripped of inexorable movement toward its realization, the goal of a classless society enters a utopian register, becoming what Jean-François Lyotard termed a 'desirevolution'.[51] While Eisler adhered to the Marxist orthodoxy of the socioeconomic base as the ultimate determining factor, many post-Marxists have rejected the idea of determination, the base/superstructure binary and with them the view that there can be straightforward correspondences between a socioeconomic cause and an artistic effect. Furthermore, while Eisler's writings treat music as a component within a unified whole, post-Marxism has chipped away at the idea of social formations as cohesive and intelligible structures (we will return to this issue later in the chapter).[52] In addition to these theoretical divergences, there are fundamental political differences between post-Marxism and earlier phases of Marxism. For Eisler, Marxism revolved around class struggle and the victory of the proletariat; for post-Marxists, this focus has been replaced by a plurality of fluid radical democratic struggles.[53]

Attali's *Bruits*

Attali's *Bruits: Essai sur l'économie politique de la musique* (Noises: Essay on the Political Economy of Music), first published in 1977, is one of the most influential discussions of music's political efficacy from the last fifty years, while its analysis of the relationship between music and neoliberal capitalism now seems acutely prescient. Yet it is also a sketchy and frustrating text, reliant on assertion rather than argumentation and marred by conceptual imprecision (while Attali accords music an unrivalled socio-political significance, what he means by music is often left unclear). Attali's book is post-Marxist not merely through its political context (admirably reconstructed in a recent article by Eric Drott) but through its aims and methods, which turn upside-down conventional Marxist accounts of the relationship between music and socioeconomic structures.[54] His point of departure is that contemporary work in social, political and economy theory is deficient as a result of its failure to listen to music: 'music, as a mirror of society, calls this truism to our attention: society is much more than economistic categories, Marxist or otherwise, would have us believe.'[55]

Attali's remedy is to make music the engine driving history or, failing that, the phenomenon in which historical change manifests itself first. This approach is remarkable, given the long European tradition of music being sidelined as in Nietzsche's words the 'late fruit of every culture'.[56] The Marxist context of Attali's writing makes this strategy particularly audacious, creating the impression that he is inverting the categories of base and superstructure; he argues that music has a 'prophetic role' in the progress through modes of production, functioning as an 'immaterial recording surface' for human aspirations and as a 'herald of times to come':

Music is prophecy. Its styles and economic organization are ahead of the rest of society because it explores, much faster than material reality can, the entire range of possibilities in a given code. It makes audible the new world order that will gradually become visible, that will impose itself and regulate the order of things; it is not only the image of things, but the transcending of the everyday, the herald of the future.[57]

For Jameson, Attali's claim that the music of one epoch prefigures the socioeconomic system of the next is a boldly original 'dialectical reversal', placing the superstructure rather than the base in the driving seat; in this way, according to Jameson, he was the first theorist in the Marxist tradition to take Engels's idea of 'reciprocal effects' (see Box 3.2) to its logical conclusion, 'namely, the possibility of a superstructure to *anticipate* historical developments'.[58]

It is probably Jameson's commentary, rather than Attali's own argument, that is responsible for the authoritative status that the latter's analysis acquired; as Drott notes, the idea that music has primacy over the socioeconomic sphere has become 'a commonplace within contemporary music studies'.[59] But Jameson's gloss is puzzling, since the idea that music might sonically encode the key facets of a future socioeconomic order is not the same as the view that it can bring them to fruition. There is little in Attali's text to suggest that music acts causally on the socioeconomic base (even if he is clearly floating the idea of such a reversal), still less an explanation of how this might be possible (the nearest he comes to this is the vague causal claim that what happens in music then 'spreads throughout the entire economy').[60] In the absence of causal mechanisms, the idea of an inversion of base and superstructure becomes unsustainable; we are left with the weaker idea that music anticipates or heralds future development, making Attali's music resemble Chanticleer, the rooster who thinks his crowing makes the sun rise.

More sympathetically, the reason Attali merely hints at the inversion of base and superstructure is that he is aiming at a more complex relationship between music and the politico-economic sphere. Rather than moving in parallel, or one nudging forward the other, Attali insists that music's successive modes of production cannot be mapped neatly onto broader socioeconomic phases; he argues that 'it is deceptive to conceptualize a succession of musical codes corresponding to a succession of economic and political relations', considering instead that the points of intersection between them resemble 'a structure of interferences and dependencies'.[61] What Attali terms the 'political economy of music' is thus an autonomous system, out of sync with the broader political economy; it is this multi-layered and dislocated relationship that enables music to reproduce the current socioeconomic mode of production while at the same time prefiguring the next one.

To emphasize the difference between the conventional Marxist modes of production and the phases of the political economy of music, Attali assigns the latter labels that convey music's changing social functions:

> I would like to trace the political economy of music as a succession of *orders* ... When power wants to make people *forget*, music is ritual *sacrifice*, the scapegoat; when it wants them to *believe*, music is enactment, *representation*; when it wants to *silence* them, it is reproduced, normalized, *repetition*. Thus it heralds the subversion of both the existing code and the power in the making, well before the latter is in place. Today, in embryonic form, beyond repetition, lies freedom: more than a new music, a fourth kind of musical practice. It heralds the arrival of new social relations. Music is becoming *composition*.[62]

In spite of this rebranding exercise, Attali's categories closely map onto the kind of Marxist dissections of Western music history seen earlier in Eisler. Attali's sacrificial order is identified with pre-modern cultures, within which music's primary function is to create political order by symbolically channelling the violence of noise (see Box 2.2, page 43). In this period preceding music's entry into the market economy, it serves as a distribution network for the religious, social and political myths necessary for maintaining the existing order.[63] As in standard Marxist periodizations, this 'feudal world' is brought to an end by the French Revolution; the difference here is that the new politico-economic order it inaugurates is anticipated, decades earlier, in the transformation of music into a commodity and of musicians into bourgeois entrepreneurs.[64] Like Eisler, Attali subdivides the capitalist mode of production into two phases. But while Eisler's division is grounded in the decline of the bourgeoisie, Attali's reflects developments within capitalism: the twentieth-century shift from competitive capitalism (epitomized by the commodification of music and the rise of the concert hall) to the Fordist capitalism of mass production and consumption (epitomized by the recording industry and the 'stockpiling' of musical commodities).

Attali's future phase presents elements that link it to both conventional Marxist and post-Marxist periodizations. On the one hand, he evokes a world beyond alienation, the division of labour and the exchange principle, in which 'music, extricating itself from the codes of sacrifice, representation, and repetition, emerges as an activity that is an end in itself'.[65] Like Marx, Attali considers the creative, collective labour of the (amateur) orchestral musician to embody this 'new practice of musical production', melding together production and consumption, work and play.[66] On the other hand, Attali's musical future has features which are distinctly post-Marxist. Rather than elevating the proletariat as engine and beneficiary of radical change, it is the figure of the composer – epitome of the bourgeois intelligentsia! – who serves to epitomize the post-capitalist mode of production: 'Composition thus appears as a negation of the division of roles and labour as constructed by the old codes ... Composition, then, beyond the world of music, calls into question the distinction between worker and consumer ... to compose is to take pleasure in the instruments, the tools of communication, in use-time and exchange-time as lived and no longer as stockpiled.'[67] And while Attali shares Marx's sense of certainty his prognoses will come to fruition, the future he evokes is no communist utopia; rather, he describes the 'fragility and instability' of a world in which individuals make their own music and create their own rules, and where the ideals of tolerance and autonomy supersede Marx's vision of community.[68]

Attali's periodization retains something resembling the outline and outcome of a conventional Marxist music history. Other post-Marxist periodizations abandon all but a few bare bones of Marxist historiography or repudiate it while continuing to rely on it as an unstated background; this is the case with Foucault's histories, which reject the progressive, phased narratives of the Marxist paradigm yet locate the defining rupture of modernity so that it coincides with the French Revolution.[69] Indeed, the postmodern suspicion of grand narratives has led some post-Marxist commentators to disavow the practice of historical periodization altogether. Tellingly, even Attali makes gestures in this direction, arguing that he is not so much mapping out historical phases in the relationship between music and politics as tracing the genealogy of codes coexisting in the present.[70]

Rancière's Regimes

These traits are also present in Rancière's three aesthetico-political 'regimes', probably the best-known periodization of this kind from the last two decades. Rancière's scheme is oriented around the histories of art and literature rather than music, although he accommodates the latter within the same framework (Rancière's observations on music history have usefully been drawn together in a recent article by Jairo Moreno and Gavin Steingo).[71] As with Attali's 'orders', which serve both as historically sequential modes of production and as coexisting networks, Rancière's regimes perform a dual function. On one level, his ethical, poetic/representative and aesthetic regimes function as historical meta-contexts, each governed by a particular idea of art and by a distinct conception of art's relation to politics; rejecting notions of base and superstructure or essence and appearance, Rancière describes each as a 'historically constituted regime of perception and intelligibility'.[72] The historical nature of Rancière's categories is clearest when he is dealing with the rupture – again coinciding with the French Revolution – that inaugurates the aesthetic regime: 'the aesthetic regime of art, for example, is a system of possibilities that is historically constituted but that does not abolish the representative regime, which was previously dominant. At a given point in time, several regimes coexist and intermingle in the works themselves.'[73] On another level, however, Rancière conceives his regimes not as historical epochs but as transhistorical systems: less a means of carving up the past and more a way to grasp codes and logics that continue to coexist.[74] As Gabriel Rockhill argues, Rancière shows little interest in defining the historical or disciplinary boundaries of his regimes, approaching each instead as 'a malleable system of action, perception, and thought that takes on historically specific forms'.[75]

Each of Rancière's regimes approaches the relationship between music and politics with its own particular logic.[76] In his ethical regime, associated with Plato's *Republic*, art has no existence aside from its role in maintaining the police order; it either works positively on the ethos of individuals and the community, affirming the existing hierarchies and distribution of roles, or has no place.[77] For Rancière, art has the capability of exercising a properly political (i.e. dissensual) function only under the representative regime, which he links to both Aristotelian and eighteenth-century conceptions of artistic imitation. Rancière identifies this regime with two distinct models of art's political function. On the one hand, he connects the mimetic paradigm to the pedagogical model of art's efficacy seen earlier: the causal logic that by transmitting messages, or teaching vices and virtues, art is capable of impacting directly on the minds and behaviours of its audiences.[78] On the other hand, Rancière links mimesis to what he describes as the 'archi-ethical' paradigm of art's political efficacy: the idea that collective aesthetic experience, or better still, active participation, creates a common space and sensibility, 'framing the community as artwork' and dissolving art and politics into one another.[79] Rancière's discussions of these two models reveal the ways in which the historical and transhistorical dimensions of his regimes can come into conflict. Irked that these two models continue to dominate popular conceptions of art's political efficacy, he poses the question 'to which age do these models belong?', stressing their 'correct' location within the eighteenth-century mimetic paradigm.[80] For Rancière, the only true paradigm for art's politicality in modernity is that offered by autonomous art (see Chapter 1); he argues that this 'aesthetic regime' remains operative up to the present, rejecting the alternative paradigms offered by critical art and postmodernism.[81]

Tellingly, Rancière describes his three regimes as 'less another type of classification than a type of declassification'; in line with this logic, it could be argued that the most interesting part of his scheme is the absent fourth regime.[82] In contrast to Eisler's and Attali's goal-directed narratives, culminating in the near future, Rancière's periodization lacks a future stage. In part this reflects the broader scepticism toward teleological narratives and utopias: the view that, as Franco Berardi puts it, we are living 'after the future'.[83] But it also points to Rancière's hostility toward avant-garde and millennial diagnoses of the 'end of art'; his 'declassification' aims at neutralizing alternatives to the aesthetic regime and thus prolonging it endlessly. If in spite of this, as Joseph J. Tanke notes, Rancière's work often strikes a utopian note, this reflects the 'promise of happiness' bound up with the politics of the aesthetic.[84] But as Rancière notes in his most sustained reflection on the aesthetic regime, 'aesthetic art promises a political accomplishment that it cannot satisfy ... those who want it to fulfil its political promise are condemned to a certain melancholy.'[85]

3.3   Context, Commitment and Composition

Most arguments about contextualization can be boiled down to a basic question: should context be seen primarily as something exterior, acting on music from the outside, or is it something interior, embedded in the music itself? Is music's politicality dependent on external mediators (institutions, practices, programmes and so on), or is it symbolically coded within its materials and forms? This issue is fundamental not only to politico-contextual approaches to music but to discussions of political composition: do composers need to go out of their way to make their music engage with its political contexts, or do such contexts unavoidably imbue it with politicality? Within the Marxist tradition, both positions have been championed. Addressing composers, poets and the directors of workers' choirs, Eisler argued that 'the whole responsibility for the political and social context in this new production belongs to you'.[86] In contrast, Adorno claimed provocatively that using artworks to convey political standpoints served only to impede their true political content: 'social struggles and the relations of classes are imprinted in the structure of artworks; by contrast, the political positions deliberately adopted by artworks are epiphenomena and usually impinge on the elaboration of works and thus, ultimately, on their social truth content. Political opinions count for little.'[87]

It is in the writings of Eisler and Adorno from around 1930 that these issues first begin to receive serious attention in relation to music. The unhelpful habit, illustrated earlier, of formulating these positions as binary oppositions is not their responsibility (both present more nuanced conceptions than the quotations above suggest). Rather, it stems from the impulse, discussed in Chapter 1, to distinguish rigidly between autonomous art and political 'service' or functional art; this opposition was to have a decisive impact on attitudes toward political music over the nineteenth and twentieth centuries, in spite of being persistently challenged in theory and practice.[88] The idea of using art to convey a political message, transform political consciousness and thus strengthen opposition to the existing order has been part of the socialist tradition since its emergence in the second quarter of the nineteenth century. Since then, socialist artists and commentators have employed a wide range of concepts to describe such art: social art (*art sociale*), engaged or committed art, the learning play (*Lehrstück*), militant music (*Kampfmusik*), agitprop, interventive art, operative art and so on. While these concepts have very different connotations, they have all suffered from the misapprehension that they advocate a purely functional standpoint: in essence, that they instrumentalize art, subordinating it to an external political context. In reality, these forms of oppositional art generally aim at something more complex, seeking not to negate the principles and values of autonomous art but rather to supplement and sublate them, and in doing so, balance the claims of artistic expression, accessibility and political communication.

Box 3.3 Hanns Eisler on Revolutionary Art

Eisler reflects in 1931 on the need for a new revolutionary art to replace existing forms of musical activism, which he dismisses as '*Tendenzkunst*' (a term Eisler associates with a superseded phase of the workers' movement). The two essays presented side by side below offer similar yet clearly distinct visions of this new art. The first (left column) stresses music's educative role and its capacity to anticipate a new 'great classical age of art' in which the opposition between musical activism and art would be dissolved. The second (right column) gives priority to reconfiguring music as a teacher and weapon in the class struggle.

> It surely cannot be the task of tendency music [*Tendenzmusik*] to stir the emotions of the militant workers aimlessly. This would do nothing to bring about change. This kind of old-fashioned, outmoded music must be eliminated, and should be replaced by a revolutionary art whose main character is militant and educative . . .
>
> In a society where the broad masses are indeed united in the necessity for class struggle, but disunited in how it should be conducted – by what methods and with what means – art for the first time can become the great tutor of society.

> It will confine itself to representing the teachings of the classic [Marxist] theorists and agitators in great scenes and images distant from current reality yet capable of exercising an effect on it because of that distance. The chief task of bourgeois art is satisfying the longing for pleasure.

> It will present the theory and experiences of the class struggle in powerful scenes and images. The main purpose of bourgeois art is pleasure.

> The working class, having entered one of the most complicated and difficult periods of its class history, in which contradictions are rife in its own ranks, is faced with the real task of taking power and again embraces art as its great ally, while changing its function.

> Pleasure, which was the main purpose, even for tendency art [*Tendenzkunst*], becomes a means to an end. The text no longer has the task of satisfying the listener's need for beauty, but rather makes use of beauty to teach individuals, in order to present to them the way of thinking of the working class, dialectical materialism, in a clear and graspable form.

> Pleasure, which was the main purpose, becomes a means to an end. The text no longer has the task of satisfying the listener's need for beauty, but rather makes use of beauty to teach individuals, in order to make clear and graspable to them the way of thinking of the working class and the current problems of the class struggle.

Box 3.3 (*cont.*)

Music no longer uses its beauty as an end in itself, but rather to bring order and discipline into the confused emotions of each individual. We can see that through this a new and great change will be brought about in the function of art.

Brought forth as a teacher in the most difficult situation in class history, art sheds all those traits which naturalistic artists term 'proletarian'. It contains in strongest measure the new function of art in a classless society, and it can even be asserted that the great classical period of art in a classless society has already dawned.

Brought forth as a teacher, as a weapon in the most difficult situation in class history, art loses all that the bourgeois artist calls 'beautiful'. It already contains in strongest measure the beginnings of the new function of art in a classless society . . .

Specialists and professionals within the workers' music movement have the task of determining the changes of material and style which the new function of art necessarily entails. Workers' organizations have the task of compelling their officials to adhere to this determination and of eliminating the old opposition between engaged art and pure art . . .

Specialists and professionals within the workers' music movement have the task of determining the changes of material which the new revolutionary functions of art necessarily entail. At the same time, the broad mass of the workers and their executive have the task of compelling their music specialists to undertake this analysis and to control and appraise the results by applying them in practice . . .

If we really want to take power – and not merely believe in it like an abstract utopia – we must prepare an artistic practice which will command the interest of the new state and which beneficially directs man's receptivity for art to its proper social significance.

If we – and by that I mean the vanguard of the proletariat, the revolutionary working class – really want to take political power and not merely believe in it as an abstract, vague hope, then we must propagate an artistic practice which draws its new methods from the daily struggles of the revolutionary workers . . .

The elimination of tendency art, the elimination of everything that idiots have labelled art for the masses; onward to a new revolutionary transformation: art as a mentor in the class struggle.

A new musical culture will arise only once the workers have seized power in Germany, through the construction and completion of socialism.

> **Box 3.3** (*cont.*)
>
> ('Die Kunst als Lehrmeisterin im Klassenkampf' ('Art as Mentor in the Class Struggle', 1931), in Gesammelte *Schriften*, 131)
>
> ('Die Erbauer einer neuen Musikkultur' ('The Builders of a New Music Culture', 1931), in Gesammelte Schriften, 150–1. A translation of this text can be found in Eisler, Rebel in *Music*, 53–6)

Eisler is a case in point, since his theories and practices of political composition have often been equated with a crude, didactic functionalism. Adorno gave a succinct expression of this perspective, arguing that in composition, 'a political stance should not make itself apparent in primitive immediacy – and this is the very opinion which accounts for the difference between myself and poor Hanns Eisler.'[89] While Eisler is best-known today for his *Kampfmusik* – militant songs such as the *Solidaritätslied* and the *Kampflied gegen den Faschismus* – his writings and compositional output present a varied set of solutions to the political tasks he assigned to music. In his writings from around 1930, Eisler sometimes advocates a radically anti-aesthetic approach, envisaging art music being displaced by 'applied' music (*angewandte Musik*). But this is only one of a series of options he mooted in this period.[90]

The flexible, exploratory nature of his thinking is evident from two related passages from essays written in 1931 (see Box 3.3). Both texts stress the need for the German workers' movement to ditch its existing forms of music (male-voice choral songs that reflected the movement's origins in liberal workers' education societies) yet offer divergent solutions. The differences reflect the functions of the music under discussion and how it relates to the workers' revolutionary struggle. The first essay takes a long-term view, arguing that the workers' movement needs to lay the foundations for the new art of the post-revolutionary socialist state; here, Eisler proposes a model resembling his collaborations with Brecht – the learning-plays *Die Maßnahme* (1930) and *Die Mutter* (1931) – arguing that art should represent 'the teachings of the classic theorists and agitators in great scenes and images distant from current reality yet capable of exercising an effect on it because of that distance'. In contrast, the second essay focuses on class struggle and the immediate needs of the workers, deferring attempts to create a new musical culture until after the workers have gained power. These different focuses result in diverging conceptions of political music. The second essay, focused on aiding the 'daily struggles' of the workers, advocates a functional view of political music; in commenting on this essay, Günter Mayer is surely right to view as 'one-sided' its treatment of 'didactic music as strictly opposed to beauty and enjoyment'.[91] But the parallel passages in the first essay offer a different picture, opposing not beauty but rather well-meaning attempts to condescend to the proletariat, envisaging a 'refunctioning' of music which would usher in a new 'great classical period of art'.

Adorno too saw political art in terms of a spectrum of possibilities rather than a single viewpoint, acknowledging in the essay 'On the Social Situation of Music' that 'the agitatory value and thus the political legitimacy of proletarian community music, such as Eisler's choruses, is beyond question.'[92] He was less sympathetic, however, to the results of Eisler's endeavours at 'refunctioning' music, describing his more ambitious political compositions from this period as a 'dubious mixture of detritus from exhausted bourgeois stylistic forms, including even petit-bourgeois male-voice choir music, alongside scraps from progressive "new" music'.[93] Rather than accommodating itself passively to a 'state of consciousness suppressed and enchained through class domination', music, Adorno concludes, 'must intervene actively in consciousness through its form [*Gestalt*]'.[94]

Box 3.4 Adorno and the Politics of Form

Adorno poses the question of the contribution art music might make to social change, conceiving music's task as being to represent and critique the contradictions within society through its forms:

> The question is further the degree to which music – so far as it should intervene in the social process – will be in a position to intervene as *art*. Regardless of the answers which might be given, here at present music has the capacity to do nothing other than portray within its own structure the social antimonies which are also to blame for its own isolation. Music will be so much the better the more deeply it moulds within the contours of its own frame [*Gestalt*] the force of those contradictions and the necessity of their being overcome within society, and the more purely – through the antimonies of its own formal language – it expresses the desperation of the social situation and calls out for change through the coded language of suffering. It is to no avail if music stares in helpless horror at society: it comes closer to fulfilling its societal function if it presents the problems of society – which music bears within itself in the innermost cells of its techniques – through its own material and

Box 3.4 (*cont.*)

following its own laws of form. The task of music as art thus has a certain similarity with the task of social theory . . .

In a certain sense, the *character of cognition* is demanded of any music which today wishes to preserve its right to exist. Through its material, music must give clear expression to the problems assigned to it by this material, which is itself never purely natural material but rather a product of history and society. The solutions which music offers through this process stand on the same level as [social] theories . . .

Music is under the same obligation as theory to reach out beyond the current consciousness of the masses. Just as theory stands in a dialectical relation to praxis, not only making demands on the latter but also receiving them, so it is that music which has attained awareness of its social function stands in a dialectical relation to praxis. This is to be achieved not through the self-subordination of music to 'use', which it could do here and now only by presenting itself as a commodity with merely the illusion of immediacy, but rather by developing within music itself – in accordance with the position of social theory – all those elements whose objective is the overcoming of class domination. This music must do even where this development takes place in cell-like isolation from society during the period of class domination. It might be possible for the most advanced compositional production of the present – solely through the impulse of the immanent development of its problems – to invalidate basic bourgeois categories such as the creative personality and expression of the soul of this personality, the world of private feelings and its transfigured inwardness, setting in their place highly rational and transparent principles of construction. Even this music, however, would remain dependent on bourgeois production processes and could certainly not be regarded as 'classless' or as the true music of the future, but rather as music which fulfils its dialectic cognitive function to the utmost. The exceptionally vehement resistance which such music encounters in present society . . . appears to indicate that the dialectical function of this music is already perceptible in praxis, albeit only as a negative force, as 'destruction'. (Adorno, 'Zur gesellschaftlichen Lage', 105, 106, translation based on 'On the Social Situation of Music', in Theodor W. Adorno, *Essays on Music*, ed. Richard Leppert [Berkeley, CA, 2002], 393, 394)

The politics of form expounded earlier in Adorno's essay (see Box 3.4) raises two questions fundamental to his musical thinking: how does politicality become inscribed within a work's forms, and, once there, how is this coded material able to 'intervene actively in consciousness'? In the extract, Adorno identifies four political tasks which music has the capacity and obligation to undertake: (1) to express the problems of society through its musical materials and techniques, (2) to demand social change through its 'coded language of suffering' (*Chiffrenschrift des Leidens*), (3) to develop those elements within itself that can help overcome class domination and (4) to neutralize bourgeois aesthetic categories that help naturalize liberal individualism, such as the notion of individual creativity and of music as subjective expression. Importantly, Adorno claims here that the social critique embedded in music's contours and cells, while coded and opaque, can nonetheless be discerned by ordinary listeners. In a move that relies simply on equating artistic and political radicalism, Adorno presents the hostility of the public toward the music of Schoenberg and his school as a sign that its purportedly political dimension was already making waves. Anyone who rejects this equation as crude is likely to find Adorno's project as a whole tendentious and implausible; for the political philosopher Raymond Geuss, this standpoint is part of a 'doomed attempt to recapture that wonderful avant-garde moment around the First World War when art could be a metaphor for society and Schoenberg could speak of his compositions as "emancipation of dissonance" and associate that with real political emancipation'.[95]

In the 'Social Situation' essay, Adorno draws on two distinct strategies in explaining how the forms of musical works acquire this politicality: on the one hand, the idea that the logic inherent to musical structures and processes parallels that of social structures and processes, and on the other, the view that music should engage concretely with the social problems of its particular moment.[96] The tension between these two positions is the cause, perhaps, of the awkward way in which music's political agency is projected in the extract, apparent in particular in the image of music 'staring in horror' at social injustice and the idea that it shares the same 'obligation' as social theory. Adorno is careful here to avoid suggesting that composers, like social theorists, should consciously critique and seek to remedy the defects of society; later in the essay (in one of his notorious attempts to link Stravinsky's neoclassicism to fascism) he argues explicitly that the political consciousness of composers is not at issue in the social interpretation of music.[97] Yet the politicality Adorno ascribes to works is not just something immanent within the musical materials, even if these do come pre-inscribed with historical, social and political connotations. Rather, it emerges dialectically from the objective demands of the material and the subjective decisions of the composer, generating 'solutions' and 'social postulates' that stand on a par with those of social theory; Adorno's standpoint is that 'the dialectical composer' (the title of an essay on Schoenberg) produces acts of 'real social significance' with 'every compositional mark by his hand'.[98]

Adorno and Mediation

However attractive such claims may seem, they offer little that is concrete to explain how the politics enacted within autonomous musical works maps onto empirical reality; as Rose Rosengard Subotnik comments, the relationship Adorno posits between musical and social structures is 'indirect, complex, unconscious, undocumented, and rather mysterious'.[99] Sociologists of music have found Adorno's theories particularly frustrating, since he appears to gloss over some fundamental problems of their field; Peter Martin notes that 'for all his theoretical virtuosity, it is far from clear that Adorno did in fact provide a coherent account of the relationship he claimed between musical and social structures'; while Georgina Born argues that Adorno offers 'only a weak theorization of the relations between autonomous music and broader socio-historical processes'.[100] These problems are particularly acute in the 'Social Situation' essay, since Adorno's impulse to demonstrate music's active political engagement (a concern which, like his Marxism, was later to recede into the background) leads him to make more extravagant claims for it than are present in most of his subsequent texts. In addition, as Adorno himself concedes later in the essay, he had not formulated 'a solution to the problem of mediation' adequate enough to support his theories; indeed, as Max Paddison observes, Adorno's subsequent work sometimes gives the impression that merely invoking the term 'mediation' serves as a solution to the issues it raises.[101]

Where the politics of form is concerned, as seen already, the problem of mediation is in fact two distinct questions: how the politics gets into the musical material and how it gets out again. Mediation becomes a problem because Adorno rejects some of the most obvious ways of mediating the musical and political fields: in the extract, he is dealing with music which does not have an obvious political function, nor tangible political content, nor a connection with political institutions, nor politically engaged creators. As Antoine Hennion remarks, this rejection of standard mediations makes for an odd form of musical Marxism:

Adorno's radical theoretical rejection of all mediations brought the contradiction at the heart of discourses on art and society to a paroxysm ... For Marxists, all that matters to them is to establish connections at any price between the raft of art and the solid ground of society. Adorno casts off the theoretical moorings of art, while dialectically asserting that this casting off constitutes the social character of art.[102]

In Adorno's subsequent output, his solution to the first problem of mediation is to reduce the political demands he places on autonomous musical works. One step is to play down the idea of music as an interventive force:

the notion, as presented in the 'Social Situation' essay, that music has an obligation to 'intervene in the social process', 'represent the problems of society' and 'call out for change'. Instead, Adorno presents politicality not as a matter of choice – something music 'ought' to do – but rather as something advanced music does naturally as part of its main business. A second, related step is to concentrate the musical work's politicality on its hedgehog-like resistance to commodification and cooptation (see Chapter 6). This has the effect, observed earlier in Rancière's work, of mediating music's politicality through the politics of aesthetics. For Adorno, art does politics by (1) fiercely preserving its rights and character as art and (2) carrying out the kind of politico-aesthetic mediations he describes in paragraph three of the 'Social Situation' extract: annulling those categories of bourgeois art and aesthetics that perform political functions, such as the liberal view of art as a world of unbridled individualism, 'private feelings' and 'transfigured inwardness'.

Adorno's solution to the second problem of mediation – how the politics within musical structures communicates itself to listeners or has an effect – is to argue away the problem: communication and practical effects are in his view incidental, even irrelevant, to music's politicality. This position, broadened to encompass all art, receives its most emphatic expression in his late, incomplete work *Aesthetic Theory*. Here, Adorno lays stress on the 'highly uncertain' effect of conventional political art, contending that even Brecht's works politically impotent since they merely preached to the converted.[103] In addition to being hostages to fortune, dependent for their effect on a public already receptive to their message, Adorno regards artworks as having at best an incidental and marginal impact on politics: 'their true social effect is an extremely indirect participation in spirit that by way of subterranean processes contributes to social transformation.'[104] The minimal nature of their effect stems in part from the resistant character of advanced art, whose primary imperative is to avoid being coopted and neutralized: 'the acute reason today for the social inefficacy of artworks – those that do not surrender to crude propaganda – is that in order to resist the all-powerful system of communication they must rid themselves of any communicative means that would perhaps make them accessible to the public.'[105] But art's limited capacity to communicate politically in no way serves, according to Adorno, to diminish its political significance. While champions of engaged art such as Brecht and Eisler demand that 'art speak directly to the people, as though the immediate could realize itself immediately in a world of universal mediation', art's politics for Adorno is immanent within the artwork and refuses mediation.[106] 'Praxis' – reflection and action to change the world – 'does not lie in the effect of the work of art, but rather [is] encapsulated in its truth-content'.[107]

This standpoint is like a red rag to a bull for those commentators who, reasonably enough, expect music's politicality to have some kind of tangible presence or effect. For Geuss, the absence of the latter serves to diminish Adorno's equation of artistic and political radicalism into little more than a preference for avant-garde art:

What is the point of insisting that '*objectively*' Webern's music isn't just aesthetically revolutionary but also politically progressive, if that political progressiveness has no actual empirical counterpart or embodiment, if we have no reason to expect it ever to have such an embodiment, and if we can't even envisage a way of acting that would give it such an embodiment?[108]

Similar criticisms were voiced by Eisler, who condemned the 'Social Situation' essay for swapping 'dialectical materialism for dialectical mysticism' and for giving insufficient attention to the forces that would generate change.[109] Eisler's standpoint is rather one-sided, given that in this essay at least, Adorno builds in mediation through the politics of aesthetics, creating a route for musical works to act politically by challenging the categories and norms of bourgeois art. Given Eisler's criticisms, it is ironic that it is his music from this period, rather than Schoenberg's, that probably comes closest to realizing the prescriptions and proscriptions for interventive music which Adorno presents in his essay. I'm thinking here not of Eisler's workers' choruses or the music for Brecht's learning plays, but rather of instrumental compositions such as the *Kleine Sinfonie*, Op. 29 (1931–4): a savage, prickly work that draws together jazz idioms and instruments, advanced musical techniques and Eisler's new *Kampfmusik* style.

The *Kleine Sinfonie* has sometimes been read simply as a politically motivated attempt to create an accessible form of orchestral music.[110] But its precise, vivid gestures and montage-like succession of styles, techniques and genres suggest something altogether more ambitious: a reconfiguration of orchestral music as a form of protest and weapon in the class struggle. Eisler's comments on the work focus on its critique of bourgeois musical ideals and styles; he later described it as 'a kind of parody of a symphony, more or less composed under the principal theme "the symphony is dead"', and 'a protest against the overblown, bombastic neoclassical style of music'.[111] While Eisler retained the four-movement template, his ten-minute work ditches the grandiosity and metaphysical pretentions of the genre. Arguing that 'this art form is completely antiquated and outmoded', he claimed that the sole legitimate reason for using this and the other concert hall genres was 'for the destruction of conventional musical concepts'.[112] In the *Kleine Sinfonie*, Eisler's musical class warfare takes two forms. On the one hand, it repudiates what Eisler saw as the individualism, 'laboured naturalism' and 'fraudulent, sentimental "worldview music"' into which the bourgeois symphonic tradition had descended, aiming instead to 'purge the emotions' through clarity and rapid, trenchant contrasts.[113] On the other, it inserts the proletariat into the ideologically charged space of German symphonism by drawing on material in Eisler's *Kampfmusik* style: the scherzo second movement is adapted from his incidental music to *Kamerad Kasper*, while the third movement is a jazz reinstrumentation of the melodrama 'Lob der dritten Sache' from *Die Mutter*. While Eisler's aim was to skewer a bourgeois sacred cow, and thus contribute to the class struggle, the *Kleine Sinfonie* engages with other contemporary political contexts too. Eisler's later characterization of the first two movements as 'sorrow–protest–sorrow' and 'forceful protest–sorrow–forceful protest' are almost superfluous, given the vivid topics and gestures within the music. While this work may have started life as a critique of bourgeois musical ideals, it ended up – as Albrecht Betz observes – as a 'protest and indictment' as a nation descended into barbarism.[114]

3.4   Ideology and the Political Unconscious

So far, we have encountered three different sides of Adorno's politics of form: the idea that advanced music can (1) posit solutions to social contradictions and contribute through 'subterranean processes' toward social transformation, (2) serve as a force for resistance through the hedgehog-like intransigence of its forms and (3) negate aspects of bourgeois musical and aesthetic thinking that help sustain the existing social and political order. These three positive dimensions of music's politicality – the ways in which it can resist domination and help promote change – are only one side of the equation, however. Adorno is perhaps better known for the ways in which he freights music with a negative political side: its capacity to inculcate false consciousness and affirm the existing order. The concept of ideology is crucial to this aspect of Adorno's theorizing, yet his view of it is inflexible and one-sided, pointing to what Jameson describes as the old-fashioned nature of his Marxism.[115] To grasp the relationship between ideology and music's political unconscious, we need to evaluate Adorno's approaches to it alongside those of other Marxist commentators.

Marx, Engels and Ideology

Up to this point, we have encountered the concept of ideology in two senses: its everyday use as a synonym for a political worldview or set of principles, and my definition of it as a lens that imparts meaning to the past, brings present reality into focus and projects a transformative vision of the future. The notion of ideology as a lens transforming reality has its origins in the early writings of Marx and Engels (and ultimately in Plato's allegory of the cave), where it indicates not a project for improving the world but rather a distorted perception of it. [116] In *The German Ideology*, Marx and Engels use the term to critique the topsy-turvy logic they saw in German idealist thinking; instead of viewing the intellectual, religious and artistic spheres as outgrowths of material processes, idealism reverses the relationship, making 'men and their relations appear upside-down as in a *camera obscura* '.[117] The distorting lens of ideology does not merely invert the relationship between base and superstructure but drives a wedge between them, asserting the autonomy of the superstructural elements. In *The German Ideology*, ideology serves a similar function to the pejorative phrase 'absolute music' which Wagner coined the same year, indicating a sphere of mental labour that has tried to 'emancipate itself from the world', flattering itself that it '*really* represents something without representing something real'.[118] Ideology in this sense denies or conceals the material relationships shaping artistic and intellectual production; as Raymond Williams observes, 'ideology is then "separated theory", and its analysis must involve restoration of its "real" connections.'[119]

Although Marx and Engels largely abandoned the concept of ideology after 1848, two other important connotations for it emerge in their early writings. Rather than simply concealing the relationship between the products of mental labour and their material basis, ideology legitimates and universalizes the interests of the dominant class. For Marx and Engels, the 'ideologists' of the ruling class – intellectuals, the media, artists – 'make the formation of the illusions of the class about itself their chief source of livelihood'; another class seeking to challenge its supremacy must perform a similar operation: 'it has to give its ideas the form of universality, and present them as the only rational, universally valid ones.'[120] Here, ideology is identified not simply with the ideas animating a particular class but with its illusory self-representations; the illusion stems from the elevation of contingent class interests into givens or universal principles. This conception of ideology recurs in the *Communist Manifesto*, where the bourgeoisie is chided for its self-centred illusions: 'The selfish misconception that induces you to transform into eternal laws of nature and of reason, the social forms springing from your present mode of production and form of property – historical relations that rise and disappear in the progress of production – this misconception you share with every ruling class that has preceded you.'[121]

In another passage from *The German Ideology*, Marx and Engels offer the bare bones of an explanation of a further, crucial aspect of the concept: how the ideas of the ruling class come to be accepted by subaltern classes:

> The ideas of the ruling class are in every epoch the ruling ideas: i.e., the class which is the ruling *material* force of society is at the same time its ruling *intellectual* force. The class which has the means of material production at its disposal, consequently also controls the means of mental production, so that the ideas of those who lack the means of mental production are on the whole subject to it. The ruling ideas are nothing more than the ideal expression of the dominant material relations.[122]

Here, the ideological dimension stems from the subjection of other classes to the ideas of the ruling class. Marx and Engels's account relies on a straightforward equation of economic power with ideological heft: the commonsense idea that those in control of material production also control the circulation of ideas. What this does not explain is why the dominated classes come to internalize and acquiesce to these ideas. The concept of ideology has the function, as Balibar explains, of helping Marx and Engels to avoid the two most common explanations of this acquiescence, accounts that would have been fatal for their political project: on the one hand, the idea that it stems from the inability of the workers to think for themselves, and on the other, that it indicates their susceptibility to manipulation by the ruling class.[123] Ideology is thus called on to explain one of the oldest problems in political theory, described by the Renaissance philosopher Étienne de la Boétie as the question of 'voluntary servitude': why do individuals and classes submit to forms of domination that are against their interests?[124] Note that the servitude here is voluntary: the dominated are not passive victims of coercion, neither are they inherently incapable of grasping the injustice of their position. Rather, the prevailing nature of social relations is systematically distorted in the consciousness of the dominated classes, masking the realities of domination and exploitation.

Engels coined the problematic term 'false consciousness' to explain this phenomenon. This term has sometimes been equated with a kind of psychological manipulation: the use of distortion and disinformation to embed the interests of the ruling class and nudge the ruled into quiescence.[125] Engels's concept is more subtle, capturing how an ideological misreading of the social situation can secure compliance through leading individuals to regard the status quo as natural and unchangeable. The precise context of Engels's use of the term is often glossed over but is particularly relevant to the present discussion. Significantly, his focus here is not on the effect of ideology on the dominated classes; rather, Engels is describing how ideological distortions enter the texts of academics and artists who – by treating the sphere in which they work as autonomous from reality – fail to grasp the material relations shaping it:

> Ideology is a process ... carried out consciously by what we call a thinker, but with a consciousness that is spurious. The actual motives by which he is impelled remain hidden from him, for otherwise it would not be an ideological process. Hence the motives he supposes himself to have are either spurious or illusory. Because it is a mental process, he sees both its substance and its form as deriving solely from thought ... without inquiring whether it might not have some more remote origin.[126]

Given that here, Engels is addressing what might be described as 'white collar' false consciousness, it is understandable that he presents it in terms of misrecognition; ideology in this sense is like a pair of 'distorting spectacles' (the phrase is Žižek's) clouding or inverting how individuals see reality.[127] But by seemingly presenting false consciousness as an individual cognitive flaw, or form of self-deception, Engels's concept has been viewed as sitting uncomfortably with Marx and Engels's other explanations of ideological distortion; this has led some Marxist theorists to reject the concept of false consciousness altogether.[128] Other commentators have stressed that the falseness of false consciousness stems not from defective individual cognition but from the class illusions described above; Christopher Pines, for example, argues that 'false collective ideas and false collective modes of thinking' are consistently at the heart of Marx and Engels's conceptions of ideology, making the idea of false consciousness entirely compatible with them.[129]

Adorno and Ideology

More than for any other major Marxist figure, false consciousness dominates Adorno's conception of ideology. Indeed, he often glosses ideology as socially 'necessary false consciousness', that is, the illusions needed to sustain the status quo: 'the perpetuation of existing society is incompatible with [true] consciousness of itself, and art is punished for every trace of such consciousness. From this perspective as well, ideology – false consciousness – is socially necessary.'[130] Given the importance of false consciousness for Adorno, and the puzzling way in which most discussions of his work take the meaning of the term for granted, we need to get to grips with what exactly he aimed it to convey.

Adorno's earliest extended discussion of the relationship between music and false consciousness is presented in 'On the Social Situation', where he uses it to explain the ideological dimension of bourgeois musical consumption:

> It is incorrect to believe that no actual need lies at the basis of the consumption of music; as though all musical life were nothing but some type of resounding cultural backdrop, erected by bourgeois society for the concealment of its own true purposes, while its authentic, economic-political life takes place off-stage ... It is rather that the ideological power of music consumption is all the greater, the less it is transparent as mere illusion and as a thin surface gloss and the more precisely it communicates in terms of true needs, doing so, however, in such a way that a 'false consciousness' is the result and that the actual social situation is hidden from the consumer ... The ideological essence of 'musical life' is its ability to satisfy the needs of the bourgeoisie adequately – but to do so by means of a form of satisfaction which accepts and stabilizes the existing consciousness, rather than revealing through its own form social contradictions.[131]

Although this passage purports to explain bourgeois musical life from the perspective of its consumers' consciousness, Adorno does not share Engels's focus on individual misrecognition. Rather, his conception of false consciousness follows the model set by the Marxist aesthetician Georg Lukács the previous decade, who argued that it was the 'objective result of the economic set-up' rather than something 'subjective' and 'psychological' (Adorno's scare quotes around the term also point to Lukács's practice).[132] False consciousness here might be described as a socially programmed incapacity to think outside the box of bourgeois illusions; from this perspective, musical life serves to perpetuate these illusions and thus distract subjects from the social contradictions lurking outside in reality. Adorno also follows Lukács in mapping false consciousness onto Marx's concept of reification. For Lukács, the fetishism of the commodity under capitalism has penetrated every aspect of life, reifying human activities and relations, that is, giving them a 'phantom objectivity' that converts them into lifeless, alien things.[133] Moreover, reification has subjugated human consciousness itself, replacing active, willed behaviour with automatic, mechanical responses.[134] In addition to appropriating Lukács's idea of reified consciousness, Adorno's 'Social Situation' essay reflects the impact of figures, like Erich Fromm, who interweaved historical materialism with the psychoanalysis of the unconscious.[135] All this complicates Adorno's analyses of false consciousness as well as entwining the concept with commodity fetishism. In the 'Social Situation' essay, Adorno repeatedly associates the workings of bourgeois ideology with the unconscious, although as he later conceded, the boundaries between the unconscious and reified consciousness are hard to draw.[136]

With Adorno's reworking of false consciousness, the idea that music and ideology are intertwined becomes programmatic. This applies equally, though in different ways, to art music and to what he disparaged as the products of the culture industry. If avant-garde music, for Adorno, offers the possibility of resisting commodification, all autonomous music is on some level ideological; like Marx and Engels, Adorno regards artworks as ideological for disavowing the material relations that produced them: 'artworks, products of social labor ... seal themselves off from that they themselves are. To this extent, each artwork could be charged with false consciousness and chalked up to ideology. In formal terms, independent of what they say, they are ideology in that a priori they posit something spiritual as being independent from the conditions of its material production.'[137]

In addition, Adorno – like the other great aesthetician of the Frankfurt School, Herbert Marcuse – stresses the tendency of autonomous art to affirm the social conditions that engendered it simply through its own formal properties: 'the more binding art is to itself, the richer, denser, and more unified its works, the more it tends toward affirmation – of whatever stamp – by suggesting that its own qualities are those of a world existing in itself beyond art. This apriority of the affirmative is art's ideological dark side.'[138] Another dark side of art music, noted earlier, stems from the sociopolitical connotations that come pre-inscribed in music's materials; as Andrew Bowie argues, 'by using forms derived from society as it already is in order to articulate utopian possibilities, art is always also in complicity with what it opposes, and, as such, ideological.'[139] This entanglement of ideology with what Adorno describes as truth-content is the inescapable condition of artworks in the bourgeois era, though it takes a variety of forms. In the case of Wagner's music dramas, for example, technical inconsistencies in the music serve to puncture their ideologically dubious cultic dimension; in contrast, in Bruckner's symphonies, the use of the most modern harmonic and instrumental resources imbues the compositions with truth in spite of their regressive efforts at religious mystification.[140]

In relation to art music, Adorno's texts provided a new and much imitated model of ideological critique, polemically revealing the politically regressive aspects of the masterpieces of bourgeois culture. Adorno's approach proved much more problematic in relation to popular music, jazz and other products of what he termed the culture industry. This is not just for the obvious reasons (the authoritarian tone, the high-handed dismissal of styles and genres he knew little about and the unconcealed contempt for their listeners), but because he applies a different, flawed model of ideological critique to it. One symptom of this alternative model is the embrace of a perspective that Marx and Engels strenuously avoided: the idea that the consumers of ideology were too unthinking or vulnerable to manipulation to resist it seeping into them. Adorno's recourse to this manipulatory conception of ideology is underwritten by the idea that it acts on the unconscious; in his writings on popular culture from the 1950s and 1960s, he describes how popular music inculcates 'socially false consciousness' 'without the producers' intention and without the awareness of consumers', serving to 'train the unconscious for conditioned reflexes'.[141] The logical upshot of this perspective was to treat popular culture in its entirety as an ideological mechanism, a kind of un-truth serum blocking non-reified consciousness and thus enshrining the existing order: 'Under the banning of thought, thinking sanctions what merely is. The genuinely critical need of thought, to awaken from the phantasmagoria of culture, is ensnared, canalized, steered into false consciousness. The culture in whose environs it grew stopped thought from asking, what's it all about, and what for ... Instead of this, the now-things-are-so-and-not-otherwise is enthroned.'[142]

Adorno's view of the omnipresence of false consciousness in popular culture parallels that of Marcuse, whose *One-Dimensional Man* (1964) indicts the products of the culture industry for normalizing ideological distortion: 'the products indoctrinate and manipulate; they promote a false consciousness which is immune against its falsehood ... Thus emerges a pattern of *one-dimensional thought and behaviour* in which ideas, aspirations, and objectives that, by their content, transcend the established universe of discourse and action are either repelled or reduced to terms of this universe.'[143] Under such circumstances the concept of false consciousness is stretched to breaking point, since rather than being a distorted reflection of reality, ideology is absorbed into reality itself.[144] The idea that ideology has leached into reality is also found in Adorno's writings from this period: 'The cement that was once produced by ideologies departed from them and on the one hand seeped into the overwhelmingly existing conditions as such, on the other hand into people's psychological formation.'[145] This notion that ideology has become inseparable from reality is problematic, especially given Adorno's insistence that it no longer needs to conceal its workings. The upshot is a world divided unequally between the masses (the conscious/unconscious dupes of an overt mechanism for domination) and a small elite (which looks back with nostalgia to an age of 'authentic' false consciousness):

> In the open-air prison which the world is becoming, it is no longer so important to know what depends on what, such is the extent to which everything is one. All phenomena rigidify, become insignias of the absolute rule of that which is. There are no more ideologies in the authentic sense of false consciousness, only advertisements for the world through its duplication and the provocative lie which does not seek belief but commands silence ... The more total society becomes, the greater the reification of the mind and the more paradoxical its effort to escape reification on its own.[146]

As seen earlier, Adorno is not the only theorist of resistance whose theories make resistance seem virtually impossible. But the idea that reality itself has become 'its own self-duplicating ideology' also renders ideological critique redundant: what is the point of exposing the ideology concealed in art if it is transparent and omnipresent in society?[147]

Althusser and Ideological State Apparatuses

Adorno's view that ideology has outgrown the concept of false consciousness and seeped into territory hitherto viewed as the reality outside the ideological has been developed by other mid- and late twentieth-century theorists. But while Adorno presents the creeping ideologization of society as a sickness unique to late modernity, other commentators conceive it as ideology's normal condition. The crucial figure here is Althusser, whom we encountered briefly earlier in exploring the 'material existence' of ideologies, that is, how they work not merely through texts and ideas but through broader networks of practices. Althusser rejects Marx and Engels's conception of ideology as an illusion of consciousness – 'an imaginary assemblage [*bricolage*], a pure dream, empty and vain' – instead conceiving ideology as having an integral practical function within every society.[148] In part, Althusser justifies this approach by appealing to Marx and Engels's sporadic use of the term to indicate civil society, or that part of the superstructure not directly involved in the workings of the state (see Box 3.1); from this perspective, ideology does not carry the negative connotation of distorted communication, but rather is simply part and parcel of how societies work. Althusser defines ideology as 'a system (with its own logic and rigour) of representations (images, myths, ideas or concepts, depending on the case) endowed with a historical existence and role within a given society'; what these representations represent is not reality, but rather 'the imaginary relationship of individuals to their real conditions of existence'.[149] Rather than being consciously held ideas, ideological representations are the unconscious assumptions, values and beliefs that trigger actions; in relation to the individual subject, Althusser argues, 'his ideas are his material actions inserted into material practices governed by material rituals which are themselves defined by the material ideological apparatus from which derive the ideas of that subject.'[150]

The theory of ideology thus expands into learned behaviour and lived experience, becoming a theory of discourse (used here in its widest sense to incorporate material culture). The discursive fields within which an individual operates define the structural constraints within which he or she thinks and acts; Althusser gives the example of how religious ideology is realized through the different materialities of attending mass: 'of kneeling down, of the gesture of the sign of the cross, or of the *mea culpa*, of a sentence, of a prayer, of an act of contrition, of a penitence, of a gaze, of a handshake, of an external verbal discourse or an "internal" verbal discourse (consciousness)'.[151] As is apparent from this example, while the subject may on occasion submit such practices to reflective scrutiny, they normally work their effect unconsciously; Althusser comments more broadly that ideological structures and practices are 'perceived-accepted-suffered cultural objects', which 'act functionally on men via a process that escapes them. Men "live" their ideologies ... *not at all as a form of consciousness, but as an object of their "world"* – as their "world" itself.'[152] As the last part of this comment implies, individuals internalize ideology so that it becomes inseparable from their own selfhood, constituting or 'interpellating' them as subjects. This is a variant of the 'voluntary servitude' argument seen earlier: as free agents, individual subjects freely accept and 'work at' their own subjection through ideology.[153] The process of subject formation through subjection is fostered by Althusser's 'ideological state apparatuses' (ISAs). Althusser's claim is that multiple ISAs – schools, churches, trades unions, cultural institutions and so on – each not only inculcates its own distinct discursive rules but also reproduces the 'rules of the established order'; the 'know-how' required within each discursive frame ensures '*subjection to the ruling ideology* or the mastery of its "practice"'.[154] It is through being realized within the ISAs that the ruling ideology perpetuates itself and enables the ruling class to hold onto state power: 'no class can hold State power over a long period without at the same time exercising its hegemony over and in the State Ideological Apparatuses.'[155]

While the institutional dimension of Althusser's theory is probably the most influential aspect of his conception of ideology, it is also the most problematic. The key flaw is apparent from a musical allusion at the heart of his argument: 'this concert is dominated by a single score, occasionally disturbed by contradictions (those of the remnants of former ruling classes, those of the proletarians and their organizations): the score of the Ideology of the current ruling class.'[156] Althusser's conception of the ruling ideology demands, unrealistically, that the multiple, supposedly autonomous ISAs (even organizations such as trade unions) all sing in perfect unison from the same hymn sheet. A second aspect of this problem, highlighted by Stuart Hall, is the way in which the very idea of 'ideological state apparatuses' forecloses a key issue in media and cultural studies: why exactly do free, independent bodies such as media outlets view the world through such a narrow ideological lens when they are under no compulsion to do so?[157] Althusser's conception of how ISAs sustain the ruling ideology also raises a second, now familiar problem: how is resistance possible under such conditions? Or rather, given that he acknowledges the possibility of unsuccessful resistance (Althusser praises as heroic those teachers who 'teach against the ideology, the system and the practices in which they are trapped'), how is it possible for the existing system to be overthrown?[158] Althusser's response – that class struggle goes on beyond the ISAs – only serves to underscore their apparent stranglehold.

From the perspective of music, the advantage of Althusser's account of ideology is that it offers concrete ways of understanding how works and practices can be conditioned ideologically: not by some totalizing discourse but by more local, small-scale discursive fields. A particular musical text might be located at the intersection of a range of different institutional and discursive frames, each of which imparts its own parameters and constraints as well as, indirectly, those of the ruling ideology. Althusser's own brief, gnomic accounts of the relationship between art and ideology give little attention to the question of how ideology comes to have a material existence in the artwork (he simply comments that 'every work of art is born of a project both aesthetic and ideological', and goes on to argue that artists, whether consciously or not, are responsible for 'the ideological *effects* necessarily produced by its existence').[159] This emphasis on effects is crucial to how he views the ideological functions of artworks, since the latter are assigned the capacity 'to make us "see", "perceive" or "feel" the reality of the ideology' of the world they inhabit.[160] Althusser's argument appears to be that by inserting aesthetic distance between themselves and this ideology, artworks act like honest brokers, concealing their ideological potency:

> Perhaps one might even suggest the following proposition, that as the specific function of the work of art is to make *visible* (*donner à voir*), by establishing a distance from it, the reality of the existing ideology . . ., the work of art *cannot fail to exercise* a directly ideological effect, that it maintains far closer relations with ideology than any other *object*, and that it is impossible to think the work of art, in its specifically aesthetic existence, without taking into account the privileged relation between it and ideology, i.e. *its direct and inevitable ideological effect*. [161]

Beyond Ideology Critique

Althusser's view that artistic institutions, discourses, texts and practices produce ideological effects was crucial in triggering the growth of cultural studies in the 1970s, 1980s and beyond. Similarly, Adorno's conception of false consciousness as sedimented content was a factor behind ideology critique becoming a cottage industry in arts disciplines in the same period.[162] More recently, theorists have increasingly questioned the validity and usefulness of unmasking the ideology supposedly at work within artworks, turning against 'paranoid reading' strategies intent on exposing the concealed or repressed underbelly of texts.[163] One factor behind the move away from ideology critique is the broader scepticism toward the oppositions of true and false consciousness, essence and appearance, depth and surface, reality and illusion on which its operations depend; as Rancière argues, 'once we could have fun denouncing the dark, solid reality concealed behind the brilliance of appearances. But today there is allegedly no longer any solid reality to counter-pose to the reign of appearances, nor any dark reverse side to be opposed to the triumph of consumer society.'[164] Another factor behind the waning of the critique of ideology is the rejection of the idea that consumers of culture are dupes ripe for political manipulation, a standpoint that, as Jameson argues, relies on 'a peculiarly unconvincing notion of the psychology of the viewer, as some inert and passive material on which the manipulatory operation works'.[165]

One familiar cavil against the Marxist brand of ideology critique is that by unmasking the repressive politics lurking within the masterpieces of Western musical culture, it effectively surrenders their ownership to the right wing. The best-known example of such self-sabotage is probably Adorno's *Versuch über Wagner* (Essay on Wagner, 1937–8), a text that set out to resist the Nazi appropriation of Wagner. As Benjamin noted in a letter to Adorno, the latter's aim of salvaging the progressive sides of Wagner's oeuvre and disentangling them from those aspects he regarded as proto-fascist was undermined by the fiercely polemical ideology critique burning through the text.[166] The danger of burying canonic works under the rubble of their negative historical connotations is not unique to ideology critique, but rather is a problem for contextualization in general. Music historians, like their counterparts in cognate disciplines, have proved adept at using ideological exposés of the Western canon as an outlet for their political energies. Yet 'contextual politics', as James Currie provocatively terms this mode of critique, risks stripping away the positive political values such works can still possess for us, reducing them to being exemplars of historical ideologies and immuring them inertly in the past.[167]

Žižek makes a similar point in critiquing historicist approaches to interpreting Wagner. Rejecting the 'leftist ideologico-critical' approach to the *Ring* and *Parsifal* initiated by Adorno, Žižek praises Hans-Jürgen Syberberg's film version of *Parsifal* (1982) for its multilayered, pluralistic approach to the work's historical resonances:

Syberberg is right to reject historicist readings that yearn to elucidate the true meaning of Wagnerian tropes (Hagen as masturbating Jew, Amfortas's wound as syphilis, and so on). Wagner, so the argument goes, was mobilizing historical codes known to everyone in his own time: when a person stumbles, sings in cracking high tones, or makes nervous gestures, 'everyone knew' this was a Jew. However, do we really learn anything salient in this way? What if such historicist contextualization were not only superfluous, but an active obstacle? . . . One needs to abstract from historical trivia, to decontextualize the work, to tear it out of the context in which it was originally embedded.[168]

For Žižek, historicist endeavours to strip bare the reactionary ideologies concealed within Wagner's symbols and characters fail on two levels. One is that they reduce multiple strata of significance to a singular, originary meaning, treating works merely as symptoms of their initial historical moment. The other is that they take that meaning at face value, rather than probing how the trope of syphilis or, more controversially, the anti-Semitic conception of the Jew are themselves ciphers for broader ideological and social antagonisms, and thus require further decoding.[169] In contrast to such approaches, Žižek sketches provocative counterinterpretations,

reading the *Ring* as a critique of fascism *avant la lettre* and *Parsifal* as
anticipating the Brechtian *Lehrstück*: 'Why not leave behind this search for
the "proto-Fascist" elements in Wagner and, rather, in a violent gesture of
appropriation, reinscribe *Parsifal* in the tradition of radical revolutionary
parties?'[170]

The details of Žižek's communist readings of the *Ring* and *Parsifal* are
less important than the goal behind them: that of rethinking the politics of
these works in ways that liberate them from the constraints of contextualism and the negativism of ideology critique. Žižek theorizes the relationship between his approach and contextualism through the distinction
between historicism and historicity. From this perspective, contextual
approaches drastically narrow our political engagement with historical
texts, anchoring their meanings, values and uses in the local, particular
and contingent. In contrast to this debilitating historicist emphasis on
difference, historicity stresses the non-historical kernel of texts, graspable
only through their relationships with Others: historicism is 'historicity
minus the unhistorical kernel of the Real ... which returns as the Same
through all historical epochs'.[171] An unhistorical referent, or the figure of
the universal, is crucial to politicized interpretation, just as it is to all forms
of radical politics; universality serves as the unattainable yet indispensable
stimulus to strive beyond an existing reality.[172] This does not mean that
ideological critique is no longer necessary, but rather that its target shifts
from historical texts to contemporary culture (including the critique of
contemporary culture through the interpretation of historical texts). At a
time when what Balibar terms the 'real universality' of neoliberal
capitalism has gained a global stranglehold, the critique of ideology is
essential to clearing a space for the 'ideal universality' of emancipatory
projects.[173] The kind of present-minded interpretation that unlocks the
positive politicality of historical texts has a role to play in this process.

4 | Propaganda, Ritual and Sovereign Power

So far, I have explored the relationship between music and domination from the coercive side of the power spectrum: music as violence and as a vehicle for social control. Most scholarship on music and domination, however, focuses on soft power, that is, music's capacity to express, promote and instil hegemonic ideologies, values and interests. The concept of propaganda looms large here, and before going any further, we need to chase down and quarantine it. At one time, propaganda was one of the most commonly invoked terms in the lexicon of music and politics, serving to encompass virtually all forms of proselytizing through music or ways in which it can be pressed into the service of power. While the concept continues to serve as convenient shorthand, its Cold War glory days are long past; today, its usefulness may well seem slight given its pejorative connotations, limitations as an analytical tool and restricted frame of reference. This is not to suggest that propaganda is absent from the contemporary political scene (this is far from the case, as a glance at the videos issued by Egypt's Department of Morale Affairs or the 'fake news' produced by Russia's Internet News Agency will attest), but rather that the concept is an obstacle to understanding the phenomenon.[1]

Part of the problem with the idea of propaganda is that it hives off one form of political promotion from all the others, singling it out on account of its biased and distorted character: a move which assumes the possibility of unbiased and undistorted political expression.[2] Propaganda has not always been synonymous with manipulative and misleading communication. As Jason Stanley notes, the term was employed positively or neutrally by American commentators in the early twentieth century, and as late as 1954 Martin Luther King Jr referred to the 'noble sense in which propaganda can be used'.[3] But this kind of special pleading cannot easily cancel out the negative associations that the term acquired in the era of Hitler and Stalin. In recent years, there have been several attempts to redefine propaganda, whether through expanding it to encompass positive forms of persuasion or through equating it with political publicity *in toto*. Yet the more such studies succeed in expanding our understanding of political communication, the more they underscore the failings of the concept they are seeking to rehabilitate.[4]

The indelible link between propaganda and totalitarian demagoguery reinforces, and is in turn reinforced by, the concept's circumscribed historical range. While Jim Samson argues that 'the concept knows no boundaries, either of time or of place', its usefulness rapidly diminishes when applied beyond the short twentieth century (1914–89) or to music that is not under totalitarian control.[5] While the term itself has seventeenth-century origins (its formal use can be traced back to the Catholic Sacra Congregatio de Propaganda Fide, or organization for propagating the faith, founded in 1622), its association with the systematic control of information and with modern publicity media limits its horizons to the twentieth century.[6] During the height of the Cold War, it was common for scholars to project the idea of propaganda back into earlier epochs, perhaps most notably Tudor England, Reformation-era Germany and the France of Louis XVI. More recently, however, historians of these periods have reacted sceptically to talk of coordinated, top-down propaganda and the use of the ubiquitous phrase 'propaganda machine'; Greg Walker argues that 'the instincts of observers conditioned by 20th-century political propaganda may not be a sure guide to the precise impact and import of politicized imagery from the very different culture of the Tudor court', while Tatiana C. String rejects propaganda as 'a severely limited and inadequate concept when applied to sixteenth-century communicative culture'.[7] The idea of propaganda can be no less problematic when applied to present-day media and politics. Today, the concept seems crude and anachronistic, a relic of an age of cinema newsreels, colourful posters and kitschy heroic monuments. As John Corner observes, the sophistication of contemporary political publicity, and the omnipresence of promotional activity in contemporary political life, create 'conditions very different from the ones in which ideas of propaganda gained their suggestiveness and force'.[8]

Box 4.1 Hitler on Art and Propaganda

[Propaganda] is nothing but a weapon, and indeed a most terrifying weapon in the hands of those who know how to use it ... It must always address itself to the masses. For the intelligentsia, or what passes for it today, propaganda is not suitable but only rational arguments. Propaganda has as little to do with intellectual content as an advertisement poster has to do with art, so far as the form in which it presents its message is concerned. The artistry of the advertisement poster consists in

Box 4.1 (*cont.*)

the ability of the designer to attract the attention of the crowd through the form and colours he chooses. The poster for an art exhibition serves merely to publicize the art on display; the better it does that, the more successful is the art of the poster as such. The poster must convince the public of the importance of the exhibition, but should in no way set itself up as a substitute for the art presented at it. They are something entirely different ... A similar relationship pertains with regard to what we today describe as propaganda. The purpose of propaganda is not the academic instruction of the individual, but rather to attract public attention to certain facts, actions, imperatives etc., the importance of which can be brought home to the masses only by this means.

The art of propaganda consists in putting a matter so clearly and forcibly before the minds of the people as to create a general conviction regarding the reality of a certain fact, the necessity of a certain action, the just character of something that is essential, and so on. But as this art is not an end in itself and because its purpose must be exactly that of the advertisement poster – to attract the attention of the crowd and not by any means to convey intellectual doctrines to those who already have an educated grasp of matters or are striving to form such insights – it must target its effects on the feelings of the masses and only very minimally impinge on their reasoning powers.

All propaganda must be presented in a popular form and must fix its intellectual level so as not to be above the heads of the least intellectual of those to whom it is directed ... The more it is addressed exclusively to the feelings of the masses, the more decisive will be its success. This is the best test of the value of a piece of propaganda, and not the approbation of a coterie of intellectuals or callow aesthetes.

Thus the art of propaganda lies in being able to awaken the imagination of the masses through an appeal to their feelings, by finding the appropriate psychological form that will grip the attention and then the hearts of the multitude. (Adolf Hitler, *Mein Kampf*, vol. I (1925) (Munich, 1943), 196–7; translation based on *Mein Kampf* (London, 1939), 146–8)

The problems multiply when the term 'propaganda' is applied to the arts, since it triggers the kind of unhelpful polarizations of free and applied art examined in Chapter 1. The view that propaganda offers a narrowly functional, instrumentalized form of artistic expression is epitomized by one of Hitler's discussions of propaganda in *Mein Kampf* (see Box 4.1). Here, Hitler cautions against treating propaganda as an end in itself or infusing it with excessive intellectual or artistic content; to illustrate his point, he cites the functional and qualitative chasm separating a poster advertising an exhibition and the art within that exhibition, arguing that the value of propaganda lies solely in popularizing a message or cause. Yet this kind of rigid distinction is contradicted by some of the propaganda produced in the Third Reich: most notably, Leni Riefenstahl's 1935 film *Triumph des Willen* (Triumph of the Will), a production that is regularly acclaimed not only as supremely successful propaganda but as a 'cinematic masterpiece'.[9] The problem posed by *Triumph of the Will* is not that it juxtaposes moments of exemplary political promotion with moments of supreme artistry. Rather, what is striking is that the most effective scenes from a propaganda standpoint are precisely the ones which seem most successful in artistic terms.

Much of the film is given over to well-edited but unremarkable scenes of marching, popular adulation and speechifying from the Nazi hierarchy. But two scenes stand out as being on an altogether different level. I'm not thinking here of the most overtly didactic part of the film – its conclusion – at which Rudolf Hess delivers a trite summation of its message: 'The party is Hitler! But Hitler is Germany, just as Germany is Hitler!' Rather, I have in mind those portions of the film where the work of propaganda is assigned solely to non-diegetic music and the visual image. The first of these is the celebrated opening, in which Hitler's plane descends through the clouds to Nuremberg to the accompaniment of Herbert Windt's orchestral variations on the *Horst Wessel Lied*.[10] While much has been made of the messianic dimensions of the scene, its exemplary propaganda value lies in its normalization of Nazism, a task accomplished by the music; Windt takes the *Horst Wessel Lied* – emblem of Nazism as a thuggish, paramilitary force – and transforms it into something respectable, stitching it contrapuntally into German bourgeois culture. A similar function is performed by Windt's use of the Act III prelude from Wagner's *Die Meistersinger* to accompany dawn over Nuremberg.[11] Wagner's prelude itself embodies nostalgia for a German golden age, making its use in the film doubly nostalgic; here, the score, in association with comforting images of old Nuremberg, serves to reassure bourgeois audiences that Hitler's vision of national reawakening remains anchored firmly in tradition.

Judging from *Triumph of the Will*, propaganda in practice is a lot subtler than the concept itself seems to allow. One further factor circumscribing the usefulness of the term is its association with official government publicity: a connotation derived from early twentieth-century usage and reinforced by some recent literature, including the writings of the

American philosopher and activist Noam Chomsky.[12] The danger here is that in discussing particular cases, merely invoking the term can serve to exaggerate the closeness of the relationship between music and the state; in the paranoid world of propaganda, any kind of correspondence between a government agenda and a musical text seems like evidence of musicians' toadying or collusion with power. As well as avoiding the term (or drastically limiting its scope), we need to guard against carrying over this and its other drawbacks.

4.1   Political Promotion and Affirmation

The following discussion uses the concepts of promotion and affirmation to explore some of the ways in which music serves hegemonic power. I use the word 'promotion' to convey not only music's contribution to image-making, publicity and persuasion, but also the projection of power itself (in each of the following categories, 'state' could be replaced by any other hegemonic body):

1. formal promotion: state-sponsored 'official' music, or compositions commissioned by state agencies for promotional purposes;
2. informal promotion: music which endorses a particular state initiative, policy or figure but which is not state-sponsored; and
3. affirmation: music that actively but indirectly endorses the ruling order, perhaps by mediating its politics through allegory or historical subject matter. What I have in mind here resembles Marcuse's description of political art as 'performing an essentially dependent, affirmative-ideological function, that is to say, glorifying and absolving the existing society'.[13]

Formal Promotion

The category of formal promotional music encompasses not only national anthems but all forms of official and ceremonial music which publicize, project and endorse state and sovereign power: as Esteban Buch puts it, 'music seen as gesture, as political discourse, music produced and interpreted by the state itself'.[14] For Sabine Mecking and Yvonne Wasserloos, 'state ceremony is scarcely conceivable without the symbolic power of music': the extent to which music is indispensable within royal display is apparent in the common use of the phrase 'drum-and-trumpet history' to disparage popular histories oriented around monarchs and dynasties.[15]

Alongside music's role of choreographing rituals and displays of power (coronations, funerals, entries, parades and so on), the category of formal promotion includes state-sponsored presentation music such as cantatas and odes for birthdays, name days and other royal occasions.[16] Historically, such celebratory or commemorative music would in general have been heard by small audiences of courtiers and diplomats, rather than by the broader populace; even so, its promotional techniques can be every bit as insistent as those of twentieth-century mass propaganda. Consider, for example, Georg Frideric Handel's *Ode for the Birthday of Queen Anne* (1713), which hails the successful negotiation of the peace Treaty of Utrecht with a refrain drummed home in no fewer than seven movements ('The Day that gave great Anna birth, / Who fix'd a lasting Peace on Earth').[17] It is in cases such as this, where music is used to help impose an official standpoint or sanctioned reading of events, that it seems legitimate to speak of propaganda; here, the repetition built into the libretto and music draws to mind Hitler's definition of propaganda as 'putting a matter so clearly and forcibly before the minds of the people as to create a general conviction regarding the reality of a certain fact'.

Most examples of formal promotional music, such as Handel's ode, involve the collaboration of state officials and librettists as well as composers, making it difficult to determine precisely whose political agency and agenda are to the fore. In a surprisingly large number of cases, monarchs and ministers have taken a direct role in musical promotion, whether by penning librettos, participating in performances or even composing the music. Some leaders, such as the seventeenth-century Holy Roman Emperor Ferdinand III, have used their own compositions – in his case, predominantly Catholic sacred works – to shape perceptions of their image.[18] Similarly, the Prussian kings Friedrich II (Fredrick the Great) and Friedrich Wilhelm III both composed marches for their own military parades; as the standard inspection march of the German army, the *Präsentiermarsch Friedrich Wilhelms III* remains today a key component of German state and military ceremonies.[19] Perhaps the most striking contemporary examples of musical self-promotion come from Zimbabwe, where a succession of Zanu-PF ministers have used their own music to help secure public support for their policies. During his period as Minister for Information and National Commissar for Zanu-PF (2000–5), Jonathan Moyo was in charge of popularizing President Robert Mugabe's land reform programme, using musical albums and commercials to incite army veterans and other supporters into violent action: 'Zanu-PF slogans like "land is the economy and the economy is land" and "Zimbabwe will never be a colony again", all of that was me, including the *Hondo Yeminda* music jingles I composed on my guitar. But Jonathan Moyo never beat anyone up.'[20] The saturation broadcasting of Zanu-PF campaign songs during election periods, combined (as described earlier) with the informal censorship and intimidation of musicians opposing the regime, were undoubtedly a factor that helped Mugabe to cling onto power. Mugabe himself provided an unlikely contribution to this musical self-promotion with a 2011 voiceover to the song 'Toita Sei?' ('What should we do?) by the Zanu-PF–affiliated band Born Free Crew.[21]

Informal Promotion

My second category takes us beyond music composed or commissioned by state officials and outside the sphere of government publicity. Much of what is generally referred to as propaganda falls into this category, aligning itself unofficially to the state by promoting ideologies, myths and narratives which further its interests. In relation to Germany during the First World War, for example, Dietrich Helms emphasizes that there is no evidence that the state exercised a direct influence on the production of music that supported the war effort; instead, it was composers, promoters and publishers who cultivated music's potential as a 'decentralized influencing factor', producing what he terms 'unofficial propaganda'.[22] The compositions Helms refers to – mostly bluff songs and marches in praise of the kaiser and of military top brass – seem to fit in unproblematically with this perspective (though as we will see, the category of unofficial propaganda or informal promotion is ill-suited to some of the music which did ideological work during the First World War).

Another example of informal promotional music is Beethoven's cantata *Der glorreiche Augenblick* (The Moment of Glory), Op. 136 (1814), composed to honour the assemblage of crowned heads gathered at the Congress of Vienna following the defeat of Napoleon.[23] The ideological ground and dominant tropes of *Der glorreiche Augenblick* overlap with those of another work produced at the time of the Vienna Congress: the painting *Die heilige Allianz* (The Holy Alliance) by the Prussian artist Heinrich Olivier (Figure 4.1). Both cantata and painting draw on readily understood stock devices in order to make their political messages vivid and unambiguous. Olivier exalts the Holy Alliance between Friedrich Wilhelm III of Prussia (left), Tsar Alexander I of Russia (right) and Emperor Franz II of Austria as an affirmation of absolutist monarchy, symbolically cladding the rulers in ornate medieval armour. While

Figure 4.1 Heinrich Olivier, *Die heilige Allianz* (The Holy Alliance), 1815, showing the alliance between the dominant absolutist powers of Europe, represented by Friedrich Wilhelm III of Prussia (left), Tsar Alexander I of Russia (right) and the host of the Vienna Congress Emperor Franz II of Austria (centre).
Dessau, Staatliche Galerie. By permission of Bildarchiv Foto, Marburg.

dynastic emblems abound in the painting, modern symbols of nationhood that might compete with the monarchs for the limelight, such as flags, are entirely absent. Like Olivier, Beethoven draws on musical emblems that by this point were well-established markers of sovereign power; in relation to

Der glorreiche Augenblick, Nicholas Mathew speaks of how the grandiose choral effects of Handel's *Messiah* and Haydn's *Creation* had 'frozen into symbols of sublimity, symbols that were constantly recycled for explicitly political ends'.[24] The practice of employing such musical gestures and topics as shorthand – described by Nicholas Cook as 'composition with genres' – should not be taken as a sign that promotional music required and received desultory attention from composers.[25] Rather, pieces destined for one-off performances of necessity drew on materials guaranteed to strike the right note and elicit the correct response; this form of political music left no room for ambiguity.

Both Beethoven's cantata and Olivier's painting are striking for the way in which they stage and frame the monarchs at their heart. In the third movement of the cantata – the number that seems to have made the most impression on Beethoven's audience – each of the crowned heads is announced in turn as if making an entrance, greeted by musical accolades appropriate to their rank; this dramatic evocation of the monarchs ('what a spectacle!' [*Welch' Schauspiel*], notes the soloist personifying Vienna) is crucial to the overall message of the cantata.[26] Olivier's painting is, if anything, even more theatrical, grouping its monarchs like an operatic trio; their clasped hands, upturned eyes and the blessing offered by the tsar make the moment resemble a reactionary inversion of the oath-taking scenes common in French revolutionary opera.[27] While revolutionary oath-taking, as Elizabeth Bartlet notes, negated traditional social hierarchies, Olivier's scene vividly reinstates and sanctifies them.[28] The religious symbols in Olivier's painting – most notably the gothic cathedral interior and the crusader imagery on the monarchs' armour – are at the heart of its meaning. As in nostalgic evocations of the Middle Ages such as Novalis's 'Die Christenheit oder Europa' (1799), the rulers' response to the upheavals and secularism of the French Revolution is to pledge to safeguard Christianity and absolutism throughout Europe. A similar, if marginally less reactionary vision of Christianity and Europe is presented in the penultimate movement of Beethoven's cantata, which places God at the heart of the process of reconstructing Europe and enabling 'the old times to finally reappear on earth'. But Beethoven's cantata includes an additional element that arguably makes it more effective as promotion than Olivier's painting. While Olivier's monarchs are presented as if on stage, there is no audience in the painting to represent their subjects; indeed, the geography of the scene places them directly in front of the cathedral's high altar, making God the only witness to their oath taking. But if Olivier offers a vision, as Jürgen Angelow puts it, of 'religion and monarchy iconographically bound together', Beethoven's cantata inserts the populace into what his librettist Aloys Weissenbach describes as the union of 'heart, heaven and sceptre': its choruses of women, children and men combine to pay homage to the gathered monarchs and to celebrate this 'glorious moment' of absolute consensus. What better way to promote an idea than to make the very notion of dissent seem unthinkable, at least for a moment?

Affirmation

My third category encompasses music that actively yet less directly endorses hegemonic power. One way to see how affirmation differs from promotion is by looking at other forms of music connected to the contexts explored earlier, the Congress of Vienna and the First World War. In recording music from the Great War for a recent project, I have been struck by the extent to which composers – even when writing in genres seemingly remote from politics – reproduced the tropes and narratives used by state and religious authorities to maintain enthusiasm for the war.[29] In only a handful of cases, however, such as patriotic marches and pieces marking battle victories, does the concept of promotional music seem relevant or helpful; instead, much of this repertory offers more oblique affirmations of sanctioned war narratives. Charles Stanford's Sonata No. 2 'Eroica', Op. 151 (1917), for example, makes use of religious and national musical symbols to project a story of French wartime tribulation, resurgence and anticipated victory; similarly, Max Reger's *Sieben Stücke*, Op. 145 (1915–16) interweaves chorale melodies to convey a similar proleptic narrative, tracing Germany's Christ-like journey from sacrificial suffering to its expected triumph.[30]

For different reasons, the concept of promotion ill suits some nineteenth-century compositions that idealize the monarchical order. One example connected to the Congress of Vienna – though operating at several removes from reality – is Carl Loewe's 'Die Kaiserjagd im Wienerwald' (The Emperor's Hunt in the Vienna Woods), Op. 108, No. 1. Loewe's ballad, setting a poem by Johann Nepomuk Vogl, narrates a scene at a hunting party during which the visiting Russian tsar takes pity on an injured roe deer:

Den blickt es an in seinem Schmerz,
als wollt' zu ihm es fleh'n:
O rette mich, du starker Mann,
sonst ist's um mich gescheh'n!

. . .

Und um den Russenherrscher steht
bewegt der bunte Schwarm,
doch Östreichs Kaiser drückt dem Zar
die Hand gar fest und warm;

'Nie werde diesem Reh hinfort
gekrümmt auch nu rein Haar,
es soll an Euer edles Herz
mich mahnen immerdar!'

(In its agony, it looks at him as if in supplication: O rescue me, you
   strong man, or it will be the end of me! . . .
And all around the Russian ruler, the assorted assembly was moved,
   but Austria's Emperor took the Tsar's hand and squeezed it firmly and
   warmly:
'Henceforth, no-one will ever hurt this deer in any way; it shall remind
   me evermore of your noble heart!')[31]

Vogl's scene offers a sentimental variant on what is arguably the single
most important metaphor for monarchical power: the apostrophization of
the ruler as a shepherd tending his flock, in what Foucault describes as the
'pastoral modality of power'.[32] Familiar musical examples of this trope
include J. S. Bach's aria 'Schafe können sicher weiden' ('Sheep may safely
graze'); far from praising Christ the shepherd, as is sometimes assumed, the
aria has the more mundane figure of Duke Christian of Saxe-Weissenfels in
its sights (the cantata from which it comes, *Was mir behagt, ist nur die
muntre Jagd* BWV 208, was composed for a hunting party marking the
duke's birthday).[33] While Bach's aria promotes the qualities of a particular
ruler, the deceased monarchs remembered in Vogl's poem had little to gain
from his panegyrics. Rather, for Vogl and Loewe – who set the poem in the
heightened political climate shortly before the 1848 revolution – the quasi-
allegorical scene served as the premise for a more generalized idealization of
monarchical benevolence; instead of promoting a particular monarch, the
ballad functions as a broader statement of ideological affinity.

4.2   Ritual and the Politics of Acclamation

In several of the examples of promotional and affirmative music explored
above, the appropriation of religious symbolism plays a crucial role in
communicating and legitimizing sovereign power. The extent to which
secular power draws on the sacred for its validation is most obviously

apparent in royal ceremonies and similar forms of ritual action, particularly those from the medieval and early modern periods. We need to tread carefully in exploring the relationship between ritual and sovereign power, since in this area as elsewhere the legacy of the propaganda model can still be felt. For earlier generations of scholars – working in the shadow of fascism or during the Cold War – pursuing the parallels between totalitarian displays of power and the royal rituals of earlier periods proved hard to resist; as a result, figures such as the sociologist Norbert Elias and the historian Ernst Kantorowicz treated coronations, royal processions and other ceremonies as calculated and systematically choreographed vehicles for state propaganda.[34] More recently, historians have increasingly challenged these kinds of readings of royal ritual as anachronistic and constraining.[35] One issue is that the propaganda model exaggerates the degree of centralized planning that went into rituals in these periods; as Dougal Shaw argues, there is surely a need 'to acknowledge a qualitative difference between the mindset of an early modern courtier engaged in a pageant and Leni Riefenstahl filming a rally, or a twenty-first-century "spin doctor" managing a media campaign'.[36] Another problem with this model is that it presupposes that medieval and early modern ceremonies project purposeful, coherent 'messages'. Like most other liturgical ceremonies, however, royal rituals such as coronations and funerals tend to be loose assemblages of heterogeneous musical, textual and performative ingredients; as a result their symbolism can be multivalent and ambiguous. In addition to assuming that rituals convey unitary messages, the propaganda model takes it as read that their function was to manipulate the ruler's subjects and thus secure their quiescence. But as John Adamson notes, it is important to distinguish between 'a generalized intention of conveying meanings that relate to the exercise of rule and the deliberately opinion-forming objectives of propaganda'; the symbols and gestures of royal ritual relate to power in ways that go beyond transmitting messages or securing subjugation.[37]

One of the most significant challenges to the propaganda model is that presented by the anthropologist Clifford Geertz, who assigns ritual an altogether different relationship to power. In *Negara*, his study of ritual and politics in nineteenth-century Bali, Geertz argues against perspectives that instrumentalize ritual, that is, treat it simply as a vehicle for political ends:

The stupendous cremations, tooth filings, temple dedications, pilgrimages, and blood sacrifices, mobilizing hundreds and even thousands of people and great quantities of wealth, were not means to political ends: they were the ends themselves, they were what the state was for. Court ceremonialism was the driving force of court politics; and mass ritual was not a device to shore up the state, but rather the state, even in its final gasp, was a device for the enactment of mass ritual. Power served pomp, not pomp power.[38]

Here, Geertz's focus on the 'theatre state' of Bali results in a startling inversion of the usual view of how power and state ceremony relate to one another. In general, however, his writings stress the complex reciprocity between domination and its symbolic forms and practices: 'the easy distinction between the trappings of rule and its substance becomes less sharp, even less real; what counts is the manner in which, a bit like mass and energy, they are transformed into each other.'[39] Rather than functioning as a material expression of a pre-existing political verity, rituals are a formative force, generating and reproducing power; as the historian Alejandro Cañeque notes, 'political rituals embody the very production and negotiation of power relations and are not merely the instrument of power, politics, or social control (which are usually seen as existing before or outside the ritual activities).'[40]

Religious Ritual and the 'Politics of Glory'

A similar emphasis on the role of ritual in generating power is present in Giorgio Agamben's recent study of the 'politics of glory':

If power is essentially force and efficacious action, why does it need to receive ritual acclamations and hymns of praise, to wear cumbersome crowns and tiaras, to submit itself to an inaccessible ceremony and an immutable protocol[?] ... The simple instrumental explanation that states that this is a stratagem of the powerful to justify their ambition or a mise-en-scène to produce reverential fear and obedience in the subjects ... is not able to account for the deep and original connection that involves not only the political sphere but also the religious one.[41]

Exploring how politics and religion became locked together through the politics of glory takes us to the heart of Western rituals of sovereign power. While some aspects of medieval and early modern rituals can be traced back to imperial Rome, their principal prototype was not something lost in the distant past but rather part of the living present: the liturgy of the Catholic mass. It is hard to exaggerate the impact that the rituals of the mass had on perceptions of the relationship between sacred and secular power. In these periods, the Catholic liturgy provided regular revelations of the capacity of ritual to work miracles, serving no less a function than conjuring into existence the body and blood of Christ.[42] The belief that Catholic ritual possessed such awesome transformative power lent a particular significance to political ceremonies – crucially, coronations – that were intertwined with it. This is particularly apparent in the coronation rituals of the Holy Roman Empire, held initially in St Peter's basilica in Rome and later in the seat of the Imperial Diet in Frankfurt. The coronation of Charlemagne (AD 800) initiated the tradition of monarchs being crowned by clergy (in this case the pope) and of such ceremonies being embedded within the celebration of mass. As well as formally conferring the Church's approval, coronation by the clergy reflected the 'two powers' doctrine promulgated by the fifth-century pope Gelasius I, which distinguished between the sacred authority (*auctoritas*) of the church and the royal power (*potestas*) it delegated to earthly rulers.[43] In addition, the sacralization of the coronation ceremony enabled Christian monarchs to retain something of the untouchable mystique of the classical Roman emperors; as Adrian Hastings notes, church ceremonial 'ensured that the legacy of a "divine" Caesar survived with an apostolic, quasi-episcopal, face-lift'.[44] In the Holy Roman Empire and other countries whose ceremonies it influenced, coronations appropriated the symbols and gestures normally used for the consecration of bishops, giving the monarch what Sergio Bertelli describes as 'an autonomous Christ-like sacerdotal function'.[45]

Music and ritual played a crucial role in the process of transforming an earthly prince into a Christ-like successor to the Caesars. The chanting of the *Laudes regiae* (royal praises) immediately following the consecration of the emperor was pivotal, serving as the formal acclamation of the ruler by both the church and his subjects. Kantorowicz's famous study of the *Laudes regiae* meticulously traces the derivation of the opening section ('Christus vincit, Christus regnat, Christus imperat') and peroration ('Feliciter! Tempora bona habeas') from ancient Roman imperial acclamations.[46] But the worldly political function of the acclamations is evident from the text alone, with its evocation of a warrior Christ reigning supreme with the aid of his earthly proxies. Anne Walters Robertson argues that 'the intent of this royal chant is blatantly deifying' as a result of its systematic association of the monarch with Christ; similarly, Craig Wright describes the *Laudes* as 'flagrantly political in their import' as a result of the chant's endeavour 'to correlate the heavenly and earthly realms and thereby effect an apotheosis of the ruler'.[47] What Kantorowicz describes as the 'dissolving' of the earthly world into the transcendental one may seem from a modern perspective to be exemplary propaganda, securing control over the ruler's subjects by ventriloquizing the divine.[48] But to the medieval mentality, this coming together of worldly and earthly concerns offered a supreme moment of truth; as Aron Gurevich argues, 'truth manifested itself in the contiguity of both worlds, and properly only in those instances when through the transient phenomena of this world the other world shone through and genuine truths were revealed to the believer's gaze.'[49]

Crucial to the effect of this ritual moment is the near trance-like state generated by repetition and 'unisonance' (Benedict Anderson's term for keeping together in time through group singing).[50] Intensely repetitive chanting, such as the central litany of saints in the *Laudes regiae*, can make participation automatic and unconscious, pushing the subject toward absorption in the collective.[51] For Agamben, it is at this point, when sheer repetition renders verbal meaning subordinate to incantation, that the ritual performance of the *Laudes* exercises its desired effect: 'in the sphere of doxologies and acclamations, the semantic aspect of language is deactivated and appears for a moment as an empty rotation; and, yet, it is precisely this empty turning that supplies it with its peculiar, almost magical, efficacy: that of producing glory.'[52] What this moment produces is not simply an affirmation of a pre-existing political truth. Acclamation, as Kantorowicz notes, involved more than simple endorsement; it meant 'to "create" a new ruler and to recognize him publicly in his new dignity'.[53] The *Laudes* therefore served a constitutive role, establishing the ruler's legitimacy and authority through glorification; sovereign power is constituted by acting as if it exists.[54]

The maintenance of sovereign power is similarly dependent on it being regularly reaffirmed, making reiteration a crucial aspect of the political efficacy of ritual. One extraordinary symptom of this in the medieval period was the phenomenon of *coronamenta*, or repeated crownings – festivals at which the coronation of the ruler was repeated – as well as the display of the crown on major church festivals (at which the *Laudes regiae* would be reiterated). The use of the crown as a surrogate for the ruler initiated a multiplicity of forms of symbolic representation geared around making the absent monarch present, each of which had its own rituals.[55] Johann Wolfgang von Goethe's definition of the symbol as 'the thing, without being the thing, but nonetheless the thing' resonates with some medieval and early modern descriptions of symbolic representations of rulers.[56] In colonial Mexico, the accession of a new Habsburg ruler was marked by the ceremonial reception of the new royal seal, which was greeted in exactly the same way that the absent monarch would have been; according to Alejandro Cañeque, 'the ritual of reception of the seal made the king "present"', to the extent that as with the host in the Catholic mass, 'the seal did not represent or symbolize the king – it *was* the king.'[57] Whether in European colonies or in annexed territory closer to home, these kinds of ceremonies remained common well into the nineteenth century. In 1837, for example, the *Allgemeine musikalische Zeitung* reported on a royal festival staged in Erfurt (ceded to Prussia in 1802) held to demonstrate the town's loyalty to the Prussian monarchy. On the second day of the festival, the citizenry paid homage to a bust of the king, placed on a stage underneath a ceremonial canopy and illuminated by coloured lanterns; a chorus and concealed orchestra performed suitably laudatory music, including Carl Maria von Weber's *Jubel-Cantate*, Op. 58.[58] As the noisy choruses in Weber's cantata, Beethoven's *Der glorreiche Augenblick* and similar nineteenth-century productions attest, simulating popular acclamation for monarchy acquired a new importance in an age when it was under threat.

Far from being a musical museum piece, the *Laudes regiae* chant is still in use today as a key ingredient in the making of a modern ruler. Last heard in this capacity at the inauguration of Pope Francis in 2013, the *Laudes* were reintroduced into papal ritual in the early twentieth century, a move motivated in part by the then pressing need to redefine the authority of the papacy in the wake of the loss of its territorial power.[59] As a result, the text of the version of the *Laudes* used in papal inaugurations repeatedly stresses the supranational nature of the pope's authority:

Francisco Summo Pontifici,
in unum populos doctrina congreganti, caritate:
Pastori gratia, gregi obsequentia.

(For Francis Supreme Pontiff, who gathereth into one all peoples
    through doctrine, in charity: let there be grace for the shepherd
    and obedience for the flock.)[60]

To some extent, the functions served by the *Laudes* in the inauguration of a pope are similar to those the chant had in medieval coronations, elevating a prince of the church into the Vicar of Christ through acclamation. But in papal inaugurations, this process coincides with another transformation effected through music and ritual: the new pope's identification with the first Catholic pope, St Peter. In the early medieval period, the idea that the pope was Peter reborn was crucial to papal power; as Kantorowicz notes, this notion can be seen from one of the earliest sets of papal lauds, which hailed Pope Gelasius I with the words 'we see the apostle Peter before us!'[61] The mystical identification of the pope with

St Peter recalls medieval conceptions of the 'king's two bodies', which distinguished between the king's mortal natural body and his immortal 'Body Politic [which] contains the Office, Government, and Majesty royal'.[62] The remnants of this identification could still be discerned in the rituals that launched Pope Francis's so-called Petrine ministry. The ceremony began following the pope's emergence from the tomb of St Peter, where the papal pallium and Ring of the Fisherman were stored overnight prior to the ceremony. Following the imposition of the pallium and bestowal of the ring, the new pope was heralded with Palestrina's motet *Tu es Petrus* (You Are Peter); the iteration of this acclamation at subsequent papal ceremonies (whether in Palestrina's setting or more recent versions) serves as a regular reminder of the source of his authority.

4.3   Contemporary Rituals of Acclamation

If royal and ecclesiastical ceremonies have largely declined into political irrelevance in modernity, the same cannot be said of acclamatory rituals. For both Kantorowicz and Agamben, collective gestures and chants of glorification played their most crucial role not in medieval monarchies but in twentieth-century dictatorships: not in the age of 'Vivat rex' or 'Christus vincit' but in that of 'Heil Hitler' and 'Duce duce'.[63] As these examples suggest, acclamation is by no means the same as assent (or at least, not the same as individual, freely given, rational assent). Acclamation, as the political scientist Mitchell Dean argues, is a social institution which presents individuals with a preformed choice and foists it on them, regardless of their thoughts and inclinations.[64] Most readers will have experienced the sense of unease that stems from feeling obliged – compelled – to participate against one's will in a standing ovation or similar collective ritual. More is at stake in collective acts of acclamation, however, than mere social awkwardness. Today, as in the middle ages or the fascist era, the prominence of acclamation is a sign of democratic deficit: a situation where the figure of the people, the nation or the Dear Leader has vastly outgrown the individuals whose assent sustains the hegemonic order.

It is all too easy to turn to North Korea for contemporary examples of how individual rights can be trampled in the quest to stage collective assent. All forms of political authority draw on the theatrical in staging rituals of acclamation, whether through inaugurations, anniversary parades, mass rallies or liturgical ceremonies. But in North Korea, as

Figure 4.2 Rehearsing a parade in Kim Il-sung Square, Pyongyang, North Korea, 2008, photograph by stephan, www.flickr.com (https://creativecommons.org/licenses/by/2.0/).

Suk-Young Kim explains, theatricality has spread from the ceremonial realm into everyday reality, making life a performance, an attempt to act out the state's vision: 'North Korea is a theatrical state par excellence precisely because it forces a utopian illusion to mandate conditions of real life. Perpetually obsessed with appropriating the utopian narrative for staging its ideal self-image and directing its citizens as if they were actors ... the North Korean state, with its well-developed propaganda apparatus, fabricates the foundation of every sociocultural reality.'[65] The most obvious symptoms of this preoccupation with staging public assent are the rallies and parades held to commemorate national festivals and the birthdays of Kim Il-sung, Kim Jong-il and Kim Jong-un (see Figure 4.2); as Bruce Cumings notes, 'the regime takes great pride in its truly awesome choreographed mass marches through the great central square in Pyongyang, with literally a million people marching in step in fifty parallel columns.'[66] Yet these grandiose acclamatory ceremonies – whose success depends on coerced participation – are less important as a mechanism for social control than the arduous process of preparation that goes into them. Rehearsals over six months, through which the state's musical beat is drilled daily into its citizens, serve to generate not only compliance but pride and enjoyment in collective activity. However objectionable or puzzling to Western eyes, this culture of rehearsal succeeds in securing the complicity of the individuals involved, making it in Suk-Young Kim's view 'North Korea's most efficient governing strategy'.[67]

In the contemporary West, the politics of acclamation is less clumsily coercive yet no less pervasive. In his 1962 book *Strukturwandel der Öffentlichkeit* (The Structural Transformation of the Public Sphere), the German philosopher Jürgen Habermas anticipated the eclipsing of the critical public sphere – oriented around political debate and deliberation – by a manipulative display 'merely staged for the purpose of acclamation'.[68] More recently, Agamben has argued that under the neoliberal regime, deliberative democracy has been replaced by a culture of glorification:

What was confined to the spheres of liturgy and ceremonials has become concentrated in the media and, at the same time, through them it spreads and penetrates at each moment into every area of society, both public and private. Contemporary democracy is a democracy that is entirely founded upon glory, that is, on the efficacy of acclamation, multiplied and disseminated by the media beyond all imagination.[69]

What Agamben is describing here is how, under neoliberalism, consensus politics as moulded by the media has displaced democratic contestation; this development is epitomized by the transformation in the 1990s and 2000s of British party conferences and US political conventions into stage-managed, debate-free zones. But the idea of a politics based around acclamation also resonates with political developments in the present decade, in particular the polarization of political culture fuelled by digital media. For Mitchell Dean, political engagement through social media is increasingly acclamatory in nature, spurning rational debate in favour of one-note acclamations of praise or disapproval (this development, he notes, is epitomized by the 'like' button on Facebook, whose symbol is the 'thumbs up' sign of the Roman arena).[70] Similarly, Frances Dyson highlights how 24/7 TV news demands that consumers 'respond with a modern-day "Amen"', presenting viewer tweets in the news ticker as if they were breaking stories.[71] In this climate of polarized viewpoints and intolerance to dissent, even well-intentioned protest tactics, such as the Occupy protest's human microphone, point to this shift toward the acclamatory politics of the mob.

Many of the other tools of political persuasion and protest – including music – also become suspect within this context of acclamatory politics.

Indeed, the terms used by Habermas and Agamben to criticize the latter echo the age-old objections to music as a dangerous, manipulative antithesis to rational political discourse. To an extent, suspicion of acclamation and of music as irrational reflect (and have always reflected) the fears of a political class whose privileged management of public affairs seems under threat.[72] But it is hard not to be troubled by the nexus of populism, acclamatory spectacle and music when it displaces democratic debate. One symptom of this is the prominence of music in the series of post-inauguration rallies that, at the time of writing, President Trump continues to stage on a monthly basis. The playlists for the 'Make America Great Again' rallies are predictably middle-of-the-road, combining testosterone-packed Americana (Lee Greenwood's 'God Bless the USA'), inanely portentous instrumental numbers ('Sirius' by the Alan Parsons Project), angry rock anthems (Twisted Sister's 'We're Not Gonna Take It'), and acclamatory classics (including the ubiquitous 'Ode to Joy'). But if the song choices are unexceptionable, other aspects of Trump's use of 'authoritarian hold music' are more troubling.[73] Played on a loop over extended periods, the ever-increasing decibels serve not only to pump up the crowd but to make dissent or even conversation impossible, transforming citizens into inert spectators. Just like the chants of 'lock her up!' and 'build a wall' that pervade such events, Trump's rally music signals that the vacant space of politics has been filled by something infantilizing and inimical to democratic participation.

5 | Performing Protest

Music and Activism

The idea that resistance is locked into a relationship of mutual dependency with power seems particularly relevant to protest, at least in its contemporary Western variants. At present, when optimism and belief in the possibility of genuine change are in short supply, the concepts of protest activism and protest song may seem like relics of an earlier age: products of what Jameson describes as 'the halcyon era of the 1960s when the world was still young'.[1] Rather than promising radical transformation, protest may seem today to be at best an impotent gesture and at worst a masquerade that merely serves to affirm existing power structures. Readers who have participated in protest actions may have been struck by the collaborative spirit that can develop between activists and the authorities, enabling both parties to go away satisfied with a job well done while power relations remain entirely undisturbed. Žižek gives a salutary example of this, describing the 'strange symbiotic relationship' between power and protest observable in the London anti-war protests of 2003:

The protesters saved their beautiful souls – they had made it clear that they did not agree with the government's policy on Iraq – while those in power could calmly accept it, even profit from it: not only did the protests do nothing to prevent the (already decided upon) attack on Iraq, paradoxically, they even provided an additional legitimization for it, best rendered by none other George Bush, whose reaction to the mass demonstrations protesting his visit to London was: 'You see, this is what we are fighting for: so that what people are doing here – protesting against their government policy – will be possible also in Iraq!'[2]

From this perspective, protest activism resembles a kind of licensed naysaying, furthering the interests of the existing order rather than mounting a serious challenge to it. In one way, Žižek's view of the 2003 demonstration is remarkably similar to that of President Bush, in that both treat it as an essentially unthreatening application of the liberal-democratic principles of free assembly and free speech. Bush's view of protest as a harmless exercise of democratic rights points to two features characteristic of contemporary Western democracies. On the one hand, it reflects how protest activism has become part of everyday political life since the 1960s, a normalization that stems in part from the strategies of accommodation that governments have adopted in order to neutralize dissent; as a result, protesters have had to resort to ever more unconventional methods to get their message heard and put pressure on those in authority.[3] On the other hand, it confirms the stranglehold of neoliberalism within Western politics in the twenty-first century (the issue of whether protest is futile today is returned to in the Postscript).

In spite of the obstacles in the path of contemporary activism, we should avoid drawing the conclusion that protest is always and everywhere powerless or that it is simply part of the machine it rages against. Although protest can be neutered and contained by governments of every stripe, its nature lies in defying authority and pushing beyond state-sanctioned modes of dissent. While protest may seem to be simply 'an extension of democratic principles', as Ron Eyerman puts it, its very existence points to failings within mainstream political processes.[4] Forced to operate outside normal channels, protest activism draws into the public square issues and grievances that are excluded from or shunted to the margins of official political discourse.[5]

5.1   Protest Music and Social Movements

The interpretation of musical protest takes its cue from wider work on protest activism, in particular the ever-growing body of scholarship on social movements from the fields of sociology, political science and cultural studies. While protest music can serve the needs of other types of groups (e.g. political parties and pressure groups), its development over the twentieth century has been defined by its relationship with social change movements: the labour and civil rights movements, for example, or more recently the environmental and anti-globalization movements. Within social movement research, protest tends to be defined broadly as a public, collective display which challenges power holders to remedy an injustice or redress a grievance (a social movement, for Charles Tilly, amounts simply to clusters of such protest performances, rather than necessarily indicating a more cohesive or permanent grouping).[6] Theorists disagree however about the kind of activities that qualify as protest activism, largely as a result of the distinction – highlighted above – between protest as an extension of mainstream political processes and as a counterforce against them. Thus some commentators, such as the cultural theorist T. V. Reed, restrict protest to unconventional tactics outside the political mainstream, differentiating between the 'dramatic actions' staged by protesters and the methods utilized by their 'tamer, more institutionalized cousins, political parties and lobbyists'.[7] Others have adopted more capacious (and arguably problematic) definitions; for the sociologists Verta Taylor and Nella Van Dyke, for example, the 'toolkit' of protest encompasses 'conventional strategies of political persuasion such as lobbying, voting, and petitioning; confrontational tactics such as marches, strikes, and demonstrations that disrupt the day-to-day life of a community; violent acts that inflict material and economic damage and loss of life; and cultural forms of political expression such as rituals, spectacles, music, art, poetry, film, literature, and cultural practices of everyday life'.[8]

Given the breadth of ways in which protest is conceived, it would be unrealistic to posit a restrictive definition of protest music. While the term had its origins in the US labour movement of the 1920s, protest song quickly became associated with a wider range of causes and, in the process, drew into its fold related genres such as the rebel song, fight song, anti-war song and so on.[9] Protest song has come to be indelibly defined by the music of the 1960s, just as that decade continues to shape broader perceptions of social movements and their methods. While the vast majority of American popular music from the 1960s is – to quote Jeffrey Roessner – 'strikingly apolitical', three distinct models of protest song flourished in this period.[10] One strand, folk-protest song, grew directly out of left-wing political activism, engaging explicitly with contentious topical events, figures and issues. Representative here is the work of the 'singing journalist' Phil Ochs, who neatly defined the genre in introducing his anti-war song 'I Ain't Marching Anymore': 'a protest song is a song that's so specific that you cannot mistake it for bullshit.'[11] The scorching lyrics and simple chant-like melodies in Ochs's songs (such as 'Love Me, I'm a Liberal' and 'Here's to the State of Mississippi') point to the didactic model of political communication animating them. Another strand within protest music, aptly described by Jerry Rodnitsky as 'hazy message songs', engages more abstractly with political concerns, yet it is this model that has most come to epitomize 1960s musical activism.[12] In contrast to the finger-pointing mode, songs from this second strand do not directly address specific issues, instead offering more generalized evocations of emancipation and solidarity. The classic examples (all predating the 1960s) are 'We Shall Overcome', 'We Shall Not Be Moved' and Pete Seeger and Lee Hays's 'If I Had a Hammer', as well as Bob Dylan's 'Blowin' in the Wind' (1962). A third strand, emerging around the time of the Civil Rights Act (1964) and developing alongside the Black Power movement, is radical soul music. The template for this form of protest song was Sam Cooke's 'A Change Is Gonna Come', which swiftly inspired a host of other politicized soul hits such as Curtis Mayfield's 'Keep on Pushing' and 'People Get Ready', James Brown's 'Say It Loud (I'm Black and I'm Proud)', and Aretha Franklin's feminist classic 'Respect'.[13]

Ever since the 1960s, commentators have regularly dismissed protest music as ineffective or as a distraction from 'real' politics. Such viewpoints are understandable, given the inflated claims that folk and rock musicians have sometimes made about the political efficacy of their songs. In 1962, for example, the folk singer Oscar Brand quipped that 'protest songs move the body, move the mind, and move the government', a notion echoed by Tom Morello following the break-up of Rage Against the Machine: 'I was confident that, given the right dice throw of historical circumstance, that rock band could have started a social revolution in the United States of America that would have changed the country irrevocably. I put no ceiling on what the potential impact a cultural force like that could have.'[14] While this kind of optimism is a necessary fuel for the hard slog of political struggle, few protest musicians would claim that their music is capable of producing change by itself (making it unfair to attempt to measure its efficacy on that basis); as Billy Bragg argues, 'political rock 'n' roll can only really be effective against a backdrop of social pressure, rather than just working on its own.'[15] More broadly, it is rarely possible to demonstrate a straightforward causal relationship between protest activism of any form and political change. Indeed, as the political philosopher Jón Ólafsson notes, where protest is concerned, success can be as hard to define as it is to achieve: 'protest groups are rarely successful in the sense of actually being granted what they demand, and success in that sense is almost never expected.'[16]

Rather than changing the world by itself, protest music supports the broader work of social change movements. The extent to which musicians and songs are integrated within the work of social movements varies substantially. In some cases, such as Morello's participation in the Occupy Wall Street protest in October 2011 (see Figure 5.1), music is directly embedded within a broader protest event and allied unambiguously with the aims of the movement.[17] But many performers and songs associated with protest music have a less direct relationship to activism, leading some commentators to dismiss them as politically ineffective or irrelevant; the classic example is the pioneering sociologist of protest song, R. Serge Denisoff, who argued in 1970 that 'for maximum effectiveness, protest songs must be linked to some supportive organizational form such as a

Figure 5.1 Tom Morello performing on day 28 of the Occupy Wall Street protest, 2011, photograph by David Shankbone, www.flickr.com (https://creativecommons.org/licenses/by/2.0/).

social movement. Otherwise, the message is intellectualized without some possible social action.'[18] While few would argue with the first part of Denisoff's claim, the second is more tendentious, reflecting his agenda to distinguish rigidly between protest songs 'on the top forty and those of the streets'. In reality, the loose, porous nature of social movements makes it hard to sustain such distinctions, at least in such black and white terms. Music need not be directly embedded within broader activism in order to contribute to the cultural work of a social movement, and some of the musicians most closely identified with particular movements (for example, Bob Dylan and the civil rights movement) have remained largely aloof from non-musical forms of activism.[19]

The Functions of Protest Song

In an influential 1966 article, Denisoff categorized the key ways in which protest songs help social movements achieve their aims. Revisiting and amplifying his categories gives a useful point of entry to thinking about the functions of protest songs and performances:

1. The song attempts to solicit and arouse outside support and sympathy for a social or political movement.
2. The song reinforces the value structure of individuals who are active supporters of the social movement or ideology.
3. The song creates and promotes cohesion, solidarity, and high morale in an organization or movement supporting its world view.
4. The song is an attempt to recruit individuals for a specific social movement.
5. The song invokes solutions to real or imagined social phenomena in terms of action to achieve a desired goal.
6. The song points to some problem or discontent in the society, usually in emotional terms.[20]

Denisoff's first and fourth categories deal with the external-facing role of protest songs and performances: their function as a means to generate support and recruits for social change movements. Rather than simply preaching to the choir, protest music can communicate the ideas and values of a movement in a palatable and attractive form to those outside it, functioning like advertisements for their cause. While there are limits to music's capacities for seduction, the most effective protest songs can break through listeners' cynicism or force them to question their own prejudices. Such songs often have a Marmite effect, attracting or repulsing listeners in the course of making their point; one example that retains its force is Ochs's 'Love Me, I'm a Liberal', which pulls the rug out from under flip-flopping liberals by pointing the finger at their hypocrisy and double standards. Subsequent covers have updated Ochs's message for the internet generation; a recent version by the British psych-folk singer Chris T-T, for example, denounces the 'clicktivist sensibilities and "me, me" sensitivity of hipsters on social media, displaying their colours and doing not much else'.[21] Both versions of the song aim at nudging – or shaming – lukewarm sympathizers into becoming committed activists, a function of protest song highlighted in Denisoff's fourth category. It is probably in this area of recruitment that the effectiveness of protest song is most evident, since it provides one of the most important entry points for social movements from across the political spectrum. Perhaps the best-known example of how protest singing can recruit supporters for a social movement is the Freedom Singers, whose performances played a vital role in the civil rights movement by drawing support for the Student Nonviolent Coordinating Committee (SNCC). As one of the original singers, Rutha Mae Harris comments, 'without the songs of the movement, personally I believe that there wouldn't have been a movement.'[22]

The second and third of Denisoff's categories highlight the role of protest song as a tool for sustaining and mobilizing activists and building a sense of collective identity. At the most basic level, songs can encapsulate a movement's core ideas and values, serving – as Reed puts it – to 'provide information in compact, often highly memorable and emotionally charged ways, both to educate new recruits and refocus veterans'.[23] But songs do more than simply rehearse the ideas and values animating a movement, contributing to the process of framing and interpreting them. A song can serve to embed a particular protest event within a shared narrative of struggle or can function as a microcosm of the experience of participating in the movement. As such, protest songs function as what Eyerman and Jamison describe as 'exemplary actions', drawing together the cognitive and affective dimensions of individual and collective experience and embodying everything the movement stands for.[24] This crucial role is apparent in Martin Luther King Jr's well-known paean to the songs of the civil rights movement: 'The freedom songs are playing a strong and vital role in our struggle. They give the people new courage and a sense of unity. I think they keep alive a faith, a radiant hope, in the future, particularly in our most trying hours.'[25] As this reference to a 'sense of unity' attests, participation in the performance of protest songs serves both to display and to consolidate collective identity. Separate from their efficacy as protest actions, the performance of songs at demonstrations and parades generates feelings of belonging, solidarity and group loyalty, while reiterated performances help stitch together a movement's collective memory and story.[26]

Only in his last two categories does Denisoff address what might seem the most important aspects of protest song: drawing attention to social problems and presenting solutions to them. Denisoff's wording points to both the strengths and limitations of 'message' music. While protest song can 'point to' social injustices and angrily denounce them, it cannot offer a detailed analysis of social problems and often does not go beyond 'individualistic statements of vexation'.[27] And in Denisoff's formulation, its positive message is limited to encouraging listeners to take action, that is, to pursue the other forms of protest that a social movement engages in (making protest song seems like a kind of secondary activism).

Other commentators, too, have stressed the limitations of protest song as a vehicle for conveying political messages or highlighted the factors that can neutralize or depoliticize them. One issue, endemic since at least the mid-1960s, is that of listeners treating protest song as just another musical genre or as an aesthetic expression of generalized rebellion rather than a political intervention. Other problems centre on how listeners hear and mishear lyrics. As Deena Weinstein argues, 'the point of the song, its message of protest, can be entirely lost' as a result of listeners fixing only on the refrain (as, for example, in Bruce Springsteen's 'Born in the USA') or not understanding political allusions in the lyrics (as in 'Last Train to Clarksville' by the Monkees).[28] This issue reaches levels of absurdity in relation to National Socialist black metal and other forms of extreme metal: Just how can such music serve as a supposed 'gateway drug' into right-wing extremism if the lyrics are entirely inaudible? The ease with which the message of protest songs can be lost sight of reflects a broader tension, identified by Reed, between music's value as a means of diffusing political ideologies and its potential merely to defuse them. For Reed, the 'ongoing, irresolvable, creative tension between defusion and diffusion' is fundamental to the relationship between music and social movements.[29]

This line of argument assumes that the verbal message is the core ingredient in a protest song and that its political value diminishes if its lyrics are misheard, inaudible or simply vague to begin with. But the fact that protest songs can so easily become detached from the causes that gave rise to them – becoming floating signifiers ripe for appropriation by other movements – should give us pause for thought. Many of the best-known protest songs have been adopted by multiple movements and organizations: 'We Shall Overcome', for example, became part of freedom struggles in countries as diverse as Bangladesh, South Africa and the Czech Republic.[30] In part, this capacity for cross-movement transfer reflects the common pool of symbols and metaphors from which emancipatory movements draw: 'having a dream', 'being brothers together' and so on. But it also points to how the gestural, performative and affective dimensions of protest music communicate their own layers of meaning, distinct from those of the verbal text.

This plurality of layers can help us understand the strange phenomenon of listeners from one side of the political spectrum identifying strongly with protest songs from the other. One example is the Republican congressman Paul Ryan's much derided, but perfectly understandable, claim to 'like the sound' but 'hate the lyrics' of Rage Against the Machine.[31] Another is the puzzling attraction of 1980s Republican admen to Springsteen's 'Born in the USA'. Earlier, I suggested that this attraction stemmed from a misreading of the song's title and chorus, a failure to register the hostility to the Reagan government expressed in the verses of the song. Yet this line of interpretation, as Weinstein argues, oversimplifies matters by attempting to tidy the song's mixed messages into a single, consistent meaning; instead, we need to acknowledge the double coding present in the lyrics, their combination of both affirmative and dissensual elements.[32] The postmodern idea of double coding, or communication on two (or more) levels simultaneously, is particularly apposite here, since the mixed messages in the lyrics are compounded by the testosterone-packed gestures of the music as well as by Springsteen's heroically masculine mode of performance; small wonder, therefore, that journalist Brian Doherty posed the question, 'Who's to say Reagan wasn't right to insist the song was an upper? When I hear those notes and that drumbeat, and the Boss' best arena-stentorian, shout-groan vocals come over the speakers, I feel like I'm hearing the national anthem.'[33]

5.2   Auteur-Activists: Bob Dylan and Fela Kuti

The double nature of Springsteen's 'Born in the USA' points to a broader tension within protest music from the 1960s onward. One of the key developments in the early 1960s was the emergence of a new, dual role for the protest singer: on the one hand, conscience and mouthpiece for the collective, and on the other, transgressive individualist and political visionary. The first of these functions was familiar from earlier folk-protest singing, with figures such as Guthrie and Seeger content to view themselves as 'people's artists' and their music as a vehicle for the cause. The second – the singer-songwriter as freewheeling political truth-teller – was largely without precedent in the field of popular music, although some classical composers such as Wagner had aspired to a similar role and influence (see Section 6.1). In many ways, the relationship between popular music and political activism since the early 1960s has been defined by how the tension between these positions played out. One obvious symptom of this is the elevation of rock stars as global political players crusading against the establishment and the transformation of pop concerts into vehicles for political lobbying on a grand scale (most notably through Live Aid and Live 8). Figures such as Bob Geldof and Bono have proved extraordinarily successful in converting their fame and music-industry connections into political capital, yet it is far from clear which constituency these millionaire mavericks speak for. (Can it be assumed that all those who attended the Live 8 concerts or watched them on television endorsed Geldof's stance on international aid and debt relief?)[34]

The tension between individual expression and speaking for a broader movement has had a defining impact on two key figures in the history of protest music: Bob Dylan and Fela Kuti. Both can be described as auteur-activists, in that their work in critiquing society and envisioning change owes more to their own fiercely independent political and artistic creativity than to the movements with which they were connected. The way in which this tension unfolded was different in each case. Although both were born at roughly the same time, Dylan's brief phase as a protest artist was over well before Fela's began. While Dylan was initially happy to take on the role of mouthpiece for his generation, he swiftly withdrew from it, adopting more freewheeling forms of political expression before disavowing politics altogether. Even at the height of his political involvement, Dylan rejected the concept of protest song: in part due to generic purism (he regarded songs like 'The Ballad of Emmett Till' as topical songs rather than protest songs) but mainly because he resisted the implication that he was singing on behalf of a movement. In introducing 'Blowin' in the Wind' in 1963, Dylan famously claimed that 'this here ain't a protest song or anything like that, 'cause I don't write protest songs ... I'm just writing it as something to be said, for somebody, by somebody.'[35] The following year, while recording *Another Side of Bob Dylan*, he told his liner note writer Nat Hentoff that 'there aren't any finger pointing songs [here] ... I don't want to write for people anymore. You know – be a spokesman.'[36]

In contrast to Dylan, Fela's political engagement became stronger and more vehement over the course of his career, intensifying as a result of repeated harassment, beatings and imprisonment by the Nigerian authorities. While Dylan abjured the role of spokesman, Fela embraced it, founding a political party to sweep away corruption, styling himself 'The Black President' and increasingly treating the whole of Africa as his constituency (though as John Howe notes, 'when Fela spoke – as he often did – in the name of "Africa", he may have been projecting some of the attitudes of a famous, eccentric, successful, Westernized, upper-class Yoruba anarchist and bohemian on a largely uncomprehending continent').[37] Unlike Dylan, Fela was content in theory to instrumentalize his music as a vehicle for political change, arguing in the documentary *Music Is a Weapon* (1981) that only fully liberated societies could afford the luxury of music as a mere entertainment:

Yes, if you're in England, you sing of enjoyment. You sing of love or ... who you're going to bed with *next*! But my society is underdeveloped because of an alien system imposed on my people. So there's no music for enjoyment, for love, when there's such a struggle for people's existence. So as an artist, politically, artistically, my whole idea about my environment must be represented in the music ... Music must awaken people to do their duty as citizens and act.[38]

In practice, Fela's view of the social responsibilities of the artist was in continual conflict with his unruly individualism, summed up by Tejumola Olaniyan as a 'pervasive and enduring narcissism composed of gross sexual exhibitionism, a huge egotistical striving for effect, and a broad outrageous sensationalism'.[39] The tension between these sides of Fela's art is immediately apparent in the sheer hedonistic length of many of his protest songs, with some such as 'Beasts of No Nation' (1989) weighing in at more than twenty-five minutes. Much of this length stems from extended instrumental passages – highly unusual in protest songs of any kind – giving Fela's performances a double coding to which we will return below.

Dylan's career as a protest singer is often seen as coming to an abrupt end in the spring of 1964, as a part of a broader disenchantment with liberal activism and the folk movement. Yet some songs from after this point retain a strongly political dimension, while very few from his earlier period resemble conventional folk-protest songs. Rather than talking of distinct phases, it is better to highlight four overlapping categories or elements within his political songs, each of which gradually recedes from view. The first category is the straightforward finger-pointing song on a topical theme, epitomized by 'Masters of War' (the twist in the tail in this song is the highly personal tone of Dylan's denunciation of the arms industry). The second consists of ballads critiquing a particular social injustice: songs such as 'The Death of Emmett Till', 'With God on Our Side', and 'The Lonesome Death of Hattie Carroll'. While these ballads resemble finger-pointing songs, their focus is more on the listener than on the events or their perpetrators, in line with Dylan's view that protest songs should 'show people a side of themselves that they don't know is there'.[40] Dylan's approach is to castigate those who stand by and allow injustices to be perpetrated, and thus spur his listeners into political action. Yet by the time of the last of these songs, 'The Lonesome Death of Hattie Carroll', Dylan's faith in the political capacities of white middle-class liberals – 'you who philosophize disgrace and criticize all fear' – was on the wane; as Barry Shank argues, Dylan's weary, almost nihilistic harmonica solos seem to point to the impotence of activism and political song in the face of the 'stubborn, inertial recalcitrance of hatred and injustice'.[41]

Some of Dylan's best-known protest songs – 'Blowin' in the Wind', 'The Times They Are A-Changin'' and 'When the Ship Comes In' – fall into the third category, presenting more abstract statements in support of progressive change. These hazy message songs, inspired in part by the extraordinary success of Peter, Paul and Mary's 1962 cover of 'If I Had a Hammer', are carefully calculated to appeal to the broadest possible activist coalition. 'Blowin' in the Wind', for example, manages to allude to the concerns not only of the civil rights movement but of anti-war and anti-nuclear protest, while the biblical imagery and tone of 'When the Ship Comes In' seem designed to speak to black as well as white civil rights activists.[42] Each of these songs presents change as an inevitable consequence of the zeitgeist – something 'in the wind' that just needs to be grasped and pinned down – evoking an imminent future in which all people will be free and equal. Lingering behind these songs, however, is Dylan's growing frustration that liberals were not up to job of realizing their own aims and a sense that his own rhetoric had helped fuel complacency and inertia. In *Another Side to Bob Dylan* (1964), song after song highlights his unsuitability as a spokesman for the Movement ('It ain't me you're lookin' for, babe'), repudiating liberal preaching, self-righteous zeal and black and white thinking as well as his own political naivety ('Ah, but I was so much older then, I'm younger than that now').[43] This rebuttal of his earlier viewpoints comes across even more strongly in the extended poems that serve as the album's liner notes, where he speaks dismissively of 'the tone of principles' and 'piles of paper slogans': 'I tell you there are no politics.'[44]

The 'politics' that Dylan rejected in 1964 was that of governments, parties and movements, yet he retained a pressing interest in thematizing social injustice and communicating his own political viewpoints. The fourth category of Dylan's protest songs, those which offer a more personalized form of political critique, had emerged in 'A Hard Rain's A-Gonna Fall' (1962), a song that pioneered a new kind of poetic-prophetic content and tone; Eyerman and Jamison allude to this song in describing how Dylan introduced

a musical variant of critical social theory, mixing into the political discourse a new kind of insight, derived not so much from literature or philosophy as from a rural populist tradition, in which the lone individual – Dylan's 'blue-eyed son' – could come back from his wanderings, tell of the horrors and the visions that he had seen, and proclaim a poetic truth: 'it's a hard rain's a-gonna fall.'[45]

As well as consolidating his role as truth-telling outsider, the songs in what Lawrence Wilde describes as Dylan's 'social expressionist' mode exhibit a new concern for poetic innovation.[46] Here, the plain language of folk protest is replaced by self-consciously literary symbols and allusions, resulting in a more oblique – but no less vivid – form of political commentary. Perhaps the stand-out examples are 'Gates of Eden' (*Bringing It All Back Home*) and 'Desolation Row' (*Highway 61*

Revisited), both of which contrast a dystopian present with a problematic alternative reality. Both evoke worlds of alienation and despair, in which humanity's moral compass has become 'time-rusted' and language has lost its capacity to convey truth. Enslaved by consumerism, social convention and government control, the figures populating these songs lifelessly act out pre-ordained roles; potentially redemptive forces such as art are neutered through navel-gazing, while political activists merely 'whisper in the wings', fearful of the Orwellian agents that 'round up everyone / That knows more than they do'. The alternative realities that Dylan conjures up have little in common with conventional post-revolutionary utopias or with the kind of community envisaged by Dylan's liberal fans, instead seeming either unattainable (Eden) or unappealing ('Desolation Row'). According to Al Kooper, one of the backing musicians on *Highway 61 Revisited*, Dylan modelled his Desolation Row on New York's Eighth Avenue, then 'an area infested with whore houses, sleazy bars, and porno-supermarkets'; escape from reality thus seems limited to temporary intoxication and sexual relief, rather than the kind of permanent fixes Dylan advocated in his earlier protest songs.[47]

Box 5.1 Marcuse on Dylan and Revolutionary Language

The traditional language somehow seems to be dead. It seems to be incapable of communicating what is going on today, and archaic and obsolete compared with some of the achievements and force of the artistic and the poetic language, especially in the context of the opposition against this society among the protesting and rebellious youth of our time. When I saw and participated in their demonstration against the war in Vietnam, when I heard them singing the songs of Bob Dylan, I somehow felt, and it is very hard to define, that this is really the only revolutionary language left today . . .

The traditional concepts and the traditional words used to designate a better society, that is, a free society (and art has something to do with freedom), seem to be without any meaning today. They are inadequate to convey what man and things can be and ought to be. These traditional concepts pertain to a language which is still that of a pre-technological and pre-totalitarian era in which we no longer live . . . Thus, since the thirties, we see the intensified and methodical search for a new language, for a poetic language as a revolutionary language, for an artistic language

> **Box 5.1** (*cont.*)
>
> as a revolutionary language. This implies the concept of the *imagination* as a cognitive faculty, capable of transcending and breaking the spell of the Establishment.
>
> In this sense, the Surrealist thesis as it was developed during this period elevates the poetic language to the rank of being the only language that does not succumb to the all-embracing language spoken by the Establishment, a 'meta-language' of total negation – a total negation transcending even the revolutionary action itself. In other words, art can fulfil its inner revolutionary function only if it does not itself become part of any Establishment, including the revolutionary Establishment . . .
>
> Poems and songs assume a new Form and function: namely they want to be consciously and methodically destructive, disorderly, negative nonsense anti-art. And today in a world in which sense and order, the 'positive', must be imposed with all available means of repression, these arts assume by themselves a political position: a position of protest, denial and refusal. (Herbert Marcuse, 'Art in the One-Dimensional Society' (1967), in *Collected Papers*, vol. IV, 113–15.)

Dylan's social expressionist songs mark a shift from interventive political music to what I described earlier as 'intra-musical politics' or the politics of culture. This should not be regarded as a move from 'real' politics to 'art' politics, but rather as a means of preserving an authentically radical voice at a time when the Movement seemed to offer just another set of dogmas and constraints. The significance of what Dylan accomplished in these songs was grasped by one of his most politically perceptive fans, the philosopher Herbert Marcuse. In *One-Dimensional Man*, Marcuse had argued that 'the realm of the irrational becomes the home of the really rational', a perspective that he later applied directly to Dylan's social expressionist songs (Marcuse apparently analyzed the emancipatory elements in *Bringing It All Back Home* in his lectures at the University of California, San Diego).[48] According to Marcuse, 'the totalitarian tendencies of the one-dimensional society render the traditional ways and means of protest ineffective', with the result that only society's 'outcasts and outsiders' – precisely the motley characters depicted in 'Desolation Row' – had a chance of breaking the system.[49] Elsewhere, Marcuse argued that Dylan's songs modelled a new 'revolutionary language', breaking free from the prison-house of traditional language that hamstrung other forms of oppositional politics (see Box 5.1). While Marcuse continued to view Dylan's songs as a model of artistic negation, he revised his opinion of their revolutionary potential in the wake of the failures of 1968: 'It seems that the poems and the songs of protest and liberation are always too late or too early: memory or dream. Their time is not the present; they preserve their truth in their hope, in their refusal of the actual.'[50]

Dylan's 'refusal of the actual' entailed not only repudiating existing society but cutting himself off from organized opposition. If Fela was similarly isolated, it was for different reasons. Ruled by a succession of authoritarian and corrupt military dictatorships, Fela's Nigeria lacked effective institutions and forums for dissent; as a result, his songs and weekly press column 'Chief Priest Say' catapulted him into being what Olaniyan describes as 'virtually a one-man countergovernment in the popular realm'.[51] Each of the phases within the evolution of Fela's musical activism was triggered by an act of government interference or repression. After his return from the United States in 1970, Fela's prime concern was with using his new Afrobeat style to promote radical black nationalism and pan-Africanism (focuses apparent in his early albums *Why Black Man Dey Suffer* and *Afrodisiac*).[52] It was only following his detention in 1974 on fabricated drug-dealing charges that Fela began to confront the Nigerian authorities openly, taking on police brutality in *Expensive Shit* (1975) and holding up the military regime to ridicule in *Zombie* (1976). The regime's response was to order a full-scale attack on Fela's compound the Kalakuta Republic, during which members of the singer's entourage were beaten, bayoneted and raped while his mother was thrown out of a window. It was this attack, and in particular the death of his mother shortly afterward, that elicited Fela's most explicit and caustic musical attacks on the regime, in albums such as *Sorrows, Tears and Blood* (1977), *Unknown Soldier* (1979) and *Coffin for Head of State* (1980).

Fela drew heavily on his personal suffering and persecution by the Nigerian state in his songs, embedding his broader political observations within experiential narratives. Perhaps the best example is 'Unknown Soldier', Fela's response to a government investigation that concluded that the destruction of his compound was the fault of 'an exasperated and unknown soldier'.[53] Fela's song opens with the kind of story-telling formula that often precedes his narratives – 'Make you no go anywhere / Just wait make I tell you something' – a device that places him in the position of a pedagogue politically educating his listeners (this didactic dimension is underscored by the call and response exchanges with the chorus). Fela frames the narrative of the army attack on his compound with scathing jibes at the 'government magic' that enables the regime to conceal its crimes. But the political power of the song derives from its central section, in which Fela's voice breaks as he describes the army's treatment of his mother:

Dem throw my mama

78 year old mama

Political mama

Ideological mama

Influential mama

Dem throw my mama

Out of window

Dem kill my mama.[54]

As these lines illustrate, Fela's songs have little in common with the hazy message music encountered earlier, drawing on vivid personal testimony and caustic barbs to ruthlessly skewer their targets. Fela's lyrics are far from artless (at an earlier point in 'Unknown Soldier' the chorus sing a barrage of nonsense syllables to evoke the commotion of the army attack).[55] But every line is geared around emphatic, unambiguous communication, underscored by Fela's use of Nigerian pidgin (the everyday language of the urban working classes), frequent repetition and song structures that ram home the connections he wishes to make.

For Olaniyan, Fela's conception of protest song was characterized by 'pedagogic anxiety': 'what is unique about Fela was his obsessive double anxiety to teach and to make sure that we get the message of the teaching completely.'[56] Fela's anxiety is understandable, since he saw his task as being to correct the miseducation that continued subconsciously to enslave Africans in what he described as a 'colo-mentality' ('Colonial Mentality', 1977). His most ambitious songs, most notably 'Beasts of No Nation' and 'Teacher Don't Teach Me Nonsense', aim at comprehensively re-educating the listener, overturning the everyday assumptions and narratives that keep the subordinate classes in voluntary servitude.[57] But if his lyrics are uncompromisingly didactic, Fela's music models an alternative kind of truth-telling, in which the transgressive, libertarian side of his political personality comes to the fore. Fela's saxophone frequently intervenes sardonically, commenting on the lyrics or making explicit something withheld from them (it is only Fela's mocking version of the Assembly bugle call at the end of 'Zombie' that makes the song's target fully explicit). More often, Fela's extended solos, placed at the start of a song, have the function of imagining freedom musically, presenting a sonic analogue to the alternative reality he constructed in the Kalakuta Republic. Fela draws attention to this function in the song 'Teacher Don't Teach Me Nonsense', where the lyrics are presented as a recipe for realizing the freedoms embodied in his saxophone playing:

Let's get down, to the underground spiritual game

We all sing together, play music together in happiness

All you have to do is sing what I play on my horn.[58]

5.3   Beyond Protest Song: Contemporary Musical Activism

Since at least the late 1960s, media commentators have regularly lamented the waning of the protest song or written the genre's obituary. At the same time, any and every hit song referencing politics has been hailed as marking its rebirth and instantly incorporated into the canon of protest classics. These anxious tropes of death and reawakening reflect how protest music has come to serve as a barometer of the health of both popular music and broader oppositional activism. But they have the result of freezing what was a fluid genre into a narrow set of models, as well as projecting problematic expectations onto it. Our nostalgia-fuelled view of protest song gives it a strange composite form, welding together ingredients and functions that in practice hardly ever came together. Earlier we saw the tension between two of these elements: on the one hand, the protest singer as mouthpiece for the collective and, on the other, as the embodiment of transgressive individualism. This tension points to a broader conflict between protest song as a tool for political struggle and as a consumable product aimed at a mass audience. In our idealized view – shaped by the sounds and images of the 1960s – this music is inseparable from social movements and protest events, serving to galvanize communities, instil hope and help produce change. Yet perceptions of protest song generally focus on high-profile artists and hit records, treating it as a commercial genre within the musical mainstream. What laments at the decline of the genre correctly discern is the scarcity of songs that can satisfy these competing demands.

Another factor fuelling talk of the death of protest song is the sense that the two dominant models of the genre, as well as the politics they embodied, are no longer fit for purpose. In the red corner, we have the folk-protest idiom of the 1950s and 1960s epitomized by 'We Shall Overcome' and 'If I Had a Hammer', songs embedded in protest activism. One reason why these songs evoke such fierce nostalgia is their manichean politics; they seem to stem from a simpler world of black-and-white certainties, in which change for the better would be assured if only the bad guys could be swept from power. While the project to insert folk-protest song into mainstream popular culture has long since faded, this model of song remains a common vehicle for musical opposition; its limitations are all too apparent in some recent anti-Trump songs, such as Joan Baez's 'Nasty Man' (2017), which function as little more than liberal virtue-signalling. It is this kind of song that music critic Conrad Amenta has in mind in describing protest as 'an entrenched and unresponsive dialect which speaks for, or rather in place of, reality, not so much unreal as *anti*-real, frozen in the past, a code of dilemmas packaged with their resolutions'.[59] In the blue corner, we have the tradition of rock rebellion initiated by the Beatles' 'Revolution' and the Rolling Stones' 'Street Fighting Man': music whose politics is focused inward rather than having an interventive function. The extent to which rock in general came to be defined by the mythology of countercultural rebellion has often been highlighted, as has the connection between its values and those of consumer capitalism. For the political commentator Thomas Frank, fantasies of resistance and individual empowerment have become hard-wired into advertising and corporate ideology, making us all wannabe street fighting men: 'We consume not to fit in, but to prove, on the surface at least, that we are rock 'n' roll rebels, each one of us as rule-breaking and hierarchy-defying as our heroes of the 60s, who now pitch cars, shoes, and beer.'[60] But while the rock rebel helped to reshape capitalist consumption, the symptoms of this process included the fragmentation of popular music and the marginalization of more interventive forms of protest music.

Until recently, protest song seemed a thing of the past within mainstream popular music. For Rou Reynolds of the British band Enter Shikari, the contemporary scene is 'devoid of its Marleys, its Lennons, its Dylans and is now saturated with utterly insipid music with little to no lyrical content other than the glorification of violence or greed and the glamorisation of narcissism'.[61] On one level, the marginalization of protest music reflects the intensification of tendencies seen already in the Live Aid era: celebrity musicians do not need to produce protest songs to make a political statement when they can lobby world leaders or just post a tweet. On another level, the ties linking protest music to social change movements have continued to loosen, with the result that contemporary protests are often accompanied by seemingly non-political music. The 2010 student protests in the United Kingdom, for example, had a soundtrack of grime, dancehall and chart rap rather than songs with explicitly political lyrics.[62]

Recently, however, politicized songs have made a dramatic re-entry into both chart music and protest activism. The Black Lives Matter movement, protesting police violence against black Americans, has stimulated R&B and hip-hop artists including Beyoncé, Miguel, Jay-Z and D'Angelo to explore new ways of articulating protest through music. The best-known example of this trend is Kendrick Lamar's song 'Alright' (2015), whose hook – 'We gon' be alright' – was chanted defiantly by protesters in Cleveland, Ohio, in July 2015 following a confrontation with the police; rapidly the song was acclaimed as 'the unifying soundtrack to Black Lives Matter protests nationwide'.[63] The song's catchy chorus, trenchant text ('We hate po-po [the police] / Wanna kill us dead in the street fo sho') and above all its connection with street activism led many media commentators to elevate it to the protest song canon; in an example of the premature historicization typical of 24/7 media, one journalist hailed the song as 'the protest song of a generation', comparing it to Nina Simone's 'Mississipii Goddamm' and Billie Holiday's 'Strange Fruit', while others described it as a new black national anthem to replace 'Lift Every Voice and Sing' and 'We Shall Overcome'.[64]

This urge to crowbar 'Alright' into the American protest songbook exemplifies the trope of rebirth described earlier. But the move to read it through the lens of protest song arguably oversimplifies both this song and broader tendencies in contemporary musical activism. In some ways, 'Alright' is self-consciously designed to fit into the protest song tradition; its hook echoes the spiritual 'I'll Be All Right', one of the source texts for 'We Shall Overcome', while its experiential narrative relates it to civil rights–era classics such as 'Say It Loud (I'm Black and I'm Proud)' and 'What's Going On'. Lamar's impulse to align the song with protest activism is apparent in a stage performance from June 2015 in which he perched on top of a smashed-up police cruiser while an American flag fluttered in the background; even before the song's release, he predicted (correctly) that 'it will be taught in college courses someday'.[65]

But there is an additional layer or two of complexity to 'Alright' that makes it more like a post- or meta-protest song, reflecting on the nature of activism and on Lamar's role within it. One issue here is his previously ambivalent attitude toward the Black Lives Matter movement; on one level, the song can be read as one man's journey from being 'conflicted' to embracing political commitment. But while Lamar takes on the role of spokesman for the movement in the song's chorus ('Nigga, we gon' be alright'), its verses and in particular the poem framing the song present him as still looking for answers. This textual contrast is underlined by the music; the confident, steady rhythms of the chorus ('WE gon' BE al-RIGHT') are dissolved in the verses by an unstable recurring 3+2+3 pattern emphasized by bleak minor ninth chords. The 'we' of the chorus and the 'I' of the rest of the song are not wholly reconciled, pointing to its wavering between interventive politics and transgressive individualism. Rather than marking a return to protest song, therefore, 'Alright' initiates a more conditional connection to the genre and stages the tensions within it. As with other recent examples of rap activism, it gestures at collective utterance, yet inscribes its politicality within what Spencer Kornhaber aptly describes as the 'pissed-and-personal' attitude characteristic of rap.[66]

6 | Critique, Subversion and Negation

Coded politicality, or the use of political symbols and gestures comprehensible only to insiders, can be found in the music of all periods and places. As with propaganda, however, the use of music as a vehicle for conveying hidden messages of dissent or for staging secret acts of resistance is primarily associated with the totalitarian regimes of the twentieth century. The idea that a musical text or performance might enact a masked political critique – that is, a concealed or indirect indictment of oppression, injustice or an entire system, requiring the aural equivalent of reading between the lines to be understood – requires a particular combination of conditions in order to flourish. It needs a regime in which open opposition is not tolerated or in which overt political communication through art is regarded as aesthetically suspect, a milieu in which music is taken seriously as a medium for disclosing truths about the world and a politicized social group accustomed to producing and understanding oblique forms of political expression.

In practice, it can be difficult to distinguish between the kinds of veiled political meanings invested in texts through the agency of writers, artists and composers – through symbolism, metaphor, allegory, allusion and so on – and those read into works by listeners or critics. Indeed, it is a moot point whether a technique like allegory is a mode of artistic production or a mode of reading or listening. Even where artists have given detailed explanations of the aims of a particular political allegory, as in the case of George Orwell's *Animal Farm* (1945), this has in no sense precluded multiple alternative interpretations.[1] While the political value of allegory relies on its message being readily decipherable, its artistic success may seem dependent on a capacity to sustain diverse, even conflicting readings. With music, these complications are compounded. While music has often been drawn into allegorical constructions within Western culture, its ambiguous, volatile nature seems to fight against this mode of representation (or at least the kind of allegorizing that relies, like a bad translation, on frozen one-to-one correspondences).

6.1   Wagner's *Ring* and Music as Political Critique

Given all this, it is perhaps surprising that within modern European culture, the most prominent and elaborate example of political allegory is a work of music: Wagner's epic operatic cycle *Der Ring des Nibelungen* (1848–74). The potency that the *Ring* retains up to the present owes much to its continuing grip on the political imagination: the sense that it has something pressing to say about the political conditions and possibilities of modernity. Yet far from offering a straightforward message or programme, Wagner's saga of gods, dwarves and heroes is decidedly more ambiguous; while most allegories offer a combination of didactic directness and cryptic density, the balance in the *Ring* is weighted decisively in favour of the latter.[2] These ambiguities extend to the question of whether the work can really be regarded as a political allegory at all. In spite of persuasive advocates, chief among them the dramatist George Bernard Shaw, it is by no means clear that the *Ring* presents a cohesive allegory – an extended metaphor worked out consistently throughout the cycle – or whether it merely offers a series of isolated political resonances.[3] Similarly, it is a moot point whether the work is a politicized critique, interrogating the conditions of Wagner's own age, or whether it presents a more universal examination of power and social relations. In addition, even Wagner's most ardent political exegetes – Shaw included – have conceded that there is more to the *Ring* than politicized critique and that his ambitions for the cycle shifted significantly over the course of its composition.

Wagner's aim of staging a critique of capitalism and modern civilization is apparent in a series of texts produced during the revolutions of 1848–9.[4] One of the most intriguing from the perspective of the politics of the *Ring* is the article 'Die Revolution', published anonymously shortly before Wagner's participation in the Dresden uprising of May 1849. While the concept of critique may today suggest an abstruse or academic refutation, it functioned very differently in the writings of the Left Hegelians and other early socialists of the 1840s. For Marx, who explored the concept at length in his 'Zur Kritik der Hegelschen Rechtsphilosophie' (On the Critique of Hegel's Philosophy of Right, 1844), critique serves as a means 'not to refute but to *destroy* ', being a weapon in his ongoing '*war* on conditions in Germany'.[5] Critique does not offer detailed programmes or solutions, but rather a scathing indictment of existing power relations; for Foucault, in terms that echo Marx,

critique doesn't have to be the premise of a deduction that concludes: 'this, then, is what needs to be done.' It should be an instrument for those who fight, those who resist and refuse what is. Its use should be in processes of conflict and confrontation, essays in refusal. It doesn't have to lay down the law for the law. It isn't a stage in a programming. It is a challenge directed to what is.[6]

'Die Revolution' falls firmly within this radical tradition of critique, sweeping aside every aspect of the existing order in order to liberate humanity from the forces and institutions constraining it: government, religion, property, law and even marriage. In common with other Hegelian socialists writing around 1848, Wagner conceives political change from the perspective of Hegel's phased conception of the course of history; this leads him to present the revolution as inaugurating a complete transformation in all aspects of human relations.[7] Liberation from domination and socioeconomic equality will result, for Wagner, in nothing less than the eradication of envy and antagonism from human relations; having attained this higher form of humanity, 'man raised to divinity' can dispense with religion and dedicate himself to proclaiming a new secular 'gospel of happiness'.[8] As well as anticipating the view of revolution and the historical process presented in the *Ring*, Wagner's article sketches a series of revolutionary character types which, to varying degrees, presage characters from the *Ring* and illuminate their functions (see paragraphs one and two of Box 6.1): the anxious ruler, aware that the game is up yet reluctant to relinquish the trappings of power (Wotan); the cunning courtier entirely free from moral scruples (Loge); the rapacious capitalist always seeking to maximize his assets (Alberich); and the blinkered bureaucrat who prizes codices and contracts over 'the hearts of living men' (Fricka).[9] The most startling anticipation of the characters of the *Ring*, however, is the eponymous heroine of Wagner's article: the goddess of revolution (Brünnhilde), riding 'on the wings of the storm', annihilating the existing order and inaugurating a new humanity.

Box 6.1 Wagner's 'Revolution'

The old world, we can see, is about to collapse; from it a *new* world will arise, for the sublime goddess of *Revolution* comes thundering in on the wings of the storm, lightning flashing round her august head, a sword in her right hand, torch in her left, her eye so dark, so vengeful, so cold ... But behind her there is revealed to us, bathed in glowing sunshine, an unsuspected paradise of happiness, and where her foot has passed in destruction, sweet-scented flowers spring from the ground and the joyful

Box 6.1 (*cont.*)

hallelujahs of liberated mankind fill the air, which is yet re-echoing with the din of conflict.

And now look around you. There you see some mighty prince, his heart beating anxiously, his breath hesitant, struggling to put on a calm and collected air as he tries to deny to himself and to others what he nevertheless clearly sees is inescapable. And there you see another, his leathery old face furrowed with every vice, fishing out and bringing into play all those crafty little tricks which have already earned him many a little title and many a little medal ... And there is yet a third, calculating the approach of the phenomenon, then running to the stock exchange to study and assess the rise and fall of the stocks, haggling and bargaining, trying to squeeze out the last ounce of speculative profit, until with one stroke his whole shabby business is blown to smithereens ...

Lift your eyes and look up to where thousands upon thousands are gathering on the hillsides to await the new sun, full of joyful expectation! Look at them, they are your brothers, your sisters, they are the host of all the poor, those wretches who have never yet known *anything* from life but *suffering*, who were strangers on this earth of joy; they are all longing for just *this* Revolution, which *you* are afraid of, to set them free from this world of despair, to create a new world of happiness for *everyone*! ...

They look out with fervent gaze upon the approaching phenomenon, and listen in silent rapture to the roar of the rising storm as it brings to their ears the greeting of the Revolution: 'I am the ever-rejuvenating, ever-creating life! Where I am not is death! ... All that exists must pass away, that is the eternal law of nature, the rule of life, and I, the eternal destroyer, have come to fulfil the law and create the eternally youthful life. I will utterly annihilate the established order in which you live, for it springs from sin, its flower is misery and its fruit is crime; but the seed has ripened and I am the reaper. I will destroy the domination of one over the other, of the dead over the living, of the material over the spiritual, I will shatter the power of the mighty, of the law and of property. Man's master shall be his *own* will, his *own* desire his only law, his *own* strength his only property, *for only the free man is holy and there is nought higher than he.*

Let there be an end to the injustice that makes man subject to his own works, to property. Man's highest possession is his creative power, that is the spring from which all happiness for ever rises and your greatest real pleasure lies not in *what is produced* but in the *act of production*, in the use of *your own power* ... Let there be an end to everything that oppresses you and makes you suffer, and from the ruins of this old world a *new* one shall arise, full of undreamed of happiness. Let there be no more hate, nor

Box 6.1 (*cont.*)

envy, nor ill-will, nor enmity among you; you shall see yourselves as *brothers – all* you who live in it – and be free to recognize the value of life, free in your desires, free in your actions, free in your pleasures . . .

No longer are they the poor, the starving, bowed down by misery, their proud figures arise, with the glow of enthusiasm transfiguring their faces, their eyes are alight with excitement and, with the heaven-shaking cry '*I am a man!*', the millions, the living Revolution, man raised to divinity, burst forth into the valleys and the plains and proclaim to the whole world the new gospel of happiness! (Extract from Richard Wagner, 'Die Revolution', in *Der junge Wagner: Dichtungen, Aufsätze, Entwürfe 1832–1849*, ed. Julius Kapp (Berlin and Leipzig, 1910), 487–95, trans. based on *Wagner: A Documentary Study*, ed. Herbert Barth, Dietrich Mack and Egon Voss (London, 1975), 170–3)

Wagner famously reflected on the allegorical dimensions of the *Ring*, as well as its intended political function, in a letter to his fellow revolutionary August Röckel from 1856. Here, Wagner describes how the personality of the cycle's hero Siegfried was designed to convey the pain-free life of a future humanity, while the staging of the Nibelung myth had the aim of 'showing the original injustice out of which a whole world of injustice grew and thereby came to destruction, so as to teach us a lesson how to recognize injustice, tear it out root and branch, and establish a just world in its place'.[10] Wagner's conception recalls what Rancière terms the pedagogical model of art's political efficacy: the notion that theatrical representations convey clear messages to audience members and thus shape their views and behaviour. As seen earlier, Rancière's treatment of this model reflects his broader hostility to conceiving the relationship between art and politics in causal terms. But the problem with Wagner's claim is not that it oversimplifies causality but that it assumes that the *Ring* transmits straightforward, easily absorbable messages. In commenting on how similar claims animated Enlightenment drama, Rancière argues that they treat theatrical representation as a transparent 'language of natural signs':

The stage was thought of as a magnifying mirror where spectators could see the virtues and vices of their fellow human beings in fictional form . . . That ability to produce the dual effect of intellectual recognition and appropriate emotion was itself predicated on a regime of concordance inherent in representation. The performance of the bodies on the stage was an exhibition of signs of thoughts and emotions that could be read without any ambiguity.[11]

Elements of this pedagogic model can be found in the *Ring*, particularly in *Das Rheingold*, whose didactic directness led John Deathridge to quip that it resembles a Brechtian *Lehrstück*.[12] In general, however, Wagner's approach to 'teaching a lesson' is neither transparent nor straightforward, reflecting how within his thinking and practice, this model vied with alternative conceptions of how music drama might function politically. Broadly speaking, Wagner's writings from this period articulate three distinct takes on the relationship between art and politics: (1) that true art is an impossibility under contemporary conditions and that it can re-emerge only following a social and political revolution; (2) that political art, offering a realistic portrayal of the vices and injustices of modernity, is a necessary evil in the present; and (3) that individual artists can anticipate, albeit imperfectly, aspects of the post-revolutionary community of the future and thus help bring it to fruition. All three of these strands of thought are also present in the writings of other Left Hegelian and socialist commentators from the mid-nineteenth century, which is not to suggest that they sit easily together. Although Wagner conceived the *Ring* as an intervention in the social and political issues of his time, he never entirely abandoned the dichotomized view of political versus autonomous art discussed in Chapter 1; like most German musicians and critics of the period, he regarded overtly political art with suspicion, considering it to be ephemeral, tendentious and narrow in comparison with the supposed universality of autonomous art.[13] In his treatise *Oper und Drama*, Wagner dissected the failings of the most prominent form of political art of his day, the social novels of the French writer Eugène Sue and his imitators. Here, Wagner argues that artists cannot shirk the duty of critiquing the injustices of the present, yet complains that in transforming novels into 'revolutionary weapons', writers had vitiated their value as art: 'Novel writing became journalism, its content was dispersed in political articles, its artistry turned into platform rhetoric, the breath of its speech an appeal to the people. Thus has the art of the poet become politics: no one can poeticize without politicking.'[14] Wagner's concern to avoid such rhetorical tub-thumping and to reconcile political content with artistry is evident in a letter to Röckel, where he argues in favour of a more ambiguous, concealed politicality:

I believe my instincts are correct in striving to guard against the urge to make everything too obvious, because it has become clear to me that too overt disclosure of one's agenda may well get in the way of correct understanding. Drama – and the same is true of works of art in general – has its effect not through expounding propositions but through making what is represented appear natural and inevitable. It is this which distinguishes my poetic material from the kind of political material that seems to be prevalent these days.[15]

As well as being driven by what Gerald Raunig terms the aesthetic imperative of ambiguity, Wagner's turn to allegory points to broader trends within mid-nineteenth-century oppositional art.[16] The practice of mediating political expression through historical subjects was familiar enough in Germany in this period, enabling composers and dramatists to tackle themes that would otherwise have fallen foul of government censorship. A case in point is the enthusiasm for bourgeois heroes from the distant past such as Cola di Rienzo, who inspired not only Wagner's opera *Rienzi* but an abortive libretto by none other than Friedrich Engels.[17] Yet Wagner's turn to myth – justified at length in *Oper und Drama* – was not motivated primarily by the need to cloak contentious topical material; indeed, Wagner's scepticism toward overtly political art stemmed in part from the belief that the standpoints he was expounding were so fundamental to humankind's development that they transcended mere politics. Instead of scrutinizing the sociopolitical conditions of his age through a microscope in the manner of the social novel, Wagner takes a macrohistorical approach akin to that of Marx, using mythology to present a telescoped narrative of humanity's past, present and future. The idea that myth could serve as a vehicle for such metapolitical insights is explored in *Oper und Drama* in relation to Sophocles' *Oedipus Rex* and *Antigone*. Wagner's interpretations of these plays do not simply assign them contemporary political relevance, but rather discern within them the unfolding of larger historical processes; this is clearest in his allegorical reading of *Oedipus Rex*: 'Even today, we need only read [*deuten*] the Oedipus myth in a manner faithful to its innermost essence in order to gain a clear picture of the entire history of humanity, from the origins of society up to the inevitable downfall of the state. The necessity of this downfall is sensed in advance in the myth; it is the task of actual history to bring it about.'[18]

Here, Wagner identifies his allegorical interpretation with the essence of the myth itself. A similar validation was claimed by Shaw for his politicized reading of the *Ring*, which proceeds from the premise that the work is 'a drama of today' that 'could not have been written before the second half of the nineteenth century, because it deals with events which were only then consummating themselves'.[19] As this comment suggests, Shaw treats the allegorical dimension of the *Ring* as fundamental and pervasive; comparing Wagner's approach with that of John Bunyan's *Pilgrim's Progress*, Shaw argues that the Nibelung myths served as 'the merest pretext' for a drama that in reality 'demanded modern costumes, tall hats for Tarnhelms, factories for Nibelheims, villas for Valhallas, and so on'.[20] The notion that the primary layers of meaning of the *Ring* are more or less incidental may seem to take matters too far. Yet the impulse to produce a socialist critique of capitalism and existing power relations was, at least in the early 1850s, more important for Wagner than the precise mythic vehicle he chose to clothe his ideas.[21] The most impressive aspect of Shaw's interpretation is the way in which he draws out and elaborates this critique, reading the *Ring* as allegorizing the clash between the established social, political and religious order and the forces unleashed by industrialized capitalism. Thus, for example, the magic fire conjured up at the end of *Die Walküre* conveys the Church's reliance on hellfire for the 'intimidation and subjection of the masses', while the depiction of Nibelheim in scene iii of *Das Rheingold* offers 'a poetic vision of unregulated industrial capitalism as it was made known in Germany in the middle of the nineteenth century by Engels's *Condition of the Labouring Classes in England*'.[22] Shaw's technique is to interweave such politicized elaborations with summaries of the plots of each drama, with the effect that these elements seem inseparable.

Shaw's conception of the allegorical politics of the *Ring* has become deeply embedded within the work's subsequent history, informing numerous productions as well as critical interpretations. Several key elements within it are problematic, however. One is his assigning of more or less frozen meanings to each character, symbol and setting (a procedure that recalls the contemporary mania for fixing verbal labels to Wagnerian leitmotifs); accordingly, characters who fail to exhibit consistent allegorical associations (such as Fricka, whose association with the rigidity of 'state law' emerges only in Act II scene ii of *Die Walküre*) are explained as departures from Wagner's supposed norms.[23] Another issue that stems from treating the *Ring* as if it were *Pilgrim's Progress* is Shaw's equation of the dwarfs, giants, gods and heroes with moral types; this has the effect of neutralizing the relationship between these categories and social class, as well as obscuring the putative racial dimensions of Wagner's typology.[24] Perhaps most problematically, Shaw's view that the *Ring* is 'about' the nineteenth century oversimplifies what is arguably the most impressive aspect of Wagner's allegory: its macro-level approach to human development and historical change. This can be seen by comparing how Wagner and Shaw approach one of the key symbols in the *Ring*, the Nibelung hoard of gold. For Shaw, Alberich's zeal to pile up gold at the expense of his workers is something 'frightfully real, frightfully present, frightfully modern', symbolizing the social cost of the sterile accumulation of wealth.[25] This interpretation takes its cue from Wagner's libretto, in which Wotan asks Alberich 'what good is the hoard, since Nibelheim's joyless and naught can be bought here with wealth?'[26] But while Wagner, like Shaw, drew contemporary analogies in describing the symbols in the *Ring* (famously comparing the ring itself to a 'stock-exchange portfolio'), his critique of capitalism took a long-term view.[27] Just as Engels turned to Cola di Rienzo in dissecting early capitalist relations of production, so Wagner took a historical approach to the Nibelungs' hoard, linking it with the decline of the feudal system and the emergence of the idea of private property.[28]

The best-known flaw in Shaw's interpretation is his dismissal of the last scene of *Siegfried* and the whole of *Götterdämmerung* – that is, all the action following Siegfried's vanquishing of Wotan – as irrelevant to Wagner's otherwise 'perfectly clear allegorical design'.[29] Shaw's official explanation for this manoeuvre is the notion that the latter part of the *Ring* merely reverts to grand opera and adds nothing to Wagner's critique of modernity. But Shaw's strategy also reflects his lack of sympathy for the anarchist strand within Wagner's politics, as well as frustration with what to him seemed woolly-minded utopianism. Shaw's notion that the story of the *Ring* ends with Wotan's emasculation is understandable, given that he reads the entire work from the perspective of critique. But the function of critique is not merely to challenge an existing order, but to try to catch hold of an alternative political logic. For Judith Butler, critique is 'a practice in which we pose the question of the limits of our most sure ways of knowing': a mode of thinking that searches for liberty by going beyond the horizons and constraints imposed by a particular discursive regime.[30] The difficulties involved in thinking the unthinkable were captured by one of Wagner's models for Siegfried, the anarchist Michael Bakunin, who famously challenged Marx to explain how a free, egalitarian society could emerge if socialists configured themselves as an authoritarian organization.[31] Wagner himself explored a similar dilemma during the early gestation of the *Ring*, locating Wotan at the limits of the knowable and conceiving Siegfried as anticipating life beyond them:

Siegfried alone (man alone) is not the perfected, complete human: he is just one half, and it is only with Brünnhilde that he becomes the liberator. Look well at [Wotan], since he resembles us in every last detail. He represents the limits of present-day intelligence, while Siegfried is the man of the future we wish and long for yet who cannot be brought to realization by us, since he must create himself by his own efforts through our destruction.[32]

For Shaw, Wagner's efforts to think the unthinkable through Siegfried and Brünnhilde amounted merely to utopian cliché ('love as the remedy for all evils and the solvent of all social difficulties').[33] In the event, Siegfried and Brünnhilde's union offers only a temporary anticipation of what a future social utopia might look like: a brief glimpse of a new humanity, liberated from religion, capitalism and the blandishments of the state. It is left to the world that emerges at the end of the *Ring* to carry out the work of post-revolutionary reconstruction. What Wagner leaves us with, perhaps in spite of himself, is a message of what Jonathan Lear terms radical hope, a commitment to strive toward 'a future goodness that transcends the current ability to understand what it is'.[34]

If Wagner lost faith in this radical vision – talk of his supposed 'conversion' to Schopenhauer's pessimism oversimplifies matters – this reflects the recent adage, variously attributed to Jameson or Žižek, that it is easier to imagine the end of the world than the end of capitalism. For those convinced by the idea that there is no alternative to the current order, Wagner's politics, like that of Marx, can at best be of merely historical interest. In a shock-jock editorial for the 2012 bicentenary, for example, the musicologist Leon Botstein argued that Wagner's concerns now seemed 'quaint' and that 'the political relevance is gone entirely' from his dramas.[35] In contrast, some of the greatest contemporary left-wing thinkers, including both Jameson and Žižek, have stressed the continuing political stimulus offered by Wagner's works, renewed through ever more inventive and provocative productions. For Jameson, contemporary stagings of the *Ring* and Wagner's other dramas go beyond the kind of strong readings or ideology critiques described in Section 3.4; instead, they bring the latent contradictions within the dramas into resonance with present-day concerns, functioning as 'an extraordinarily sensitive registering apparatus for all the tremors and vibrations of the age'.[36] Similarly, Žižek argues that Wagner productions serve as a unique contemporary point of reference, giving 'the most accurate registration of our global spiritual and political preoccupations'; precisely because of the ambiguous, mutable meanings of Wagner's dramas, 'it is through a new staging of Wagner that we make it clear to ourselves where we stand, in the most radical existential sense.'[37] As both Jameson and Žižek stress, it is the multilayered, enigmatic nature of Wagner's works which enables them to continue to strike fresh political resonances. While Wagner may have failed to produce the kind of world-changing didactic dramas he at one stage envisaged, the slow-burning effect that they continue to exercise is no less remarkable.

6.2   Shostakovich, Subversion and Secret Dissidence

Resistance is often used as a catch-all term for oppositional activism, or treated as more or less interchangeable with protest. But as seen earlier, the term also carries more specific connotations, being associated with micro actions rather than grand spectacles and with subversive activities rather than open dissent. While protest activism centres on public actions, resistance can work quietly under the radar, often in circumstances where more overt opposition would be dangerous or futile. Thus while protest music, for Dave Laing, offers 'explicit statements of opposition to the political, economic or social status quo', the 'music of resistance' is more 'coded or opaque in its expression of dissidence'.[38] If protest is an active, visible form of opposition, resistance – for Marita Fornaro Bordolli – can involve 'immobility and invisibility': 'not attending an event, not broadcasting the National Anthem in celebrations imposed by the dictatorial government, not "being present" as ways of denial'.[39] And while protest generally entails organized collective action, resistance can centre on uncoordinated individual initiatives: the production of texts or acts whose singular potential may be slight, yet which cumulatively chip away at the structures of power.

A brief detour into the world of film can highlight some of the strengths and limitations of such musical subversion. I'm not thinking here of the extraordinary dual between the *Marseillaise* and *Die Wacht am Rhein* fought out in *Casablanca* (1942): a moment of open and provocative dissent, in which the French refugees resist their space being sonically occupied by the forces of the Reich. Rather, I have in the mind the more clandestine use of a national anthem in a film released earlier the same year: Michael Powell and Emeric Pressburger's *One of Our Aircraft Is Missing* (1942), a wartime flag-waver set in the Netherlands under German occupation. Unusually for the period the film has no composed soundtrack, an omission which heightens the potency and symbolic significance of its diegetic moments of resistance. When German soldiers interrupt a Catholic service searching for six downed British airmen, the church organist distracts them by surreptitiously playing the forbidden Dutch national anthem (*Het Wilhelmus*). Knowing full well that the organ is the source of the sound yet reluctant to appear foolish, the soldiers beat a hasty retreat as the congregation lustily takes up the anthem. Later in the film, a patriotic schoolboy plays a trick on the Germans by swapping a parcel of gramophones destined for the soldiers' mess with recordings of the *Wilhelmus*; outraged at this musical insult, the unamused soldiers search for the culprit with fixed bayonets. Although both examples arguably strain credibility, they point to some key aspects of clandestine musical resistance. One is the element of risk involved, since this is the factor behind the need to disguise either the acts of resistance or their perpetrators; no matter how trivial, gestures of musical subversion antagonize power and place their instigators in jeopardy. Another is the dual function of such acts, since as well as challenging power they promote cohesion among those resisting it. The examples of musical resistance in *One of Our Aircraft Is Missing* may seem little more than pranks, generating no lasting effects; yet they engineer moments of solidarity among the occupied townspeople as well as undercutting the authority of the occupiers. Moreover, for Anita Jorge, the playing of the *Wilhelmus* serves as a means of sonically recapturing spaces ceded to the Germans, temporarily transposing listeners to a future when the anthem can again sound forth freely.[40]

Shostakovich

No less fictional, perhaps, is the supposed secret dissidence lurking within the music of Dmitri Shostakovich. The idea that Shostakovich's works – in particularly, the Fifth and Seventh Symphonies – conceal subversive content beneath their robustly Soviet exteriors was championed by Solomon Volkov following the composer's death; in spite of vigorous resistance from musicologists, it became common currency in the 1980s and 1990s, propelling a spectacular revival in interest in Shostakovich and his music.[41] In Russia, the reinvention of Shostakovich as a dissident was a form of rehabilitation, repurposing his music to make it fit in with the changed climate of the perestroika and post-Soviet eras. In the West, particularly in the years surrounding the collapse of Communism, the idea that the leading composer of the Stalin era was attacking the system from within flattered the liberal illusion that at heart everyone shares the values of liberal democracy. Within musicology, thanks to a series of interventions from Laurel E. Fay and Richard Taruskin, the so-called Shostakovich wars have been consigned to the past, even though a few keepers of the flame cling to the view of Shostakovich as dissident.[42] Yet within broader culture, this perspective remains deeply embedded, continuing to dominate popular perceptions of the composer (one recent example of this is Julian Barnes's 2016 novel *The Noise of Time*).[43]

Two aspects of this familiar tale are worth revisiting here. The first, which has received substantial attention, concerns interpretation: What exactly is being claimed by those who hear masked anti-Soviet dissidence in Shostakovich's works, and how does that content relate to their other layers of meaning? The second, which has seldom been addressed, is what – if any – political function such purely musical subversion might serve, and whether secret dissidence is a meaningful concept. For the leading champion of the 'new Shostakovich', the British music critic Ian MacDonald, there can be no doubt that the composer was 'scathingly anti-Communist': a 'secret dissident waging, from behind the many masks of his music, a campaign of protest against the very system which had paraded him as its laureate'.[44] Earlier, in exploring the critique of ideology, we encountered the impulse to strip away the brilliant facades of the masterpieces of the Western tradition in order to reveal the hidden reactionary politics at their heart. MacDonald's approach is similarly reductive yet serves a different end, aiming not to debunk the works of his hero dissident but rather to ensure that they outlive the Soviet culture that begat them. While the critique of ideology is fuelled by historicism (damning a work on the basis of its dubious historical origins), MacDonald's approach is resolutely present-minded, stripping away the original connotations of the music in order to reinvent Shostakovich as a dissident in the mould of Aleksandr Solzhenitsyn.

For MacDonald, Shostakovich's 'guerilla war' on Stalin and 'dissident critique' of Soviet society leave their mark on all the symphonies.[45] It is his interpretations of the Fifth and Seventh Symphonies, however, that have provoked the most discussion. For MacDonald, the first movement of the Symphony No. 5, Op. 47 (1937) – purportedly the composer's 'Practical Creative Reply to Just Criticism' – offers nothing less than a satirical portrait of Stalin himself:

A startling cinematic cut sends us tumbling out of the world of abstraction and into representation of the most coarsely literal kind. We are at a political rally, the leader making his entrance through the audience like a boxer flanked by a phalanx of thugs. This passage (the menace theme dissonantly harmonised on grotesquely smirking low brass to the two-note goosestep of timpani and basses) is a shocking intrusion of cartoon satire. Given the time and place in which it was written, the target can only be Stalin – an amazingly bold stroke.[46]

The most controversial of MacDonald's interpretations, however, was his revisionist reading of the march from the Symphony No. 7 'Leningrad' (1941), which argues that its official programme was a red herring designed to conceal the composer's true agenda: 'The simplest explanation is that, like the rest of the symphony, the *Leningrad* march is two things at once: superficially an image of the Nazi invasion; more fundamentally a satirical picture of Stalinist society in the thirties. That is to say: the "war symphony" legend, along with the composer's programme and movement titles, was, like the Fifth's similar accoutrements, a bodyguard of lies for his deeper intentions.'[47]

What provoked controversy was not MacDonald's revisionist agenda (this kind of politicized critique was familiar enough by 1990) but his insistence that his interpretations conveyed the composer's intentions (via Volkov) and thus possessed a unique and indisputable legitimacy. From this perspective, anyone dissenting from the idea of Shostakovich as dissident simply isn't 'in tune with the composer's *intentions* ' or hasn't got 'ears to listen'.[48] This impulse to impose a party line reached its nadir in an article by the British journalist Norman Lebrecht, who identified a 'striking symmetry' between refusal to embrace the 'new Shostakovich' and holocaust denial.[49] Given that contemporary musicologists were busy stressing interpretative contingency and pluralism, such dogmatism was fiercely challenged. The most compelling rebuttals came from Taruskin, who argued that rather than enriching our picture of the composer, the new Shostakovich simply offered a trivialized inversion of the existing one: 'black and white have been conveniently reversed, all grey still resolutely expunged.'[50] While sharing MacDonald's view that Shostakovich intended his music to convey 'deep content', Taruskin counters one-sided readings that attempt 'to contain meaning and foreclose interpretation'.[51] Instead, he stresses the polysemous, protean nature of its meanings, rejecting the tendency to reduce individual works – and the Shostakovich oeuvre – to a 'single, endlessly repeated and paraphrased content'.[52]

Rejecting black and white thinking – or, to quote a *New York Times* headline, the view of Shostakovich as either 'sly dissident or Soviet tool' – need not of course entail the complete dismissal of dissident readings of the composer's works. Neither does it imply that audiences – then and now – are wrong to hear dissidence in his music.[53] Perhaps here, as in 'Born in the USA', we are dealing with a case of double coding or, as Shostakovich scholars would call it, doublespeak.[54] Enter Žižek, whose 2008 discussion offers two related perspectives on the doubled nature of Shostakovich's music. His first move is to mediate the two extremes highlighted above by arguing that if Shostakovich's music is Stalinist, it is precisely because the composer strained against the official world he was bound up with: 'the gap between "public" allegiance to the regime and "private" dissidence was part of the very identity of the Stalinist subject.'[55] His second move is to argue that this gap between public and private character resulted not simply in concealed dissident content but in a music that works simultaneously on two different levels satisfying two different codes: 'one, public, intended for the ruling ideological gaze, and another which transgresses the public rules, but remains, as such, its inherent supplement'.[56] Žižek invokes a cinematic parallel for Shostakovich's approach, arguing that it resembles the signals used in films made under the Hollywood Production Code of the 1930s and 1940s to compensate for the absence of sex scenes. Thus in *Casablanca*, in the scene when Ilsa visits Rick in his room, a cutaway shot of an airport tower and the obligatory post-coital cigarette enables viewers minded to do so to read between the lines, without the censors feeling the need to intervene. *Casablanca* 'contains' no sex scene, but rather relies on the viewer to construct one on the basis of the symbols it presents. Similarly, for Žižek, Shostakovich's symphonies do not contain political content, but merely cultivate a 'double-talk idiom ... combining external accommodation with inner bitterness and sadness'.[57]

All of which returns us to the second question posed above. In describing Shostakovich's double talk, Žižek limits the private layer of his music to 'inner bitterness and sadness', rejecting the idea that the concept of dissidence can be applied in this context. Dissidence, he notes, can be at issue only in public discourse, and dissidents can refer only to those who disturb its mechanisms.[58] Similarly, Taruskin rejects the term 'dissidence' in relation to Shostakovich, regarding it as pure myth-making to elevate him as 'the Soviet dissident supreme: an omnipotent anti-Stalin, able at the height of the Stalinist terror to perform heroic acts of public resistance (absolutely transparent to all his fellow dissidents but absolutely opaque to those in power) ... Private grumbling and joking are not "dissidence", as the term is normally used. Dissidence is public.'[59] This conception of dissidence may well seem merely common sense. Yet in circumstances in which overt opposition is well-nigh unthinkable, such a standpoint seems to set the bar for dissidence impossibly high. How do we measure the difference between 'real' dissidence and other forms? The danger here, as resistance theorist James Scott observes, is that 'all that is being measured may be the level of repression that structures the available options.'[60] When overt public dissidence is not an option, dissident energies either dissipate or get channeled into different directions, perhaps becoming indistinguishable from private grumbling, bitterness and sadness. That being said, acknowledging that dissidence operates on a continuum does not lend support to the notion that Shostakovich was somehow able – as if by telepathy – to communicate 'secret dissidence' to sympathetic listeners.[61] If Shostakovich's music provided Soviet-era audiences with consolation and hope as a result of what Taruskin describes as its 'blessed polysemy', it was left to them to translate its portentous gestures into political content.[62]

It would be easy to stop there. But as seen earlier, in discussing how music's receivers can confer political agency onto it, it is problematic to make a rigid distinction between Shostakovich's music and what listeners hear and have heard in it. Regardless of whether Shostakovich encoded dissidence within his works, and regardless of the critical consensus on the issue, his music has over time undergone a process of resemanticization, absorbing the meanings and preconceptions projected onto it by successive generations of musicians and listeners.[63] Until another dominant resemanticization comes to displace the trope of Shostakovich as dissident, the latter seems entirely likely to retain its grip on the collective imagination.

6.3   Negation and Critical Composition

Like protest and resistance, the concept of negation came to prominence within musical discourse and practice in the 1960s and remains one of the key terms in the Marxist aesthetico-political lexicon. For musicologists, negation and the aesthetics of negativity are most closely associated with Adorno, whose *Negative Dialektik* (1966) and *Ästhetische Theorie* (1970) influenced a generation of West German composers including Helmut Lachenmann and Nicolaus A. Huber. However, the importance of negation for avant-garde music goes well beyond the impact of Adorno and this generation. Although the concepts of *musica negativa* and critical composition emerged in Adorno's wake, earlier composers – most notably Luigi Nono – had engaged directly with Marx and Engels's conception of negation or had drawn on Marcuse's aesthetics and politics of refusal.[64] And while some theorists treat critical composition as a historical category, a phenomenon that petered into insignificance around the time of the fall of the Berlin wall, its impact continues to be felt in avant-garde music from the present decade.[65]

On one level – as a broader phenomenon within music and culture of the 1970s – negation can be seen as a response to the failure of the radical hopes of 1968, channelling political energies in a negative direction. The Marxist art theorist John Roberts glosses negation as 'withdrawal, non-reconcilability, disaffirmation, distantiation, dissension, subtraction, displacement, denial': concepts which overlap with but should not be confused with nihilism.[66] Nihilism rejects political solutions, either as a result of world-weary scepticism ('it's all pointless') or by allowing non-political means (terrorism, martyrdom, jihad) to overtake and engulf whatever political aims were originally in sight.[67] In contrast, negation retains a faith in the necessity for political struggle, channelling it not in positive directions but in relentless negativity toward the existing order. When wrong is firmly entrenched in power, and when wrong thinking squeezes out or neutralizes alternatives, negativity becomes a force for preserving right.

On another level, negation gains its traction from Marxist dialectics, in particular from Marcuse's and Adorno's 'negative' dialectics. For Marx and Engels, negation is a component within the dialectical engine governing the historical process. Engels famously presents the dialectic as three laws, framing them in terms derived from Marx's analyses of capitalism: dialectical development, or 'the transformation of quantity into quality and vice versa' (the idea that small quantitative changes generate epoch-making qualitative ones); dialectical contradiction, or the 'interpenetration of opposites' (that antagonistic forces are at work in any system or process); and 'the negation of the negation' (that change is driven not only by one force overcoming another, or first negation, but by that force in turn being negated, or second negation).[68] Thus something that initially seems like a unified given – such as the capitalist mode of production – is in fact gradually mutating as a result of the antagonistic forces within it, contradictions which will eventually generate fundamental change. The concepts of first and second negation can be seen in the following passage from *Capital*, where Marx analyzes how the capitalist mode of property ownership is being superseded, just as it superseded earlier forms of ownership:

The capitalist mode of appropriation, the result of the capitalist mode of production, produces capitalist private property. This is the first negation of individual private property . . . But capitalist production begets, with the inexorability of a law of Nature, its own negation. It is the negation of negation. This does not reestablish private property for the producer, but gives him individual property based on the acquisitions of the capitalist era: i.e., on co-operation and the possession in common of the land and of the means of production.[69]

Individual private property is negated as a result of capitalism's centralizing, monopolistic drives, yet the latter is in turn negated by socialized production, establishing a new collective form of ownership. Two aspects of Marx's analysis are worth highlighting. First, while it is clear that Marx views the outcome of this process at the macro level as positive, qualitative change, his dialectics draw out both negative and positive outcomes at the micro level; the emergence of collective property is facilitated by capitalist centralization as well as by the growth of cooperative forms of production.[70] Second, Marx presents common property not merely as a goal but as a certain outcome, elevating the negation of negation – the superseding of the capitalist system – as an inexorable natural law.

The 'negative' in negative dialectics has Hegel rather than Marx in its sights, aiming at overturning Hegel's affirmation of existing society. For Marcuse, Hegel's system 'accentuates the positive emphatically', over-reaching itself by attempting to reconcile antitheses into a unified whole; similarly, Adorno's *Negative Dialectics* sets out to counter Hegel's 'equation of the negation of the negation with positivity'.[71] For Adorno, Hegel's 'identity thinking' – synthesizing contradictory elements, or stressing the identity between identity and non-identity – affirms the status quo and thus neuters the political potential of the dialectic. Instead, Adorno argues that second negation does not revoke the first, but rather 'proves that it was not negative enough': each negation is just one more step in a limitless process, provoked by capitalism's seemingly endless capacity to reinvent itself.[72] If Hegel is the primary target, negative dialectics also dismantles key aspects of Marx and Engels's thinking. For Adorno and Marcuse, just as for Marx and Engels, 'dialectics is the ontology of the false condi-tion', a tool for chipping away at the existing order: but while Marx's dialectics scrutinize a negative condition from the vantage point of its positive solution, Adorno rejects formulating the negation of the negation in terms of a 'happy end'.[73] There are no certainties in negative dialectics: none of Marx and Engels's reliance on 'historical necessity' and no inexor-able motion toward a pre-determined endpoint.[74] Neither is there any guarantee that what Marcuse describes as 'the power of negative thinking' can penetrate beyond the world of philosophy: Marcuse argues that the gap between thought and action is one of the symptoms of the unfreedom of the present, but there is little in his or Adorno's writing to suggest that it can be overcome:

Since the established universe of discourse is that of an unfree world, dialectical thought is necessarily destructive, and whatever liberation it may bring is a liberation in thought, in theory. However, the divorce of thought from action, of theory from practice, is itself part of the unfree world. No thought and no theory can undo it; but theory may help to prepare the ground for their possible reunion.[75]

For Adorno and Marcuse, art shares critical theory's task of contradict-ing established reality: 'the common element is the search for an "authentic language" – the language of negation as the Great Refusal to accept the rules of a game in which the dice are loaded.'[76] Earlier, we saw how Marcuse elevated Surrealist poetry and the lyrics of Dylan's expressionist phase as models of a '"meta-language" of total negation': 'a destructive, disorderly, negative nonsense anti-art' that negates existing art as well as adopting a political position of 'protest, denial and refusal' (see Section 5.2). This twofold negation – of artistic tradition and of present society – is epitomized by the fictional cantata *Dr Fausti Weheklag* (Dr Faust's Lamentation) at the heart of Thomas Mann's novel *Dr Faustus* (1947); Mann's Adornian anti-hero, composer Adrian Leverkühn, produces a 'formal negation' of Beethoven's Ninth, 'an inversion, an austere and proud upending of meaning'.[77] For Marcuse, such negation was an entirely necessary response to the role that bourgeois culture plays in affirming the 'repressive Establishment':

One must revoke the Ninth Symphony not only because it is wrong and false (we cannot and should not sing an ode to joy, not even as a promise), but also because it is there and is true in its own right. It stands in our universe as the justification of that 'illusion' which is no longer justifiable. However, the revocation of a work of art would be another work of art. As far as one can go in revocation of the Ninth Symphony, I think Stockhausen has achieved it.[78]

For Adorno, as for Marcuse, it falls to avant-garde art to stand fortress-like against society and thus to preserve a space from which it can be subjected to critique. Earlier, we saw that for Adorno, art works politically through its material and forms, rather than through offering explicit messages. In his essay 'Engagement' from 1962, Adorno argues that 'it is not the office of art to spotlight alternatives, but to resist by its form alone the course of the world, which permanently puts a pistol to men's heads ... There is no material content, no formal category of artistic creation ... which did not originate in the empirical reality from which it breaks free.'[79] Music's capacity to negate empirical reality derives not simply from cutting itself off from that reality but from actively contradicting it; for this to happen, a work needs to have a relation to existing music (and through it, a relation to broader culture and society) even as it repudiates it. Thus for Adorno, if a composer 'turns critically against tradition through the use of an autonomous material, one completely purged of concepts such as consonance, dissonance, triad, and diatonicism, the negated is nevertheless retained in the negation. Such works speak by virtue of the taboos they radiate; the falseness or, at the least, the shock of every triad that they permit makes this obvious enough.'[80]

What is it, then, that transforms avant-garde music into the music of political negation? In dealing more broadly with avant-garde art, Roberts argues that 'if the challenge of negation in art is not simply the supersession or transgression of tradition or art itself, then it must conform, following Hegel, to a process of *determinate* negation in which reversal, chiasmus, parody and other rhetorical strategies of displacement and reinscription prevail.'[81] As determinate negation, art engages the contradictions at work at a particular social moment, revealing for Marcuse 'the basic factors and forces which make for its destructiveness, as well as for the possible alternatives beyond the status quo'; similarly, Adorno argues that 'by determinate negation artworks absorb the *membra disjecta* of the empirical world and through their transformation organize them into a reality that is a counterreality.'[82]

Nono, Huber and Spahlinger

Adorno's image of art soaking up and remodelling fragments of reality resonates strongly with the avant-garde music of the 1960s, in particular with Nono's use of found materials in his tape compositions. Yet the kind of intra-musical negation that Adorno envisaged diverges significantly from the more interventive approach Nono took in this period. Rather than negating existing society obliquely by annulling artistic conventions, works such as *La fabbrica illuminata* (1964), *Die Ermittlung* (1965), *Contrappunto dialettico* (1968) and *Non consumiamo Marx* (1968–9) combine this with direct assaults on industrialized capitalism, imperialism and the still lingering shadow of fascism. The most straightforward of these compositions is *La fabbrica illuminata* (The Illuminated Factory) for soprano and four-channel magnetic tape, inspired by Giovanni Carocci's 1960 report on workers' conditions at the Fiat factory in Turin. Nono's composition uses recordings he made in the Italsider steel foundry in Genoa, including the voices of workers as well as noises from the furnace; in addition, it draws on a text compiled by Giuliano Scabia from clauses in union contracts and observations heard in the factory.[83] It was probably the contentious workers' banter – 'factory of the dead they call it', 'concentration camp more like' – that led to the first performance being cancelled by the state broadcaster RAI.[84] Nono's incendiary aims are evident from the work's programme note, in which he highlights how the factory enacts in microcosm Marx's negation of the negation:

A factory is a story, a situation of struggle, a moment of immense passion and life within the workers' movement, where the negation of the negation is being put into practice. How can one learn about today's world from this situation and illuminate it by means of invention and construction? ... No *mimesis*, no reflection. No industrial arcadia. No populist or popular naturalism. Only a semantically precise music-idea about the man of today at the scene of his servitude and liberation, the negation of the negation fixed in a form, committed to overcoming the one-sidedness, be it subjective or objective, that is dominant today not only in music.[85]

For Nono, the modern factory illuminates Marx's negation of the negation, epitomizing not only the workers' alienation under capitalism but also how the socialization of labour will enable their liberation. In a letter to the workers who participated in his recordings, Nono noted that 'each of our factories, where the power of capital is opposed and contested . . . indicates and prepares for the true communist nature of the finally liberated man.'[86] The dialectical nature of the compositional materials and performance media (live and recorded sounds, human voices and machine noises, singer and loudspeakers) enables Nono to 'fix in a form' the antagonisms fuelling the workers' movement; the composition thus functions as an educative tool, enabling his worker audiences to understand their situation.[87] Nono's keenness to expose the workers themselves to the music points to its second object of critique. As well as enacting political negation, *La fabbrica illuminata* is negational in relation to the institutions and practices of art music. For Nono, studio composition marked a release from his problematic dependence on bourgeois musical institutions, enabling him to take his music out of the concert hall and into more politically sympathetic spaces.

For Nono's former student and mouthpiece, Lachenmann, compositions such as *La fabbrica illuminata* suffered as a result of simultaneously tackling political and artistic issues. Instead, Lachenmann advocated the Adornian negation of aesthetic norms: 'A serious critique of Nono's music should try to defend it from his own ambitions, in which artistic and political problems today run the risk of reciprocally playing each other down. The mere setting to music of slogans and ideological programmes can never have a socially altering effect; the direct way to influence and shake people up – and that is art's best chance today – is via their aesthetic taboos.'[88]

A similar agenda is at work in Huber's programmatic essay 'Kritisches Komponieren' (Critical Composition) from 1972. For Huber, the political dimension of avant-garde music is not a matter of 'political text or dedications to political victims' (although he concedes that texts can have a value in preventing misinterpretation).[89] Rather, politics is enacted in and through music itself, and critical composition consists of drawing out and bringing to the fore this hidden politics. On one level, the critical composer produces a kind of meta-music, critiquing the premises and norms of musical practice. On another, the dialectical interaction between music and society means that such a musical and aesthetic critique is at the same time a political statement:

All thinking, regardless of how differentiated, specialized and smart it is, will produce senseless and arbitrary results if the working, thinking through and analysis are only carried out in alienated spheres ... Once one has attained, in consciousness and practice, the foundation where the human being is the centre point – rather than music just because one happens to be a composer – stale wafts of fog begin to clear up. Then, one is no longer producing culture, but carrying out labour that is useful to humans – that is, humans as a species – oriented consciously in a determinate historical epoch and under determinate historical conditions.[90]

At the core of critical composition, therefore, is reconnecting music with other spheres of human practice: neutralizing the 'autonomous tendency of sounds', refusing the work concept and the idea of music as an end in itself, and rejecting the concert hall as a forum for critical music-making and listening.[91] Instead, composers need to discover ways to fold together the different spheres of human experience, ignoring every 'aesthetic, political, technological or avant-garde taboo' in the quest for 'dialectical radicality'.[92]

    For Claus-Steffen Mahnkopf, Huber's compositions from this period amount to 'didactic illustrations of theoretical considerations whose tenets are themselves questionable, as they are not inspired by any genuinely artistic thoughts'.[93] This perspective seems off the mark on two grounds: not only was Huber's aim to explode notions of the 'genuinely artistic', but his theories and compositions do not map as neatly onto each other as Mahnkopf assumes. Huber himself identified his period of critical composition primarily with the years 1968–72, during which he produced *Aion* (1968), *Versuch über Sprache* (1969), *Anerkennung und Aufhebung (Georg Lukács)* (1971–2) and *Harakiri* (1971).[94] In these compositions, the musico-aesthetic dimension of negation comes across more emphatically than in his essay, while their political claims are less clear. In each, Huber scrutinizes and annuls a particular aspect of bourgeois art music or its performance tradition. The most notorious of these compositions is *Harakiri*, in which Huber enacts nothing less than the ritual suicide of art music itself. Earlier, Huber had described his *Aion* as more a 'working paper' than a composition, a description that conveys the intent of *Harakiri* too. *Harakiri* consists of a ten-minute drone note played on slack, detuned strings, followed by a long crescendo, a loud thunderclap, a pause, a sound effect of heavy rain, and an oral declaration denouncing the use of the crescendo, climaxing with the words:

Are crescendos worth the effort? The practice of crescendo and decrescendo is found in war and peace, work and play, in the everyday and in holidays, in taking a life and in sparing it, in sunrise and sunset, in oppression, in moods, in pleasure, in destruction ...

Crescendos are not value-free.

Music conceals their dangerous nature, mystifies their use.

One should no longer, under the cover of structure, dress up crescendos into something more than they are![95]

Of interest here is not the debate about aesthetic value which the work provoked, but whether its musical and textual ingredients amount to political as well as artistic negation. Huber's critique of crescendos focuses on their manipulatory, aggrandizing dimension: they make something seem what it is not, or promise a breakthrough which they do not deliver. If this hints at a denunciation of the rhetorical dimension of politics, it relies on a rhetorical gesture – the concluding agitprop-style speech – to imbue it with the whiff of political radicalism. Rather than being excessively didactic, as Mahnkopf argued, Huber's compositions, as the composer himself stressed, are 'dependent on the help of critical listeners' to find political resonances in their musical processes. Disappointed at the level of response that this and other pieces elicited, Huber rapidly became aware of the scarcity of such listeners and of the political limitations of this strain of avant-gardism.[96] His subsequent compositions, such as *Darabukka* (1976) and *Morgenlied* (1980), incorporate politicized musical materials and texts in order to make their political dimension more tangible; similarly, in revising *Harakiri* for its eventual première, Huber replaced its original peroration with a more explicit interweaving of aesthetic and political negation: 'Fight the intellectual profiteers / fight the uninterested pleasure / fight the subjective expression / fight the exploiters of human underdevelopment / fight empiricism / fight the finished works / dispossess the possessors of music.'[97]

If Huber's *Harakiri* worked through the limitations of immanent musical critique, this did not prevent other composers from taking up this model of critical composition. The most prominent, rigorous and enduring among these is Mathias Spahlinger, whose engagement with negative dialectics in music began in the early 1970s and continues to the present. For Spahlinger, avant-garde music is both a space for metapolitical reflection and a vehicle for a kind of long-haul interventive action. In his 2015 essay 'Political Implications of the Material of New Music', Spahlinger argues that the value of such music for reflecting on the most fundamental issues of politics stems from the consistency of its practices of negation; new music has jettisoned all givens and 'driven the auto-reflection of its own categories to the point of self-sublation', making it a model of negative thinking.[98] The significance of this model has nothing to do with direct traffic between the musical and political fields; Spahlinger has repeatedly engaged compositionally with music's 'inability to speak directly ... in the face of concrete suffering'.[99] Rather, music 'refers to that which is outside itself solely through its inner relational network and via its logic', generating political insights analogically rather than directly.[100] Spahlinger's writings offer a striking example of the politics of aesthetics, fuelled by the conviction that the findings of compositional practice can be translated into political strategies. This is apparent in particular in the idea that the way in which new music constitutes and regulates itself offers a model of democratic socialism:

new music does not establish any new conventions that are either obvious, or capable of 'conditioning' us ... [form] is in contention with both itself and an emergent system of rules. the analogy with democracy is clear to see, and apparently only remains concealed to its private and sinister enemies: the legitimate possibility to legally and fundamentally convert state and society into consensual partners.[101]

One of the ways in which music can point to a future polity, according to Spahlinger, is through modelling a new mode of production, free from exploitation and domination.[102] Spahlinger explored one aspect of this in his vocal composition *vorschläge – konzepte zur ver(über)flüssigung der funktion des komponisten* (proposals – concepts on liquidizing/rationalizing the function of the composer, 1993), and another in his *doppelt bejaht* (doubly affirmed, 2009), etudes for orchestra without conductor. The title of the latter is taken from one of Marx's early essays, in which the alienation of labour under capitalism is contrasted with work as life-affirming activity; under the second form of labour, producers are 'doubly affirmed' through the enjoyment of productive activity and through gratifying the needs of those who benefit from it.[103] Spahlinger's piece functions on several different levels as a critique of politics, music and musical politics under capitalism. Its starting point is negating the idealized view of the orchestra as a paradigm of unalienated labour and community of free, fulfilled individuals, a cliché found even in the writings of Marx (see Box 1.2). In scotching this view, Spahlinger's commentary stresses the hierarchical nature of the musical establishment and its rigid division of labour, claiming that 'the means of power and production are as omnipresent and as unconscious as they are in the realm of politics more narrowly defined.'[104] For Spahlinger, the reluctance to move beyond conductor-led, traditionally notated music is a mark of the political as well as aesthetic anachronism of orchestral music-making; by preserving the power of the composer and conductor, such music denies orchestral musicians the freedom to express themselves as individuals. While Spahlinger's commentary takes on the task of critiquing existing practices, the music inhabits a terrain somewhere between critique and utopian projection; if a successful performance might vindicate his vision of emancipated individual expression, a flawed one would serve to demonstrate the constraining effect of traditional orchestral practices on musicians' development. Spahlinger describes his four-hour piece as a space for musicians and listeners 'to learn, practice and understand what new music is or still could become'. Yet, as he notes, 'freedom requires practice': for modern orchestral musicians, whose daily fare is certainly not improvisational avant-garde scores, performing in isolation while members of the public wandered freely among the musicians must have been an uncomfortably unfamiliar task.[105]

The reception of *doppelt bejaht* demonstrates the overwhelming challenges that confront critical composition today. Media accounts of the premiere gleefully oversimplified Spahlinger's aims, greeting the work as an attempt to abolish the orchestra or reorganize it along Marxist lines.[106] More caustically, they derided the composer as a last-ditch fighter for Adornian modernism, or as simply stuck in 1968.[107] Spahlinger would doubtless retort that his critique of music under capitalism is as valid now as it was at the start of his career and that new music plays an even more marginal role in the life of orchestras now than it did back then. His critics, in turn, might respond that the notion of compositionally denouncing the orchestra as an anti-democratic institution, or interrogating its complicity in capitalist production, is tired and stale (had not Spahlinger himself contributed to this discourse with *morendo* from 1975?). Not only has avant-garde music made all these political points before, the argument might go, but it did so at a time when such music and its composers had significantly more cultural heft than they do in the present; in the 1970s, a work like *doppelt bejaht* might have provoked genuine consternation rather than cynicism, indifference or what Marcuse describes as the 'benevolent neutrality' that punctures art's critical potential.[108]

Such objections by no means rob such compositions of their political value, however, at least from the perspective of the aesthetics of negation. Critical composition is not a form of proselytizing, aiming to convert listeners to a particular political viewpoint; neither does it aim at producing immediate effects in the political field. The priority for negation is merely to preserve a space in which to refuse that which exists and to nurture an alternative to it. While rethinking musical hierarchies of production cannot bring about political change, it can prefigure it and serve as its precondition; for Spahlinger, 'so little about the world can be changed, either as a consequence of music or solely using it. despite this, i maintain that "if change does not take place in thinking, and does not take place in music, then it does not take place anywhere."'[109]

7 | Nationalism, Racism and Fascism

7.1 Political Identity, Culturalization and the New Racism

For much of the last three decades, identity has displaced ideology as the main point of contention within Western politics and as the dominant focus for political work in the humanities. On the global stage, many of the headline political events – from the Yugoslav wars, via 9/11 to Brexit – stem from tensions around ethnic, religious or national identity; at the same time, race, gender, sexual orientation and disability have come to prominence within domestic political agendas. Over the course of this period, academic conceptions of identity have become increasingly sophisticated, reflecting the complexity of lived identity in late modernity. Thus rather than seeing identities as closed, fixed and singular, theorists have stressed their open, fluid and pluralistic nature, viewing even indigenous identity as constructed rather than 'an accident of birth'.[1] Balibar, for example, argues that 'no identity is either given or acquired once and for all'; rather, identities have a 'hypothetical or fictive nature', requiring an ongoing process of validation and reinforcement.[2] Similarly, Judith Butler presents identities as contingent and mutable, acquiring stability only though performative acts that inscribe them as marks of our existence.[3] Contemporary theory also emphasizes the multiple, overlapping identities at play within each individual, celebrating the cosmopolitan nature of the modern global citizen. One recent example is from Nicolas Bourriaud's book *The Radicant*, whose title aims to capture the 'self-rooting' nature of today's identities in contrast to the fixed roots of traditional identity discourse:

Rather than set one fixed root against another, a mythologized 'origin' against an integrating and homogenizing 'soil', wouldn't it make more sense to assign them to other conceptual categories, ones suggested by a global imagination in the process of mutation? . . . To be radicant means setting one's roots in motion, staging them in heterogeneous contexts and formats, denying them the power to completely define one's identity.[4]

The notion that identities can be playfully taken up and discarded, like carnival masks, certainly rings true for the globalized art world that is

Bourriaud's focus of attention. Bourriaud presents nomadic cosmopolitanism as if it were a lifestyle choice, a matter of liberation and personal growth open to all willing to discard their fictive roots. From this viewpoint, clinging to an inherited culture is a sign of regressive thinking, a childish dependency on outmoded cultural logics. This liberal pluralist perspective, to say the least, makes it hard to understand or empathize with those for whom a particular identity is a matter of deep need and something to be defended at all costs. Rather than simply treating such attitudes as outmoded or regarding them as symptoms of a 'social pathology', we need to probe the logics behind such thinking, since they are at the core of conflicts between different identity groups.[5] At issue here is a set of closely related concepts – essentialism, identitarianism and culturalism – which together correspond to the view (1) that cultures are bounded wholes; (2) that each culture possesses its own unique, unchanging essence; (3) that people locked into them come pre-programmed with certain qualities and unique characteristics and (4) that as a result of this uniqueness, the differences between cultures are insurmountable. The main topic explored in this section is how this matrix continues to shape attitudes toward ethnic, racial and national identity, even in supposedly 'post-racial' and 'colour-blind' countries such as the United Kingdom and the United States. A second theme is how the culturalized racism that stems from such essentialism impacts on attitudes toward citizenship, supposedly a non-racial category.

It is not hard to find examples of how music can rehearse or reinforce cultural essentialism in relation to national or racial identity. Consider Figure 7.1, which shows a Parades Commission notice targeted at Orange Order marching bands participating in the Belfast march of 12 July 2013. Held annually to commemorate the victory of the Protestant king William of Orange at the Battle of the Boyne in 1690, these parades provide a ritualized affirmation of cultural difference, with music being one of the most provocative ingredients. The Commission's instruction for 'only respectful hymn tunes' to be played in the vicinity of St Patrick's Catholic Church was apparently not heeded, with Catholic residents reporting that the band played the Ulster Protestant anthem 'The Sash', interspersed with shouts of 'stick a poker up the pope's hole'.[6]

White Nationalism and Classical Music

No music is immune from being coopted as a symbol of political identity or totem of cultural difference. Thus for so-called white nationalists and others on the extreme right, classical music often serves as an emblem of

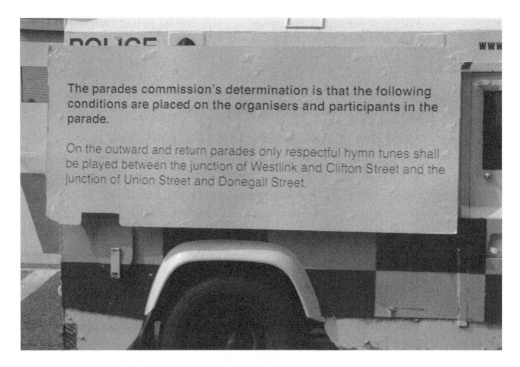

Figure 7.1 Parades Commission notice, Belfast, 12 July 2013,
photograph by Dominic Bryan www.flickr.com (https://creativecommons.org/licenses/by/2.0/).

whiteness and racial superiority.[7] The online forum of Stormfront.org, the oldest and most popular extreme-right website in the United States, contains thousands of posts extolling the racial dimensions of classical music. In a thread entitled 'A chance to BE WHITE: Classical Music', the contributor 'Karajan' – who identifies himself as a student at the University of Florida – argues that he feels empowered by such music, 'as if I am fully participating in complete white culture'.[8] One respondent notes 'a fairly high correlation between classical music lovers and white nationalists . . . it does seem to be a kind of cultural marker', while for another, listening to such music is 'the number one way to teach racial and cultural pride to one's children'.[9] Rather than simply acclaiming such music as an embodiment of unalloyed whiteness, contributors tend to treat it – and the race that produced it – as being under an existential threat. Thus for 'Karajan', listening to classical music is a racial imperative, essential for the future health of white culture:

Rap, hip-hop is destroying our youth and elevates negro culture while promoting miscegenation. *We have to act right here, right now to PROHIBIT black music from our ears as much as humanly possible while replacing that garbage with pro white music.* It is essential to our survival as a race that we do this. I want to challenge *everyone* to listen to more classical music ... The more you listen to it, the more you understand that such beauty, such majesty, can only be the work of white FOR WHITES. The masters, Mozart, Bach, Beethoven, Tchaikovsky, Wagner, Vivaldi (to name but a few) ... Only if we fail to insure the survival of our white race will the beauty of classical music disappear.[10]

This kind of explicitly racist thinking is utterly taboo in the United States, as elsewhere in the Western world. Yet similar sentiments, shorn of the kind of 'biological' racism found here, are regularly voiced by mainstream politicians and commentators. One controversial example is a speech given by President Trump during his 2017 state visit to Poland, in which he invokes the symphony as an exemplar of the values and achievements of Western civilization. We need to tread carefully here, since while the concept of Western civilization comes with unsavoury baggage, it is not in itself enough to justify accusations of 'blood and soil nationalism'.[11] A generation ago, it would have been unproblematic to speak of the West and take pride in its accomplishments, since the term would have been understood to mean 'the free world' or the countries of the NATO alliance. But while Trump's speech refers to NATO at several points, he treats the West in essentialist terms as a homogenized culture, united by deeper affinities than just the values of liberal democracy:

We must work together to confront forces ... that threaten over time to undermine these values and to erase the bonds of culture, faith and tradition that make us who we are ... The world has never known anything like our community of nations. We write symphonies. We pursue innovation. We celebrate our ancient heroes, embrace our timeless traditions and customs ... Those are the priceless ties that bind us together as nations, as allies, and as a civilization. What we have, what we inherited ... from our ancestors has never existed to this extent before. And if we fail to preserve it, it will never, ever exist again.[12]

What is most troubling in the speech is not Trump's equation of Western civilization with civilization *tout court*, or the idea that it is locked in mortal combat with the forces of barbarism; both these tropes were employed by earlier Republican presidents too.[13] Rather, it is his presentation of 'Westernness' in terms of Christianity, European heritage and whiteness, resonances all too apparent at the speech's peroration: 'the West will never, ever be broken. Our values will prevail. Our people will thrive. And our civilization will triumph.' Trump's reference to 'our people' and his evocation of a culture under threat present clear parallels to the explicitly racist rhetoric of the likes of 'Karajan'. Even so, it seems an exaggeration to accuse him of 'white-nationalist dog-whistling' or to describe it as an 'alt-right' speech.[14] Rather than deliberately setting out to appeal to a white nationalist constituency, Trump's speech is an example of the kind of casual, unthinking cultural racism that has become pervasive within contemporary US and European politics. It also illustrates how the once-clear boundaries between the extreme right and the political mainstream have become muddied as a result of political populism.

The New Racism

Cultural racism or the 'new racism' is grounded not in pseudo-biological distinctions but in the cultural essentialism highlighted earlier; for Balibar 'it is a racism whose dominant theme is … the insurmountability of cultural differences, a racism which, a first sight, does not postulate the superiority of certain groups or peoples in relation to others but "only" the harmfulness of abolishing frontiers, the incompatibility of life-styles and traditions'.[15] The idea that the world is divided into multiple incompatible cultures, each of which must jealously guard its own space and demand total loyalty from its members, may seem like a phantasm of the extreme right. Yet the way in which culture is invoked by contemporary mainstream politicians and media commentators often resembles this caricature; culture is seen as defining individuals absolutely, rendering them either insiders or undesirable Others. In this context, 'culture' serves as a proxy for race, religion, customs, clothing and all the other things that make an individual or group stand out from the crowd; indeed, most of those who advocate the need to 'preserve our culture' or 'safeguard our way of life' would strenuously deny any racist intent. Recent legislation in France, Germany and elsewhere to prevent Muslim women from wearing full-face veils in public is a case in point. By taking symbolic measures to eradicate visible cultural difference, governments demonstrate their commitment to re-homogenizing the nation-state; they also placate those for whom, in the words of one French minister, there are simply 'too many Muslims'.[16]

Another symptom of the programme to re-homogenize the state is the imposition of citizenship tests on new immigrants. At first glance, these might seem nothing more than a pragmatic effort to ensure that immigrants possess the linguistic and cultural tools necessary to function in their new environments. Yet the questions posed in such tests suggest an additional agenda, pointing to how in Western nations – according to Evelien Tonkens and Jan Willem Duyvendak – citizenship is now 'less defined in terms of civic, political or social rights, and more in terms of adherence to norms, values and cultural practices'.[17] Thus immigrants to the United Kingdom are quizzed on their knowledge of Christmas traditions, patron saints and Jane Austen novels, while those taking the Dutch Civic Integration Exam are expected to give the right answers to a series of culturally loaded questions such as 'Are women in the Netherlands allowed to choose with whom they want to marry?'[18] The use of citizenship tests to enforce cultural norms is just one of the ways in which political processes can become slanted to discriminate against minorities. In the Netherlands, for example, the nation's self-image is tightly bound up with secularism, individual freedom and sexual liberation; the resulting cocktail of liberal values, provocatively described by Paul Mepschen and Jan Willem Duyvendak as 'sexual nationalism', has proved to be virulently illiberal where Muslims are concerned.[19] What is surprising about the Dutch case is the ease with which populist politicians, such as Geert Wilders, have exploited the issue of gay rights as a means to fuel hostility toward Muslims; according to this logic, those unwilling to embrace the progressive sexual freedoms of the West are backward, repressed and intolerant.[20] This is an example of what Wendy Brown describes as the use of tolerance as a form of 'identity management': our culture of tolerance is at risk, or so the argument goes, if we continue to tolerate Muslim immigration.[21]

One way to tackle such intolerant tolerance is by poking fun at the racist stereotypes that engender it. The best-known musical response to Dutch hostility toward migrants is a song by the Dutch-Moroccan rapper Raymzter, released shortly after 9/11. Inspired by a Dutch politician's microphone gaffe, *Kutmarokkanen* (Moroccan cunts) gives a personalized account of how media misrepresentations have led to Moroccan immigrants being vilified and socially excluded ('they look at me as if I was flying into the Twin Towers').[22] The popularity of Raymzter's song, which was number one in the Dutch charts for several weeks, served not only to help break down barriers within Dutch society but to demonstrate the poverty of assimilationist models of culture. Rather than attempting to conform to any unitary ideal, *Kutmarokkanen* and the video accompanying it present a playful melange of ethnic codes, juxtaposing not only Arabic pop and African American hip-hop but also North African and Dutch cultural stereotypes.

7.2   Fascism and the Aestheticization of Politics

The idea that 'we are all fascists now' has become something of a cliché among journalists and bloggers, most often invoked to attack the supposed

encroachment of the state over individual rights and freedoms.[23] Part of
the shock value of this phrase lies in the perceived remoteness of fascism as
a functioning ideology; in spite of the continuing pervasiveness of
the politics of nationalism and racism, fascism itself may seem tied to the
period 1922–45 and of little significance beyond that context. Yet even if
treated as a purely historical phenomenon, fascism remains by far the most
important political ideology to have emerged over the last century, and
aspects of its influence continue to resonate within contemporary politics.
One aspect of its influence lies in what the philosopher Karl Löwith
described in 1935 as the 'total politicization of everything, even of seemingly neutral domains of life'; with fascism, politics extends its sway
irrevocably into Aristotle's realm of bare life.[24] For Agamben, the fascist
concentration camp is the symbol and epitome of the broader mission
creep of politics into all aspects of human existence, making the camp the
'biopolitical paradigm of the modern' and 'the hidden matrix of the politics
in which we still live'.[25] Another aspect of the enduring impact of fascism is
its aestheticization of politics. While all forms of politics have an aesthetic
dimension, the idea that it has become aestheticized implies an excess or
imbalance: the ascendancy of emotional appeal over rational argument and
the displacement of democratic debate by mediatized spectacle. The continuing relevance of this concept is immediately apparent, given that we are
experiencing a new era of post-truth politics, of charismatic populists
tilting against the establishment and of acclamatory rallies on a grand scale.

In coining the term 'aestheticization of politics' (*Ästhetisierung der
Politik*) in 1935–6, Benjamin gives it several distinct connotations. What
is immediately clear is that he is not merely talking about the use of
symbols, images, rhetoric and spectacle, elements which are merely part
of the 'routine' aesthetic dimension of politics. Rather, he links aestheticization to the excesses of aestheticism or *l'art pour l'art* (art for art's sake):
in this context, the notion that the claims of art, beauty and aesthetic
pleasure reign supreme over all other rationales for human action, justifying violence, cruelty and destruction so long as they serve aesthetic ends.[26]
Benjamin links this viewpoint to the Italian Futurists, in particular the
fascist poet and theorist Filippo Tommaso Marinetti, whose 1935 essay
'Estetica futurista della guerra' (Futurist aesthetic of war) celebrated the
beauty of Mussolini's use of the full panoply of techniques of modern
industrialized warfare in his Ethiopian campaign; for Benjamin, such
aesthetic posturing marks the 'consummation of *l'art pour l'art*' and the
nadir of humanity's self-alienation, the point at which it can 'experience its
own annihilation as a supreme aesthetic pleasure'.[27]

A second aspect of the aestheticization of politics identified by Benjamin is the appropriation of what he saw as the outmoded shibboleths of bourgeois aesthetics. Thus life – the authentic communal life of the idealized *Gemeinschaft* – is transformed into a work of art, presided over by an artist-genius whose followers model the kind of enrapt engagement previously associated with aesthetic contemplation.[28] It is this aspect of Benjamin's concept that maps most closely onto fascist statements on this theme, such as Joseph Goebbels's and Mussolini's notorious comparisons of the masses to passive, shapeless material requiring the manipulative skills of the artist-politician to mould them into a unified whole.[29] Finally, and perhaps most importantly, Benjamin uses the concept of aestheticized politics to convey the coming together of modern technology, atavistic ritual and the magical aura formerly possessed by art, a combination which serves to render the masses susceptible to domination. The fascist use of cinema and spectacle to this end has been deftly analyzed by Lutz Koepnick, who argues that aestheticized politics serves

to colonize the structures of modern experience, to engage popular sentiments, and to discipline sense perception with the ambition of integrating society and mobilizing the masses for future warfare. The fascist spectacle massages minds and emotions in such a way that modern postauratic perception loses its progressive thrust and succumbs to the signifiers of vitalistic power . . . It causes individuals to identify with that which forces them into submission and conformity and, ultimately, fosters their destruction.[30]

With fascism, aestheticization is not simply an add-on, a complementary but ultimately subordinate element within a primarily verbal ideological field. Indeed, it would be easier to make the opposite case, conceiving fascism as primarily aesthetic in orientation and only secondarily a matter of doctrines and programmes. Attempts to boil fascism down to a set of verbal principles – the so-called fascist minimum – have been notoriously unsuccessful, leading some commentators, most famously George Orwell, to dismiss the concept as meaningless.[31] This is perhaps unsurprising, given that fascism is not so much a cohesive 'ism' as a generic label or ideal type (whose definition is drastically affected by quite basic questions such as whether Francoist Spain or movements post 1945 are part of the picture).[32] In addition, the endeavour to define fascism as a set of principles or political philosophy is hampered by its protagonists' reluctance to conceive it in such terms; as Robert O. Paxton notes, Hitler and Mussolini considered their personalities and actions to define their ideals, rejecting formal programmes as the 'cheap promises' of mere politicians.[33] It is telling that the best-known recent attempt to summarize fascism as a verbal principle – Roger Griffin's definition of it as 'palingenetic ultra-nationalism', or an extreme form of nationalism hinging on myths of national rebirth – was formulated in the context of a volume on fascism and theatre.[34] The inextricability of the aesthetic from fascism reflects its emergence in the age of mass politics and mass media. While the great 'isms' of the nineteenth century – liberalism, conservatism, socialism and anarchism – were grounded in philosophical systems and debated within civil society, the appeal of fascism rested on gut feelings, fiery rhetoric and aesthetic spectacle, pointing to its nature 'not as a political text but as a system of the arts'.[35] It was precisely this aesthetic dimension that led many contemporaries to underestimate the allure fascism exercised; as the German-American historian George L. Mosse noted, 'we failed to see that the fascist aesthetic itself reflected the needs and hopes of contemporary society, that what we brushed aside as the so-called superstructure was in reality the means through which most people grasped the fascist message.'[36]

Acknowledging the primacy of the aesthetic in fascism is not to suggest that it lacked ideas, but rather that its messages were conceived and presented in aesthetic terms. There is no verbal core that can be separated out from the aesthetic and affective dimensions of fascist ideology. All of which makes it difficult to pin down just what, if anything, makes fascist art fascist, or differentiates it from art with wholly different ideological freight.[37] This is not merely a historical issue, but one that frequently confronts fans of contemporary hard rock and industrial metal: How is it possible to distinguish the music of parody fascist and neo-Nazi bands from the real thing? Judging from social media, even bands that signal their parodic intentions with a sledgehammer – such as the American industrial duo Hanzel und Gretyl – are regularly mistaken as genuinely fascist. Known for their faux German, Mel Brooks–style humour and extravagant headgear, Hanzel und Gretyl offer what they describe as a 'parody on wheels' of the Nazi era, with song titles such as 'Born to Be Heiled', 'Third Reich from the Sun' and 'Lederhosen Macht Frei'.[38] Yet German record distributors refused to distribute their album *Über Alles*, while fans complained to Spotify for including songs by what is 'clearly a neonazi band celebrating the third reich'.[39]

Laibach and Rammstein

While Hanzel und Gretyl's parodic distancing is never really in doubt, other bands – most notably the Slovenian group Laibach and the German band Rammstein – have engaged more provocatively with the aesthetics of fascism. Both have drawn directly on symbols and imagery from the Nazi era and have persistently been labelled as far-right bands by the media. Yet their relationship to fascism is by no means one of straightforward affiliation or appropriation, and their songs have little in common with those of the right-extremist groups examined in the next section.

One reason why Rammstein have provoked controversy is that their songs, performances and videos have been held responsible for bringing back into circulation materials from the Third Reich that had up until then been taboo in Germany. Two of their songs, the Depeche Mode cover 'Stripped' (1998) and 'Links 2–3–4' (2001), draw on or allude to the films of Riefenstahl, though not in a way that suggests a straightforward endorsement of fascist ideology. Indeed, both songs are calculatedly ambiguous. 'Stripped' softens the sexual violence present in the original version of the song, yet strengthens its atavistic quest for a humanity stripped of the accretions of civilization; in the video, the use of striking images from the opening of Riefenstahl's *Olympia* (1938) appears entirely without irony or distancing. In contrast, the lyrics of 'Links 2–3–4' – which allude to Brecht's *Einheitsfrontlied* and to the Social Democrat politician Oscar Lafontaine's phrase 'the heart beats on the left' (*Das Herz schlägt links*) – aim at distancing the band from right-wing extremism. Yet the song's militaristic tone and provocative video, in which an army of ants re-enacts scenes from *Triumph of the Will*, play to the band's reputation for far-right sympathies.[40] Earlier, we have seen that such double coding can be a sign of trying to draw diverse interest groups into a loose coalition, or simply of trying to please multiple constituencies. In 'Links 2–3–4', Rammstein attempt to keep at least three balls in the air, seeking on one level to rebut allegations of far-right sympathies, while at the same time feeding the controversy that generated their success and retaining the loyalty of their right-wing fans. Given this juggling act, it is not hard to see why some critics accuse the band of playing 'an irresponsible game with fascist aesthetics'.[41]

Žižek offers a more sympathetic take on Rammstein, although aspects of his interpretation rely on a problematic conception of fascist ideology. The problem here is that he seems to conceive fascist ideology in verbal terms, arguing that Rammstein 'de-semanticize' fascist ideology by presenting merely the empty shell of its gestures and rhetoric without the kernel of ideas.[42] Žižek presents a similar version of this argument in his film *The Pervert's Guide to Ideology*:

The minimal elements of the Nazi ideology enacted by Rammstein are something like pure elements of libidinal investment. Enjoyment has to be, as it were, condensed in some minimal ticks – gestures which do not give any precise ideological meaning. What Rammstein does is that it liberates these elements from the Nazi articulation. It allows us to enjoy them in their pre-ideological state. The way to fight Nazism is to enjoy these elements, ridiculous as they may appear, by suspending the Nazi corrosion of media. This way you undermine Nazism from within.[43]

As seen earlier, it is not feasible to separate the verbal and non-verbal dimensions of ideology and dismiss the latter as pre-political. While the meanings of 'Stripped' and 'Links 2–3–4' are multilayered, the fascist elements within them are neither minimal nor disconnected from Nazi articulation. The second dimension of Žižek's argument – that the way to undermine fascism is through hyperbole, emphatically exaggerating its gestures and rhetoric so as to make them ridiculous – is more persuasive. In defending the work of Laibach from the charge of fascism, Žižek argues that the kind of approach demanded by postmodern critics, ironic distancing, is no longer effective in a world in which such cynical detachment is the norm.[44] Instead, Žižek stresses that Laibach offer an emphatic over-identification with fascism, a 'public staging of the obscene fantasmatic kernel of an ideological edifice'.[45]

Over-identification, as Žižek diagnoses it, has much in common with the Russian aesthetic known as *stiob* that flourished in the late Soviet era: a mode of parody that replicates to the point of absurdity the images, codes and conventions of an official ideology.[46] In the case of Laibach (see Figure 7.2), the point of this hyperbolic identification is not to ridicule fascism as a historical phenomenon but rather to expose the concealed fascistic mechanisms at work within contemporary society. Two striking examples can be found on the group's third album *Opus Dei* (1987): 'Life Is Life', a cover of the Austrian band Opus's hit 'Live Is Life' (1984), and 'Geburt einer Nation' (Birth of a Nation), a reworking of Queen's 'One Vision' (1986). Thanks in part to the Pythonesque promotional videos that accompany the songs, their strange potency is still vividly apparent today. In the case of 'Life Is Life', Laibach draw to the surface the nostalgia for the Nazi era infusing Opus's celebration of folk, blood and soil, revealing how exclusionary ideologies can lurk within even the most vacuous Euro hit.[47] Small textual changes play a part in this transformation, but music is the prime factor, from the portentous orchestral opening to the apocalyptic fanfares that replace the easygoing hook in the original. Queen's 'One Vision', the 1980s stadium rock anthem par excellence, may seem a less obvious target for such a musical critique of ideology, until you

Figure 7.2 Laibach 'Einkauf' (shopping) performance action in Ljubljana, 2003, photograph by Sašo Podgoršek. By permission of Laibach.

contemplate the frightening resonances of a slightly built, moustachioed man effortlessly holding a stadium-full of followers in the palm of his hand. As with 'Life Is Life', Laibach make minimal textual changes in order to draw out the totalitarian demagoguery implicit in the original anthem:

One flesh, one bone, one true religion.
One voice, one hope, one real decision. (Queen)
Ein Fleisch, ein Blut, ein wahrer Glaube.
Eine Rasse und ein Traum, ein starker Wille. (Laibach)

Here too, it is the militaristic musical arrangement and guttural bass of Milan Fras that bring home the dangers inherent in Queen's lazy-hazy universalism. Another focus of the cover's critique, as Alexei Monroe notes, is the parallels it posits between 'the structures of unquestioning adulation (and obedience) common to both totalitarian mass mobilization and capitalist mass consumption'.[48] Some of the musical omissions are as telling as the reworkings: within Laibach's hyper-fascistic world, there is no place for Brian May's supremely individualistic guitar solo.

7.3   Metapolitical Activism and the Extreme Right

Scholarly interest in music's role in extreme right-wing movements has mushroomed over recent years, stimulated by the new prominence that the internet has given to the white nationalist, neo-fascist and neo-Nazi music scenes. Much academic research in this area shares the campaigning spirit and tone of organizations such as the Southern Poverty Law Center (US) and Unite Against Fascism and *Searchlight* magazine (UK); quite understandably, politically committed researchers relish taking on the role of crusaders against fascism, battling against an 'international web' of Nazis and white supremacists using 'hate music' to corrupt the innocent and undermine democracy.[49] The problem with this, to put it bluntly, is that crusading researchers tend to find what they are looking for: they have a vested interest in accentuating music's importance for the extreme right, stressing the dangers it poses for young people and linking it to incidents of racial violence. My aim here is not to minimize the threat posed by right-wing extremism but rather to encourage scholars in this area to jettison sensationalist language and outmoded theoretical models. Phrases like 'hate music' have no analytical value, while the view that such music serves as a 'gateway drug', drawing the young and innocent into the world of right-wing extremism, relies on the long-discredited 'magic bullet' model of communication (see Section 1.2).

Rather than approaching this music as a weapon or as a magic potion for converting the unwary, this section explores its changing role within the protest activism of the extreme right.[50] The concept of protest music may seem to jar when applied to the extreme right and is seldom encountered in discussions of its music. Yet the concepts of protest and resistance are fundamental to how right-wing extremist bands represent themselves and articulate their music's role. Exploring how music relates to broader protest strategies within the extreme right can help us understand why this music has mutated in recent years. In particular, it enables us to grasp how music that might initially seem unrelated to extreme-right ideologies in fact ties in closely with the movement's broader tactics.

Protest Activism and the Extreme Right

Since the 1990s, protest activism has played a crucial role within German right-wing extremism, with hundreds of parades, demonstrations and smaller events being staged each year. In 1997, the Nationaldemokratische Partei Deutschlands (NPD) adopted 'struggle on the streets' as one of its three strategic imperatives, and other right-extremist groups have also relied on protest activism to help retain and galvanize their members.[51] These protests are exhaustively chronicled by both participants and anti-fascist organizations, as well as by the German media, and a large selection of videos of such events can be found on social media websites. What is strikingly apparent from these videos is the diversity of contemporary right-wing extremist protest forms and tactics.[52] While some events suggest that the extreme right remains yoked to the National Socialist past, others create an entirely contemporary impression. Many of these protests conform with what we might expect to see and hear at an extreme right-wing parade or demo: aggressive, middle-aged skinheads, an array of Nazi-era symbols (most prominently the black, white and red *Reichsflagge*, standing in for the illegal swastika) and music associated with the Third Reich (whether songs connected to the Hitler Youth or bleeding hunks of Wagner).[53] But if these ingredients suggest the extreme right is incapable of moving beyond its default gestures and tactics, other elements within its protest repertory give compelling evidence of an impulse to adapt and modernize.

One key strategy is using issues that resonate with a broader constituency to help embed the movement's deeper agenda. Often, as in the case of the annual Dresden and Magdeburg parades commemorating the victims of Allied bombings in the Second World War, sham pressure groups are used to conceal the extreme-right organizations behind such events. This tactic of coopting topical issues – or as the German Ministry for the Interior puts it, 'making instrumental use of socially relevant themes by which the right-wing extremist origin of the events is cloaked' – is at the heart of the demonstrations and smaller-scale events staged by the NPD, Die Rechte and other extreme-right groups.[54] The majority of these demonstrations make no kind of reference to the Third Reich or to National Socialism, reflecting the NPD politician Jürgen Gansel's strategic line that 'Adolf Hitler and the NSDAP are past . . . while globalization, immigration and EU interference are the cruel realities of the present.'[55] The most regular tactic of the NPD is to appropriate issues that are the traditional territory of populist right-wing parties, such as hostility to immigration, asylum seekers, multiculturalism and the European Union. These protest themes are employed not to deliver a short-term aim, but as a strategy for working toward the movement's longer-term goals: those of displacing parliamentary democracy and creating a racially homogenized nation.

A contrasting approach to normalizing the extreme right can be seen in demonstrations by the youth wings of the NDP and Die Rechte. Perhaps the most surprising aspect of these demonstrations is that, aside from the prominent black, white and red flags, there is little to differentiate them from any other youth-oriented protest event, with slogan T-shirts, flyers, and a loud soundtrack of heavy metal to create an edgy, rebellious atmosphere. These elements point not merely to the aim of attracting the young, but to the tactic of broadening the extreme right's appeal by mimicking themes and protest tactics associated with left-wing groups. This approach is evident in the wide range of anti-establishment causes promoted in the movement's banners and placards. One example of this tactic is the annual Dortmund Antikriegstag (anti-war day), which has served as the focal point for a range of different protest actions since 2005.[56] These events present themselves as protests against Western imperialism, capitalism and liberal democracy, seeking to exploit public hostility to the wars in the Middle East and Afghanistan. This kind of cooption of themes associated with the left is particularly characteristic of a relatively new grouping within the German extreme right: the Autonomous Nationalists (AN). In addition to adopting the principle of autonomous activism from the radical left, the AN have appropriated its fashion codes, symbols and protest rhetoric as a means to reach beyond the extreme right's traditional constituency. As Jan Schedler notes, the AN align themselves not only with anti-capitalism and hostility to globalization but also environmentalism and animal rights, seeking to make the full gamut of left-wing protest themes their own.[57]

In addition to appropriating symbols and themes from the left, German extreme-right groups have also made use of left-wing protest forms. The most visible example is the so-called black block – tightly massed activists, dressed uniformly in black with hoodies and masks – a demonstration tactic employed by groups on the radical left since the 1980s.[58] Another protest tactic borrowed from the tool-kit of left-wing activism is the flash mob: a group of activists mobilized through social media to perform a predetermined yet quasi-spontaneous action in a public space. The most striking examples of right-extremist flash mobs are the protests staged by the Spreelichter network, active from around 2008 until it was banned by the South Brandenburg state government in 2012, and by a similar group named Die Unsterblichen (The Immortals).[59] The protests staged by these groups range from large-scale torchlight parades (taking their cue from similar events in the Third Reich) to impromptu interventions at public festivals and clandestine incursions into buildings such as Schloss Colditz.[60] All these actions are oriented around youth and the new media; the stunts staged by these networks were conceived to have an impact primarily through internet dissemination and include media-friendly branding such as the ubiquitous slogan 'democrats are destroying our people' (*Demokraten bringen uns den Volkstod*).

The diversification of protest tactics described above is by no means unique to Germany and can be seen in various forms in extreme-right organizations across Europe. The most striking example is Italy's Casa-Pound movement which, like the German right-wing extremist groups, has coopted leftist themes and tactics to serve its own ends. Just as the German AN have sought to reactivate the socialist dimension of National Socialism, CasaPound offers a socially revolutionary 'fascism for the third millennium', combining anti-capitalist rhetoric with right-wing populism.[61] The leader of CasaPound, Gianluca Iannone, is also the lead singer of the band ZetaZeroAlfa, which has played a crucial role in helping to make this mixture of political stances cohere and appeal to a youth audience. As Franco Berteni, Denis Giordano and Caterina Sartori argue, the organization's music scene has enabled a link to be forged between 'the subcultural dimension of a youth experience that finds its raison d'être in a generically rebellious and anti-conformist identity, and the experiences of a more ideologically defined political militancy'.[62]

Music and Contemporary Right-Wing Extremism

As the case of ZetaZeroAlfa illustrates, music plays a significant role in shaping and articulating the shift in tactics within the extreme right. The kinds of singers and bands that have been crucial to this shift diverge significantly from our received picture of right-extremist music, a picture defined by the skinhead band Skrewdriver and the wave of German rock and heavy metal groups that first brought this music to prominence in the 1980s.[63] Until very recently, this model continued to dominate government and media representations of right-extremist music, particularly German *Rechtsrock*.[64] Table 7.1 outlines some of the ways in which the newer model of right-wing extremism and its music diverge from the earlier one.

Perhaps the most obvious difference is in how these models treat the National Socialist past. The earlier German bands revelled in glorifying the Nazi regime, and some drew on its buzzwords for their names (e.g. Freikorps, Gestapo, Reichsfront) or for album titles (e.g. Landser, *Das Reich kommt wieder* (1992), and Arisches Blut, *Ein Führer* (1999)). In this music, words and slogans associated with the Third Reich function as ideological shorthand, adding crucial definition to the starkly oppositional landscape they articulate. In Landser's 'Arische Kämpfer' from

Table 7.1 Phases within right-wing extremism and its music

Older Model	Newer Model
Promotion of violence/overthrow of parliamentary democracy	Long-term metapolitical strategy of cultural resistance/changing consciousness
Glorification of National Socialist era, with heavy use of Nazi slogans and symbolism	References to Nazism or neo-Nazi culture subtle, coded or entirely absent (replaced by broader oppositional rhetoric)
White Power message combined with exclusionary, statist nationalism	Pan-European white nationalism
Explicitly racist and anti-Semitic	Islamophobic, hostile to immigrants, sometimes pro-Israel
Authoritarian; *Volksgemeinschaft* versus individualism	Generally conforms with the rock ideal of the rebel individual
Homophobic, chauvinistic	Aggressively masculine (but homophobic lyrics uncommon)
'Rock against Communism'	Hostile to capitalism and economic globalization
Preaches to the converted	Proselytizes or at least aims to sell records to a broader constituency
'Message' music	More veiled or intentionally ambiguous in content

Das Reich kommt wieder, for example, isolated references to 'Aryan fighters' and 'National Socialists' are the sole ideologically specific ingredient within a generalized message of resistance. As well as keeping alive the fantasy of an Aryan community, these songs relive the conflicts of the Nazi era, elevating Nazism as a bulwark against communism. The label 'Rock against Communism' was crucial to promoting *Rechtsrock* as protest music, and the idea that communism is to blame for the evils of the present continued to flourish well beyond the fall of the Berlin wall. This can be seen from the 2001 song 'Ein Volk, ein Reich, ein Führer' by Arische Kämpfe, which anticipates the annihilation of the left by a reawakened SS (this song, available on YouTube, epitomizes the DIY quality of much *Rechtsrock*, with its meagre, chant-like music and cliché-ridden, grossly racist text).

In contrast, references to the Nazi era in more recent right-wing-extremist rock tend to be subtle, coded or entirely absent.[65] Similarly, the newer model largely abandons the explicitly racist and anti-Semitic lyrics found in the work of earlier bands. Instead, the songs often articulate or allude to white nationalist ideas, in particular the notion that the white race is threatened with extinction and that Western democracy is hastening its decline. As with Skrewdriver and its German imitators, the more recent right-extremist bands treat their music as a form of protest or resistance. In place of the 'Rock against Communism' platform, the newer bands have taken up a range of different causes. The best example of this direction within classic *Rechtsrock* is the band Sleipnir, whose shift in protest tactics mirrors that of the broader extreme-right movement. The band's second album *Kriegsverbrechen* (War Crimes) offers a musical equivalent of the neo-Nazi commemorative parade, protesting against the injustice of regarding 'the brutal murderous crimes of the allies as legal'.[66] More recently, the list of causes espoused by Sleipnir parallels those coopted by the NPD and Die Rechte: the band has produced songs protesting against American imperialism, the Iraq War, global capitalism and the European Union, and in 2016–17 the band participated in a series of 'Rock against Immigration' concerts.[67]

In spite of my division of this scene into two columns, these strands are not wholly distinct and the first model has not been ousted by the second. Much of this music scene continues to resemble an ever-expanding tribute album to Skrewdriver, and many of the old *Rechtsrock* bands such as Sturmwehr are still active. Further, to speak of a new model of right-wing extremist protest music risks oversimplification, since several distinct strands can be discerned within it. Scholarship and media coverage have tended to address shifting patterns within the music of the extreme right from the perspective of genre, stressing the diversification of the scene beyond *Rechtsrock* and heavy metal. The best-known symptom of this trend is the work of the Swedish singer Saga, whose soft rock piano ballads gained notoriety in 2011 when Anders Behring Breivik cited them as an inspiration. The difference between Saga's most recent albums and classic *Rechtsrock* is not simply one of musical style. Rather, as Breivik himself argued, the political orientation of Saga and her music appears to diverge significantly from that of neo-Nazi bands:

Marxist and multiculturalist character-assassins will claim that Saga is an evil, national-socialist monsterband from hell, due to her success. However, this characteristic couldn't be anywhere further from the truth ... Saga has created several pop-tracks with nationalist oriented texts that will appeal to all conservatives, and especially revolutionary conservatives of all conservative ideological denominations ... Instead of 'physical' revolutionary or democratic resistance, she fights through her music by inspiring the best in us.[68]

Breivik's account exaggerates the distance between Saga and neo-Nazi skinhead bands, since her solo career began with three tribute albums of Skrewdriver songs.[69] Yet even in these, the lyrics are modified to remove anti-Semitic references, while Saga's own songs largely steer clear of the kind of explicit racism found in earlier extreme-right material.[70] Although Saga's songs contain relatively little reference to Nazism or the Third Reich, she sometimes alludes to contemporary right-wing extremists or draws on their lyrics.[71] The recurring theme is the fate of the white race, as in the song 'One Nation Arise' (from *On My Own*, 2007). This song presents a common right-extremist trope: the idea of the white nation as an oppressed minority, weakened by apathy and enfeebled by democracy.

Compared with the lyrics of the neo-Nazi bands cited above, Saga's songs might seem to amount to what Richard Stöss identified in the political realm as 'right-extremism light'.[72] But if their political message is soft-pedalled, this is still message music, relentlessly circling around the white nationalist vision of racial conflict; as Emily Turner-Graham comments, 'much of her material is firmly of the far reaches of the extreme right.'[73] Other bands have cultivated a more subtle approach, avoiding lyrics that articulate political messages and instead relying on a few key buzzwords to convey their drift. In such cases, extreme right-wing politics are often more evident from their interview, webpage and social media sites than from the lyrics of their songs. One example is the Magdeburg acoustic band Agharta, whose first album – significantly entitled *Zwischen den Zeilen* (Between the Lines) – appeared in 2011. Agharta perform regularly alongside neo-Nazi bands Sleipnir and Heiliges Reich, and this album was released by the Wolfszeit label, which records exclusively right-extremist material. Yet this record offers, in the words of Agharta's publicity blurb, a 'non-conformist album of a different kind'.[74] Rather than engaging explicitly with the familiar themes of *Rechtsrock*, it just makes fragmentary, passing allusions to them: 'the world is full of deceptions and falsehoods'; 'our own people do not know that they must save themselves'; 'like a tree I stand firm on Germany's soil'; 'the day of reckoning draws ever closer'; 'it is your deeds which will change things for your children's future!'; 'it is your deeds which will set you free!'[75]

Even reading 'between the lines', this kind of material may seem to have little in common with *Rechtsrock* or with protest music in the conventional sense. But this shift away from explicit political messages can be found in a significant number of current German bands, particularly those working within the hardcore genre. As Jan Raabe and Martin Langebach note, contemporary National Socialist Hardcore (NSHC) bands rarely spell out their political standpoint in their lyrics, instead taking a more self-consciously poetic and ambiguous approach.[76] Like Sleipnir, some of the older NSHC bands have gradually moved away from articulating openly racist and neo-Nazi views, reinventing themselves to suit broader trends in extreme-right activism. The Magdeburg band Daily Broken Dream is a case in point, since prior to 2007 it went by the name Race Riot. In explaining this name change, the band sheds light on why they and other NSHC groups have moved away from the hyper-explicit lyrics of earlier bands:

[We] want to be seen as a band providing political, critical and inventive lyrics about social problems, the downfall of nations, the loss of values etc. . . . Our lyrics deal with many aspects of NS ideas or general critical statements about the modern lifestyle, about drug abuse, about wars, US imperialism etc. – in general, we prefer lyrics that are not too straightforward – we want our listeners to think about our words, to find own interpretations and to be more critical than they'd need to be when listening to 'in-your-face' lyrics about violence.[77]

As Rainer Fromm observes, other NSHC bands who are outspoken about their right-extremist views in interviews often entirely avoid such material in their song lyrics, instead lambasting capitalism and globalization while occasionally addressing environmental themes.[78] This focus on protest issues more often associated with the left reflects the close relationship between the NSHC scene and the AN.[79] But within NSHC, just as in the music of Saga and Agharta, most songs offer a generalized message of resistance rather than a precise programme, stressing the need for right-thinking individuals to join the struggle rather than acquiesce to the existing order. A recent album by Brainwash, *Time to Act* (2013), is entirely given over to this theme, offering a call to action to those disaffected and alienated by contemporary society, the political system and the global order.

Like some of the protest tactics described earlier, the themes and lyrics of these songs could plausibly stem from either the far left or right of the political spectrum. They provide a generic message of resistance which has the capacity to resonate with listeners beyond the reach of classic *Rechtsrock*, while also enabling initiates to read 'between the lines' and respond to their 'true' content. Before pursuing further the parallels between developments in the music and protest tactics of the extreme right, it is necessary to understand some of the practical factors responsible for this change in approach. In Germany and elsewhere in northern Europe, right-wing-extremist organizations have been in decline now for more than a decade, while more moderate, populist right-wing groups have surged in numbers. The most recent figures indicate that no more than

24,350 people in Germany (0.03% of the population) are involved with extreme-right organizations, while just 5,800 (less than 0.01%) are active neo-Nazis.[80] Small wonder that activists and bands have turned to material that can draw in a broader right-wing constituency, fixated not on the Nazi past but on contemporary issues like immigration and multiculturalism. In a 2007 interview, Maik, the bass guitarist from Daily Broken Dream, observed that it was easier to draw people into the right-extremist scene through more moderate material than through the kind of explicit, aggressive lyrics favoured by 'Landser & Co.':

> Just recently we had a discussion in the band about whether music needs to convey 'unambiguous' messages in order to be a useful tool for propaganda. My view is that music like ours, which takes its lead from models entirely outside of the 'right-wing scene', does not necessarily have to have extreme political texts in order to produce an effect. I've often heard people from the hardcore scene respond enthusiastically if I play them CDs by the likes of Teardown or Path of Resistance; in this way, talk has naturally turned to politics. Since then, some of these people have become active in the nationalist movement. If I'd played them music by Landser & Co. they would surely have been scared off (at least back then), and above all found little to interest them in such unsophisticated music.[81]

Another factor motivating this shift is the tough legislative and policing regime that has confronted the extreme right since the late 1990s, particularly in Sweden and Germany. In Sweden, mass arrests of participants in extreme-right rock concerts seriously weakened the White Power scene and diminished the place of live music within it.[82] Similarly, in Germany, the imprisonment of members of several bands under hate speech legislation has served as an incentive to tone down both behaviour and lyrics. Government censorship of recordings remains rigorous, and bands have to contend with intensive police surveillance of live performances, risking prosecution if their language or gestures breach the law. In recent years, however, the most pressing factor encouraging bands to moderate their lyrics and to strive to appeal to a wider public has been the collapse of the market for recorded music. While in the late 1990s, right-extremists viewed online music sales as a means to bankroll the entire movement, the ubiquity of free music downloads has drastically reduced this income.[83]

Metapolitical Activism

The new approach adopted by Saga, Agharta and the NSHC bands is more than just a means to compensate for declining sales. We need to tread cautiously in probing the motives behind this shift, however, since it is all too easy to read it as a cynical ploy to seduce the unwary. As mentioned earlier, much of the literature on right-extremist music is predisposed to treating it as a form of manipulation, calculated to beguile and brainwash listeners exposed to it. From this viewpoint, the turn toward material with a broader appeal represents an attempt to conceal the music's true underlying ideology, and thus dupe listeners into embracing right-extremist views. This line of interpretation does not sit well with the views of Maik from Daily Broken Dream quoted earlier. Rather than aiming to dupe listeners, bands are seeking to proselytize more effectively for their cause. Their change of tack, like the broader shift within protest tactics, reflects a recognition that the strategies, behaviour and language of the earlier phase of right-extremism had comprehensively failed to advance the movement; as one far-right blogger puts it, the White Power scene of the 1980s and 1990s offered only 'oppositional defiance' and 'nihilism', rendering it impotent as a political force.[84] In contrast, more recent right-extremist activists have adopted what they describe as a metapolitical approach, a term which in this context simply means preparing the political ground for their ideas by embedding them first in the cultural sphere.

In one form or another, metapolitics has been a component within the thinking of the extreme right since the 1980s, most often serving to convey the idea that consensus building through cultural and intellectual work is a necessary precondition for political transformation. For the publicist and ideologue Pierre Krebs, metapolitics proceeds from the realization that the worldview of the extreme right is utterly foreign not only to most contemporary Europeans but to the hegemonic liberal-democratic order. Accordingly, Krebs and his circle argued that the only way to dislodge this entrenched order is by transforming values and constructing a new consensus: 'the metapolitical strategy consists therefore of conducting an ideological struggle and inculcating a new system of cultural values.'[85] The idea of using culture to win hearts and minds and thus create a new consensus was derived from Gramsci, although the conception of cultural hegemony elaborated by the Thule Seminar members departs from the original in fundamental ways.[86] Paraphrasing Gramsci, Krebs argues that

in order to make it possible for the new political message to find a firm footing (party activity) one must first influence thinking and behaviour within civil society (metapolitical or cultural activity). A political majority is thus grounded on a cultural, that is, ideological majority ... These efforts must therefore gain a wider influence in order to work their effect on strata of culture, through poetry, theatre, popular music, film, the fine arts, the press and other areas.[87]

The work of Saga, Agharta and NHSC bands like Daily Broken Dream similarly aims at cultural transformation, filtering and repackaging right-extremist views to draw in the largest possible constituency. As with the types of protest action discussed earlier, their music represents a distinct form of activism, aimed not at securing particular goals but rather at the long-haul task of transforming values. Even though specific themes or causes may serve as the focus for particular protest or lyrics, these are merely premises serving to help build up a counterculture. This kind of metapolitical activism has proved successful in Italy, largely as a result of the practical form it acquired under the leadership of CasaPound; for Iannone, the ultimate goal – 'retake everything' – demands that 'we have to renew the language, symbolism, esthetics … if we can't communicate with "the others" it is not always their fault. We try to communicate in a radical mode and renew our dream. We want to launch it and give it a new spin. It could be through music or art.'[88] But if this metapolitical strategy appears to be paying off in Italy, there are few signs of similar success in Sweden and Germany. There is little evidence that the new approaches pursued by musicians such as Saga, Agharta and the NSHC bands have enabled them to attract more people to the extreme right than the earlier *Rechtsrock* bands did or that they have been able to avoid the legal and practical obstacles faced by more overtly extremist groups. Although the casual listener who comes across their songs on YouTube might assume that bands such as Agharta and Daily Broken Dream are harmlessly nationalist or non-conformist, the authorities and anti-fascist activists work zealously to counter such misconceptions. Both bands were recently included in a list of right-extremist bands published by the government of Saxony-Anhalt, and one of Agharta's 2014 concerts was interrupted and closed down by the police (who were criticized in Parliament for failing to prevent it taking place altogether).[89]

Aside from such external factors, there are pressing internal reasons for the failure of metapolitical strategies to expand the extreme-right base. Gramsci's concept of cultural hegemony was not simply about converting hearts and minds, but about the practical work of building alliances with other movements.[90] But the extreme right's embrace of metapolitics has not even served to patch over the divisions within its own ranks and has resulted rather in an incoherent mixture of messages and tactics. While music may serve as a kind of metapolitical glue in holding the scene together, it alone cannot fuse these disparate elements into a common front or a coherent force. This does not mean that the extreme right and its music should no longer be regarded as a threat. But rather than sensationalizing this music and the dangers it poses for democracy, we should recognize – as seen earlier in the chapter – that in both the United States and Europe the major threat lies in the breakdown of the boundaries between right-wing extremism and supposedly mainstream right-wing populism. In Germany, the new protest strategies of the extreme right – especially its focus on issues like immigration – seems merely to have fostered support for populist right-wing parties, in particular Alternative für Deutschland (AfD). Like Trump, AfD politicians have resorted to dog-whistle tactics to expand their support into the far reaches of the right, even invoking coded Nazi language in condemning their opponents.[91] Given this blurring of the boundaries between the populist and extreme right, we need to rethink how we conceptualize music's relationship to the latter. Rather than serving as a gateway drawing listeners into the world of extremism, music is one of the conduits through which extremism percolates into mainstream culture and becomes normalized. The term 'grey zone' is often used within the extreme right to describe bands at the margins of its music scenes, groups that share its platforms yet merely toy with its ideology or present it in a more publicly acceptable form. A similar grey zone has opened up within American and European politics, with cultural racism and dog-whistling enabling its dispersion into the mainstream.

⌇ | Postscript

Music and Politics after the Future

Earlier, I defined political ideology as a lens that imparts meaning to the past, brings reality into focus and projects a transformative vision of the future. Yet this kind of ideology, promising radical change, has been consigned to the margins for decades now and may seem merely a quirk of a brief phase of history, a blip in the otherwise smooth advancement of global capitalism. From the perspective of neoliberal theorists, the fall of the Berlin wall and the collapse of the USSR marked the definitive end of ideology; yet it was the global financial crisis of 2007–11 – generating years of hardship yet not triggering a serious challenge to the system – that seemingly confirmed that 'there is no alternative.' We live in an age 'after the future', as Berardi puts it, stripped of the belief in the possibility of change that fuelled earlier radical politics; at this point, 'the future no longer appears as a choice or a collective conscious action', but rather as an 'unavoidable catastrophe that we cannot oppose in any way'.[1]

Back in the mid-nineteenth century, Marx had diagnosed how the estrangement of workers from their humanity was compounded by the breakdown of social structures, a perpetual state of flux and the relentless acceleration of life: 'Constant revolutionizing of production, uninterrupted disturbance of all social conditions, everlasting uncertainty and agitation distinguish the bourgeois epoch from all earlier ones. All fixed, fast-frozen relations ... are swept away, all new-formed ones become antiquated before they can ossify. All that is solid melts into air.'[2] If Marx's diagnosis already resembles our contemporary situation, alienation is compounded under neoliberalism by the sense of being trapped in a mechanism that is not only outside our control, but out of control. For Berardi, the angry, 'purely negative' gestures of resistance that followed the financial crisis exemplify this new phase of alienation:

This rage is impotent and inconsequential, as consciousness and coordinated action seem beyond the reach of present society. Look at the European crisis. Never in our life have we faced a situation so charged with revolutionary opportunities. Never in our life have we been so impotent. Never have intellectuals and militants been so silent, so unable to find a way to show a new possible direction.[3]

Accepting the current lack of alternatives and abandoning utopian thinking might seem a counsel of despair, yet for Žižek these are the necessary preconditions for radical thought today: 'The true courage is not to imagine an alternative, but to accept the consequences of the fact that there is no clearly discernible alternative: the dream of an alternative is a sign of theoretical cowardice, functioning as a fetish that prevents us from grasping the deadlock of our predicament.'[4] Under these conditions, many of the standard forms of activism, musical and otherwise, seem ineffective or irrelevant. At a time when mass demonstrations held in major cities can go entirely unreported by mainstream media, it is drastically evident how futile some of the staples of the activist repertory have become. For Micah White, the failure of the Occupy movements demonstrates that protest is 'broken', while for Berardi, the seeming impossibility of change renders all activism part of the 'fake show of politics', a charade that merely breeds resentment and depression.[5] In place of activism, Berardi advocates refusal and withdrawal, arguing that only through seceding from the system can a space be created for the long-term process of reconstruction: 'withdrawal means creation of spaces of autonomy where solidarity can be rebuilt, and where self-relying communities can start a process of proliferation, contagion, and eventually, of reversal of the trend.'[6]

Berardi is probably right in arguing that activism has little to offer this long, slow battle to inculcate a new idea. But such a timescale is not feasible for other pressing global challenges – I'm thinking in particular of climate change – and here activism still has a crucial role to play in raising public awareness. Conventional forms of protest and resistance are problematic, given the ease with which they can miss their target, be defused by governments or be reframed by the media. By far the best-known example of musical activism from the last decade, Pussy Riot's 'Punk Prayer', exemplifies at least one of these problems, given the way in which the media diluted its political message into one of rock rebellion. But there are plenty of other recent examples of how musicians are reinventing activism, breaking down the barriers between it and mainstream musical genres, embedding it in everyday spaces and giving it the capacity to engage substantively with contemporary issues. Kendrick Lamar's 'Alright' is one standout example, negotiating the boundaries between interventive politics and intramusical transgression while making full use of rap's lyrical breadth. Within contemporary classical music, new forms of political engagement are serving to reinvigorate art music as well as activism. One striking example is *Extinct Birds* (2013), by the Australian-British composer and environmental activist David Holyoake, which combines chamber ensemble and voice, live electronics and sound recordings of extinct and endangered songbirds. Given the extent to which humans, and presumably birds, define themselves through their music, there is something incredibly poignant about hearing such voices from beyond being juxtaposed with the sounds of the species that robbed them of life.[7] Such sonic experiences have the ability to cut through the roster of denials and excuses we customarily offer for climate change, bringing home just how much is at stake; as Holyoake comments succinctly, 'there is no music on a dead planet. Time to get involved.'[8]

Whether academic writing about music can usefully contribute to activism is a moot point. Would it not be more worthwhile to engage in practical forms of political work or to follow the example of the German musicologist Georg Knepler and write a radical manifesto for change?[9] After all, the politicization of music studies since the 1990s has been compellingly read as a form of transference or compensation, filling the void created by the absence of meaningful antagonism in real-life politics under the neoliberal consensus.[10] Academic activism, in particular in fields such as this, may seem to amount to nothing more than virtue-signalling, 'slacktivism' or what Žižek calls 'radical chic', constructing a politicized persona without taking the time or trouble to engage in real political commitments.[11] But as we have seen, the folds of reality work in more complex ways than such binaries imply. Moreover, given that neoliberalism ruthlessly effaces the boundaries between private and public and between work and life, its opponents have an obligation to follow suit. Rather than being mutually exclusive, political action and thinking – in whatever reality compartment they take place – are complementary activities serving the same ends. As Foucault put it, outlining the prerequisites of a new politics, 'do not use thought to ground a political practice in Truth; nor political action to discredit, as mere speculation, a line of thought. Use political practice as an intensifier of thought, and analysis as a multiplier of the forms and domains for the intervention of political action.'[12]

Notes

1 Music and Politics: Key Concepts and Issues

1. Aage Borchgrevink, *A Norwegian Tragedy: Anders Behring Breivik and the Massacre on Utøya*, trans. Guy Puzey (Cambridge, 2013), 232.
2. Ibid., 268, 243.
3. For an overview of the music which Breivik claimed inspired and motivated him, see Joe Stroud, 'The Importance of Music to Anders Behring Breivik', *Journal of Terrorism Research* 4/1 (2013), http://ojs.st-andrews.ac.uk/index.php/jtr/article/view/620/537.
4. See Jonathan Pieslak, *Radicalism and Music: An Introduction to the Music Cultures of al-Qa'ida, Racist Skinheads, Christian-Affiliated Radicals, and Eco-Animal Rights Militants* (Middletown, CT, 2015), 89–95.
5. Andrew Berwick [Anders Behring Breivik], *2083: A European Declaration of Independence* (2011), original version from andersbreivik.co.uk. Breivik refers to the reorchestrated version of *Lux Aeterna* used in the trailer for *Lord of the Rings: The Two Towers*.
6. Erica Buist, 'That's Me in the Picture: Markiyan Matsekh Plays the Piano for Riot Police in Kiev', *The Guardian* (5 December 2014), www.theguardian.com/artanddesign/2014/dec/05/.
7. Chervonaruta, 'Protest Piano: Revolutionary Art against Violence by "Fascist Extremists"', *Voices of Ukraine* (12 February 2014), http://maidantranslations.com/2014/02/12/; '#BBCtrending: Playing the Piano to Riot Police in Ukraine' (30 January 2014), www.bbc.co.uk/news/magazine-25955350.
8. Anna Wittmann, 'Framed Performance: The Innocence of the Piano' (July 2015), *The Potential of Art and Literature in the Context of Political Crisis and War: Current Tendencies in Ukrainian Literature and Art*, http://aesthetic-potential.com/about/essays/framed-performance-the-innocence-of-the-piano/.
9. Ioan Grillo, 'There Are Already Dozens of Ballads Celebrating the Escape of Chapo Guzman', *Time* (14 July 2015), http://time.com/3956838/.
10. Lupillo Rivera, 'El Chapo otra fuga mas' (13 July 2015), www.youtube.com/watch?v=_rBMU430Y_Y.
11. The ways in which the narcocorrido draws on the traditions of the corrido genre are explored in John H. McDowell, *Poetry and Violence: The Ballad Tradition of Mexico's Costa Chica* (Urbana, IL, 2000), 199–207; Mark Pedelty, *Musical Ritual in Mexico City: From the Aztec to NAFTA* (Austin, TX, 2004),

134–5; and Helena Simonett, '*Los gallos valientes*: Examining Violence in Mexican Popular Music', *Trans: Revista Transcultural de Música* 10 (2006), www.sibetrans.com/trans/articulo/149/.

12. Deborah Hastings, 'Hundreds March in Mexico for Release of Drug Lord Joaquin "El Chapo" Guzman', *New York Daily News* (27 February 2014), www.nydailynews.com/news/world/mexicans-demonstrate-release-drug-lord-el-chapo-guzman-article-1.1703832.

13. John P. Sullivan, 'Criminal Insurgency: Narcocultura, Social Banditry, and Information Operations', *Small Wars Journal* 8/12 (3 December 2012), http://smallwarsjournal.com/jrnl/iss/201212.

14. Miriam Elder, 'Pussy Riot Sentenced to Two Years in Prison Colony over Anti-Putin Protest', *The Guardian* (17 August 2013), www.theguardian.com/music/2012/aug/17/pussy-riot-sentenced-prison-putin.

15. Tom Parfitt, 'Sir Paul McCartney Supports Pussy Riot', *The Telegraph* (16 August 2012), www.telegraph.co.uk/news/worldnews/europe/russia/9479937/Sir-Paul-McCartney-supports-Pussy-Riot.html. See also Nicholas Tochka, 'Pussy Riot, Freedom of Expression, and Popular Music Studies after the Cold War', *Popular Music* 32/2 (2013), 303–11.

16. Anon., 'Pussy Riot, Western Media Manipulation and Just How Liberal Is Russia', *GRANews* (2 May 2012), www.granews.info/content/pussy-riot-western-media-manipulation-and-just-how-liberal-russia. See also Vadim Nikitin, 'The Wrong Reasons to Back Pussy Riot', *New York Times* (20 August 2012), www.nytimes.com/2012/08/21/opinion/the-wrong-reasons-to-back-pussy-riot.html?_r=0.

17. Bill Osgerby, 'Subcultures, Popular Music and Social Change: Theories, Issues and Debates', in *Subcultures, Popular Music and Social Change*, ed. The Subcultures Network (Cambridge, 2014), 1–45.

18. Polly McMichael, 'Defining Pussy Riot Musically: Performance and Authenticity in New Media', *Digital Icons: Studies in Russian, Eurasian and Central European New Media* 9 (2013), 103. See also Yngvar B. Steinholt, 'Kitten Heresy: Lost Contexts of Pussy Riot's Punk Prayer,' *Popular Music and Society* 36/1 (2013), 120–4; and Valerie Sperling, *Sex, Politics, and Putin: Political Legitimacy in Russia* (Oxford, 2015), 233–4. The original footage from the cathedral can be viewed here: 'Pussy Riot Gig at Christ the Savior Cathedral (original video)' (2 July 2012), www.youtube.com/watch?v=grEBLskpDWQ. On Pussy Riot's exploitation of new media, see Maria Chehonadskih, 'What Is Pussy Riot's "Idea"?', *Radical Philosophy* 176 (November/December 2012), 2–7.

19. Gilles Deleuze, *Negotiations*, trans. Martin Joughin (New York, 1990), 45. See also Richard Grusin, 'Radical Mediation', *Critical Inquiry* 42 (2015), 124–48.

20. See Anja Kanngieser, *Experimental Politics and the Making of Worlds* (Farnham, 2013), 48–9; see also Gerald Raunig, 'The Many Ands of Art and

Revolution', in *Art and Social Change: A Critical Reader*, ed. Will Bradley and Charles Esche (London, 2007), 384–94.

21. Slavoj Žižek, *The Ticklish Subject: The Absent Centre of Political Ontology* (London, 1999), 191.
22. Andrew Heywood, *Politics*, 4th edn. (Basingstoke, 2013), 4.
23. Aristotle, *Politics*, trans. and ed. C. D. C. Reeve (Indianapolis, IN, 1998), 4, 76.
24. See Giorgio Agamben, *Homo Sacer: Sovereign Power and Bare Life* (1995), trans. Daniel Heller-Roazen (Stanford, CA, 1998), 9–10.
25. The best starting point for the study of civil society is Michael Edwards (ed.), *The Oxford Handbook of Civil Society* (Oxford, 2011).
26. Francis Fukuyama, 'The Worldwide Liberal Revolution', in *The End of History and the Last Man* (New York, 1992), 44–5. For an introduction to liberalism, see John Gray, *Liberalism*, 2nd edn. (Buckingham, 1995); Paul Kelly, *Liberalism* (Cambridge, 2005); and Norberto Bobbio, *Liberalism and Democracy*, trans. Martin Ryle and Kate Soper (London, 2005). On neoliberalism, see Nick Couldry, *Why Voice Matters: Culture and Politics after Neoliberalism* (London, 2010); Stuart Hall, 'The Neo-Liberal Revolution', *Cultural Studies* 25/6 (2011), 705–28; and Jeremy Gilbert, 'What Kind of Thing Is "Neo-Liberalism"?', *New Formations* 80 and 81 (2013), 7–22.
27. See David Moxon, 'Consumer Culture and the 2011 "Riots"', *Sociological Research Online* 16/4 (2011), www.socresonline.org.uk/16/4/19.html.
28. Mark Lilla, 'The Truth about Our Libertarian Age', *New Republic* (18 June 2014), https://newrepublic.com/article/118043/our-libertarian-age-dogma-democracy-dogma-decline.
29. Jacques Rancière, *Disagreement: Politics and Philosophy* (1995), trans. Julie Rose (Minneapolis, MN, 1999), 135.
30. Simon Critchley, *Infinitely Demanding: Ethics of Commitment, Politics of Resistance* (London, 2012), 111–14, 13.
31. Rancière, *Disagreement*, 29, 30; see also Rancière, *Dissensus: On Politics and Aesthetics*, ed. and trans. Steve Corcoran (London, 2010), 36–7, 205–7.
32. The relationship between Rancière and this tradition is probed in Samuel A. Chambers, 'Jacques Rancière and the Problem of Pure Politics', *European Journal of Political Theory* 10/3 (2011), 303–26. A broader survey of the use of this opposition is given in Oliver Marchant, *Post-Foundational Political Thought: Political Difference in Nancy, Lefort, Badiou and Laclau* (Edinburgh, 2007), 35–60.
33. Carl Schmitt, *The Concept of the Political* (1932), 2nd edn., trans. and ed. George Schwab (Chicago, IL, and London, 2007), 26–7, 29.
34. Chantal Mouffe, *The Democratic Paradox* (London, 2000), 101. See also Mouffe, *The Return of the Political* (London, 1993), 3; and Mouffe, *On the Political* (London, 2005), 9–16.
35. For a survey of different conceptions of biopolitics, see Thomas Lemke, *Biopolitics: An Advanced Introduction*, trans. Eric Frederick Trump (New York, 2011);

see also Sarah C. E. Riley, Christine Griffin and Yvette Morey, 'The Case for "Everyday Politics"; Evaluating Neo-Tribal Theory as a Way to Understand Alternative Forms of Political Participation, Using Electronic Dance Music Culture as an Example', *Sociology* 44/2 (2010), 345–63.

36. One indicator of this proliferation of concepts is the numerous attempts to update Raymond Williams's classic *Keywords: A Vocabulary of Culture and Society* (London, 1976), the most recent of which is Kelly Fritsch, Clare O'Connor and A. K. Thompson (eds.), *Keywords for Radicals: The Contested Vocabulary of Late-Capitalist Struggle* (Chico, CA, 2016).

37. Fredric Jameson, 'Interview with Leonard Green, Jonathan Culler, and Richard Klein', in *Jameson on Jameson: Conversations on Cultural Marxism*, ed. Ian Buchanan (Durham, NC, 2007), 16.

38. Fredric Jameson, *Valences of the Dialectic* (London, 2009), 350.

39. John Hoffman, *A Glossary of Political Theory* (Edinburgh, 2007), 119–20. For Reinhart Koselleck, the temporal character of political concepts is a fundamental characteristic of modernity ('The Temporalisation of Concepts', *Finnish Year-book of Political Thought* 1 (1997), 16–24). See also Kari Palonen, *The Struggle with Time: A Conceptual History of 'Politics' as an Activity* (Berlin, 2014), 17–19.

40. Alain Badiou, *Metapolitics*, trans. Jason Barker (London, 2005), 24.

41. Gary Tomlinson, *The Singing of the New World: Indigenous Voice in the Era of European Contact* (Cambridge, 2009), 37; Ana María Ochoa, 'On the Zoopolitics of the Voice and the Distinction between Nature and Culture', in *The Routledge Companion to Art and Politics*, ed. Randy Martin (Abingdon, 2015), 20.

42. Martin Luther King's 'I Have a Dream' speech (18 August 1963) can be heard here: https://archive.org/details/MLKDream.

43. Hanan Sabea, '"I Dreamed of Being a People": Egypt's Revolution, the People and Critical Imagination', in *The Political Aesthetics of Global Protest: The Arab Spring and Beyond*, ed. Pnina Werbner, Martin Webb and Kathryn Spellman-Poots (Edinburgh, 2014), 75. See also Charles Tripp, *The Power and the People: Paths of Resistance in the Middle East* (Cambridge, 2013), 9.

44. For a broad exploration of music's capacity to occupy and reconfigure space, see Georgina Born, 'Introduction – Music, Sound and Space: Transformations of Public and Private Experience', in *Music, Sound and Space: Transformations of Public and Private Experience*, ed. Born (Cambridge, 2013), 1–69.

45. Nathan Jurgenson, 'Occupy Audio: The Soundscape of the Protest', *The Atlantic* (28 November 2011), www.theatlantic.com/technology/archive/2011/11/occupy-audio-the-soundscape-of-the-protests/249123/.

46. Rossana Reguillo, 'Human Mic: Technologies for Democracy', *NACLA* (autumn 2012), https://nacla.org/article/human-mic-technologies-democracy.

47. James Deaville, 'The Envoicing of Protest: Occupying Television News through Sound and Music', *Journal of Sonic Studies* 3 (2012), http://journal.sonicstudies.org/vol03/nr01/a05.

48. Alain Badiou, *Peut-on penser la politique?* (Paris, 1985), 96, as quoted in Alberto Toscano, 'Politics in Pre-Political Times', *Politics and Culture* (1 September 2014), https://politicsandculture.org/2014/09/01/politics-in-pre-political-times-by-alberto-toscano/.

49. See John J. McGavin, 'Robert III's "Rough Music": Charivari and Diplomacy in a Medieval Scottish Court', *Scottish Historical Review* 74/2 (1995), 144–58; E. P. Thompson, 'Rough Music Reconsidered', *Folklore* 103/1 (1992), 3–26; and Emma Dillon, *The Sense of Sound: Musical Meaning in France, 1260–1330* (New York, 2012), 92–128.

50. See Pauline Greenhill, *Make the Night Hideous: Four English-Canadian Charivaris, 1881–1940* (Toronto, 2010); and Mark McKnight, 'Charivaris, Cowbellions, and Sheet Iron Bands: Nineteenth-Century Rough Music in New Orleans', *American Music* 23/4 (2005), 407–25.

51. Beverly Bell, *Walking on Fire: Haitian Women's Stories of Survival and Resistance* (Ithaca, NY, 2001), xiii, 97; and Isabeau Doucet, 'With Pots and Pans, IDPs Protest Expulsions' (15 October 2010), http://isabeaudoucet.org/2010/10/15/with-pots-and-pans-idps-protest-expulsions/.

52. Gage Averill, *A Day for the Hunter, A Day for the Prey: Popular Music and Power in Haiti* (Chicago, IL, 1997), 14.

53. Jacques Rancière, 'The Paradoxes of Political Art', in Rancière, *Dissensus*, 135–6. Rancière refers to Rousseau's *Lettre à M. D'Alembert sur les spectacles* (1758) (for an English translation, see Jean-Jacques Rousseau, *Politics and the Arts: Letter to M. D'Alembert on the Theatre*, ed. and trans. Allan Bloom (Ithaca, NY, 1968)).

54. See, for example, Anthony M. Giovacchini, 'The Negative Influence of Gangster Rap and What Can Be Done about It', *Poverty & Prejudice: Media and Race* (4 June 1999), https://web.stanford.edu/class/e297c/poverty_prejudice/mediarace/negative.htm; and Edward G. Armstrong, 'Gangsta Misogyny: A Content Analysis of the Portrayals of Violence against Women in Rap Music, 1987–1993', *Journal of Criminal Justice and Popular Culture* 8/2 (2001), 96–126. Rap's relationship to violence is placed in broader context in Jeanita W. Richardson and Kim A. Scott, 'Rap Music and Its Violent Progeny: America's Culture of Violence in Context', *Journal of Negro Education* 71/3 (2002), 175–92. For a useful overview of the debate, see Anthony F. Lemieux and Lisa LaViers, 'Effects of Violent Content in Rap Lyrics', in *Encyclopedia of Media Violence*, ed. Matthew S. Eastin (Thousand Oaks, CA, 2013), 304–8.

55. David Gauntlett, 'Ten Things Wrong with the Media "Effects" Model', in *Approaches to Audiences: A Reader*, ed. Roger Dickinson, Ramaswami Harindranath and Olga Linné (London, 1998), 120–30.

56. Peter J. Martin, 'Music, Identity, and Social Control', in *Music and Manipulation: On the Social Uses and Social Control of Music*, ed. Steven Brown and Ulrik Volgsten (New York, 2006), 59.

57. See Mahmut Kural, *Rechtsrock: Einstiegsdroge in rechtsextremes Gedankengut?* (Saarbrücken, 2007); and Romano Sposito, 'Einstiegsdroge Musik: Wie NPD & Co. versuchen Jugendliche zu ködern', in *Bundeszentrale für politische Bildung: Dossier Rechtsextremismus* (23 April 2007), www.bpb.de/politik/extremismus/rechtsextremismus/41758/.

58. Landesamt für Verfassungsschutz Sachsen, *Rechtsextremistische Musik: Lockmittel und Szenekitt* (Dresden, 2008), 10.

59. As quoted in Laura Mason, *Singing the French Revolution: Popular Culture and Politics, 1787–1799* (Ithaca, NY, 1996), 126.

60. François Marchant, *La constitution en vaudevilles, suivie des droits de l'homme, de la femme & de plusieurs autres vaudevilles constitutionnels* (Paris, 1792).

61. Herbert Schneider, 'The Sung Constitutions of 1792: An Essay on Propaganda in the Revolutionary Song', in *Music and the French Revolution*, ed. Malcolm Boyd (Cambridge, 1992), 236.

62. David Hesmondhalgh, *Why Music Matters* (Chichester, 2013), 146.

63. Mark Carroll, 'Introduction. Of Swords and Ploughshares: Perspectives in Music and Ideology', in *Music and Ideology*, ed. Carroll (Farnham, 2012), xi.

64. Marcello Sorce Keller, 'Why Is Music so Ideological, and Why Do Totalitarian States Take It so Seriously? A Personal View from History and the Social Sciences', *Journal of Musicological Research* 26 (2007), 99.

65. Crispin Sartwell, *Political Aesthetics* (Ithaca, NY, 2010), 2.

66. Louis Althusser, 'Ideology and Ideological State Apparatuses (Notes towards an Investigation)', in *Mapping Ideology*, ed. Slavoj Žižek (London, 1994), 100–40 (125–8).

67. Jameson, *Valences*, 345, 350.

68. The most important sources for this positive view are Karl Marx and Friedrich Engels, *The German Ideology*, *Collected Works*, ed. Jack Cohen et al., trans. Clemens Dutt, W. Lough and C. P. Magill, 50 vols. (London, 1976), vol. V; and Karl Marx, 'Critique of the Gotha Programme', in Marx and Engels, *Collected Works*, vol. 24. See also David Leopold, *The Young Karl Marx: German Philosophy, Modern Politics, and Human Flourishing* (Cambridge, 2007); Ian Forbes, *Marx and the New Individual* (Abingdon, 2015); Bertell Ollman, 'Marx's Vision of Communism: A Reconstruction', *Critique* 8/1 (1977), 4–41; and Bertell Ollman, 'Marx's Vision of Communism: The First Stage', www.nyu.edu/projects/ollman/docs/marxs_vision.php.

69. The impact of Saint-Simon on the musical world is explored in Ralph P. Locke, *Music, Musicians, and the Saint-Simonians* (Chicago, IL, 1986).

70. G. A. Cohen, *Karl Marx's Theory of History: A Defence*, 2nd edn. (Oxford, 2000), 335.

71. Karl Marx, 'The Eighteenth Brumaire of Louis Bonaparte', in *Selected Writings*, ed. David McLellan, 2nd edn. (Oxford, 2000), 329.

72. Karl Marx and Friedrich Engels, *The Communist Manifesto*, ed. Gareth Stedman Jones, trans. Samuel Moore (London, 2002), 243–4.

73. Alain Badiou, 'The Idea of Communism', in *The Idea of Communism*, ed. Costas Douzinas and Slavoj Žižek (London, 2010), 1–14.

74. Félix Guattari, *Chaosmosis: An Ethico-Aesthetic Paradigm*, trans. Paul Bains and Julian Pefanis (Bloomington, IN, 1995), 9.

75. Plato, *Laws*, trans. Trevor J. Saunders, in *Complete Works*, ed. John M. Cooper (Indianapolis, IN, 1997), 1460. For a detailed commentary on this passage, see Francesco Pelosi, *Plato on Music, Soul and Body*, trans. Sophie Henderson (Cambridge, 2010), 15–17.

76. For a critique of 'effect' theories of music, see Steven Brown, 'Introduction: "How Does Music Work?" Toward a Pragmatics of Musical Communication', in Brown and Volgsten (ed.), *Music and Manipulation*, 18–19.

77. Friedrich Nietzsche, *On the Birth of Tragedy and Other Writings*, ed. Raymond Geuss and Ronald Speirs, trans. Ronald Speirs (Cambridge, 1999), 17.

78. Friedrich Schiller, 'On the Pathetic' (1792), in *Essays*, ed. Walter Hinderer and Daniel O. Dahlstrom (New York, 1993), 49

79. Nietzsche, *Birth of Tragedy*, 18. In his later writings, particularly the anti-Wagnerian texts from his final active years, Nietzsche was to decry music's sensual power in terms very similar to Schiller's.

80. Judith O. Becker, *Deep Listeners: Music, Emotion, and Trancing* (Bloomington, IN, 2004), 43. See also Gilbert Rouget, *Music and Trance: A Theory of the Relations between Music and Possession*, trans. Brunhilde Biebuyck (Chicago, IL, 1980), xviii.

81. Sarah Thornton, *Club Cultures: Music, Media and Subcultural Capital* (Cambridge, 1995), 97.

82. Jeremy Gilbert and Ewan Pearson, *Discographies: Dance Music, Culture and the Politics of Sound* (London, 2002), 183.

83. Steve Goodman, *Sonic Warfare: Sound, Affect, and the Ecology of Fear* (Cambridge, MA, 2010), 67.

84. Examples of this model include Patricia T. Clough, 'The Affective Turn: Political Economy, Biomedia, and Bodies', in *The Affect Theory Reader*, ed. Melissa Gregg and Gregory J. Seigworth (Durham, NC, 2010), 206–25; and, in relation to music, Srđan Atanasovski, 'Consequences of the Affective Turn: Exploring Music Practices from Without and Within', *Muzikologija* 18 (2015), 57–75. For a critique of the scientific premises underpinning this model, see Ruth Leys, 'The Turn to Affect: A Critique', *Critical Inquiry* 37 (2011), 434–72.

85. Brian Massumi, *Politics of Affect* (Cambridge, 2015), ix. Similarly, Gilles Deleuze and Félix Guattari characterize affects as 'becomings' (*A Thousand Plateaus: Capitalism and Schizophrenia*, trans. Brian Massumi, Minneapolis, MN, 1987, 256).

86. Jeremy Gilbert, 'What Does Democracy Feel Like? Form, Function, Affect, and the Materiality of the Sign', in *Discourse Theory and Critical Media Politics*, ed. Lincoln Dahlberg and Sean Phelan (Basingstoke, 2011), 92, 91. See also

Margaret Wetherell, 'Affect and Discourse – What's the Problem? From Affect as Excess to Affective/Discursive Practice', *Subjectivity* 6/4 (2013), 349–68.

87. Luiz Pessoa, 'On the Relationship between Emotion and Cognition', *Nature Reviews Neuroscience* 9 (2008), 148–58 (148).

88. Benedict de Spinoza, *A Spinoza Reader: The Ethics and Other Works*, ed. and trans. Edwin Curley (Princeton, NJ, 1994), 154–5.

89. Britta Timm Knudsen and Carsten Stage, 'Introduction', in *Global Media, Biopolitics and Affect: Politicizing Bodily Vulnerability* (New York, 2015), 20.

90. On which see Inder S. Marwah, 'A Dangerous Turn: Manipulation and the Politics of Ethos', *Constellations* (2015), https://doi.org/10.1111/1467-8675.12176.

91. 'Bernie Sanders Campaign Political Ad – America', www.youtube.com/watch?v=LIZW5trdE5o.

92. Alexander Zaitchik, 'A Hippy Song for a Political Ad? Only Sanders Can Pull That Off', *The Guardian* (27 January 2016), www.theguardian.com/commentis free/2016/jan/27/bernie-sanders-political-ad-america-simon-garfunkel-hippy-song-alexander-zaitchik; Benedict Pringle, 'Commentary on Political Advertising: from Amnesty to Zanu-Pf' (17 February 2016), https://politicaladvertising .co.uk/.

93. Alvin Chang, 'Democrats and Republicans Both Loved This Bernie Sanders Ad', *Vox: Policy and Politics* (14 March 2016), www.vox.com/policy-and-politics/2016/3/14/11219138/.

94. 'I like Ike' is discussed in Benjamin S. Schoening and Eric T. Kasper, *Don't Stop Thinking about the Music: The Politics of Songs and Musicians in Presidential Campaigns* (Lanham, MD, 2012), 124–6.

95. Music package 'Political Attack! Background Music for Negative Campaign Ads', Music Cult: World Class Music for TV and Film, www.musiccult.com/mcc/archive/Dangerous/Dark-Music/Political-Attack-Background-Music-for-Negative-Campaign-Ad/499914.

96. 'Attack Ads and Transitions', Firstcom Music: Creative Solutions, www.firstcom.com/#!/themed-playlists.aspx?playlistId=521.

97. See Ron Rodman, 'Music in Political Ads', *OUPblog* (20 November 2012), http://blog.oup.com/2012/11/music-in-political-ads/.

98. Marco Rubio channel, 'Morning Again', www.youtube.com/watch?v=Lp80DfHgJ8k. On the original Reagan ad, see Paul Christiansen, '"It's Morning Again in America": How the Tuesday Team Revolutionized the Use of Music in Political Ads', *Music & Politics* 10/1 (2016), http://dx.doi.org/10.3998/mp.9460447.0010.105.

99. AmericanCrossroads channel, 'Cool', www.youtube.com/watch?v=lhXGkeMdOJs.

100. Quoted in Joanna Love, 'Branding a Cool Celebrity President: Popular Music, Political Advertising, and the 2012 Election', *Music & Politics* 9/2 (2015),

http://dx.doi.org/10.3998/mp.9460447.0009.203. For a broader survey of the music of the 2012 US election, see Dana Gorzelany-Mostak and James Deaville, 'On the Campaign Trail(er): Deconstructing the Soundscape of the 2012 U.S. Presidential Election', *Music & Politics* 9/2 (2015), http://dx.doi.org/10.3998/mp.9460447.0009.201. See also Ted Brader, 'Striking a Responsive Chord: How Political Ads Motivate and Persuade Voters by Appealing to Emotions', *American Journal of Political Science* 49/2 (2005), 388–405.

101. The connotations of these samples are explored in Love, 'Branding a Cool Celebrity', 12–13.

102. Tim Hanrahan, 'Top Web Ads: "Cool", "One Chance" Climb Up Charts', *Wall Street Journal* (30/4/2012), https://blogs.wsj.com/washwire/2012/04/30/top-web-ads-cool-one-chance-climb-up-charts/.

103. See Raffaele Marchetti, 'Introduction: Political Agency in the Age of Globalization', in *Contemporary Political Agency: Theory and Practice*, ed. Bice Maiguashca and Raffaele Marchetti (Abingdon, 2013), 1–13 (4).

104. Barry Shank, 'The Political Agency of Musical Beauty', *American Quarterly* 63/3 (2011), 833.

105. See Esteban Buch, *Beethoven's Ninth: A Political History*, trans. Richard Miller (Chicago, IL, 2003), 220–67.

106. Jane Bennett, *Vibrant Matter: A Political Ecology of Things* (Durham, NC, 2010), xvi, viii.

107. Ibid., xvi.

108. Ibid., 32. Bennett refers to Jacques Derrida, 'Marx & Sons', in Jacques Derrida et al., *Ghostly Demarcations: A Symposium on Jacques Derrida's Specters of Marx*, ed. Michael Sprinker (London, 1999), 248–9.

109. Theodor W. Adorno, *Aesthetic Theory*, ed. Gretel Adorno and Rolf Tiedemann, trans. Robert Hullot-Kentor (London, 1997), 82, 311. See James Gordon Finlayson, 'The Artwork and the *Promesse du Bonheur* in Adorno', *European Journal of Philosophy* 23/3 (2015), 392–419.

110. Shank, 'Political Agency', 835.

111. Ibid., 838.

112. Bennett, *Vibrant Matter*, 12.

113. James Garratt, *Music, Culture and Social Reform in the Age of Wagner* (Cambridge, 2010), 144.

114. John Platoff, 'John Lennon, "Revolution," and the Politics of Musical Reception', *Journal of Musicology* 22/2 (2005), 241–67. On the distinction between interventive politics and politics as culture, see Reiichi Miura, 'What Kind of Revolution Do You Want? Punk, the Contemporary Left, and Singularity', *Mediations* 25/1 (2010), 61–80 (63).

115. Marie Thompson and Ian Biddle, 'Introduction: Somewhere between the Signifying and the Sublime', in *Sound, Music, Affect: Theorizing Sonic Experience*, ed. Thompson and Biddle (London, 2013), 1–24 (2–4).

116. Timothy Morton, *Realist Magic: Objects, Ontology, Causality* (Ann Arbor, MI, 2013), 69.
117. Chang, 'Democrats and Republicans'.
118. Mieke Bal and Miguel Á. Hernández-Navarro, 'Introduction', in *Art and Visibility in Migratory Culture: Conflict, Resistance, and Agency*, ed. Bal and Hernández-Navarro (Amsterdam, 2011), 9–20 (14).
119. I've borrowed the term 'exemplary causality' from theology, where it is used to convey the idea that the essence of the divine is reflected in creation (see Vivian Boland, *Ideas in God According to Saint Thomas Aquinas: Sources and Synthesis* (Leiden, 1996), 326).
120. Jacques Rancière, *Aesthetics and Its Discontents*, trans. Steve Corcoran (Cambridge, 2009), 25.
121. Rancière, 'Paradoxes of Political Art', 140.
122. Ibid., 151.
123. Ibid., 142.
124. Jacques Rancière, *The Politics of Aesthetics: The Distribution of the Sensible*, trans. Gabriel Rockhill (London, 2004), 63.
125. Gerald Raunig, 'Singers, Cynics, Molecular Mice: The Political Aesthetics of Contemporary Activism', *Theory, Culture & Society* 31/7–8 (2014), 69.
126. Rancière, 'Paradoxes of Political Art', 134, 149, 139.
127. Ibid., 148.
128. Lawrence Grossberg, *Cultural Studies in the Future Tense* (Durham, NC, 2010), 189, 191.
129. William E. Connolly, *A World of Becoming* (Durham, NC, 2011), 171.
130. Ibid., 173.
131. Rancière, *Politics of Aesthetics*, 19.
132. See, for example, Erica Fox Brindley, *Music, Cosmology, and the Politics of Harmony in Early China* (Albany, NY, 2012)
133. On musical metaphors in politics and political theory, see Nancy S. Love, *Musical Democracy* (Albany, NY, 2006).
134. Slavoj Žižek, *The Ticklish Subject: The Absent Centre of Political Ontology* (London, 1999), 101–2.
135. Paul Bekker, *The Story of the Orchestra* (New York, 1936), 117, as quoted in Love, *Musical Democracy*, 56.
136. Rachel Beckles Wilson, 'Whose Utopia? Perspectives on the West-Eastern Divan Orchestra', *Music and Politics* 3/2 (2009), http://dx.doi.org/10.3998/mp.9460447.0003.201.
137. For a nuanced discussion of this issue, see Currie, *Politics of Negation*, 139–77.
138. Hans Georg Nägeli, *Die Pestalozzische Gesangbildungslehre* (Zurich, [1810]), 53–4, as quoted in Garratt, *Music, Culture and Social Reform*, 41.
139. Claude Lévi-Strauss, *The Naked Man*, vol. 4 of *Mythologiques*, trans. John Weightman and Doreen Weightman (New York, 1981), 659, as quoted in Tia De Nora, 'Practical Consciousness and Social Relation in *MusEcological*

Perspective', in *Music and Consciousness: Philosophical, Psychological, and Cultural Perspectives*, ed. David Clarke and Eric Clarke (Oxford, 2011), 317.

140. Theodor W. Adorno, 'Some Ideas on the Sociology of Music', in *Sound Figures*, trans. Rodney Livingstone (Stanford, CA, 1999), 3.

141. Immanuel Kant, *Kritik der Urteilskraft, Schriften zur Ästhetik und Naturphilosophie*, ed. Manfred Frank and Véronique Zanetti (Frankfurt am Main, 1996), sections 15, 43, and 54 (all translations based on Immanuel Kant, *Critique of Judgment*, trans. Werner S. Pluhar [ndianapolis, IN, 1987]). See Garratt, *Music, Culture and Social Reform*, 10–26.

142. Kant, *Critique of Judgment*, 328; Friedrich von Schiller, 'Briefe an den Herzog Friedrich Christian von Augustenberg', in *Werke und Briefe*, ed. Otto Dann et al., 12 vols. (Frankfurt am Main, 1988–2002), vol. III, 498.

143. Hans Georg Nägeli, 'Versuch einer Norm für die Recensenten der musikalischen Zeitung', *Allgemeine musikalische Zeitung* 5 (1802–3), 225–37, 265–74 (267–8, 273),

144. See Richard T. Gray, *Stations of the Divided Subject: Contestation and Ideological Legitimation in German Bourgeois Literature, 1770–1914* (Stanford, CA, 1995), 157.

145. Carl Dahlhaus, 'Thesen über engagierte Musik', in *Musik zwischen Engagement und Kunst*, ed. Otto Kolleritsch (Graz, 1972), 7–19.

146. As quoted in Richard Taruskin, 'Of Kings and Divas', in *The Danger of Music and Other Anti-Utopian Essays* (Berkeley, CA, 2009), 217.

147. Mieke Bal, *Of What One Cannot Speak: Doris Salcedo's Political Art* (Chicago, IL, 2010), 2.

148. Lydia Goehr, *The Quest for Voice: On Music, Politics, and the Limits of Philosophy* (Oxford, 1998), 15.

149. Ibid., 13.

150. Ibid.; Lydia Goehr, 'Political Music and the Politics of Music', *Journal of Aesthetics and Art Criticism* 52/1 (1994), 106.

151. Alain Badiou, 'Does the Notion of Activist Art Still Have a Meaning?', lecture of 13 October 2010 transcribed by Richard James Jermain, www.lacan.com/thesymptom/?page_id=1580. Further criticisms of Rancière's conception of autonomy are presented in Ruben Yepes, 'Aesthetics, Politics, and Art's Autonomy: A Critical Reading of Jacques Rancière', *Evental Aesthetics* 3/1 (2014), 40–64.

152. Georgina Born, 'Music and the Materialization of Identities', *Journal of Material Culture* 16/4 (2011), 381.

153. Jean Baudrillard, *The Transparency of Evil: Essays on Extreme Phenomena*, trans. James Benedict (London, 1993), 9.

154. Sartwell, *Political Aesthetics*, 63.

155. Chantal Mouffe, '"Every Form of Art Has a Political Dimension": Chantal Mouffe, Interviewed by Rosalyn Deutsche, Branden W. Joseph, and Thomas Keenan', *Grey Room* 2 (2001), 99–125 (100).

2 Power and Counterpower

1. Bruno Latour, 'The Powers of Association', in *Power, Action and Belief: A New Sociology of Knowledge?*, ed. John Law (London, 1986), 264–80 (266), as quoted in Steven Lukes, *Power: A Radical View*, 2nd edn. (Basingstoke, 2005), 64.

2. Lukes, *Power*, 14–29; and John Gaventa, 'Finding the Spaces for Change: A Power Analysis', *Institute of Development Studies Bulletin* 27/6 (2006), 23–33.

3. See Leo Benedictus, 'Backing Bands: Which Musicians Endorse Which US Presidential Candidates?', *The Guardian* (1 February 2016), www.theguardian.com/us-news/2016/feb/01/backing-bands-which-musicians-endorse-which-us-presidential-candidates. The literature on music and power is extensive: see in particular the collections *Music, Power, and Politics*, ed. Annie J. Randall (New York, 2005); and *Music and the Play of Power in the Middle East, North Africa and Central Asia*, ed. Laudan Nooshin (Farnham, 2009).

4. Maro Pantazidou, 'What Next for Power Analysis? A Review of Recent Experience with the Powercube and Related Frameworks', Institute of Development Studies Working Paper 400 (London, 2012), 12.

5. On which see Ali Parchami, *Hegemonic Peace and Empire: The Pax Romana, Britannica, and Americana* (Abingdon, 2009); Paul Kennedy, *The Rise and Fall of the Great Powers: Economic Change and Military Conflict from 1500 to 2000* (London, 1987).

6. Terry Eagleton, *Ideology: An Introduction* (London, 1991), 115–16; Michèle Barrett, *The Politics of Truth: From Marx to Foucault* (Stanford, CA, 1991), 54.

7. Antonio Gramsci, 'Selections from the Prison Notebooks', in *The Gramsci Reader: Selected Writings 1916–1935*, ed. David Forgacs (New York, 2000), 306–7.

8. Ibid., 235.

9. Ibid., 210, 261.

10. Ibid., 348. Gramsci's conception of cultural hegemony is explored in greater detail in Chantal Mouffe, 'Hegemony and Ideology in Gramsci', in *Gramsci and Marxist Theory*, ed. Mouffe (London, 1979), 168–203.

11. Laclau and Mouffe, *Hegemony*, xviii.

12. Richard J. F. Day, *Gramsci Is Dead: Anarchist Currents in the Newest Social Movements* (London, 2005), 8.

13. Scott Lash, 'Power after Hegemony: Cultural Studies in Mutation?', *Theory, Culture & Society* 24/3 (2007), 55–78; see also Yannis Stavrakakis, 'Discourse Theory, Post-Hegemonic Critique and Chantal Mouffe's Politics of the Passions', *Parallax* 20/2 (2014), 118–35.

14. Joseph Nye Jr, 'Soft Power', *Foreign Policy* 80 (1990), 161.

15. Nudge theory entered the political theory lexicon in 2008. It contends that gentle hints and incentives work more successfully in influencing human behaviours than direct instruction or coercion (see Richard H. Thaler and

Cass R. Sunstein, *Nudge: Improving Decisions about Health, Wealth and Happiness* (New Haven, CT), 2008).

16. Hannah Arendt, *Crises of the Republic* (New York, 1972), 142.

17. Carl von Clausewitz, *Vom Kriege*, 5th edn. (Berlin, 1905), 19; Remi Peeters, 'Against Violence, but Not at Any Price: Hannah Arendt's Concept of Power', *Ethical Perspectives: Journal of the European Ethics Network* 15/2 (2008), 169–92.

18. Žižek, *Ticklish Subject*, 191; see also Žižek, *Living in the End Times* (London, 2011), 387–9.

19. Slavoj Žižek, *Violence: Six Sideways Reflections* (New York, 2008), 9. For a more expansive discussion of this text, see Susan Fast and Kip Pegley, 'Introduction', in *Music, Politics, and Violence*, ed. Fast and Pegley (Middletown, CT, 2012), 1–33 (esp. 4–12).

20. Žižek's argument expands on the use of this opposition in Étienne Balibar, 'Violence, Ideality and Cruelty', in *Politics and the Other Scene*, trans. Christine Jones, James Swenson and Chris Turner (London, 2002), 143.

21. Žižek, *Violence*, 12, 14.

22. Slavoj Žižek, *The Sublime Object of Ideology* (London, 1989), 4; Mirjana Kiš, 'Euphemisms and Military Technology' *Hieronymous* 1 (2014), 123–37.

23. See John T. Hamilton, 'Torture as an Instrument of Music', in *Thresholds of Listening: Sound, Technics, Space*, ed. Sander van Maas (New York, 2015), 143–52; and Bruce W. Holsinger, *Music, Body, and Desire in Medieval Culture* (Stanford, CA, 2001), 53–60.

24. Juliette Volcler, *Extremely Loud: Sound as a Weapon*, trans. Carol Volk (New York, 2013), 91.

25. Jacques Attali, *Noise: The Political Economy of Music*, trans. Brian Massumi (Minneapolis, MN, 1965), 24.

26. Anon., 'The Rock 'n' Roll Assault on Noriega. U.S. SOUTHCOM Public Affairs after Action Report Supplement, "Operation Just Cause" Dec. 20, 1989–Jan. 31, 1990', *National Security Archive* (6 February 1996), facsimile pp. 4–6, http://nsarchive.gwu.edu/nsa/DOCUMENT/950206.htm.

27. J. Martin Daughtry, *Listening to War: Sound, Music, Trauma, and Survival in Wartime Iraq* (Oxford, 2015), 240.

28. Suzanne G. Cusick, 'Music as Torture/Music as Weapon', *Trans: Revista transcultural de música* 10 (December 2006), www.redalyc.org/articulo.oa?id=82201011; see also J. Martin Daughtry, 'Aural Armor: Charting the Militarization of the iPod in Operation Iraqi Freedom', in *The Oxford Handbook of Mobile Music Studies*, ed. Sumanth Gopinath and Jason Stanyek, vol. I (Oxford, 2014), 221–58.

29. Morag J. Grant, 'Pathways to Music Torture', *Transpositions: Musiques et sciences sociales* 4 (2014), 4–5.

30. Bruce Johnson and Martin Cloonan, *Dark Side of the Tune: Popular Music and Violence* (Farnham, 2009), 152.

31. Cusik, 'Music as Torture'; see also Suzanne G. Cusick, 'Musicology, Torture, Repair', *Radical Musicology* 3 (2008), www.radical-musicology.org.uk/2008/Cusick.htm; and Suzanne G. Cusick, 'Towards an Acoustemology of Detention in the "Global War on Terror"', in Born (ed.), *Music, Sound and Space*, 275–91.

32. Johnson and Cloonan, *Dark Side*, 154–5. See also Morag J. Grant, 'The Illogical Logic of Music Torture', *Torture* 23/2 (2013), 4–13.

33. Eberhard Schmidt, *Ein Lied – ein Atemzug. Erinnerungen und Dokumente*, ed. Manfred Machlitt (Berlin, 1987), as quoted in Guido Fackler, 'Music in Concentration Camps 1933–1945', trans. Peter Logan, *Music & Politics* 1/1 (2007), http://dx.doi.org/10.3998/mp.9460447.0001.102.

34. Jon Ronson, *The Men Who Stare at Goats* (London, 2004), 121; Ben Anderson, *Encountering Affect: Capacities, Apparatuses, Conditions* (Farnham, 2014), 62–3.

35. Anabela Duarte, 'Acousmatic and Acoustic Violence and Torture in the Estado Novo: The Notorious Revelations of the PIDE/DGS Trial in 1957', *Music & Politics* 9/1 (2015), http://dx.doi.org/10.3998/mp.9460447.0009.101.

36. Johnson and Cloonan, *Dark Side*, 24.

37. Lesley Gill, 'Torture Is US: Public Amnesia and the School of the Americas', in *Rethinking America: The Imperial Homeland in the 21st Century*, ed. Jeff Maskovsky and Ida Susser (Abingdon, 2016), 66–82 (78).

38. Bernard Zuel, 'Katy Perry, David Guetta, Dolly Parton Used to Calm APEC Protesters in the Philippines', *Sydney Morning Herald* (20 November 2015), www.smh.com.au/entertainment/music/20151120-gl3h7s.html.

39. Jessica Duchen, 'Mind the Bach: Classical Music on the Underground', *The Independent* (26 March 2008), www.independent.co.uk/arts-entertainment/music/features/mind-the-bach-classical-music-on-the-underground-800483.html; see also Lily E. Hirsch, *Music in American Crime Prevention and Punishment* (Ann Arbor, MI, 2012), 12–14; and Nicholas Cook, 'Classical Music and the Politics of Space', in Born, *Music, Sound and Space*, 224–5.

40. Johnson and Cloonan, *Dark Side*, 185.

41. Bennett Capers, 'Crime Music', *Ohio State Journal of Criminal Law* 7 (2010) 749–70 (766).

42. Stephen Halliwell, 'Plato', in *The Routledge Companion to Philosophy and Music*, ed. Theodore Gracyk and Andrew Kania (Abingdon, 2011), 307–16 (314, 315).

43. Plato, *Laws*, 1363, 1471.

44. Ibid., 1389–90.

45. Plato, *Republic*, as presented in *Greek Musical Writings*, vol. I: *The Musician and His Art*, ed. Andrew Barker (Cambridge, 1984), 139–40.

46. Plato, *Laws*, 1469–70.

47. The contemporary political theorist Peter L. P. Simpson presents a no less stringent view of music's relationship to moral virtue (*Political Illiberalism: A Defense of Freedom* [New Brunswick, NJ, 2015], 198–205).

48. For a more detailed discussion of the term, see Martin Cloonan, 'Call That Censorship? Problems of Definition', in *Policing Pop*, ed. Martin Cloonan and Reebee Garofalo (Philadelphia, 2003), 13–29. Other useful recent studies of music censorship include John Street, *Music and Politics* (Cambridge, 2012), 9–23; and Marie Korpe, Ole Reitov and Martin Cloonan, 'Musical Censorship from Plato to the Present', in Brown and Volgsten (ed.), *Music and Manipulation: On the Social Uses and Social Control of Music*, ed. Steven Brown and Ulrik Volgsten (New York, 2006), 239–63; see also the articles and reports available on the Freemuse organization website (freemuse.org).

49. Heather Stur, 'Borderless Troubadour: Bob Dylan's Influence on International Protest during the Cold War', in *Highway 61 Revisited: Bob Dylan's Road from Minnesota to the World*, ed. Colleen J. Sheehy and Thomas Swiss (Minneapolis, MN, 2009), 122–32 (125).

50. Anon., 'Protest Singer Ibrahim Kashoush Had His Throat Cut', *Freemuse* (6 July 2011), http://freemuse.org/archives/5054; Elie Chalala, 'Silencing the Singer', *Al Jadid: A Review & Record of Arab Culture and Arts* 16/63 (2011), www.aljadid.com/content/silencing-singer.

51. Manuel Roig-Franzia, 'Mexican Drug Cartels Leave a Bloody Trail on YouTube', *Washington Post* (9 April 2007), www.washingtonpost.com/wp-dyn/content/article/2007/04/08/AR2007040801005.html.

52. Anon., 'Murders of Kombo Kolombia Attributed to Los Zetas', *Borderland Beat* (9 February 2013), www.borderlandbeat.com/2013/02/murders-of-kombo-kolumbia-attributed-to.html.

53. Quoted in Sergei I. Zhuk, 'Fascist Music from the West: Anti-Rock Campaigns, Problems of National Identity, and Human Rights in the "Closed City" of Soviet Ukraine, 1975–84', in *Popular Music and Human Rights*, vol. II: *World Music*, ed. Ian Peddie (Farnham, 2011), 147–59. See also Sabrina P. Ramet, *Social Currents in Eastern Europe: The Sources and Consequences of the Great Transformation* (Durham, NC, 1995), 237–8.

54. Ali Akbar Dareini, 'Can't Stop the Music, say Young Iranians after Ban', *The Washington Post* (26 December 2005), www.washingtonpost.com/wp-dyn/content/article/2005/12/25/AR2005122500690.html.

55. Mawlavi Enayatullah Baligh, 'Letter from the Cultural and Social Affairs Department of General Presidency of Islamic State of Afghanistan', as presented in 'Humanity Denied: Systematic Denial of Women's Rights in Afghanistan', Human Rights Watch Report 13/5 (October 2001), 23–4, www.hrw.org.

56. John Baily, *War, Exile and the Music of Afghanistan: The Ethnographer's Tale* (Farnham, 2015), 105.

57. Abubakar Siddique, 'Understanding the Taliban's Campaign against Music', *Freemuse* (23 June 2009), http://freemuse.org/archives/4689.

58. John Baily, 'Music and Censorship in Afghanistan, 1973–2003', in Nooshin (ed.), *Play of Power*, 143–63 (143).

59. Carlos Chávez, 'Mexico: Two More States ban Narcocorridos' (9 March 2016), http://freemuse.org/archives/11902.

60. Giles Tremlett, 'Cuba Cracks Down on "Vulgar" Reggaeton Music', *The Guardian* (6 December 2012), www.theguardian.com/world/2012/dec/06/cuba-crackdown-vulgar-reggaeton-music.

61. Braden Goyette, '"Blurred Lines" Banned by University Student Union', *Huffpost Women* (14 September 2013), www.huffingtonpost.com/2013/09/14/blurred-lines-banned_n_3927594.html.

62. See Adam Bychawski, 'Robin Thicke's "Blurred Lines" Banned from University of Edinburgh', *NME* (12 September 2013), www.nme.com/news/robin-thicke-0/72627; and Matt Grimes, 'Censorship and University Student Unions', *Index: The Voice of Free Expression* (26 February 2014), www.indexoncensorship.org/2014/02/censorship-university-student-unions/.

63. Wendy Brown, *Regulating Aversion: Tolerance in the Age of Identity and Empire* (Princeton, NJ, 2006), 5. See also Žižek, *Violence*, 140–77.

64. Brendan O'Neill, 'Zero Tolerance for Anti-Zionists? The Right Is Now as PC as the Left', *The Spectator* (3 May 2016), http://blogs.spectator.co.uk/2016/05/zero-tolerance-for-anti-zionists-the-right-is-now-as-pc-as-the-left/. The quotation is from John Stuart Mill, *On Liberty*, 2nd edn. (Boston, 1863), 135.

65. Leon Botstein, 'German Jews and Wagner', in *Richard Wagner and His World*, ed. Thomas S. Grey (Princeton, NJ, 2009), 151–99.

66. Robert Everett-Green, 'Controversial Ukrainian-Born Pianist Dropped from TSO Concerts', *The Globe and Mail* (6 April 2015), www.theglobeandmail.com/arts/music/ukrainian-born-soloist-dropped-from-tso-for-her-political-views/article23812295/.

67. Michael Scammell, 'Censorship and Its History – A Personal View', in *Article 19 World Report 1988: Information, Freedom and Censorship*, ed. Kevin Boyle (New York, 1988), 1–19 (10).

68. As quoted in Marie Korpe (ed.), *Shoot the Singer! Music Censorship Today* (London, 2004), back cover.

69. Banning Eyre, *Playing with Fire: Fear and Self-Censorship in Zimbabwean Music* (Copenhagen, 2001). See also Diane Thram, 'ZVAKWANA! – ENOUGH! Media Control and Unofficial Censorship of Music in Zimbabwe', in *Popular Music Censorship in Africa*, ed. Michael Drewett and Martin Cloonan (Abingdon, 2006), 71–89.

70. Lingson Adam, 'Self-Censorship and Fear in the "Island Paradise"', *Freemuse* (22 January 2008), http://freemuse.org/freemuseArchives/freerip/freemuse.org/sw24251.html. See also Kelly M. Askew and John Francis Kitime, 'Popular Music Censorship in Tanzania', in Drewett and Cloonan (ed.), *Music Censorship*, 137–56.

71. Jocelyn A. Hollander and Rachel L. Einwohner, 'Conceptualizing Resistance', *Sociological Forum* 19/4 (2004), 533–54.

72. See, for example, Tim Gee, *Counterpower: Making Change Happen* (Oxford, 2011).

73. Rich Cross, '"There Is Not Authority but Yourself": The Individual and the Collective in British Anarcho-Punk', *Music & Politics* 4/2 (2010), http://dx.doi .org/10.3998/mp.9460447.0004.203. See also Brian Cogan, '"Do They Owe Us a Living? Of Course They Do!" Crass, Throbbing Gristle, and Anarchy and Radicalism in Early English Punk Rock', *Journal for the Study of Radicalism* 1/ 2 (2007), 77–90; George McKay, *Senseless Acts of Beauty: Cultures of Resistance since the Sixties* (London, 1996), 73–102; Pete Dale, *Anyone Can Do It: Empowerment, Tradition and the Punk Underground* (Abingdon, 2016), 134–40; and Mark Mattern, *Anarchism and Art: Democracy in the Cracks and on the Margins* (Albany, NY, 2016), 39–60.

74. Stephen Duncombe, 'Introduction', in *Cultural Resistance Reader*, ed. Stephen Duncombe (London, 2002), 1–15 (5).

75. See, for example, Ian Peddie, 'Introduction', in *The Resisting Muse: Popular Music and Social Protest*, ed. Peddie (Aldershot, 2006), xix.

76. Marion Leonard, *Gender in the Music Industry: Rock, Discourse and Girl Power* (Aldershot, 2007), 95; Lawrence Grossberg, 'The Media Economy of Rock Culture: Cinema, Post-Modernity and Authenticity', in *Sound and Vision: The Music Video Reader*, ed. Simon Frith, Andrew Goodwin and Lawrence Grossberg (London, 1993), 202.

77. Federico Reuben, 'Imaginary Musical Radicalism and the Entanglement of Music and Emancipatory Politics', *Contemporary Music Review* 34/2–3 (2015), 232–46.

78. T. V. Reed, *The Art of Protest: Culture and Activism from the Civil Rights Movement to the Streets of Seattle* (Minneapolis, MN, 2005), 304.

79. Bradford Martin: '"... And You Voted for That Guy": 1980s Post-Punk and Oppositional Politics', *Journal of Popular Music Studies* 16/2 (2004), 142–74 (144).

80. Joe Wood, 'Malcolm X and the New Blackness', in *Malcolm X: In Our Own Image*, ed. Wood (New York, 1992), 1–17 (14).

81. Duncombe, 'Introduction', 6–7.

82. Gerald Raunig, *Art and Revolution: Transversal Activism in the Long Twenti-eth Century*, trans. Aileen Derieg (Cambridge, MA, 2007), 50.

83. Michel Foucault, *History of Sexuality*, vol. I [*The Will to Knowledge*], trans. Robert Hurley (New York, 1978), 95.

84. Michel Foucault, 'The Ethics of the Concern of the Self as a Practice of Freedom' (1984), in *Ethics, Subjectivity and Truth: The Essential Works of Michel Foucault, 1954–1984*, vol. 1, ed. Paul Rabinow, trans. Robert Hurley et al. (London, 1997), 291–2.

85. Foucault, *History of Sexuality*, 95.

86. Michel Foucault, 'The Subject and Power', in *Power: The Essential Works of Michel Foucault 1954–1984*, ed. James D. Faubion, vol. 3 (London, 1997), 340.

87. Foucault, 'Ethics', 283, 292.

88. Foucault, *History of Sexuality*, 95.

89. Foucault, 'Sex, Power and the Politics of Identity', in *Ethics, Subjectivity and Truth*, 167.

90. Ibid.

91. John Holloway, *Change the World without Taking Power: The Meaning of Revolution Today* (London, 2002), 26.

92. Žižek, *Ticklish Subject*, 256, 252.

93. Foucault, *History of Sexuality*, 95.

94. Foucault, 'Prison Talk', in *Power/Knowledge*, 39.

95. Barrett, *Politics of Truth*, 136; see also Fabio Vighi and Heiko Feldner, *Žižek: Beyond Foucault* (Basingstoke, 2007), 97; Saul Newman, *Power and Politics in Poststructuralist Thought: New Theories of the Political* (Abingdon, 2005), 52–3.

96. Gilles Deleuze, 'Postscript on the Societies of Control', *October* 59 (1992), 3–7.

97. Lash, 'Power after Hegemony', 61.

98. Michael Hardt and Antonio Negri, *Empire* (Cambridge, MA, 2000), 24.

99. Lash, 'Power after Hegemony', 70–1; Hardt and Negri, *Empire*, 23.

100. Byung-Chul Han, *Psychopolitik: Neoliberalismus und die neuen Machttechniken* (Frankfurt am Main, 2015), 10.

101. Ibid., 25–6, 16.

102. Ibid., 19.

103. James C. Scott, *Weapons of the Weak: Everyday Forms of Peasant Resistance* (New Haven, CT, 1985), and Scott, *Domination and the Arts of Resistance: Hidden Transcripts* (New Haven, CT, 1990). See also Stellan Vinthagen and Anna Johansson, '"Everyday Resistance": Exploration of a Concept and Its Theories', *Resistance Studies Magazine* 1 (2013), 1–46.

104. Deleuze, *Negotiations*, 176.

105. As quoted in Cross, 'Individual and the Collective', 10.

106. Michael Hardt and Antonio Negri, *Commonwealth* (Cambridge, MA, 2009), 56.

107. Holloway, *Change*, 18–27; Antonio Negri, *Insurgencies: Constituent Power and the Modern State*, trans. Maurizia Boscagli (Minneapolis, MN, 1999).

108. Michael Hardt and Antonio Negri, 'Globalization and Democracy' (2001), in *Implicating Empire: Globalization and Resistance in the 21st Century World Order*, ed. Stanley Aronowitz and Heather Gautney (New York, 2003), 109–21.

109. Negri, *Insurgencies*, 10. See also Antonio Negri, 'Communism: Some Thoughts on the Concept and Practice', in Douzinas and Žižek (eds), *Idea of Communism*, 155–65.

110. Negri, *Insurgencies*, 13.

111. Michael Hardt and Antonio Negri, *Declaration* (New York, 2012), not paginated.

112. See Mark Wenman, *Agonistic Democracy: Constituent Power in the Era of Globalisation* (Cambridge, 2013), 3–27.
113. Kanngieser, *Experimental Politics*, 53.
114. Simon O'Sullivan, *Art Encounters Deleuze and Guattari: Thought beyond Representation* (Basingstoke, 2006), 80.
115. Hardt and Negri, 'Globalization and Democracy', 120.
116. Connor T. Jerzak, 'Ultras in Egypt: State, Revolution, and the Power of Public Space', *Interface: A Journal for and about Social Movements* 5/2 (2013), 240–62 (247).
117. Ibid., 245.
118. Dalia Abdelhameed Ibraheem, 'Ultras Ahlawy and the Spectacle: Subjects, Resistance and Organized Football Fandom in Egypt', Master's dissertation, American University in Cairo, 2015, 52.

3 History, Ideology and the Politics of Context

1. Fredric Jameson, *The Political Unconscious: Narrative as a Socially Symbolic Act* (London, 2002).
2. Key musicological texts on contextualism from this period include Gary Tomlinson, 'The Web of Culture: A Context for Musicology', *19th-Century Music* 7/3 (1984), 350–62; Philip V. Bohlman, 'On the Unremarkable in Music', *19th-Century Music* 16/2 (1992), 203–16; Gary Tomlinson, 'Musical Pasts and Postmodern Musicologies: A Response to Lawrence Kramer', *Current Musicology* 53 (1993), 18–24; and Lawrence Kramer, 'Music Criticism and the Postmodernist Turn: In Contrary Motion with Gary Tomlinson', *Current Musicology* 53 (1993), 25–35.
3. William H. Sewell Jr, *Logics of History: Social Theory and Social Transformation* (Chicago, IL, 2005), 10.
4. On discourse and parametric causation, see Dave Elder-Vass, 'The Causal Power of Discourse', *Journal for the Theory of Social Behaviour* 41/2 (2010), 143–60.
5. Walter Benjamin, 'Reply to Oscar A. H. Schmitz', in *Selected Writings*, ed. Howard Eiland and Michael W. Jennings, trans. Rodney Livingstone et al. (Cambridge, MA, 1996–2003), vol. II, part ii, 16–17.
6. Ernst Bloch, 'Nonsynchronism and the Obligation to Its Dialectics', *New German Critique* 11 (1977), 22–38.
7. Martin Jay, 'Historical Explanation and the Event: Reflections on the Limits of Contextualization', *New Literary History* 42/4 (2011), 560.
8. Shank, *Political Force*, 14.
9. Rita Felski, 'Context Stinks!', *New Literary History* 42/4 (2011), 577.
10. Ibid., 589.
11. Georgina Born and David Hesmondhalgh, 'Introduction: On Difference, Representation, and Appropriation in Music', in *Western Music and Its Others: Difference, Representation, and Appropriation in Music*, ed. Born and Hesmondhalgh (Berkeley, CA, 2000), 1–58 (5).

12. Marx and Engels, *German Ideology*, 53–4.

13. See, for example, Badiou, *Metapolitics*.

14. Hanns Eisler, '[Die Kunst als Lehrmeisterin im Klassenkampf]', in *Gesammelte Schriften 1921–1935*, ed. Tobias Faßhauer and Günter Mayer, *Hanns Eisler Gesamtausgabe*, ser. IX, vol. 1.1 (Wiesbaden, 2007), 124 (unless otherwise indicated, all the other Eisler essays cited are from this source).

15. Ibid., 123–4.

16. Eisler, 'Einiges über das Verhalten der Arbeiter-Sänger und -Musiker in Deutschland', 221.

17. Eisler, 'Die Erbauer einer neuen Musikkultur', 148.

18. Eisler, '[Rundfunkmusik]', 99.

19. Eisler, 'Über moderne Musik', 47.

20. Stuart Hall, 'Re-Thinking the "Base-and-Superstructure" Metaphor', in *Class, Hegemony and Party*, ed. Jon Bloomfield (London, 1977), 43. See also Jorge Larrain, 'Base and Superstructure', in *Dictionary of Marxist Thought*, 2nd edn., ed. Tom Bottomore (Oxford, 1991), 45–8.

21. This example is borrowed from Étienne Balibar's analysis of the 1859 preface (*The Philosophy of Marx*, trans. Chris Turner [London, 2014], 94).

22. Louis Althusser and Étienne Balibar, *Reading Capital*, trans. Ben Brewster (London, 1970), 140.

23. Alex Callinicos, *Making History: Agency, Structure, and Change in Social Theory*, 2nd edn. (Leiden, 2004), xxxii.

24. Jameson, *Valences*, 46–7.

25. Karl Marx, *Capital: A Critique of Political Economy*, in Marx and Engels, *Collected Writings*, vol. XXXV, 331. On 'social productive forces', see Derek Sayer, *The Violence of Abstraction: The Analytic Foundations of Historical Materialism* (Oxford, 1987), 34–9.

26. Marx and Engels, *German Ideology*, 89, 36–7.

27. Ibid., 36.

28. Ibid., 36–7.

29. Friedrich Engels, letter to Joseph Bloch of 21–22 September 1890, in *The Marx-Engels Reader*, 2nd edn., ed. Robert C. Tucker (New York, 1978), 762.

30. Jameson, *Valences*, 47.

31. Marx and Engels, *German Ideology*, 53.

32. Karl Marx, 'Economic Manuscript of 1861–63 [Theories of Surplus Value]', in Marx and Engels, *Collected Works*, vol. XXXI, 182.

33. Friedrich Engels, letter to Franz Mehring of 14 July 1893, in Marx and Engels, *Collected Works*, vol. L, 165.

34. Friedrich Engels, letter to Conrad Schmidt of 27 October 1890, Marx and Engels, *Collected Works*, vol. XLIX, 58, 61.

35. Engels, letter to Bloch, 760–1.

36. Ernest Mandel, 'How to Make No Sense of Marx', in *Analyzing Marxism: New Essays on Analytical Marxism*, ed. Robert Ware and Kai Nielsen (Calgary, 1989), 105–32.

37. Alasdair MacIntyre, 'Notes from the Moral Wilderness', *The New Reasoner* 7 (1958–9), 98; Raymond Williams, *Culture and Materialism: Selected Essays* (London, 2005), 34.

38. Max Paddison, *Adorno's Aesthetics of Music* (Cambridge, 1993), 79.

39. Eisler, 'Die Hochzeit des Figaro', 80. *Le nozze di Figaro* was actually composed and premiered in 1786, three years before the storming of the Bastille.

40. Eisler, 'Lectures', 96.

41. Eisler, 'Die Erbauer', 138–9.

42. The view of Mozart as a rococo figure had recently been popularized through Ernst Bücken, *Die Musik des Rokoko und der Klassik* (Wildpark-Potsdam, 1927).

43. Eisler, 'Die Erbauer', 136, 137, 140. A slightly abridged translation of this text can be found in Hanns Eisler, *A Rebel in Music: Selected Writings*, ed. Manfred Grabs, trans. Marjorie Meyer (London, 1999), 36–58.

44. Ibid., 142.

45. Ibid., 135.

46. Ibid., 152.

47. Ibid., 147.

48. On which see, for example, Wolfgang Martin Stroh and Günter Mayer (eds.), *Musikwissenschaftlicher Paradigmenwechsel? Zum Stellenwert marxistischer Ansätze in der Musikforschung* (Oldernburg, 1999); Anne C. Shreffler, 'Berlin Walls: Dahlhaus, Knepler, and Ideologies of Music History', *Journal of Musicology* 20/4 (2003), 498–525; and Elaine Kelly, *Composing the Canon in the German Democratic Republic: Narratives of Nineteenth-Century Music* (New York, 2014).

49. Eisler, '[Die Kunst als Lehrmeisterin]', 123.

50. Ernesto Laclau and Chantal Mouffe, 'Post-Marxism without Apologies', *New Left Review* 166 (1987), 80.

51. Jean-François Lyotard, 'Desirevolution', in *Dérive à partir de Marx et Freud* (Paris, 1973), 30–5, as quoted in Eve Tavor Bannet, *Postcultural Theory: Critical Theory after the Marxist Paradigm* (Basingstoke, 1993), 20.

52. See Stuart Sim, *Post-Marxism: An Intellectual History* (London, 2000), 65–6.

53. See Ernesto Laclau and Chantal Mouffe, *Hegemony and Socialist Strategy: Towards a Radical Democratic Politics*, 2nd edn. (London, 2014), 133–55.

54. Eric Drott, 'Rereading Jacques Attali's *Bruits*', *Critical Inquiry* 41 (2015), 721–56.

55. Attali, *Noise*, 4.

56. Friedrich Nietzsche, *Human, All Too Human: A Book for Free Spirits*, trans. R. J. Hollingdale (Cambridge, 1996), 252–4.

57. Attali, *Noise*, 43, 9, 4, 11.

58. Jameson, *Valences*, 44; Jameson, 'Foreword', in Attali, *Noise*, xi.

59. Dott, 'Attali's *Bruits*', 724.

60. Attali, *Noise*, 42.

61. Ibid., 19.

62. Ibid., 19, 20.

63. Ibid., 25.

64. Ibid., 57, 47.

65. Ibid., 134, 135.

66. Ibid., 140–1.

67. Ibid., 135 (on the context for Attali's elevation of the composer, see Drott, 'Attali's *Bruits*', 736–8).

68. Ibid., 147.

69. Michel Foucault, *The Order of Things: An Archaeology of the Human Sciences* (London, 2002), 285–6, 224.

70. Attali, *Bruits*, 45.

71. Jairo Moreno and Gavin Steingo, 'Rancière's Equal Music', *Contemporary Music Review* 31/5–6 (2012), 487–505.

72. Rancière, *Politics of Aesthetics*, 50.

73. Ibid.

74. See in particular Rancière, *Dissensus*, 207–10.

75. Gabriel Rockhill, *Radical History and the Politics of Art* (New York, 2014), 149; and Jean Philippe Deranty, 'Regimes of the Arts', in *Jacques Rancière: Key Concepts*, ed. Deranty (Durham, NC, 2010), 116–30.

76. Rancière's three regimes of art are paralleled elsewhere in his output by three regimes of politics (see Rancière, *Disagreement*, 65–93); aside from the first component of both sets, these regimes are not designed to map onto one another.

77. Rancière, *Politics of Aesthetics*, 20–1.

78. Rancière, *Dissensus*, 135–6.

79. Ibid., 136–7.

80. Ibid., 135 (see also Jacques Rancière, *The Emancipated Spectator*, trans. Gregory Elliott [London, 2011], 61–3).

81. Ibid., 144.

82. Ibid., 205.

83. Franco Berardi, *After the Future*, ed. Gary Genosko and Nicholas Thoburn, trans. Arianna Bove et al. (Oakland, CA, 2011).

84. Joseph J. Tanke, 'Why Rancière Now?', *Journal of Aesthetic Education* 44/2 (2010), 15.

85. Jacques Rancière, 'The Aesthetic Revolution and Its Outcomes', in *Dissensus*, 133.

86. Hanns Eisler, 'Labor, Labor Movement and Music: Speech to the International Ladies' Garment Workers Union', in Eisler, *Musik und Politik*, 427.

87. Adorno, *Aesthetic Theory*, 232.

88. Some of these challenges are explored in Garratt, *Music, Culture and Social Reform*.

89. Theodor W. Adorno, letter to Hans Bunge of 11 February 1964, as quoted in Günter Mayer, 'Eisler and Adorno', in *Hanns Eisler: A Miscellany*, ed. David Blake (Luxembourg, 1995), 137.

90. Hanns Eisler, '[Thesen]' (1931), *Gesammelte Schriften*, 114. For useful surveys of Eisler's attitudes toward political music, see Georg Knepler, 'Hanns Eisler the Thinker', in Blake (ed.), *Hanns Eisler*, 441–52; and Georg Knepler, 'Hanns Eisler and "Interventive Thought"', *Journal of Musicological Research* 17/3 (1998), 239–60.

91. Mayer, 'Eisler and Adorno', 142.

92. Theodor W. Adorno, 'Zur gesellschaftlichen Lage der Musik', *Zeitschrift für Sozialforschung* 1/1–2 (1932), 103–24 and 1/3 (1932), 356–78 (124).

93. Ibid.

94. Ibid.

95. Raymond Geuss, 'Art and Criticism in Adorno's Aesthetics', *European Journal of Philosophy* 6/3 (1998), 313.

96. Richard Leppert, 'Introduction', in Adorno, *Essays on Music*, 74. For extended commentaries on how these two strategies interact, see Paddison, *Adorno's Aesthetics*, 108–48; and Peter J. Martin, *Sounds and Society: Themes in the Sociology of Music* (Manchester, 1995), 98–112.

97. Adorno, 'Zur gesellschaftlichen Lage', 117.

98. Adorno, 'The Dialectical Composer', in *Essays on Music*, 207.

99. Rose Rosengard Subotnik, 'Adorno's Diagnosis of Beethoven's Late Style: Early Symptom of a Fatal Condition', *Journal of the American Musicological Society* 29/2 (1976), 271.

100. Martin, *Sounds and Society*, 112; Born, 'On Musical Mediation', 12.

101. Adorno, 'Zur gesellschaftlichen Lage', 117; Paddison, *Adorno's Aesthetics*, 108.

102. Antoine Hennion, *The Passion for Music: A Sociology of Mediation*, trans. Margaret Rigaud and Peter Collier (Farnham, 2015), 67.

103. Adorno, *Aesthetic Theory*, 242.

104. Ibid.

105. Ibid., 243.

106. Theodor W. Adorno, *Noten zur Literatur* (Frankfurt am Main, 1981), 120, as quoted in Fredric Jameson, *Late Marxism: Adorno or the Persistence of the Dialectic* (London, 2007), 188.

107. Adorno, *Aesthetic Theory*, 247 (I have borrowed the translation in Jameson, *Late Marxism*, 188).

108. Geuss, 'Art and Criticism', 314. Cf. Terry Eagleton, *The Ideology of the Aesthetic* (Oxford, 1990), 363.

109. Eisler, 'Zur Krise der bürgerlichen Musik', *Gesammelte Schriften*, 170.

110. Reinhold Brinkmann, 'Ästhetische und politische Kriterien der Kompositionskritik', *Darmstädter Beiträge zur Neuen Musik*, vol. XIII (Mainz, 1973), 28–41.

111. Bernd Sponheuer, 'Angewandte Instrumentalmusik: Hanns Eislers Kleine Sinfonie op. 29', *Die Musikforschung* 32/3 (1979), 271.

112. Hanns Eisler, 'Einges über die Lage des modernen Komponisten [I]', *Gesammelte Schriften*, 249; Hanns Eisler, 'The Crisis in Music' (1935), in *Rebel in Music*, 114.

113. Eisler, 'Einges über die Lage', 249; Günter Mayer, liner notes, *Hanns Eisler Edition* (Brilliant Classics 9430, 2014), www.brilliantclassics.com/media/594812/9430-Hanns-Eisler-Edition-Liner-Notes-download.pdf.

114. Mayer, liner notes; Albrecht Betz, *Hanns Eisler: Political Musician*, trans. Bill Hopkins (Cambridge, 1982), 128.

115. Jameson, *Late Marxism*, 230.

116. For a more detailed survey of Marx and Engels's use of the term, see Barrett, *Politics of Truth*, 3–17.

117. Marx and Engels, *German Ideology*, 36.

118. Ibid., 45 (on the connotations of Wagner's 'absolute music', see Mark Evan Bonds, *Absolute Music: The History of an Idea* (New York, 2014), esp. 129–40).

119. Raymond Williams, *Marxism and Literature* (Oxford, 1977), 66.

120. Marx and Engels, *German Ideology*, 60.

121. Marx and Engels, *Communist Manifesto*, 238–9.

122. Marx and Engels, *German Ideology*, 59.

123. Balibar, *Philosophy of Marx*, 46.

124. Étienne de la Boétie, *Discours de la servitude volontaire ou le Contr'un* (Paris, 1574).

125. Callinicos, *Making History*, 158.

126. Engels, Letter to Franz Mehring, 164.

127. Slavoj Žižek, 'How Did Marx Invent the Symptom?', in *Mapping Ideology*, 312.

128. See Christopher L. Pines, *Ideology and False Consciousness: Marx and His Historical Progenitors* (Albany, NY, 1991), 2–6.

129. Ibid., 158.

130. Theodor W. Adorno, 'Ideologie', in *Soziologische Exkurse* (Frankfurt am Main, 1974), 169, as quoted in Michael Rosen, *On Voluntary Servitude: False Consciousness and the Theory of Ideology* (Cambridge, MA, 1996), 1; Adorno, *Aesthetic Theory*, 312.

131. Adorno, 'On the Social Situation', 421.

132. Georg Lukács, *History and Class Consciousness: Studies in Marxist Dialectics*, trans. Rodney Livingstone (London, 1971), 54.

133. Ibid., 83, 86.

134. Ibid., 86–7, 99–100.

135. An important essay by Fromm appeared in the same issue of the *Zeitschrift für Sozialforschung* as Adorno's 'Social Situation' article (Erich Fromm, 'Über Methode und Aufgabe einer analytischen Sozialpsychologie', *Zeitschrift für Sozialforschung* 1/1–2 (1932), 28–54).

136. Adorno, 'On Popular Music', in *Essays on Music*, 468.

137. Adorno, *Aesthetic Theory*, 227.

138. Ibid., 160. See also Herbert Marcuse, 'The Affirmative Character of Culture' (1937), trans. Jeremy J. Shapiro, in *Collected Papers of Herbert Marcuse*, vol. IV: *Art and Liberation*, ed. Douglas Kellner (London, 2007), 82–112.

139. Andrew Bowie, *From Romanticism to Critical Theory: The Philosophy of German Literary Theory* (London, 1997), 271.

140. Adorno, 'Some Ideas', 12; Adorno, *Aesthetic Theory*, 192.

141. Theodor W. Adorno, *Einleitung in die Musiksoziologie: Zwölf theoretische Vorlesungen* (Frankfurt am Main, 1975), 72, 70.

142. Theodor W. Adorno, *Negative Dialectics*, trans. Dennis Redmond (2001), 93, http://monkeybear.info/ND_Full.pdf.

143. Herbert Marcuse, *One-Dimensional Man: Studies in the Ideology of Advanced Industrial Society* (London, 2002), 14.

144. Ibid., 13.

145. Theodor Adorno and Max Horkheimer, 'Ideologie' (1956), in Adorno, *Gesammelte Schriften* (Frankfurt am Main, 1973–86), vol. VIII, 18, as quoted in Jan Rehmann, *Theories of Ideology: The Powers of Alienation and Subjection* (Leiden, 2013), 94.

146. Theodor W. Adorno, *Prisms*, trans. Samuel Weber and Shierry Weber (Cambridge, MA, 1981), 34.

147. Adorno, *Aesthetic Theory*, 255.

148. Louis Althusser, 'Ideology and Ideological State Apparatuses (Notes towards an Investigation)', in *Mapping Ideology*, ed. Slavoj Žižek (London, 1994), 100–40 (123).

149. Louis Althusser, *For Marx*, trans. Ben Brewster (London, 2005), 231; Althusser, 'Ideology', 123.

150. Althusser, 'Ideology', 127.

151. Ibid.

152. Althusser, *For Marx*, 233.

153. Althusser, 'Ideology', 135–6.

154. Ibid., 104.

155. Ibid., 112.

156. Ibid., 118.

157. Stuart Hall, 'Signification, Representation, Ideology: Althusser and the Post-Structuralist Debates', *Critical Studies in Mass Communication* 2/2 (1985), 100–1.

158. Althusser, 'Ideology', 119.

159. Louis Althusser, 'Cremonini, Painter of the Abstract' (1966), in *Lenin and Philosophy and Other Essays*, trans. Ben Brewster (New York, 1971), 241, 242.

160. Louis Althusser, 'A Letter on Art in Reply to André Daspre', in *Lenin*, 223.

161. Althusser, 'Cremoni', 241–2. Alternatively, Althusser could be arguing that art performs ideology in a way that stages its own alienation effect, enabling the consumer to be exposed to the ideological effects while also perceiving them as ideology. For a range of other interpretive possibilities, see Thomas Albrecht, 'Donner à voir l'idéologie: Althusser and Aesthetic Ideology', *Bulletin de la Société Américaine de Philosophie de Langue Français* 14/2 (2004), 1–28.

162. Key musicological examples include Rose Rosengard Subotnik, 'The Role of Ideology in the Study of Western Music', *Journal of Musicology* 2 (1983), 1–12, repr. in Subotnik, *Developing Variations: Style and Ideology in Western Music* (Minneapolis, MN, 1991), 3–14.

163. Eve Kosofsky Sedgwick, *Touching Feeling: Affect, Pedagogy, Performativity* (Durham, NC, 2003), 123–51.

164. Rancière, *Emancipated Spectator*, 25.

165. Jameson, *Political Unconscious*, 277.

166. Walter Benjamin, letter to Theodor W. and Gretel Adorno, 19 June 1938, as presented in Theodor Adorno and Walter Benjamin, *The Complete Correspondence 1928–1940*, ed. Henri Lonitz, trans. Nicholas Walker (Cambridge, MA, 1999), 259. For a recent survey of Adorno's text, see Mark Berry, 'Adorno's *Essay on Wagner*: Rescuing an Inverted Panegyric', *The Opera Quarterly* 30/2–3 (2014), 205–227.

167. James Currie, 'Music after All', *Journal of the American Musicological Society* 62/1 (2009), esp. 155–71.

168. Slavoj Žižek, 'Afterword: Wagner, Anti-Semitism and "German Ideology"', in Alain Badiou, *Five Lessons on Wagner* (London, 2010), 163–4. Žižek's comments on the critique of anti-Semitism in Wagner's music dramas are targeted in particular at Marc A. Weiner, *Richard Wagner and the Anti-Semitic Imagination* (Lincoln, NE, 1995).

169. Slavoj Žižek, 'Why Is Wagner Worth Saving?', *Journal of Philosophy and Scripture* 2/1 (2004), 18–30 (25).

170. Ibid., 23.

171. Slavoj Žižek, *Enjoy Your Symptom! Jacques Lacan in Hollywood and Out*, 2nd edn. (London, 2001), 94.

172. On which see Slavoj Žižek, 'Class Struggle or Postmodernism? Yes Please!', in Judith Butler, Ernesto Laclau and Slavoj Žižek, *Contingency, Hegemony, Universality: Contemporary Dialogues on the Left* (London, 2000), 90–135; Mads Anders Baggersgaard and Jakob Ladegaard (eds.), *Confronting Universalities: Aesthetics and Politics under the Sign of Globalisation* (Aarhus, 2011); and Newman, *Power and Politics*, 134–52.

173. Étienne Balibar, 'Ambiguous Universality', in *Politics and the Other Scene*, trans. Christine Jones, James Swenson and Chris Turner (London, 2002), 165.

4 Propaganda, Ritual and Sovereign Power

1. Bel Trew, 'Welcome to the Department of Morale Affairs: Belly Dancers, Billboards, and Egypt's Propaganda Machine', *Foreign Policy* (15 January 2014), http://foreignpolicy.com/2014/01/15/welcome-to-the-department-of-morale-affairs/; Adrian Chen, 'The Agency', *New York Times Magazine* (2 June 2015), www.nytimes.com/2015/06/07/magazine/the-agency.html?_r=0

2. On which see John Corner, 'Mediated Politics, Promotional Culture and the Idea of Propaganda', *Media, Culture & Society* 29/4 (2007), 670; and Sheryl Tuttle Ross, 'Understanding Propaganda: The Epistemic Merit Model and Its Application to Art', *Journal of Aesthetic Education* 36/1 (2002), 16–30.

3. Jason Stanley, *How Propaganda Works* (Princeton, NJ, 2015), 37–8.

4. See, for example, Stanley B. Cunningham, *The Idea of Propaganda: A Reconstruction* (Westport, CT, 2002); Nicholas O'Shaughnessy, *Propaganda and Politics: Weapons of Mass Seduction* (Manchester, 2004); and Stanley, *How Propaganda Works*.

5. Jim Samson, 'Propaganda', in *Aesthetics of Music: Musicological Perspectives*, ed. Stephen Downes (New York and London, 2014), 261.

6. Evonne Levy, *Propaganda and the Jesuit Baroque* (Berkeley, CA, 2004), 56.

7. Greg Walker, *Persuasive Fictions: Faction, Faith, and Political Culture in the Reign of Henry VIII* (Aldershot, 1996), 88–90; and Tatiana C. String, 'Henry VIII and Holbein: Patterns and Conventions in Early Modern Writing about Artists', in *Henry VIII and the Court: Art, Politics and Performance*, ed. Thomas Betteridge and Suzannah Lipscomb (Farnham, 2013), 131–41 (133). Musicologists working in these areas have tended to acknowledge this revisionism while continuing to use the term; see, for example, Georgia J. Cowart, *The Triumph of Pleasure: Louis XIV and the Politics of Spectacle* (Chicago, IL, 2008), xxi; and Alexander J. Fisher, *Music, Piety, and Propaganda: The Soundscape of Counter-Reformation Bavaria* (Oxford, 2014), 16.

8. Corner, 'Mediated Politics', 669.

9. Mary Devereaux, 'Beauty and Evil: The Case of Leni Riefenstahl's *Triumph of the Will*', in *Philosophy of Film and Motion Pictures: An Anthology*, ed. Noël Carroll and Jinhee Choi (Malden, MA, 2006), 347–61 (358).

10. Recent discussions of the music include Stefan Strötgen, '"I Compose the Party Rally . . .": The Role of Music in Leni Riefenstahl's *Triumph of the Will*', *Music and Politics* 2/1 (2008), http://dx.doi.org/10.3998/mp.9460447.0002.101; Celia Applegate, 'To Be or Not to Be Wagnerian: Music in Riefenstahl's Nazi-Era Films', in *Riefenstahl Screened: An Anthology of New Criticism*, ed. Neil Christian Pages, Mary Rhiel and Ingeborg Majer-O'Sickey (New York, 2008), 179–202; and Huw Hallam, 'Political Sound: National Socialism and its Musical Afterlives', PhD dissertation, King's College London, 2013, 43–9.

11. Windt had already used this music to accompany a similar sequence in the film *Der Sieg des Glaubens* (1933).

12. Noam Chomsky, *Media Control: The Spectacular Achievements of Propaganda*, 2nd edn. (New York, 2008).

13. Herbert Marcuse, *The Aesthetic Dimension: Towards a Critique of Marxist Aesthetics* (Boston, 1978), 11. The conception of affirmative art employed here, it should be noted, is narrower than that in Marcuse's 1937 essay 'The Affirmative Character of Culture'.

14. Buch, *Beethoven's Ninth*, 2.

15. Sabine Mecking and Yvonne Wasserloos, 'Musik – Macht – Staat: Exposition einer politischen Musikgeschichte', in *Music – Macht – Staat: Kulturelle, soziale und politische Wandlungsprozesse in der Moderne*, ed. Mecking and Wasserloos (Göttingen, 2012), 11–38 (12); Beverley C. Southgate, *History, What and Why? Ancient, Modern and Postmodern Perspectives*, 2nd edn. (London, 2001), 96–7.

16. Examples of recent studies include Fiona Kisby, '"When the King Goeth a Procession": Chapel Ceremonies and Services, the Ritual Year, and Religious Reforms at the Early Tudor Court, 1485–1547', *Journal of British Studies* 40/1 (2001), 44–75; Iain Fenlon, 'Theories of Decorum: Music and the Italian Renaissance Entry', in *Ceremonial Entries in Early Modern Europe: The Iconography of Power*, ed. J. R. Mulryne, Maria Ines Aliverti and Anna Maria Testaverde (Abingdon, 2016), 135–48; Mary Tiffany Ferer, *Music and Ceremony at the Court of Charles V: The Capilla Flamenca and the Art of Political Promotion* (Woodbridge, 2012); and Vincenzo Borghetti, 'Music and the Representation of Princely Power in the Fifteenth and Sixteenth Century', *Acta Musicologica* 80/2 (2008), 179–214.

17. On which see Rainer Bayreuther, 'Überlegungen zu einer Theorie politischer Musik am Beispiel von Händels "Ode for the Birthday of Queen Anne"', *Die Musikforschung* 63/3 (2010), 228–47; and James A. Winn, 'Style and Politics in the Philips-Handel Ode for Queen Anne's Birthday, 1713', *Music and Letters* 89/4 (2008), 547–61.

18. Andrew H. Weaver, *Sacred Music as Public Image for Holy Roman Emperor Ferdinand III: Representing the Counter-Reformation Monarch at the End of the Thirty Years' War* (Abingdon, 2016).

19. See Michael Schramm, 'Musik und Truppenzeremoniell in Deutschland', in *Militärisches Zeremoniell in Deutschland*, ed. Michael Epkenhans (Potsdam, 2008), 9–20; and Peter Moormann, Albrecht Riethmüller and Rebecca Wolf (ed.), *Paradestück Militärmusik: Beiträge zum Wandel staatlicher Repräsentation durch Musik* (Bielefeld, 2012).

20. As quoted in Blessing-Miles Tendi, *Making History in Mugabe's Zimbabwe: Politics, Intellectuals, and the Media* (Bern, 2010), 52. See also Farai Wonderful Bere, 'Infectious Beats: Urban Grooves Music's Collusion with the Zimbabwean State', in *Music, Performance and African Identities*, ed. Toyin Falola and Tyler Fleming (London, 2012), 78–93; and Katja Kellerer, '"Chant Down the System till Babylon Falls": The Political Dimensions of Underground Hip Hop

and Urban Grooves in Zimbabwe', *Journal of Pan African Studies* 6/3 (2013), 43–64.

21. Fortune Tazvida, 'Unpopular Mugabe Turns to Pop Music', *Nehanda Radio* (11 November 2011), http://nehandaradio.com/2011/11/11/unpopular-mugabe-turns-to-pop-music/.

22. Dietrich Helms, '"Das war der Herr von Hindenburg": Mythenbildung und informelle Propaganda in der deutschen Musikproduktion des Ersten Weltkriegs', in *Musik bezieht Stellung: Funktionalisierungen der Musik im Ersten Weltkrieg*, ed. Stefan Hanheide, Dietrich Helms, Claudia Glunz and Thomas F. Schneider (Göttingen, 2013), 63–100 (64).

23. Michael Ladenburger, 'Der Wiener Kongreß im Spiegel der Musik', in *Beethoven: Zwischen Revolution und Restauration*, ed. Helga Lühning and Sieghard Brandenburg (Bonn, 1989), 295.

24. Nicholas Mathew, 'Beethoven's Political Music, the Handelian Sublime, and the Aesthetics of Prostration', *19th-Century Music* 33/2 (2009), 110–50 (118); see also Nicholas Mathew, *Political Beethoven* (Cambridge, 2013), esp. 71–9.

25. Nicholas Cook, 'The Other Beethoven: Heroism, the Canon, and the Works of 1813–14', *19th-Century Music* 27/1 (2003), 22.

26. Ibid., 20.

27. The title of an earlier painting by Olivier, *Der Treueschwur* (1813), makes this link more explicit, portraying a Prussian and a Russian knight swearing an oath of allegiance (Bettina Brandt, *Germania und ihre Söhne: Repräsentationen von Nation, Geschlecht und Politik in der Moderne* [Göttingen, 2010], 187).

28. M. Elizabeth C. Bartlet, 'The New Repertory at the Opéra during the Reign of Terror: Revolutionary Rhetoric and Operatic Consequences', in Boyd (ed.), *French Revolution*, 107–57 (123). See also Mark Darlow, *Staging the French Revolution: Cultural Politics and the Paris Opéra, 1789–1794* (Oxford, 2012), 246–9.

29. Organ Music from the Great War (www.youtube.com/channel/UCUx_XDvvLRvOn9iIMSbm6HA).

30. See James Garratt, '"Ein gute Wehr und Waffen": Apocalyptic and Redemptive Narratives in Organ Music from the Great War', in *Music and War from the French Revolution to World War I*, ed. Étienne Jardin (Turnhout, 2016), esp. 389–91, 403–8.

31. Johann Nepomuk Vogl, 'Die Kaiserjagd im Wienerwald' (original title *Der Schützling*) as translated in the CD notes for Carl Loewe, *Lieder & Balladen: Complete Edition*, vol. XVI (CPO, 999 562-2, 2001).

32. Michel Foucault, '"Omnes et singulatim": Toward a Critique of Political Reason', in *Power*, 300.

33. For a broader exploration of Bach the 'devoted monarchist', see David Yearsley, 'Princes of Peace and War and Their Most Humble, Most Obedient Court Composer', *Konturen* 1 (2008), http://journals.oregondigital.org/konturen/article/view/1276.

34. Norbert Elias, *Die höfische Gesellschaft. Untersuchungen zur Soziologie des Königtums und der höfischen Aristokratie* (Frankfurt am Main, 1983), translated as *The Court Society*, trans. Edmund Jephcott (Oxford, 1983); Ernst H. Kantorowicz, *Laudes regiae: A Study in Liturgical Acclamations and Mediaeval Ruler Worship* (Berkeley, CA, 1946); and Kantorowicz, *The King's Two Bodies: A Study in Mediaeval Political Theology* (Princeton, NJ, 1957). For an overview of the relationship between politics and ritual, see David I. Kertzer, *Ritual, Politics, and Power* (New Haven, CT, 1988).

35. Alice Hunt, *The Drama of Coronation: Medieval Ceremony in Early Modern England* (Cambridge, 2008), 8.

36. Dougal Shaw, 'Nothing but Propaganda? Historians and the Study of Early Modern Ritual', *Cultural and Social History* 1 (2004), 144–5.

37. John Adamson, 'The Making of the Ancien-Régime Court, 1500–1700', in *The Princely Courts of Europe, 1500–1750*, ed. Adamson (London, 1999), 7–41 (34).

38. Clifford Geertz, *Negara: The Theatre State in Nineteenth-Century Bali* (Princeton, NJ, 1980), 13.

39. Clifford Geertz, 'Centers, Kings, and Charisma: Reflections on the Symbolics of Power', in *Culture and Its Creators*, ed. Joseph Ben-David and Terry N. Clark (Chicago, IL, 1977), 150–71 (156).

40. Alejandro Cañeque, *The King's Living Image: The Culture and Politics of Viceregal Power in Colonial Mexico* (New York, 2004), 104.

41. Giorgio Agamben, *The Kingdom and the Glory: For a Theological Genealogy of Economy and Government*, trans. Lorenzo Chiesa (Stanford, CA, 2011), 195.

42. Ibid., 105. See also Edward Muir, *Ritual in Early Modern Europe* (Cambridge, 1997).

43. Alan Cottrell, '*Auctoritas* and *Potestas*: A Reevaluation of the Correspondence of Gelasius I on Papal-Imperial Relations', *Mediaeval Studies* 55 (1993), 95–109.

44. Adrian Hastings, 'Kingship', in *The Oxford Companion to Christian Thought*, ed. Adrian Hastings, Alistair Mason and Hugh Pyper (Oxford, 2000), 372.

45. Sergio Bertelli, *The King's Body: Sacred Rituals of Power in Medieval and Early Modern Europe*, trans. R. Burr Litchfield (University Park, PA, 2001), 14–15, 6.

46. Kantorowicz, *Laudes regiae*, 16–20.

47. Anne Walters Robertson, *Guillaume de Machaut and Reims: Context and Meaning in His Musical Works* (Cambridge, 2002), 63; Craig Wright, *Music and Ceremony at Notre Dame of Paris, 500–1550* (Cambridge, 1989), 201.

48. Kantorowicz, *Laudes regiae*, 14.

49. Aron Gurevich, *Medieval Popular Culture: Problems of Belief and Perception*, trans. János M. Bak and Paul A. Hollingsworth (Cambridge, 1988), 56.

50. Benedict Anderson, *Imagined Communities: Reflections on the Origin and Spread of Nationalism*, 2nd edn. (London, 2006), 145.

51. Robert N. Bellah, 'Durkheim and Ritual', in *The Cambridge Companion to Durkheim*, ed. Jeffrey C. Alexander and Philip Smith (Cambridge, 2005), 183–210 (186–7).

52. Agamben, *Kingdom*, 232.

53. Kantorowicz, *Laudes regiae*, 76–7.

54. Ibid., 83; Agamben, *Kingdom*, 169–72.

55. On which see Louis Marin, *On Representation* (Stanford, CA, 2001), especially 38–53.

56. Johann Wolfgang von Goethe, 'Nachträgliches zu Philostrats Gemälde', as quoted in Warren Breckman, *Adventures of the Symbolic: Post-Marxism and Radical Democracy* (New York, 2013), 32.

57. Cañeque, *Living Image*, 105.

58. Anon., 'Das Königsfest in Erfurt am 3. August', *Allgemeine musikalische Zeitung* 39 (1837), 572–4. On the mushrooming of royal festivals in Prussia in this period, see Hubertus Büschel, *Untertanenliebe: Der Kult um deutsche Monarchen 1770–1830* (Göttingen, 2006), 59–60.

59. Kantorowicz, *Laudes regiae*, 182.

60. Ufficio delle celebrazioni liturgiche del sommo pontefice, 'Riti per l'inizio del ministero petrino del vescovo di Roma' (19 March 2013), www.vatican.va/news_services/liturgy/libretti/2013/20130319_inizio-ministero-petrino.pdf.

61. A. Edward Siecienski, *The Papacy and the Orthodox: Sources and History of a Debate* (New York, 2017), 256; Kantorowicz, *Laudes regiae*, 125.

62. Edmund Plowden, *Commentaries or Reports* (London, 1816), 213, as quoted in Kantorowicz, *Two Bodies*, 9.

63. Kantorowicz, *Laudes regiae*, 180; Agamben, *Kingdom*, 253–4.

64. Mitchell Dean, 'Political Acclamation, Social Media and the Public Mood', *European Journal of Social Theory* (2016), http://journals.sagepub.com/doi/pdf/10.1177/1368431016645589.

65. Suk-Young Kim, *Illusive Utopia: Theater, Film, and Everyday Performance in North Korea* (Ann Arbor, MI, 2010), 14. See also Keith Howard, 'Dancing for the Eternal President', in *Music, Power and Politics*, ed. Annie J. Randall (New York, 2005), 113–32.

66. Bruce Cumings, *North Korea: Another Country* (New York, 2003), 137.

67. Kim, *Illusive Utopia*, 17.

68. Jürgen Habermas, *The Structural Transformation of the Public Sphere: An Inquiry into a Category of Bourgeois Society*, trans. Thomas Burger with Frederick Lawrence (Cambridge, 1989), 235.

69. Agamben, *Kingdom*, 256.

70. Dean, 'Political Acclamation', 10.

71. Frances Dyson, *The Tone of our Times: Sound, Sense, Economy, and Ecology* (Cambridge, MA, 2014), 40.

72. Ernesto Laclau makes a similar argument in relation to populism (see *On Populist Reason*, London, 2005, x–xi).

73. Chris Richards, 'Authoritarian Hold Music: How Donald Trump's Banal Playlist Cultivates Danger at His Rallies', *Washington Post* (16 March 2016). On the broader music and theatrics of Trump's rallies, see Justin Patch, 'Notes on Deconstructing the Populism: Music on the Campaign Trail, 2012 and 2016', *American Music* 34/3 (2016), 365–401; and Mark Chou and Michael L. Ondaatje, 'Dramatic Rationalities: Electoral Theater in the Age of Trump', in *Why Irrational Politics Appeals: Understanding the Allure of Trump*, ed. Mari Fitzduff (Santa Barbara, CA, 2017), 191–204.

5 Performing Protest: Music and Activism

1. Fredric Jameson, *The Cultural Turn: Selected Writings on the Postmodern, 1983–1998* (London, 1998), 73–4.
2. Žižek, *End Times*, 326.
3. Bart Cammaerts, 'Protest Logics and the Mediation Opportunity Structure', *European Journal of Communication* 27/2 (2012), 121–2.
4. Ron Eyerman, 'Performing Opposition: or, How Social Movements Move', in *Social Performance: Symbolic Action, Cultural Pragmatics, and Ritual*, ed. Jeffrey C. Alexander, Bernhard Giesen and Jason L. Mast (Cambridge, 2006), 193–217 (197).
5. Charles Tilly, *Collective Violence* (Cambridge, 2003), 204.
6. Charles Tilly, 'Conclusion: From Interactions to Outcomes in Social Movements', in *How Social Movements Matter*, ed. Marco Giugni, Doug McAdam and Charles Tilly (Minneapolis, MN, 1999), 253–70 (260); see also Gemma Edwards, *Social Movements and Protest* (Cambridge, 2014), 67.
7. Reed, *Art of Protest*, xiv.
8. Verta Taylor and Nella Van Dyke, '"Get up, Stand up": Tactical Repertoires of Social Movements', in *The Blackwell Companion to Social Movements*, ed. David A. Snow, Sarah A. Soule and Hanspeter Kriesi (Oxford, 2004), 262–93 (263).
9. Vincent J. Roscigno and William F. Danaher, 'Media and Mobilization: The Case of Radio and Southern Textile Worker Insurgency, 1929 to 1934', *American Sociological Review* 66/1 (2001), 21–48. See also Vincent J. Roscigno and William F. Danaher, *The Voice of Southern Labor: Radio, Music, and Textile Strikes, 1929–1934* (Minneapolis, MN, 2004); Benjamin Bierman, 'Solidarity Forever: Music and the Labor Movement in the United States', in *The Routledge History of Social Protest in Popular Music*, ed. Jonathan C. Friedman (New York, 2013), 31–43; and Richard A. Reuss with JoAnne C. Reuss, *American Folk Music and Left-Wing Politics, 1927–1957* (Lanham, MD, 2000).
10. Jeffrey Roessner, 'That Was Now, This Is Then: Recycling Sixties Style in Post-9/11 Music', in *The Politics of Post-9/11 Music: Sound, Trauma, and the Music Industry in the Time of Terror*, ed. Joseph P. Fisher and Brian Flota (Farnham, 2011), 118. For overviews of protest music in the 1960s, see Ron Eyerman and

Andrew Jamison, *Music and Social Movements: Mobilizing Traditions in the Twentieth Century* (Cambridge, 1998), 106–39; and Sarah Hill, '"This Is My Country": American Popular Music and Political Engagement in "1968"', in *Music and Protest in 1968*, ed. Beate Kutschke and Barley Norton (Cambridge, 2013), 46–63.

11. Carnegie Hall, 19 June 1965, cited in Phil Ochs, *Farewells and Fantasies* (Elektra R273518), liner notes, 31.

12. Jerry Rodnitsky, 'The Decline and Rebirth of Folk-Protest Music', in Peddie (ed.), *Resisting Muse*, 17–29 (18).

13. See Denise Sullivan, *Keep on Pushing: Black Power Music from Blues to Hip-Hop* (Chicago, IL, 2011), 25–6, 43–4.

14. Oscar Brand, *The Ballad Mongers: Rise of the Modern Folk Song* (New York, 1962), as quoted in Mary Pipher, *Writing to Change the World* (New York, 2006), 226–7; Dorian Lynskey, *33 Revolutions per Minute: A History of Protest Songs, from Billie Holliday to Green Day* (London, 2011), 642–3.

15. Mark Willhardt, 'Available Rebels and Folk Authenticities: Michelle Shocked and Billy Bragg', in Peddie (ed.), *Resisting Muse*, 30–48 (41).

16. Jón Ólafsson, 'Defiance: A Comment on the Logic of Protest', *Trames* 4 (2007), 432–42 (440).

17. This alignment is underscored by the use of the 'human microphone' to affirm Morello's statements (see Tom Morello, 'The Fabled City' at Occupy Wall Street, 14 October 2011, www.youtube.com/watch?v=8YfZa80E1fA).

18. R. Serge Denisoff, 'Protest Songs: Those on the Top Forty and Those of the Streets' (1970), in *Sing a Song of Social Significance* (Bowling Green, OH, 1972), 151.

19. See Mark Pedelty's useful continuum of rock musicians and political commitment in 'Peter Gabriel: The Masked Activist', in *Political Rock*, ed. Mark Pedelty and Kristine Weglarz (Abingdon, 2016), 23–36.

20. R. Serge Denisoff, 'Songs of Persuasion: A Sociological Analysis of Urban Propaganda Songs' (1966), in Denisoff, *Sing a Song*, 2–3.

21. 'Christ T-T New Album "9 Green Songs"', *Xtra Mile Recordings* (6 April 2016), www.1.xtramilerecordings.com/news/2016/4/6/chris-tt-9-green-songs-out-3-june-2016.

22. Unsigned, 'Freedom Singer: "Without Music, There Would Be No Movement', *NPR Music* (28 August 2013), www.npr.org/2013/08/28/216422973/.

23. Reed, *Art of Protest*, 299.

24. Eyerman and Jamison, *Social Movements*, 23.

25. As quoted in Robert Shelton, 'Songs a Weapon in Rights Battle: Vital New Ballads Buoy Negro Spirits across the South', *New York Times* (12 August 1962), www.nytimes.com/learning/teachers/archival/19620820songsweapon.pdf.

26. Eyerman, 'Performing Opposition', 195–6.

27. Denisoff, 'Songs of Persuasion', 10.

28. Deena Weinstein, 'Rock Protest Songs: So Many and so Few', in Peddie (ed.), *Resisting Muse*, 3–16 (11–12); see also Platoff, 'John Lennon', 250–1.

29. Reed, *Art of Protest*, 313.

30. See Victor V. Bobetsky (ed.), *We Shall Overcome: Essays on a Great American Song* (Lanham, MD, 2105).

31. Colin Stutz, 'Did Paul Ryan Even Ever Really Like Rage Against the Machine?', *Billboard* (9 December 2014), www.billboard.com/articles/news/6251426/ paul-ryan-rage-against-the-machine-urban-legend.

32. Weinstein, 'Rock Protest Songs', 12.

33. Brian Doherty, 'Rage On: The Strange Politics of Millionaire Rock Stars', *reason.com* (October 2000), http://reason.com/archives/2000/10/01/rage-on/ singlepage. On Springsteen's politics, see Jim Cullen, 'Bruce Springsteen's Ambiguous Musical Politics in the Reagan Era', *Popular Music and Society* 16/2 (1992), 1–22.

34. On Live Aid, Live 8 and similar events, see Neal Ullestad, 'Rock and Rebellion: Subversive Effects of Live Aid and "Sun City"', *Popular Music* 6/1 (1987), 67–76; Reebee Garofalo, 'Understanding Mega-Events: If We Are the World, Then How Do We Change It?', in *Rockin' the Boat: Mass Music and Mass Movements*, ed. Garofalo (Cambridge, MA, 1992), 15–36; Simon Frith and John Street, 'Rock Against Racism and Red Wedge: From Music to Politics, from Politics to Music', in Garofalo (ed.), *Rockin' the Boat*, 67–80; John Street, 'The Pop Star as Politician: from Belafonte to Bono, from Creativity to Conscience', in Peddie (ed.), *Resisting Muse*, 49–61; Reed, *Art of Protest*, 156–78; C. Michael Elavsky, 'United as ONE: Live 8 and the Politics of the Global Music Media Spectacle', *Journal of Popular Music Studies* 21/4 (2009), 384–410; Street, *Music and Politics*, 62–78; and Nathan Farrell, 'Celebrity Politics: Bono, Product (RED) and the Legitimising of Philanthrocapitalism', *British Journal of Politics and International Relations* 14 (2012), 392–406.

35. Clinton Heylin, *Bob Dylan: Behind the Shades*, 2nd edn. (London, 2001), 93.

36. Clinton Heylin, *Revolution in the Air: The Songs of Bob Dylan, 1957–1973* (Chicago, IL, 2009), 206.

37. Randall F. Grass, 'Fela Anikulapo-Kuti: The Art of an Afrobeat Rebel', *Drama Review* 30/1 (1986), 131–48; John Howe, 'Fela Anikulapo Kuti: An Honest Man', *New Left Review* 225 (1997) 127–33 (130).

38. Grass, 'Fela', 142.

39. Tejumola Olaniyan, *Arrest the Music! Fela and His Rebel Art and Politics* (Bloomington, IN, 2004), 166.

40. Bob Dylan, *Chronicles*, vol. 1 (New York, 2004), 54.

41. Barry Shank, '"That Wild Mercury Sound": Bob Dylan and the Illusion of American Culture', *Boundary 2* 29/1 (2002), 97–123 (116).

42. Mike Marqusee, *Wicked Messenger: Bob Dylan and the 1960s* (New York, 2003), 59, 8.

43. Bob Dylan, 'My Back Pages', *Another Side of Bob Dylan*, https://bobdylan.com/songs/.

44. Liner notes, *Another Side of Bob Dylan*, as presented on https://williamhenryprince.com/bob-dylan-album-liner-notes-collected/.

45. Eyerman and Jamison, *Social Movements*, 123–4.

46. Lawrence Wilde, 'The Cry of Humanity: Dylan's Expressionist Period', in *The Political Art of Bob Dylan*, 2nd edn., ed. David Boucher and Gary Browning (Exeter, 2009), 104–35 (107).

47. Greil Marcus, *Like a Rolling Stone: Bob Dylan at the Crossroads* (London, 2005), 171. For an alternative reading of 'Desolation Row', see John Hughes, *Invisible Now: Bob Dylan in the 1960s* (Farnham, 2013), 125–6.

48. Marcuse, *One-Dimensional Man*, 151; Douglas Kellner, 'Introduction: Marcuse, Art, and Liberation', in Marcuse, *Collected Papers*, vol. IV, 42.

49. Marcuse, *One-Dimensional Man*, 260.

50. Herbert Marcuse, *An Essay on Liberation* (Boston, 1969), 33–4.

51. Jeremiah I. Dibua, *Modernization and the Crisis of Development in Africa: The Nigerian Experience* (Aldershot, 2006), 183; Olaniyan, *Arrest the Music*, 73.

52. Lindsay Michie and Ayoyinka Oriola, 'Afrobeat: The Music of Fela Kuti', in *Sounds of Resistance: The Role of Music in Multicultural* Activism, ed. Eunice Rojas and Lindsay Michie (Santa Barbara, CA, 2013), vol. II, 329–54 (339).

53. Ibid., 344.

54. Fela Kuti and the Africa 70, 'Unknown Soldier', Greatest Hits (Lagos, 1997), as quoted in Teresa N. Washington, *Our Mothers, Our Powers, Our Texts: Manifestations of Àjé in Africana Literature* (Bloomington, IN, 2005), 269.

55. George Ogola, Anne Schumann and Michael Olutayo, 'Popular Music, New Media, and the Digital Public Sphere in Kenya, Côte d'Ivoire, and Nigeria', in *African Media and the Digital Public Sphere*, ed. Okoth Fred Mudhai, Wisdom J. Tettey and Fackson Banda (New York, 2009), 203–22 (215).

56. Olaniyan, *Arrest the Music*, 170.

57. See Jendele Hungbo, '"Beasts of No Nation": Resistance and Civic Activism in Fela Anikulapo-Kuti's Music', in *Civic Agency in Africa: Arts of Resistance in the 21st Century*, ed. Ebenezer Obadare and Wendy Williams (Woodbridge, 2014), 167–78.

58. https://genius.com/Fela-kuti-teacher-dont-teach-me-nonsense-lyrics.

59. Conrad Amenta, 'Why Protest Albums Can't Teach Dissent: The Emergent Complexity of Post-9/11 Protest', in Fisher and Flota (ed.), *Post 9/11 Music*, 57–68 (63).

60. Thomas Frank, 'Why Johnny Can't Dissent' (1995), in *Commodify Your Dissent: Salvos from the Baffler*, ed. Thomas Frank and Matt Weiland (New York, 1997), 31–45 (32). See also Luc Boltanski and Ève Chiapello, *The New Spirit of Capitalism*, trans. Gregory Elliott (London, 2005), 419–20; and Jeffrey T. Nealon, *Post-Postmodernism: or, The Cultural Logic of Just-in-Time Capitalism* (Stanford, CA, 2012), 43–57.

61. As quoted in 'General Election 2015', *NME* (29 April 2015), www.nme.com/blogs/ nme-blogs/general-election-2015-muse-noel-gallagher-savages-du-blonde-ghetts- and-more-on-politics-and-protest-769095.

62. Dan Hancox, 'This Is Our Riot: POW!' (10 December 2010), http://dan- hancox.blogspot.co.uk/2010/12/this-is-our-riot-pow.html.

63. Joe Coscarelli, 'Kendrick Lamar on the Grammys, Black Lives Matter and His Big 2015', *New York Times* (29 December 2015), www.nytimes.com/2016/01/03/ arts/music/kendrick-lamar-on-a-year-of-knowing-what-matters.html?_r=0; see also Christopher J. Lebron, *The Making of Black Lives Matter: A Brief History of an Idea* (Oxford, 2017), 35–7.

64. Ben Gilbert, 'Kendrick Lamar's Civil Rights Anthem "Alright" Almost Didn't Happen', *Business Insider UK* (25 October 2016), http://uk.businessinsider .com/kendrick-lamar-alright-2016–10; and Aisha Harris, 'Has Kendrick Lamar Recorded the New Black National Anthem?', *Slate* (3 August 2015), www.slate.com/articles/arts/culturebox/2015/08/.

65. Jamilah King, 'The Improbable Story of How Kendrick Lamar's "Alright" Became a Protest Anthem', *Mic* (11 February 2016), https://mic.com/articles/ 134764/.

66. Spencer Kornhaber, 'Eminem and 2017's Many-Splendored Protest Songs', *The Atlantic* (26 December 2017), www.theatlantic.com/entertainment/arch ive/2017/12/eminem-revival-2017-protest-music-trump/549095/.

6 Critique, Subversion and Negation

1. Morris Dickstein, 'Animal Farm: History as Fable', in *The Cambridge Compan-ion to George Orwell*, ed. John Rudden (Cambridge, 2007), 146–59 (144).

2. See Ruth Smith, 'Allegorical Politics', in *Handel's Oratorios and Eighteenth-Century Thought* (Cambridge, 1995), 202–32.

3. George Bernard Shaw, *The Perfect Wagnerite: A Commentary on the Niblung's Ring*, 3rd edn. (New York, 1909). Other texts that discuss the *Ring* from the perspective of allegory include Jane K. Brown, *The Persistence of Allegory: Drama and Neoclassicism from Shakespeare to Wagner* (Philadelphia, 2007), 222–31; John Deathridge, *Wagner beyond Good and Evil* (Berkeley, 2008), esp. 79–84; and Lawrence Switzky, 'Allegory and Its Limits in the *Ring*: Bernard Shaw and Patrice Chéreau on Wagner', *The Opera Quarterly* 30 (2014), 1–16.

4. New translations of some of these texts are presented in Richard Wagner, *Wagner's Ring in 1848: New Translations of the Nibelung Myth and Siegfried's Death*, trans. Edward R. Haymes (Rochester, NY, 2010).

5. Karl Marx, 'A Contribution to the Critique of Hegel's Philosophy of Right. Introduction', in *Early Writings*, 246.

6. Foucault, 'Questions of Method', *Power*, 236.

7. Garratt, *Music, Culture and Social Reform*, 128, 146–7.

8. Wagner 'Revolution', 173 (translation modified).

9. Ibid., 170.

10. Richard Wagner, letter to August Röckel, 23/8/1856, *Sämtliche Briefe*, ed. Gertrud Strobel et al. (Leipzig, 1967–), vol. VIII, 152.

11. Rancière, *Emancipated Spectator*, 60–1.

12. Deathridge, *Beyond Good*, 50.

13. See Garratt, *Music, Culture and Social Reform*, 174–7.

14. Richard Wagner, *Oper und Drama*, in *Gesammelte Schriften und Dichtungen*, ed. Wolfgang Golther, vol. IV (Berlin, [1913]), 52–3.

15. Wagner, letter to Röckel of 24–25 January 1854, *Sämtliche Briefe*, vol. VI, 68–9.

16. Gerald Raunig, 'Singers, Cynics, Molecular Mice: The Political Aesthetics of Contemporary Activism', *Theory, Culture and Society* 31 (2014), 68.

17. Friedrich Engels, *Cola di Rienzi: ein unbekannter dramatischer Entwurf*, ed. Michael Knieriem (Wuppertal and Trier, 1974).

18. Wagner, *Oper und Drama*, 65.

19. Shaw, *Perfect Wagnerite*, 1.

20. Ibid., 92.

21. Deathridge, *Beyond Good*, 93.

22. Shaw, *Perfect Wagnerite*, 44, xiii.

23. Ibid., 31.

24. On the idea that Wagner's anti-Semitism shaped his portrayal of the Nibelungs Alberich, Mime and Hagen, see especially Adorno, *In Search of Wagner*, trans. Rodney Livingstone (London, 1981), 23–5; Weiner, *Richard Wagner*, 135–40; and Berthold Hoeckner, 'Wagner and the Origin of Evil', *The Opera Quarterly* 23 (2008), 151–83.

25. Shaw, *Perfect Wagnerite*, 10.

26. Richard Wagner, *Das Rheingold*, scene iii, as presented in Stewart Spencer and Barry Millington (ed.), *Wagner's Ring of the Nibelung: A Companion* (London, 1993), 96.

27. Mark Berry, *Treacherous Bonds and Laughing Fire: Politics and Religion in Wagner's Ring* (Aldershot, 2006), 92.

28. Wagner, 'Die Wibelungen', *Gesammelte Schriften*, vol. IV, 153.

29. Shaw, *Perfect Wagnerite*, 64.

30. Judith Butler, 'What Is Critique? An Essay on Foucault's Virtue', *transversal texts* (2006), http://eipcp.net/transversal/0806/butler/en.

31. Jeffrey Schantz, 'Anarchist Futures in the Present', *Resistance Studies Journal* 1 (2008), https://theanarchistlibrary.org/library/jeff-shantz-anarchist-futures-in-the-present.

32. Wagner, letter to Röckel of 24–25 January 1854, 69.

33. Shaw, *Perfect Wagnerite*, 73.

34. Jonathan Lear, *Radical Hope: Ethics in the Face of Cultural Devastation* (Cambridge, MA, 2006), 100.

35. Leon Botstein, 'Richard Wagner at Two Hundred', *The Opera Quarterly* 95 (2012), 193–206 (205, 204).

36. Fredric Jameson, 'Regieoper, or Eurotrash?', *New Left Review* 64 (2010), 111–29 (119).

37. Slavoj Žižek, 'The Politics of Redemption, or, Why Richard Wagner Is Worth Saving', in *Lacan: The Silent Partners*, ed. Žižek (London, 2006), 231–69 (267).

38. Dave Laing, 'Resistance and Protest', in *Continuum Encyclopedia of Popular Music of the World*, vol. I: *Media, Industry and Society*, ed. John Shepherd, David Horn, Dave Laing, Paul Oliver and Peter Wicke (London, 2003), 345–6 (345).

39. Marita Fornaro Bordolli, 'Communities, Territories and Genres of the Uruguayan "Resistance Music", 1962–2011', in *Protest Music in the Twentieth Century*, ed. Roberto Illiano (Turnhout, 2015), 253–75 (253).

40. Anita Jorge, 'Liminal Soundscapes in Powell & Pressburger's Wartime Films', *Studies in European Cinema* 14 (2017), 22–32.

41. Solomon Volkov (ed.), *Testimony: The Memoirs of Dmitri Shostakovich*, trans. Antonina W. Bouis (New York, 1979).

42. Laurel E. Fay, 'Shostakovich versus Volkov: Whose *Testimony*?', *Russian Review* 39/4 (1980), 484–93; Laurel E. Fay, *Shostakovich: A Life* (Oxford, 2000); Richard Taruskin, 'Public Lies and Unspeakable Truth: Interpreting Shostakovich's Fifth Symphony', in *Shostakovich Studies*, ed. David Fanning (Cambridge, 1995), 17–56; and Richard Taruskin, 'Shostakovich and Us', in *Shostakovich in Context*, ed. Rosamund Bartlett (Oxford, 2000), 1–29.

43. On which see Nikil Saval, 'Julian Barnes and the Shostakovich Wars', *The New Yorker* (26 May 2016), www.newyorker.com/books/page-turner/julian-barnes-and-the-shostakovich-wars; and Richard Taruskin, 'Was Shostakovich a Martyr? Or Is That Just Fiction?', *New York Times* (26 August 2016), www.nytimes.com/2016/08/28/arts/music/julian-barnes-the-noise-of-time-shostakovich.html.

44. Ian MacDonald, *The New Shostakovich* (Boston, 1990), 2, 7.

45. Ibid., 133, 6.

46. Ibid., 129.

47. Ibid., 159.

48. Ibid., 15; Allan B. Ho and Dmitry Feofanov, *Shostakovich Reconsidered* (Exeter, 1998), 14.

49. Norman Lebrecht, 'Dissident Notes: What Shostakovich Is Really All About', *The Telegraph* (19 January 2000), www.telegraph.co.uk/culture/4719607/Dissident-notes.html.

50. Taruskin, 'Public Lies', 54.

51. Taruskin, 'Shostakovich and Us', 8.

52. Richard Taruskin, 'Casting a Great Composer as a Fictional Hero', *New York Times* (5 March 2000), www.nytimes.com/2000/03/05/arts/spring-music-shostakovich-casting-a-great-composer-as-a-fictional-hero.html.

53. Edward Rothstein, 'Sly Dissident or Soviet Tool? A Musical War; New Evidence on Memoirs Splits Shostakovich Scholars', *New York Times* (17 October 1998), www.nytimes.com/1998/10/17/books/sly-dissident-soviet-tool-musical-war-new-evidence-memoirs-splits-shostakovich.html.

54. David Fanning, *The Breath of the Symphonist: Shostakovich's Tenth* (London, 1989), 70–6.

55. Slavoj Žižek, *In Defence of Lost Causes* (London, 2008), 236–7.

56. Ibid., 243.

57. Ibid., 245.

58. Ibid., 237.

59. Taruskin, 'Casting a Great Composer'.

60. James C. Scott, 'Everyday Forms of Resistance', *Copenhagen Journal of Asian Studies* 4 (1989), 33–62 (51).

61. In the revised edition of *The New Shostakovich* undertaken following MacDonald's death, Raymond Clarke claims that such dissidence could be expressed through a 'secret language of dissent, a hidden language of resistance', though he does not explain how music could function in this way (Ian MacDonald, *The New Shostakovich*, revised and updated by Raymond Clarke, 2nd edn. (London, 2006), 306).

62. Taruskin, 'Shostakovich and Us', 5.

63. On resemanticization, see Béatrice Joyeux-Prunel, 'Circulation and Resemanticization: An Aporetic Palimpsest', *Artl@s Bulletin* 6/2 (2017), 4–17.

64. The new music ensemble Musica Negativa was founded in 1969, while the term 'critical composition' was popularized by Huber's essay 'Kritisches Komponieren' (1972), in Nicolaus A. Huber, *Durchleuchtungen: Text zur Musik 1964–1999*, ed. Josef Häusler (Wiesbaden, 2000), 40–2; translations based on Nicolaus A. Huber 'Critical Composition', *Contemporary Music Review* 27/6 (2008), 565–8.

65. Rainer Nonnenmann, 'The Dead End as a Way Out. Critical Composition: A Historical Phenomenon?', in *Critical Composition Today*, ed. Claus-Steffen Mahnkopf (Hofheim, 2006), 88–109.

66. John Roberts, *Revolutionary Time and the Avant-Garde* (London, 2015), 56.

67. This distinction between passive and active nihilism is adapted from Critchley, *Infinitely Demanding*, 4–6.

68. Engels, *Dialectics of Nature*, in Marx and Engels, *Collected Works*, vol. XXV, 356.

69. Marx, *Capital*, vol. I, in Marx and Engels, *Collected Works*, vol. XXXV, 751.

70. Marx, *Capital*, vol. III, in *Collected Works*, vol. XXXVII, 438

71. Herbert Marcuse, 'A Note on Dialectic' (1960), in *The Essential Marcuse: Selected Writings of Philosopher and Social Critic Herbert Marcuse*, ed. Andrew Feenberg and William Leiss (Boston, 2007), 69; Adorno, *Negative Dialectics*, 192–4.

72. Adorno, *Negative Dialectics*, 194.

73. Ibid., 394.
74. Ibid., 393.
75. Marcuse, 'A Note on Dialectic', 69.
76. Ibid., 67.
77. Thomas Mann, *Doctor Faustus: The Life of the German Composer Adrian Leverkühn as Told by a Friend*, trans. John E. Woods (New York, 1997), 514. Theodore Ziolkowski has devoted an entire chapter to interpreting Leverkühn's compositions (*Music into Fiction: Composers Writing, Compositions Imitated* [Rochester, NY, 2017], 199–220).
78. Marcuse, 'Art in the One-Dimensional Society', 180, 190. Stockhausen's most direct negation of the Ninth (his proposal for compressing it into one second) postdates Marcuse's essay.
79. Theodor W. Adorno, 'Commitment' (1962), trans. Francis McDonagh, in Adorno, Walter Benjamin, Ernst Bloch, Berthold Brecht and Georg Lukács, *Aesthetics and Politics*, ed. Ronald Taylor (London, 1977), 180, 194.
80. Adorno, *Aesthetic Theory*, 148.
81. Roberts, *Revolutionary Time*, 61–2.
82. Marcuse, 'A Note on Dialectic', 68; Adorno, *Aesthetic Theory*, 321.
83. A more detailed account of the background and ingredients of *La fabbrica illuminata* is given in Gianmario Borio, 'Music as Plea for Political Action: The Presence of Musicians in Italian Protest Movements around 1968', in Kutschke and Norton (eds.), *Music and Protest*, 32–4; and Timothy S. Murphy, 'The Negation of a Negation Fixed in a Form: Luigi Nono and the Italian Counter-Culture 1964–1979', *Cultural Studies Review* 11/2 (2005), 95–109 (99–101). See also Wesley Phillips, 'Spaces of Resistance: The Adorno–Nono Complex', *Twentieth-Century Music* 9/1–2 (2013), 79–99.
84. Luigi Nono, 'La fabbrica illuminata', in *Scritti e colloqui*, vol. I (Lucca, 2001), 448, as presented on Fondazione Archivio Luigi Nono Onlus, www.luiginono.it/opere/la-fabbrica-illuminata/.
85. Ibid.
86. Luigi Nono, 'Lettera di Luigi Nono agli operai dell'Italsider di Genova-Cornigliano' (21 November 1965), *Scritti*, vol. I, 186–7, as quoted in Carola Nielinger-Vakil, *Luigi Nono: A Composer in Context* (Cambridge, 2015), 126.
87. Murphy, 'Negation of a Negation', 99–100.
88. Helmut Lachenmann, 'Luigi Nono oder Rückblick auf die serielle Musik', *Melos* 36 (1971), 225–30 (228), as translated in Ben Earle, 'The Politics of the New Music', *Music and Letters* 94/4 (2013), 664–71 (668).
89. Huber, 'Kritisches Komponieren', 41. Huber's and Lachenmann's conceptions of critical composition are compared in Ferdinand Zehentreiter, 'Sensory Cognition as an Autonomous Form of Critique: Reflections on Redefining a "Critical Form of Art"', in Mahnkopf (ed.), *Critical Composition*, 43–61; Andreas Domann, '"Wo bleibt das Negative?" Zur musikalischen Ästhetik

Helmut Lachenmanns, Nicolaus A. Hubers und Mathias Spahlingers', *Archiv für Musikwissenschaft* 62/3 (2005), 177–91.

90. Huber, 'Kritisches Komponieren', 40.

91. Ibid., 41.

92. Ibid., 42.

93. Claus-Steffen Mahnkopf, 'What Does "Critical Composition" Mean?', in Mahnkopf (ed.), *Critical Composition*, 75–87 (81).

94. Huber, '*Darabukka* – ein Versuch über Bedeutung', in *Durchleuchtungen*, 300.

95. Huber, *Harakiri*, as quoted in *Durchleuchtungen*, 400. On *Harakiri*, see Beate Kutschke, 'Aesthetic Theories and Revolutionary Practice: Nikolaus A. Huber and Clytus Gottwald in Dissent', in *Sound Commitments: Avant-Garde Music and the Sixties*, ed. Robert Adlington (Cambridge, 2009), 78–96; and Alastair Williams, *Music in Germany since 1968* (Cambridge, 2013), 190–2.

96. Huber, '*Darabukka*', 300.

97. As quoted in Kutschke, 'Aesthetic Theories', 91.

98. Mathias Spahlinger, 'Political Implications of the Material of New Music', *Contemporary Music Review* 34/2–3 (2015), 127–66 (146, 144).

99. Mathias Spahlinger, 'Commentary to *música impura*' (1983), trans. Philipp Blume, http://mathiasspahlinger.de/works-chronologically/?lang=en.

100. Spahlinger, 'Political Implications', 145.

101. Ibid., 144.

102. Mathias Spahlinger, 'This Is the Time of Conceptive Ideologues No Longer', *Contemporary Music Review* 27/6 (2008), 579–94 (586–7).

103. Karl Marx, 'Excerpts from James Mill's *Elements of Political Economy*', in Marx, *Early Writings*, 277.

104. Mathias Spahlinger, 'Commentary on *doppelt bejaht*', trans. Philipp Blume and Seth Brodsky, http://mathiasspahlinger.de/works-chronologically/?lang=en (all subsequent quotations are from this source).

105. For more details on the composition and the demands it places on performers, see Jef Chippewa, 'Practicalities of a Socio-Musical Utopia: Degrees of "Freedom" in Mathias Spahlinger's "Doppelt Bejaht"', *Nutida Musik* 3–4 (2013) (English version: http://newmusicnotation.com/chippewa/).

106. Ibid.

107. Mirko Weber, 'Wir sind so frei. Lenin, '68 und jede Menge flache Hierarchien: Die Donaueschinger Musiktage entspannen sich', *Der Tagesspiegel* (21 October 2009), www.tagesspiegel.de/kultur/donaueschinger-musiktage-wir-sind-so-frei/1619308.html; Max Nyffeler, 'Diskussionspapiere von der Orchesterbefreiungsfront', *Beckmesser: Die Seite für neue Musik und Musikkritik* (20 October 2009), www.beckmesser.de/news/donaueschingen2009.html.

108. Marcuse, 'Repressive Tolerance', 88–9.

109. Spahlinger, 'Political Implications', 142.

7 Nationalism, Racism and Fascism

1. Courtney Young, *The Moral Force of Indigenous Politics: Critical Liberalism and the Zapatistas* (Cambridge, 2008), 10.
2. Balibar, *Politics*, 27, 76.
3. Judith Butler, *Gender Trouble: Feminism and the Subversion of Identity* (London, 1990).
4. Nicolas Bourriaud, *The Radicant*, trans. James Gussen and Lili Porten (New York, 2009), 21, 22.
5. Linda Martín Alcoff. *Visible Identities: Race, Gender, and the Self* (New York, 2006), 12.
6. Henry McDonald, 'Belfast Braces for Night-Time Protests after Orange Parade Passes Peacefully', *The Guardian* (12 July 2013), www.theguardian.com/uk-news/2013/jul/12/belfast-protests-orange-parade.
7. I use the term 'extreme right' to indicate anti-democratic, anti-egalitarian individuals and organizations espousing racist, neo-fascist and neo-Nazi views. (The term 'far right' is best avoided on account of its indiscriminate use by the media.)
8. 'A Chance to BE WHITE: Classical Music', www.stormfront.org/forum/t680327/ ('Karajan', 11 February 2010).
9. Ibid. ('Harold Head', 8 February 2010; 'dsaly1969', 22 December 2016).
10. Ibid. ('Karajan', 7 February 2010).
11. Jeet Heer, 'An International Brotherhood of White Grievance', *New Republic* (6 July 2017), https://newrepublic.com/article/143746/international-brotherhood-white-grievance.
12. Donald Trump, 'Remarks by President Trump to the People of Poland' (6 July 2017), The White House: Office of the Press Secretary, www.whitehouse.gov/the-press-office/2017/07/06/remarks-president-trump-people-poland-july-6-2017.
13. Jim A. Kuypers, Stephen D. Cooper and Matthew T. Althouse, 'George W. Bush, the American Press, and the Initial Framing of the War on Terror after 9/11', in *The George W. Bush Presidency: A Rhetorical Perspective*, ed. Robert E. Denton Jr (Plymouth, 2012), 89–112.
14. Jonathan Capeheart, 'Trump's White-Nationalist Dog-Whistling', *Washington Post* (6 July 2017), www.washingtonpost.com/blogs/post-partisan/wp/2017/07/06/trumps-white-nationalist-dog-whistles-in-warsaw/?utm_term=.bd83cf6402ac; Amanda Marcote, 'Trump's Alt-Right Poland Speech: Time to Call His White Nationalist Rhetoric What It Is', *Salon* (8 July 2017), www.salon.com/2017/07/08/trumps-alt-right-poland-speech-time-to-call-his-white-nationalist-rhetoric-what-it-is/.
15. Étienne Balibar, 'Is There a "Neo-Racism"?', in Étienne Balibar and Immanuel Maurice, *Race, Nation, Class: Ambiguous Identities*, 2nd edn. (London, 2011), 17–28 (21).
16. As quoted in Alain Badiou, *The Rebirth of History: Times of Riots and Uprisings*, trans. Gregory Elliott (London, 2012), 71. See also Alana Lentin,

'Post-Race, Post Politics: The Paradoxical Rise of Culture after Multicultural-ism', *Ethnic and Racial Studies* 35 (2012), 5–6.

17. Evelien Tonkens and Jan Willem Duyvendak, 'Introduction: The Culturaliza-tion of Citizenship', in *The Culturalization of Citizenship: Belonging and Polarization in a Globalizing World*, ed. Jan Willem Duyvendak, Peter Geschiere and Evelien Tonkens (London, 2016), 1–20 (2).

18. See https://lifeintheuktests.co.uk/ and www.dutchtutor.com/en/inburgering sexamen.php.

19. Paul Mepschen and Jan Willem Duyvendak, 'European Sexual Nationalism: The Culturalization of Citizenship and the Sexual Politics of Belonging and Exclusion' *Religionresearch.org* (30 December 2012), http://religionresearch .org/closer/2012/12/30/sexual-nationalisms-culturalization-of-citizenship/.

20. Ibid.

21. Brown, *Regulating Aversion*, 14.

22. Miriam Gazzah, *Rhythms and Rhymes of Life: Music and Identification Processes of Dutch-Moroccan Youth* (Amsterdam, 2008), 201, 206; Jaap Kooij-man, *Fabricating the Absolute Fake: America in Contemporary Pop Culture* (Amsterdam, 2008), 127–8.

23. See, for example, Jonah Goldberg, *Liberal Fascism: The Secret History of the Left from Mussolini to the Politics of Meaning* (London, 2007).

24. Karl Löwith, 'Der okkasionelle Dezisionismus von C. Schmitt' (1935), as quoted in Agamben, *Sovereign Power*, 71.

25. Agamben, *Sovereign Power*, 71; Giorgio Agamben, *Means without End: Notes on Politics*, trans. Vincenzo Binetti and Cesa Te Casarino (Minneapolis, MN, 2000), 44.

26. For this reason it makes little sense to try to recuperate a positive sense of the concept as a tool for the left, a task attempted in Jon Simons, 'Aestheticisation of Politics: From Fascism to Radical Democracy', *Journal for Cultural Research* 12/3 (2008), 207–29.

27. Walter Benjamin, 'The Work of Art in the Age of Its Technological Reprodu-cibility', in *Selected Works*, vol. IV, 270.

28. Ibid., 252, 269.

29. Martin Jay, '"The Aesthetic Ideology" as Ideology; or, What Does It Mean to Aestheticize Politics?', *Cultural Critique* 21 (1992), 44–5; Erich Michaud, *The Cult of Art in Nazi Germany*, trans. Janet Lloyd (Stanford, CA, 2004), 1–3; and Simonetta Falasca-Zamponi, *Fascist Spectacle: The Aesthetics of Power in Mussolini's Italy* (Berkeley, CA, 1997), 21–5.

30. Lutz Koepnick, *Walter Benjamin and the Aesthetics of Power* (Lincoln, NE, 1999), 4.

31. George Orwell, 'What Is Fascism?', in *Complete Works*, ed. Peter Davison, 20 vols. (London, 2000) vol. XVI, 131–3.

32. The most sophisticated attempt to define fascism as a set of verbal principles is Roger Griffin, *The Nature of Fascism* (London, 1991), 1–55.

33. Robert O. Paxton, *The Anatomy of Fascism* (London, 2005), 15–17.

34. Roger Griffin, 'Staging the Nation's Rebirth: The Politics and Aesthetics of Performance in the Context of Fascist Studies', in *Fascism and Theatre: Comparative Studies on the Aesthetics and Politics of Performance in Europe, 1925–1945*, ed. Günter Berghaus (Providence, RI, 1996), 11–29 (13).

35. Sartwell, *Political Aesthetics*, 16.

36. George L. Mosse, *The Nationalization of the Masses: Political Symbolism and Mass Movements in Germany from the Napoleonic Wars through the Third Reich* (New York, 1974), as quoted in Frederic Spotts, *Hitler and the Power of Aesthetics*, 2nd edn. (Woodstock, NY, 2009), xiii. See also George L. Mosse, 'Fascist Aesthetics and Society: Some Considerations', *Journal of Contemporary History* 31 (1996), 245–52.

37. See Erik Levi, 'Toward an Aesthetic of Fascist Opera', in Berghaus (ed.), *Fascism and Theatre*, 260–76; Pamela M. Potter, 'What Is "Nazi Music"?', *The Musical Quarterly* 88 (2006), 428–55; and Pamela M. Potter, 'The Arts in Nazi Germany: A Silent Debate', *Contemporary European History* 15/4 (2006), 585–99.

38. Kevin Maimann, 'Lederhosen and Lunacy: Not Really German, Just Really Funny', *Toronto Sun* (21 May 2010), www.torontosun.com/entertainment/2010/05/20/14028071.html.

39. 'Neonazi Band in Discover Weekly', *Spotify Community* (9 May 2016), https://community.spotify.com/t5/Content-Questions/Neonazi-band-in-discover-weekly/m-p/1342810#M6122.

40. Valerie Weinstein, 'Reading Rammstein, Remembering Riefenstahl: "Fascist Aesthetics" and German Popular Culture', in Pages, Rhiel and O'Sickey (eds.), *Riefenstahl Screened*, 130–48 (140).

41. Frank Gerbert, 'Deutschrock: Im Banne der Teutonen', *Focus Magazin* 3 (18 January 1999), www.focus.de/panorama/boulevard/deutschrock-im-banne-der-teutonen_aid_177212.html.

42. Žižek, *End Times*, 385, 387.

43. Slavoj Žižek, *The Pervert's Guide to Ideology* (2012), dir. Sophie Fiennes (Zeitgeist Films).

44. Slavoj Žižek, *The Metastases of Enjoyment: Six Essays on Woman and Causality* (London, 1994), 71–2.

45. Slavoj Žižek, 'Why Are Laibach and the *Neue Slowenische Kunst* not Fascists?', in *The Universal Exception*, ed. Rex Butler and Scott Stephens (London, 2006), 64.

46. Dominic Boyer and Alexei Yurchak, 'American Stiob: Or, What Late-Socialist Aesthetics of Parody Reveal about Contemporary Political Culture in the West', *Cultural Anthropology* 25/2 (2010), 179–221.

47. For more detail on this process of reworking, see Michael Goddard, 'Noise as Cultural Subversion: The Return of Post-Punk', in *Against and Beyond: Subversion and Trangression in Mass Media, Popular Culture and Performance,*

ed. Magdalena Cieślak and Agnieszka Rasmus (Newcastle upon Tyne, 2012), 20–35 (31).

48. Alexei Monroe, *Interrogation Machine: Laibach and NSK* (Cambridge, MA, 2005), 229. See also Stevphen Shukaitis, 'Fascists as Much as Painters: Imagination, Overidentification, and Strategies of Intervention', *The Sociological Review* 59/3 (2011), 597–615.

49. See, for example, Kirsten Dyck, *Reichsrock: The International Web of White-Power and Neo-Nazi Hate Music* (New Brunswick, NJ, 2016); see also Klaus Farin et al., *Reaktionäre Rebellen: Rechtsextreme Musik in Deutschland* (Berlin, 2001).

50. A more detailed version of the research presented in this section is given in James Garratt, 'Right Extremist Protest Music and the Idea of Metapolitical Activism', in *Protest Music in the Twentieth Century*, ed. Roberto Illiano (Turnhout, 2015), 19–42.

51. See Rudolf van Hüllen, *'Modernisierter Rechtsextremismus': Eine Herausforderung für die politische Bildung* (Sankt Augustin, 2008), 36–8; and Johannes Radke, 'Der rechtsextreme "Kampf um die Straße"', *Bundeszentrale für politische Bildung: Dossier Rechtsextremismus* (14 May 2014), www.bpb.de/politik/extremismus/rechtsextremismus/184385/der-rechtsextreme-kampf-um-die-strasse.

52. For a broader survey of German right-extremist protest forms, see Fabian Virchow, 'Dimensionen der "Demonstrationspolitik" der extremen Rechten in der Bundesrepublik Deutschland', in *Moderner Rechtsextremismus in Deutschland*, ed. Andreas Klärner and Michael Kohlstruck (Hamburg, 2006), 68–101.

53. For examples, see Garratt, 'Right-Extremist Protest', 21.

54. Bundesamt für Verfassungsschutz (ed.). *Verfassungsschutzbericht 2013* (Berlin, 2014), 88.

55. Interview with Jürgen Gansel in *Deutsche Stimme* (February 2006), as quoted in Thomas Grunke, '"Sozialismus ist braun": Rechtextremismus, die soziale Frage und Globalisierungskritik', in *Strategien der extremen Rechten: Hintergründe–Analysen–Antworten*, ed. Stephan Braun, Alexander Geisler and Martin Gerster (Wiesbaden, 2009), 148–62 (150).

56. Hendrik Puls, '"Der ganze Alltag, das ganze Leben bestand eigentlich nur aus Nazi sein, Naziwelt leben und Naziaktivismus": Zur Lebenswelt "Autonomer Nationalisten" zwischen politischen Aktionen und individuellem Alltag', in *Autonome Nationalisten: Neonazismus in Bewegung*, ed. Jan Schedler and Alexander Häusler (Wiesbaden, 2011), 121–34.

57. Jan Schedler, 'Übernahme von Ästhetik und Aktionsformen der radikalen Linken – Zur Verortung der "Autonomen "Nationalisten" im extrem rechten Strategiespektrum', in Braun, Geisler and Gester (ed.), *Strategien*, 332–57. See also Raphael Schlembach, 'The "Autonomous Nationalists": New Developments and Contradictions in the German Neo-Nazi Movement', *Interface: A Journal for and about Social Movements* 5/2 (2013), 295–318.

58. See Verfassungsschutz durch Aufklärung (ed.), *Schwarze Blöcke rechts und links: Autonome Extremisten auf Gewaltkurs. Eine Veranstaltung des Verfassungsschutzes am 24. Juni 2010 in Potsdam* (Potsdam, 2010).

59. The only comprehensive discussion of this organization is Daniel Krüger, 'Völkische Ideen und Inszenierungen aus dem Spreewald: Das Internet-Projekt spreelichter.info', in *Einblicke IV: Ein Werkstattbuch*, ed. Dirk Wilking and Michael Kohlstruck (Potsdam, 2012), 51–80.

60. See 'Nichts ist zu spät – Die Unsterblichen auf Schloss Colditz' (25/05/2012), www.youtube.com/watch?v=v6sdYvX-fpI.

61. CasaPound, 'Una nazione. Il programma politico di CasaPound Italia', http://94.23.251.8/~casapoun/images/unanazione.pdf.

62. 'Moyote Project' [Franco Berteni, Denis Giordano and Caterina Sartori], 'Casa Pound and the New Radical Right in Italy', *Mute* 2/16 (20 April 2010), www.metamute.org/editorial/articles/casa-pound-and-new-radical-right-italy.

63. This initial phase of *Rechtsrock* is explored in Alenka Barber-Kersovan, 'German Nazi Bands: Between Provocation and Repression', in Cloonan and Garofalo (eds.), *Policing Pop*, 186–204; and Timothy S. Brown, 'Subcultures, Pop Music and Politics: Skinheads and "Nazi Rock" in England and Germany', *Journal of Social History* 38/1 (2004), 157–78.

64. See, for example, Bundesamt für Verfassungsschutz, *Rechtsextremistische Musik* (Cologne, 2007); and Abteilung Verfassungsschutz, *Rechtsextremistische Musik*, 3rd edn. (Berlin, 2012).

65. Useful overviews of the German *Rechtsrock* scene and details of prominent bands can be found in Farin, *Reaktionäre Rebellen*, 7–99; Martin Langebach and Jan Raabe, 'Zwischen Freizeit, Politik und Partei: RechtsRock', in Braun, Geisler and Gerster (eds.), *Strategien*, 163–88; and Chiara Pierobon, 'Rechtsrock: White Power Music in Germany', in *White Power Music: Scenes of Extreme-Right Cultural Resistance*, ed. Anton Shekhovtsov and Paul Jackson (Northampton, 2012), 7–23.

66. Sleipnir, 'Kriegsverbrechen', *Kriegsverbrechen* (Wotan Records, 2000).

67. Unsigned, '6,000 Neonazis feiern ungestört in Thüringen', *Zeit Online* (16 July 2017), http://blog.zeit.de/stoerungsmelder/2017/07/16/6-000-neonazis-feiern-ungestoert-in-thueringen_24365.

68. Breivik, *2083: A European Declaration*, 853.

69. Saga, *My Tribute to Skrewdriver*, vols. 1–3 (Midgård Records, 2000–1).

70. Andrew Hamilton, 'Voice of Swedish Nationalism: Saga and Her Music', *Counter-Currents Publishing* (16 September 2011), www.counter-currents.com/2011/09/saga-and-her-music/.

71. Two of the songs on the album *On My Own*, 'Black-Bannered Legion' and 'The Nation's Fate', have lyrics by white supremacist and convicted felon David Lane, and the album concludes with a tribute song to him ('Goodbye David Lane').

72. Richard Stöss, *Rechtsextremismus im Wandel* (Berlin, 2005), 180.

73. Emily Turner-Graham, '"Resistance never looked so good": Women in White Power Music', in Shekhovtsov and Jackson (ed.), *White Power Music*, 101–13 (110).

74. Agharta, *Zwischen den Zeilen* (Wolfszeit, 2011).

75. Ibid.

76. Jan Raabe and Martin Langebach, 'Jugendkulturelle Dynamik – Vom Hardcore über den NSHC zu den "Autonomen Nationalisten"', in Schedler and Häusler, *Autonome Nationalisten*, 154–66 (162).

77. 'Revenge', 'Daily Broken Dream Interview', *NS Revolt* (20 February 2010), http://revoltns.blogspot.co.uk/2010/02/daily-broken-dream-interview.html.

78. Rainer Fromm, '"We play NS Hardcore": Neue Tendenzen am rechten Rand – zwischen Protest und Extremismus', *BPjM-Aktuell: amtliches Mitteilungsblatt der Bundesprüfstelle für jugendgefährdende Medien* 6/1 (2008), 12–21 (14).

79. Schedler, 'Übernahme von Ästhetik', 336.

80. These percentages are calculated using the 2016 figures given in Bundesamt für Verfassungsschutz, *Verfassungsschutzbericht 2016* (Berlin, 2017), 40.

81. Interview with Race Riot (c. 2007), as quoted in Martin Langebach, David Begrich and Jan Raabe, *Sirenen des Hasses: NS Hardcore aus Sachsen-Anhalt* (Magedeburg, 2010), 20.

82. David Lagerlöf, 'The Rise and Fall of White Power Music in Sweden', in Shekhovtsov and Jackson (ed.), *White Power Music*, 35–45.

83. Ibid., 42.

84. 'Fourmyle of Ceres', blog comment of 17 September 2011 on Hamilton, 'Voice of Swedish Nationalism'.

85. Guillaume Faye, 'Warum wir kämpfen', *Elemente für die europäische Wiedergeburt* 1 (1986), 10–14 (13–14).

86. For a broader discussion of how the German Neue Rechte misused the idea of cultural hegemony, see Reinhold Gärtner, '*Neue Rechte*: Ethnocentrism, Culture and Cultural Identity', *Sociological Research Online* 5/1 (2000), www.socresonline.org.uk/5/1/gaertner.html.

87. Pierre Krebs, 'Die Flucht nach vorn – Gramscis metapolitische Wandlung', *Elemente zur Metapolitik*, II (1987), 4.

88. Joakim Andersen, 'Interview with CasaPound', *Motpol* (1 December 2010), www.motpol.nu/oskorei/2010/12/01/interview-with-casapound/.

89. 'Antwort der Landesregierung auf eine Kleine Anfrage zur schriftlichen Beantwortung: Aktuelle neonazistische Musikkultur in Sachsen-Anhalt', Landtag von Sachsen-Anhalt: Drucksache 6/233 (14 July 2011), www.landtag.sachsen-anhalt.de/fileadmin/files/drs/wp6/drs/d0233dak.pdf; 'Antwort der Landesregierung auf eine Kleine Anfrage zur schriftlichen Beantwortung', Landtag von Sachsen-Anhalt: Drucksache 6/3308 (22 July 2014), www.landtag.sachsen-anhalt.de/fileadmin/files/drs/wp6/drs/d3308dak.pdf.

90. Laclau and Mouffe, *Hegemony and Socialist Strategy*, 56.

91. Peter Foster and Justin Huggler, 'Is the Far-Right on the Rise again in Germany?, *The Telegraph* (14 March 2016), www.telegraph.co.uk/news/worldnews/europe/ germany/12193496/Is-the-far-Right-on-the-rise-again-in-Germany.html.

Postscript: Music and Politics after the Future

1. Berardi, *After the Future*, 126.
2. Marx and Engels, *Communist Manifesto*, 223.
3. Berardi, *After the Future*, 175.
4. Slavoj Žižek, *Trouble in Paradise: From the End of History to the End of Capitalism* (London, 2014), 248.
5. Micah White, *The End of Protest: A New Playbook for Revolution* (Toronto, 2016); Berardi, *After the Future*, 177, 148.
6. Berardi, *After the Future*, 177.
7. David Holyoake, '*Extinct Birds*: A New Contemporary Music Creation', www.davidholyoake.com/extinct_birds/.
8. David Holyoake, '*Extinct Birds* and Contemporary Music as Activism: An Invitation', *Resonate Magazine* (19 March 2014), www.australianmusiccentre.com.au/ article/em-extinct-birds-em-and-contemporary-music-as-activism-an-invitation.
9. Georg Knepler, *Macht ohne Herrschaft: Die Realisierung einer Möglichkeit*, ed. Stefan Huth (Berlin, 2004).
10. Currie, *Politics of Negation*, x, xiii.
11. Žižek, *The Universal Exception*, 239.
12. Michel Foucault, 'Preface', in Gilles Deleuze and Felix Guattari, *Anti-Oedipus: Capitalism and Schizophrenia*, trans. Robert Hurley, Mark Seem and Helen R. Lane (Minneapolis, MN, 1983), xi–xiv (xiv).

Select Bibliography

Adlington, Robert (ed.), *Sound Commitments: Avant-Garde Music and the Sixties* (Cambridge, 2009).

Adorno, Theodor W., *Aesthetic Theory*, ed. Gretel Adorno and Rolf Tiedemann, trans. Robert Hullot-Kentor (London, 1997).

Essays on Music, ed. Richard Leppert (Berkeley, CA, 2002).

Negative Dialectics, trans. Dennis Redmond (2001), http://monkeybear.info/ND_Full.pdf.

Prisms, trans. Samuel Weber and Shierry Weber (Cambridge, MA, 1981).

'Zur gesellschaftlichen Lage der Musik', *Zeitschrift für Sozialforschung* 1/1–2 (1932), 103–24 and 1/3 (1932), 356–78.

Adorno, Theodor, Walter Benjamin, Ernst Bloch, Berthold Brecht and Georg Lukács, *Aesthetics and Politics*, ed. Ronald Taylor (London, 1977).

Agamben, Giorgio, *Homo sacer: Sovereign Power and Bare Life*, trans. Daniel Heller-Roazen (Stanford, CA, 1998).

The Kingdom and the Glory: For a Theological Genealogy of Economy and Government, trans. Lorenzo Chiesa (Stanford, CA, 2011).

Means without End: Notes on Politics, trans. Vincenzo Binetti and Cesa Te Casarino (Minneapolis, MN, 2000).

Alcoff, Linda Martín, *Visible Identities: Race, Gender, and the Self* (New York, 2006).

Alexander, Jeffrey C., Bernhard Giesen and Jason L. Mast (eds.), *Social Performance: Symbolic Action, Cultural Pragmatics, and Ritual* (Cambridge, 2006).

Althusser, Louis, and Étienne Balibar, *Reading Capital*, trans. Ben Brewster (London, 1970).

Anderson, Benedict, *Imagined Communities: Reflections on the Origin and Spread of Nationalism*, 2nd edn. (London, 2006).

Arendt, Hannah, *Crises of the Republic* (New York, 1972).

Aristotle, *Politics*, trans. and ed. C. D. C. Reeve (Indianapolis, IN, 1998).

Atanasovski, Srđan, 'Consequences of the Affective Turn: Exploring Music Practices from Without and Within', *Muzikologija* 18 (2015), 57–75.

Attali, Jacques, *Noise: The Political Economy of Music*, trans. Brian Massumi (Minneapolis, MN, 1965).

Averill, Gage, *A Day for the Hunter, A Day for the Prey: Popular Music and Power in Haiti* (Chicago, IL, 1997).

Badiou, Alain, *Five Lessons on Wagner* (London, 2010).
　Metapolitics, trans. Jason Barker (London, 2005).
　The Rebirth of History: Times of Riots and Uprisings, trans. Gregory Elliott
　　(London, 2012).
Baggersgaard, Mads Anders, and Jakob Ladegaard (eds.), *Confronting
　Universalities: Aesthetics and Politics under the Sign of Globalisation*
　(Aarhus, 2011).
Baily, John, *War, Exile and the Music of Afghanistan: The Ethnographer's Tale*
　(Farnham, 2015).
Bal, Mieke, and Miguel Á. Hernández-Navarro (eds.), *Art and Visibility in
　Migratory Culture: Conflict, Resistance, and Agency* (Amsterdam, 2011).
Balibar, Étienne, *The Philosophy of Marx*, trans. Chris Turner (London, 2014).
　Politics and the Other Scene, trans. Christine Jones, James Swenson and Chris
　　Turner (London, 2002).
Balibar, Étienne, and Immanuel Maurice, *Race, Nation, Class: Ambiguous
　Identities*, 2nd edn. (London, 2011).
Bannet, Eve Tavor, *Postcultural Theory: Critical Theory after the Marxist
　Paradigm* (Basingstoke, 1993).
Barrett, Michèle, *The Politics of Truth: From Marx to Foucault* (Stanford, CA,
　1991).
Baudrillard, Jean, *The Transparency of Evil: Essays on Extreme Phenomena*,
　trans. James Benedict (London, 1993).
Bayreuther, Rainer, 'Überlegungen zu einer Theorie politischer Musik am
　Beispiel von Händels "Ode for the Birthday of Queen Anne"', *Die
　Musikforschung* 63/3 (2010), 228–47.
Becker, Judith O., *Deep Listeners: Music, Emotion, and Trancing* (Bloomington, IN,
　2004).
Benjamin, Walter, *Selected Writings*, ed. Howard Eiland and Michael W. Jennings,
　trans. Rodney Livingstone et al. (Cambridge, MA, 1996–2003).
Bennett, Jane, *Vibrant Matter: A Political Ecology of Things* (Durham, NC, 2010).
Berardi, Franco, *After the Future*, ed. Gary Genosko and Nicholas Thoburn, trans.
　Arianna Bove et al. (Oakland, CA, 2011).
Berry, Mark, *Treacherous Bonds and Laughing Fire: Politics and Religion in
　Wagner's Ring* (Aldershot, 2006).
Bertelli, Sergio, *The King's Body: Sacred Rituals of Power in Medieval and Early
　Modern Europe*, trans. R. Burr Litchfield (University Park, PA, 2001).
Blake, David (ed.), *Hanns Eisler: A Miscellany* (Luxembourg, 1995).
Blomann, Ulrich (ed.), *Kultur und Musik nach 1945: Ästhetik im Zeichen des
　Kalten Krieges* (Saarbrücken, 2015).
Bobbio, Norberto, *Liberalism and Democracy*, trans. Martin Ryle and Kate Soper
　(London, 2005).
Bohlman, Philip V., *The Music of European Nationalism: Cultural Identity and
　Modern History* (New York, 2004).

Bonds, Mark Evan, *Absolute Music: The History of an Idea* (New York, 2014).

Born, Georgina, 'Music and the Materialization of Identities', *Journal of Material Culture* 16/4 (2011), 376–88.

ed., *Music, Sound and Space: Transformations of Public and Private Experience* (Cambridge, 2013).

'On Musical Mediation: Ontology, Technology and Creativity', *Twentieth-Century Music* 2/1 (2005), 7–36.

'The Social and the Aesthetic: For a Post-Bourdieuian Theory of Cultural Production', *Cultural Sociology* 4/2 (2010), 171–208.

Born, Georgina, and David Hesmondhalgh (eds.), *Western Music and Its Others: Difference, Representation, and Appropriation in Music* (Berkeley, CA, 2000).

Bottomore, Tom, *Dictionary of Marxist Thought*, 2nd edn. (Oxford, 1991).

Boucher, David, and Gary Browning (eds.), *The Political Art of Bob Dylan*, 2nd edn. (Exeter, 2009).

Bourriaud, Nicolas, *The Radicant*, trans. James Gussen and Lili Porten (New York, 2009).

Bowie, Andrew, *From Romanticism to Critical Theory: The Philosophy of German Literary Theory* (London, 1997).

Boyd, Malcolm (ed.), *Music and the French Revolution* (Cambridge, 1992).

Brader, Ted, 'Striking a Responsive Chord: How Political Ads Motivate and Persuade Voters by Appealing to Emotions', *American Journal of Political Science* 49/2 (2005), 388–405.

Braun, Stephan, Alexander Geisler and Martin Gerster (eds.), *Strategien der extremen Rechten: Hintergründe–Analysen–Antworten* (Wiesbaden, 2009).

Brown, Wendy, *Regulating Aversion: Tolerance in the Age of Identity and Empire* (Princeton, NJ, 2006).

Buch, Esteban, *Beethoven's Ninth: A Political History*, trans. Richard Miller (Chicago, IL, 2003).

Butler, Judith, *Gender Trouble: Feminism and the Subversion of Identity* (London, 1990).

Butler, Judith, Ernesto Laclau and Slavoj Žižek, *Contingency, Hegemony, Universality: Contemporary Dialogues on the Left* (London, 2000).

Callinicos, Alex, *Making History: Agency, Structure, and Change in Social Theory*, 2nd edn. (Leiden, 2004).

Cammaerts, Bart, 'Protest Logics and the Mediation Opportunity Structure', *European Journal of Communication* 27/2 (2012), 117–34.

Cañeque, Alejandro, *The King's Living Image: The Culture and Politics of Viceregal Power in Colonial Mexico* (New York, 2004).

Carroll, Mark, 'Commitment or Abrogation? Avant-Garde Music and Jean-Paul Sartre's Idea of Committed Art', *Music and Letters* 83/4 (2002), 590–606.

(ed.), *Music and Ideology* (Farnham, 2012).

Chambers, Samuel A., 'Jacques Rancière and the Problem of Pure Politics', *European Journal of Political Theory* 10/3 (2011), 303–26.

Chehonadskih, Maria, 'What Is Pussy Riot's "Idea"?', *Radical Philosophy* 176 (November/December 2012), 2–7.

Chomsky, Noam, *Media Control: The Spectacular Achievements of Propaganda*, 2nd edn. (New York, 2008).

Chou, Mark, and Roland Bleiker, 'Betrayed by Democracy: Verbatim Theater as Prefigurative Politics', in *Doing Democracy: Activist Art and Cultural Politics*, ed. Nancy S. Love and Mark Mattern (Albany, NY, 2013), 231–55.

Christiansen, Paul, '"It's Morning Again in America": How the Tuesday Team Revolutionized the Use of Music in Political Ads', *Music & Politics* 10/1 (2016), http://dx.doi.orgkkk/10.3998/mp.9460447.0010.105.

Clarke, David, and Eric Clarke (eds.), *Music and Consciousness: Philosophical, Psychological, and Cultural Perspectives* (Oxford, 2011).

Cloonan, Martin, and Reebee Garofalo (eds.), *Policing Pop* (Philadelphia 2003).

Collier, Andrew, *Marx: A Beginner's Guide* (Oxford, 2004).

Connolly, William E., *A World of Becoming* (Durham, NC, 2011).

Cook, Nicholas, 'Classical Music and the Politics of Space', in *Music, Sound and Space: Transformations of Public and Private Experience*, ed. Georgina Born (Cambridge, 2013), 224–38.

'The Other Beethoven: Heroism, the Canon, and the Works of 1813–14', *19th-Century Music* 27/1 (2003), 3–24.

Corner, John, 'Mediated Politics, Promotional Culture and the Idea of Propaganda', *Media, Culture & Society* 29/4 (2007), 669–77.

Couldry, Nick, *Why Voice Matters: Culture and Politics after Neoliberalism* (London, 2010).

Critchley, Simon, *Infinitely Demanding: Ethics of Commitment, Politics of Resistance* (London, 2012).

Cullen, Jim, 'Bruce Springsteen's Ambiguous Musical Politics in the Reagan Era', *Popular Music and Society* 16/2 (1992), 1–22.

Currie, James, 'Music after All', *Journal of the American Musicological Society* 62/1 (2009), 145–204.

'Music and Politics', in *The Routledge Companion to Philosophy and Music*, ed. Theodore Gracyk and Andrew Kania (London, 2011), 546–56.

Cusick, Suzanne G., 'Music as Torture/Music as Weapon', *Trans: Revista transcultural de música* 10 (December 2006), www.redalyc.org/articulo.oa? id=82201011.

'Musicology, Torture, Repair', *Radical Musicology* 3 (2008), www.radical-musicology.org.uk/2008/Cusick.htm.

Dahlberg, Lincoln, and Sean Phelan (eds.), *Discourse Theory and Critical Media Politics* (Basingstoke, 2011).

Dahlhaus, Carl, 'Thesen über engagierte Musik', in *Musik zwischen Engagement und Kunst*, ed. Otto Kolleritsch (Graz, 1972), 7–19.

Dale, Peter, *Anyone Can Do It: Empowerment, Tradition and the Punk Underground* (Abingdon, 2016).

Daughtry, J. Martin, *Listening to War: Sound, Music, Trauma, and Survival in Wartime Iraq* (Oxford, 2015).

Day, Richard J. F., *Gramsci Is Dead: Anarchist Currents in the Newest Social Movements* (London, 2005).

Deathridge, John, *Wagner beyond Good and Evil* (Berkeley, CA, 2008).

De La Fuente, Eduardo, 'In Defence of Theoretical and Methodological Pluralism in the Sociology of Art: A Critique of Georgina Born's Programmatic Essay', *Cultural Sociology* 4/2 (2010), 217–30.

Deaville, James, 'The Envoicing of Protest: Occupying Television News through Sound and Music', *Journal of Sonic Studies* 3(2012), http://journal.sonicstudies.org/vol03/nr01/a05.

Deleuze, Gilles, *Negotiations* (1990), trans. Martin Joughin (New York, 1995). 'Postscript on the Societies of Control', *October* 59 (1992), 3–7.

Deleuze, Gilles, and Félix Guattari, *A Thousand Plateaus: Capitalism and Schizophrenia*, trans. Brian Massumi (Minneapolis, MN, 1987).

Denisoff, R. Serge, *Sing a Song of Social Significance* (Bowling Green, OH, 1972).

Deranty, Jean Philippe (ed.), *Jacques Rancière: Key Concepts* (Durham, NC, 2010).

Douzinas, Costas, and Slavoj Žižek (eds.), *The Idea of Communism* (London, 2010).

Drewett, Michael, and Martin Cloonan (eds.), *Popular Music Censorship in Africa* ingdon, 2006).

Drott, Eric, 'Rereading Jacques Attali's *Bruits*', *Critical Inquiry* 41 (2015), 721–56.

Duarte, Anabela, 'Acousmatic and Acoustic Violence and Torture in the Estado Novo: The Notorious Revelations of the PIDE/DGS Trial in 1957', *Music & Politics* 9/1 (2015), http://dx.doi.org/10.3998/mp.9460447.0009.101.

Duncombe, Stephen (ed.), *Cultural Resistance Reader* (London, 2002).

Dunlap, James, 'Through the Eyes of Tom Joad: Patterns of American Idealism, Bob Dylan, and the Folk Protest Movement', *Popular Music and Society* 29/5 (2006), 549–73.

Dyck, Kirsten, *Reichsrock: The International Web of White-Power and Neo-Nazi Hate Music* (New Brunswick, NJ, 2016).

Dyson, Frances, *The Tone of our Times: Sound, Sense, Economy, and Ecology* (Cambridge, MA, 2014).

Eagleton, Terry, *The Ideology of the Aesthetic* (Oxford, 1990). *Ideology: An Introduction* (London, 1991).

Eisler, Hanns, *A Rebel in Music: Selected Writings*, ed. Manfred Grabs, trans. Marjorie Meyer (London, 1999). *Gesammelte Schriften 1921–1935*, ed. Tobias Faßhauer and Günter Mayer, *Hanns Eisler Gesamtausgabe*, ser. 9, vol. 1.1 (Wiesbaden, 2007).

Elder-Vass, Dave, 'The Causal Power of Discourse', *Journal for the Theory of Social Behaviour* 41/2 (2010), 143–60.

Eyerman, Ron, and Andrew Jamison, *Music and Social Movements: Mobilizing Traditions in the Twentieth Century* (Cambridge, 1998).

Fackler, Guido, 'Music in Concentration Camps 1933–1945', trans. Peter Logan, *Music & Politics* 1/1 (2007), http://dx.doi.org/10.3998/mp.9460447.0001.102.

Fairclough, Pauline (ed.), *Twentieth-Century Music and Politics: Essays in Memory of Neil Edmunds* (Farnham, 2013).

Falasca-Zamponi, Simonetta, *Fascist Spectacle: The Aesthetics of Power in Mussolini's Italy* (Berkeley, CA, 1997).

Falola, Toyin, and Tyler Fleming (eds.), *Music, Performance and African Identities* (London, 2012).

Fanning, David (ed.), *Shostakovich Studies* (Cambridge, 1995).

Fast, Susan, and Kip Pegley (eds.), *Music, Politics, and Violence* (Middletown, CT, 2012).

Felski, Rita, 'Context Stinks!', *New Literary History* 42/4 (2011), 573–91.

Fisher, Mark, *Capitalist Realism: Is There No Alternative?* (Winchester, 2009).

Foucault, Michel, *History of Sexuality*, vol. 1, trans. Robert Hurley (New York, 1978).

   Power: The Essential Works of Michel Foucault 1954–1984, ed. James D. Faubion, vol. 3 (London, 1997).

   Power/Knowledge: Selected Interviews and Other Writings 1972–1977, ed. Colin Gordon (New York, 1980).

Fukuyama, Francis, *The End of History and the Last Man* (New York, 1992).

Garofalo, Reebee (ed.), *Rockin' the Boat: Mass Music and Mass Movements* (Cambridge, MA, 1992).

Garratt, James, '"Ein gute Wehr und Waffen": Apocalyptic and Redemptive Narratives in Organ Music from the Great War', in *Music and War from the French Revolution to World War I*, ed. Étienne Jardin (Turnhout, 2016), 379–411.

   Music, Culture and Social Reform in the Age of Wagner (Cambridge, 2010).

   'Right-Extremist Protest Music and the Idea of Metapolitical Activism', in *Protest Music in the Twentieth Century*, ed. Roberto Illiano (Turnhout, 2015), 19–42.

Gauntlett, David, 'Ten Things Wrong with the Media "Effects" Model', in *Approaches to Audiences: A Reader*, ed. Roger Dickinson, Ramaswami Harindranath and Olga Linné (London, 1998), 120–30.

Gaventa, John, 'Finding the Spaces for Change: A Power Analysis', *Institute of Development Studies Bulletin* 27/6 (2006), 23–33.

Geertz, Clifford, *Negara: The Theatre State in Nineteenth-Century Bali* (Princeton, NJ, 1980).

Geuss, Raymond, 'Art and Criticism in Adorno's Aesthetics', *European Journal of Philosophy* 6/3 (1998), 297–317.

Gilbert, Jeremy, *Anticapitalism and Culture: Radical Theory and Popular Politics* (Oxford, 2008).

   'What Kind of Thing Is "Neo-Liberalism?"', *New Formations* 80 and 81 (2013), 7–22.

Gilbert, Jeremy, and Ewan Pearson, *Discographies: Dance Music, Culture and the Politics of Sound* (London, 2002).

Giugni, Marco, Doug McAdam and Charles Tilly (eds.), *How Social Movements Matter* (Minneapolis, MN, 1999).

Goehr, Lydia, 'Political Music and the Politics of Music', *Journal of Aesthetics and Art Criticism* 52/1 (1994), 99–112.

 The Quest for Voice: On Music, Politics, and the Limits of Philosophy (Oxford, 1998).

Goldstein, Philip, *Post-Marxist Theory: An Introduction* (New York, 2005).

Goodman, Steve, *Sonic Warfare: Sound, Affect, and the Ecology of Fear* (Cambridge, MA, 2010).

Gorzelany-Mostak, Dana, and James Deaville, 'On the Campaign Trail(er): Deconstructing the Soundscape of the 2012 U.S. Presidential Election', *Music & Politics* 9/2 (2015), http://dx.doi.org/10.3998/mp.9460447.0009.201.

Gramsci, Antonio, *The Gramsci Reader: Selected Writings 1916–1935*, ed. David Forgacs (New York, 2000).

Grant, Morag J., 'Pathways to Music Torture', *Transpositions: Musiques et sciences sociales* 4 (2014), 2–19.

Green, Andrew, 'Rage Against the Machine, Zapatismo, and the Aesthetics of Anger', *Popular Music* 34/3 (2015), 390–407.

Grey, Thomas S. (ed.), *Richard Wagner and His World* (Princeton, NJ, 2009).

Griffin, Roger, *The Nature of Fascism* (London, 1991).

Grossberg, Lawrence, *Cultural Studies in the Future Tense* (Durham, NC, 2010).

 'The Media Economy of Rock Culture: Cinema, Post-Modernity and Authenticity', in *Sound and Vision: The Music Video Reader*, ed. Simon Frith, Andrew Goodwin and Lawrence Grossberg (London, 1993), 185–209.

Guattari, Félix, and Antonio Negri, *New Lines of Alliance, New Spaces of Liberty*, trans. Michael Ryan et al. (Brooklyn, NY, 2010).

Habermas, Jürgen, *The Structural Transformation of the Public Sphere: An Inquiry into a Category of Bourgeois Society*, trans. Thomas Burger with Frederick Lawrence (Cambridge, 1989).

Halberstam, Jack, 'Charming for the Revolution: Pussy and Other Riots', in *The Routledge Companion to Art and Politics*, ed. Randy Martin (Abingdon, 2015), 184–93.

Hall, Stuart, 'The Neo-Liberal Revolution', *Cultural Studies* 25/6 (2011), 705–28.

 'Re-Thinking the "Base-and-Superstructure" Metaphor', in *Class, Hegemony and Party*, ed. Jon Bloomfield (London, 1977), 43–72.

 'Signification, Representation, Ideology: Althusser and the Post-Structuralist Debates', *Critical Studies in Mass Communication* 2/2 (1985), 91–114.

Hamilton, John T., 'Torture as an Instrument of Music', in *Thresholds of Listening: Sound, Technics, Space*, ed. Sander van Maas (New York, 2015), 143–52.

Han, Byung-Chul, *Psychopolitik: Neoliberalismus und die neuen Machttechniken* (Frankfurt am Main, 2015).

Hanheide, Stefan, Dietrich Helms, Claudia Glunz and Thomas F. Schneider (eds.), *Musik bezieht Stellung: Funktionalisierungen der Musik im Ersten Weltkrieg* (Göttingen, 2013).

Hardt, Michael, and Antonio Negri, *Commonwealth* (Cambridge, MA, 2009).
Empire (Cambridge, MA, 2000).

Harper-Scott, J. P. E., *The Quilting Points of Musical Modernism: Revolution, Reaction, and William Walton* (Cambridge, 2012).

Hennion, Antoine, *The Passion for Music: A Sociology of Mediation*, trans. Margaret Rigaud and Peter Collier (Farnham, 2015).

Heylin, Clinton, *Revolution in the Air: The Songs of Bob Dylan, 1957–1973* (Chicago, IL, 2009).

Heywood, Andrew, *Politics*, 4th edn. (Basingstoke, 2013)

Hill, Sarah, '"This is My Country": American Popular Music and Political Engagement in "1968"', in *Music and Protest in 1968*, ed. Beate Kutschke and Barley Norton (Cambridge, 2013), 46–63.

Hirsch, Lily E., *Music in American Crime Prevention and Punishment* (Ann Arbor, MI, 2012).

Hoffman, John, *A Glossary of Political Theory* (Edinburgh, 2007).

Hollander, Jocelyn A., and Rachel L. Einwohner, 'Conceptualizing Resistance', *Sociological Forum* 19/4 (2004), 533–54.

Holloway, John, *Change the World without Taking Power: The Meaning of Revolution Today* (London, 2002).

Holloway, John, Fernando Matamoros and Sergio Tischler (eds.), *Negativity and Revolution: Adorno and Political Activism* (London, 2009).

Huber, Nicolaus A., *Durchleuchtungen: Texte zur Musik 1964–1999*, ed. Josef Häusler (Wiesbaden, 2000).

Jameson, Fredric, *The Cultural Turn: Selected Writings on the Postmodern, 1983–1998* (London, 1998).
Jameson on Jameson: Conversations on Cultural Marxism, ed. Ian Buchanan (Durham, NC, 2007).
Late Marxism: Adorno or the Persistence of the Dialectic (London, 2007).
The Political Unconscious: Narrative as a Socially Symbolic Act (Ithaca, NY, 1981; repr. London, 2002).
Valences of the Dialectic (London, 2009).
'Wagner as Dramatist and Allegorist', *Modernist Cultures* 8/1 (2013), 9–41.

Jay, Martin, '"The Aesthetic Ideology" as Ideology; or, What Does It Mean to Aestheticize Politics?', *Cultural Critique* 21 (1992), 41–61.
'Historical Explanation and the Event: Reflections on the Limits of Contextualization', *New Literary History* 42/4 (2011), 557–71.

Johnson, Bruce, and Martin Cloonan, *Dark Side of the Tune: Popular Music and Violence* (Farnham, 2009).

Kantorowicz, Ernst H., *The King's Two Bodies: A Study in Mediaeval Political Theology* (Princeton, NJ, 1957).

   Laudes regiae: A Study in Liturgical Acclamations and Mediaeval Ruler Worship (Berkeley, CA, 1946).

Keller, Marcello Sorce, 'Why Is Music so Ideological, and Why Do Totalitarian States Take It so Seriously? A Personal View from History and the Social Sciences', *Journal of Musicological Research* 26 (2007), 91–122.

Kelly, Elaine, *Composing the Canon in the German Democratic Republic: Narratives of Nineteenth-Century Music* (New York, 2014).

Kim, Suk-Young, *Illusive Utopia: Theater, Film, and Everyday Performance in North Korea* (Ann Arbor, MI, 2010).

Kitcher, Philip, and Richard Schacht, *Finding an Ending: Reflections on Wagner's Ring* (New York, 2004).

Knepler, Georg, 'Hanns Eisler and "Interventive Thought"', *Journal of Musicological Research* 17/3 (1998), 239–60.

Kutschke, Beate, and Barley Norton (eds.), *Music and Protest in 1968* (Cambridge, 2013).

Laclau, Ernesto, *Emancipation(s)* (London, 1996).

Laclau, Ernesto, and Chantal Mouffe, *Hegemony and Socialist Strategy: Towards a Radical Democratic Politics*, 2nd edn. (London, 2014).

   'Post-Marxism without Apologies', *New Left Review* 166 (1987), 79–106.

Lam, Joseph S. C., 'Ritual and Musical Politics in the Court of Ming Shizong', in *Harmony and Counterpoint: Ritual Music in Chinese Context*, ed. Bell Yung, Evelyn Sakakida Rawski and Rubie S. Watson (Stanford, CA, 1996), 35–53.

Lanning, Robert, *In the Hotel Abyss: An Hegelian-Marxist Critique of Adorno* (Leiden, 2014).

Lash, Scott, 'Power after Hegemony: Cultural Studies in Mutation?', *Theory, Culture & Society* 24/3 (2007), 55–78.

Léger, Marc James, *Brave New Avant Garde: Essays on Contemporary Art and Politics* (Winchester, 2012).

Leonard, Marion, *Gender in the Music Industry: Rock, Discourse and Girl Power* (Aldershot, 2007).

Leopold, David, *The Young Karl Marx: German Philosophy, Modern Politics, and Human Flourishing* (Cambridge, 2007).

Leys, Ruth, 'The Turn to Affect: A Critique', *Critical Inquiry* 37 (2011), 434–72.

Locke, Ralph P., *Music, Musicians, and the Saint-Simonians* (Chicago, IL, 1986).

Love, Joanna, 'Branding a Cool Celebrity President: Popular Music, Political Advertising, and the 2012 Election', *Music & Politics* 9/2 (2015), http://dx.doi.org/10.3998/mp.9460447.0009.203.

Love, Nancy S., *Musical Democracy* (Albany, NY, 2006).

Lühning, Helga, and Sieghard Brandenburg (eds.), *Beethoven: Zwischen Revolution und Restauration* (Bonn, 1989).

Lukács, Georg, *History and Class Consciousness: Studies in Marxist Dialectics*, trans. Rodney Livingstone (London, 1971).

Lukes, Steven, *Power: A Radical View*, 2nd edn. (Basingstoke, 2005).

Mahnkopf, Claus-Steffen (ed.), *Critical Composition Today* (Hofheim, 2006).

Marchant, Oliver, *Post-Foundational Political Thought: Political Difference in Nancy, Lefort, Badiou and Laclau* (Edinburgh, 2007).

Marcuse, Herbert, *The Aesthetic Dimension: Towards a Critique of Marxist Aesthetics* (Boston, 1978).

 An Essay on Liberation (Boston, 1969).

 Collected Papers of Herbert Marcuse, ed. Douglas Kellner, 6 vols. (London, 1998–2014).

 One-Dimensional Man: Studies in the Ideology of Advanced Industrial Society (London, 2002).

Marstal, Henrik, 'Taking Which Power back? Overpowerments of Rage Against the Machine', in *Protest Music in the Twentieth Century*, ed. Roberto Illiano (Turnhout, 2015), 339–88.

Martin, Peter J., 'Music, Identity, and Social Control', in *Music and Manipulation: On the Social Uses and Social Control of Music*, ed. Steven Brown and Ulrik Volgsten (New York, 2006), 57–73.

 Sounds and Society: Themes in the Sociology of Music (Manchester, 1995).

Marx, Karl, *Selected Writings*, 2nd edn., ed. David McLellan (Oxford, 2000).

Marx, Karl, and Friedrich Engels, *Collected Works*, ed. Jack Cohen et al., trans. Clemens Dutt, W. Lough and C. P. Magill, 50 vols. (London, 1976).

 The Communist Manifesto, ed. Gareth Stedman Jones, trans. Samuel Moore (London, 2002).

 The Marx-Engels Reader, 2nd edn., ed. Robert C. Tucker (New York, 1978).

Mason, Laura, *Singing the French Revolution: Popular Culture and Politics, 1787–1799* (Ithaca, NY, 1996).

Massumi, Brian, *Politics of Affect* (Cambridge, 2015).

Mathew, Nicholas, *Political Beethoven* (Cambridge, 2013).

Mayer, Günter, 'Historischer Materialstand: Zu Hanns Eislers Konzeption einer "Dialektik der Musik"', *Deutsches Jahrbuch der Musikwissenschaft* 17 (1972), 7–24.

McClary, Susan, *Reading Music: Selected Essays* (Aldershot, 2007).

McKay, George, *Senseless Acts of Beauty: Cultures of Resistance since the Sixties* (London, 1996).

McMichael, Polly, 'Defining Pussy Riot Musically: Performance and Authenticity in New Media', *Digital Icons: Studies in Russian, Eurasian and Central European New Media* 9 (2013), 99–113.

Mecking, Sabine, and Yvonne Wasserloos (eds.), *Music – Macht – Staat: Kulturelle, soziale und politische Wandlungsprozesse in der Moderne* (Göttingen, 2012).

Moormann, Peter, Albrecht Riethmüller and Rebecca Wolf (eds.), *Paradestück Militärmusik: Beiträge zum Wandel staatlicher Repräsentation durch Musik* (Bielefeld, 2012).

Moreno, Jairo, and Gavin Steingo, 'Rancière's Equal Music', *Contemporary Music Review* 31/5–6 (2012), 487–505.

Mouffe, Chantal, *Agonistics: Thinking the World Politically* (London, 2013).
  The Democratic Paradox (London, 2000).
  On the Political (London, 2005).
  The Return of the Political (London, 1993).

Mumford, Stephen, and Rani Lill Anjum, *Causation: A Very Short Introduction* (Oxford, 2013).

Murphy, Timothy S., 'The Negation of a Negation Fixed in a Form: Luigi Nono and the Italian Counter-Culture 1964–1979', *Cultural Studies Review* 11/2 (2005), 95–109.

Nealon, Jeffrey T., *Post-Postmodernism: or, The Cultural Logic of Just-in-Time Capitalism* (Stanford, CA, 2012).

Negri, Antonio, *Insurgencies: Constituent Power and the Modern State*, trans. Maurizia Boscagli (Minneapolis, MN, 1999).

Nettl, Bruno, *The Study of Ethnomusicology: Thirty-One Issues and Concepts*, 2nd edn. (Urbana, IL, 2005).

Newman, Saul, *Power and Politics in Poststructuralist Thought: New Theories of the Political* (Abingdon, 2005).

Nooshin, Laudan (ed.), *Music and the Play of Power in the Middle East, North Africa and Central Asia* (Farnham, 2009).

Nye, Joseph Jr., 'Soft Power', *Foreign Policy* 80 (1990), 153–71.

Obadare, Ebenezer, and Wendy Williams (eds.), *Civic Agency in Africa: Arts of Resistance in the 21st Century* (Woodbridge, 2014).

Ochoa, Ana María, 'On the Zoopolitics of the Voice and the Distinction between Nature and Culture', in *The Routledge Companion to Art and Politics*, ed. Randy Martin (Abingdon, 2015), 16–24.

Olaniyan, Tejumola, *Arrest the Music! Fela and His Rebel Art and Politics* (Bloomington, IN, 2004).

Paddison, Max, *Adorno's Aesthetics of Music* (Cambridge, 1993).

Pages, Neil Christian, Mary Rheil and Ingebord Majer O'Sickey (eds.), *Riefenstahl Screened: An Anthology of New Criticism* (New York, 2008).

Pasler, Jann, *Writing through Music: Essays on Music, Culture, and Politics* (Oxford, 2008).

Patch, Justin, 'Notes on Deconstructing the Populism: Music on the Campaign Trail, 2012 and 2016', *American Music* 34/3 (2016), 365–401.

Paxton, Robert, O., *The Anatomy of Fascism* (London, 2005).

Pedelty, Mark, *Musical Ritual in Mexico City: From the Aztec to NAFTA* (Austin, TX, 2004).

Pedelty, Mark, and Kristine Weglarz, *Political Rock* (Abingdon, 2016).

Pederson, Sanna, 'Beethoven and Freedom: Historicizing the Political Connection', *Beethoven Forum* 12/1 (2006), 1–12.

Peddie, Ian (ed.), *Popular Music and Human Rights*, 2 vols. (Farnham, 2011).

(ed.), *The Resisting Muse: Popular Music and Social Protest* (Aldershot, 2006).

Pelosi, Francesco, *Plato on Music, Soul and Body*, trans. Sophie Henderson (Cambridge, 2010).

Pieslak, Jonathan, *Radicalism and Music: An Introduction to the Music Cultures of al-Qa'ida, Racist Skinheads, Christian-Affiliated Radicals, and Eco-Animal Rights Militants* (Middletown, CT, 2015).

Platoff, John, 'John Lennon, "Revolution," and the Politics of Musical Reception', *Journal of Musicology* 22/2 (2005), 241–67.

Plato, *Complete Works*, ed. John M. Cooper (Indianapolis, IN, 1997).

Quinn, Eithne, *Nuthin' but a 'G' Thang: The Culture and Commerce of Gangsta Rap* (New York, 2010).

Rancière, Jacques, *Aesthetics and Its Discontents*, trans. Steve Corcoran (Cambridge, 2009).

Disagreement: Politics and Philosophy (1995), trans. Julie Rose (Minneapolis, MN, 1999).

Dissensus: On Politics and Aesthetics, ed. and trans. Steve Corcoran (London, 2010).

The Emancipated Spectator, trans. Gregory Elliott (London, 2011).

The Politics of Aesthetics: The Distribution of the Sensible, trans. Gabriel Rockhill (London, 2004).

Randall, Annie J. (ed.), *Music, Power, and Politics* (New York, 2005).

Raunig, Gerald, *Art and Revolution: Transversal Activism in the Long Twentieth Century*, trans. Aileen Derieg (Cambridge, MA, 2007).

'Singers, Cynics, Molecular Mice: The Political Aesthetics of Contemporary Activism', *Theory, Culture & Society* 31/7–8 (2014), 67–80.

Reed, T. V., *The Art of Protest: Culture and Activism from the Civil Rights Movement to the Streets of Seattle* (Minneapolis, MN, 2005).

Rehmann, Jan, *Theories of Ideology: The Powers of Alienation and Subjection* (Leiden, 2013).

Reuben, Federico, 'Imaginary Musical Radicalism and the Entanglement of Music and Emancipatory Politics', *Contemporary Music Review* 34/2–3 (2015), 232–46.

Reuss, Richard A., with JoAnne C. Reuss, *American Folk Music and Left-Wing Politics, 1927–1957* (Lanham, MD, 2000).

Richardson, Jeanita W., and Kim A. Scott, 'Rap Music and Its Violent Progeny: America's Culture of Violence in Context', *Journal of Negro Education* 71/3 (2002), 175–92.

Roberts, John, *Revolutionary Time and the Avant-Garde* (London, 2015).

Rockhill, Gabriel, *Radical History and the Politics of Art* (New York, 2014).

Roessner, Jeffrey, 'That Was Now, This Is Then: Recycling Sixties Style in Post-9/11 Music', in *The Politics of Post-9/11 Music: Sound, Trauma, and the Music Industry in the Time of Terror*, ed. Joseph P. Fisher and Brian Flota (Farnham, 2011), 115–28.

Rojas, Eunice, and Lindsay Michie (eds.), *Sounds of Resistance: The Role of Music in Multicultural Activism*, 2 vols. (Santa Barbara, CA, 2013).

Rosen, Michael, *On Voluntary Servitude: False Consciousness and the Theory of Ideology* (Cambridge, MA, 1996).

Roy, William G., *Reds, Whites, and Blues: Social Movements, Folk Music, and Race in the United States* (Princeton, NJ, 2010).

Samson, Jim, 'Propaganda', in *Aesthetics of Music: Musicological Perspectives*, ed. Stephen Downes (New York, 2014), 259–75.

Sartwell, Crispin, *Political Aesthetics* (Ithaca, NY, 2010).

Schedler, Jan, and Alexander Häusler (eds.), *Autonome Nationalisten: Neonazismus in Bewegung* (Wiesbaden, 2011).

Schmitt, Carl, *The Concept of the Political* (1932), 2nd edn., trans. and ed. George Schwab (Chicago, IL, 2007)

Schoening, Benjamin S., and Eric T. Kasper, *Don't Stop Thinking about the Music: The Politics of Songs and Musicians in Presidential Campaigns* (Lanham, MD, 2012).

Shank, Barry, 'The Political Agency of Musical Beauty', *American Quarterly* 63/3 (2011), 831–55.
    The Political Force of Musical Beauty (Durham, NC, 2014).

Shaw, Dougal, 'Nothing but Propaganda? Historians and the Study of Early Modern Ritual', *Cultural and Social History* 1 (2004), 139–58.

Shaw, George Bernard, *The Perfect Wagnerite: A Commentary on the Niblung's Ring*, 3rd edn. (New York, 1909).

Shekhovtsov, Anton, and Paul Jackson (eds.), *White Power Music: Scenes of Extreme-Right Cultural Resistance* (Northampton, 2012).

Shreffler, Anne C., 'Berlin Walls: Dahlhaus, Knepler, and Ideologies of Music History', *Journal of Musicology* 20/4 (2003), 498–525.

Shukaitis, Stevphen, 'Fascists as Much as Painters: Imagination, Overidentification, and Strategies of Intervention', *Sociological Review* 59/3 (2011), 597–615.

Simonett, Helena, '*Los gallos valientes*: Examining Violence in Mexican Popular Music', *Trans: Revista Transcultural de Música* 10 (2006), www.sibetrans.com/trans/articulo/149/los-gallos-valientesexamining-violence-in-mexican-popular-music.

Snow, David A., Sarah A. Soule and Hanspeter Kriesi (eds.), *The Blackwell Companion to Social Movements* (Oxford, 2004).

Sperling, Valerie, *Sex, Politics, and Putin: Political Legitimacy in Russia* (Oxford, 2015).

Sponheuer, Bernd, 'Angewandte Instrumentalmusik: Hanns Eislers Kleine Sinfonie op. 29', *Die Musikforschung* 32/3 (1979), 258–73.

Spotts, Frederic, *Hitler and the Power of Aesthetics*, 2nd edn. (Woodstock, NY, 2009).

Stanley, Jason, *How Propaganda Works* (Princeton, NJ, 2015).

Steinholt, Yngvar B., 'Kitten Heresy: Lost Contexts of Pussy Riot's Punk Prayer,' *Popular Music and Society* 36/1 (2013), 120–4.

Street, John, *Music and Politics* (Cambridge, 2012).

Strötgen, Stefan, '"I Compose the Party Rally . . .": The Role of Music in Leni Riefenstahl's Triumph of the Will', *Music and Politics* 2/1 (2008), http://dx.doi.org/10.3998/mp.9460447.0002.101.

Stroud, Joe, 'The Importance of Music to Anders Behring Breivik', *Journal of Terrorism Research* 4/1 (2013), http://ojs.st-andrews.ac.uk/index.php/jtr/article/view/620/537.

Subotnik, Rose Rosengard, *Developing Variations: Style and Ideology in Western Music* (Minneapolis, MN, 1991).

Sullivan, Denise, *Keep on Pushing: Black Power Music from Blues to Hip-Hop* (Chicago, IL, 2011).

Taruskin, Richard, *The Danger of Music and Other Anti-Utopian Essays* (Berkeley, CA, 2009).

 The Oxford History of Western Music, 5 vols. (New York, 2005).

Thompson, Marie, and Ian Biddle (eds.), *Sound, Music, Affect: Theorizing Sonic Experience* (London, 2013).

Thornton, Sarah, *Club Cultures: Music, Media and Subcultural Capital* (Cambridge, 1995).

Tochka, Nicholas, 'Pussy Riot, Freedom of Expression, and Popular Music Studies after the Cold War', *Popular Music* 32/2 (2013), 303–11.

Tomlinson, Gary, *The Singing of the New World: Indigenous Voice in the Era of European Contact* (Cambridge, 2009).

Valassopoulos, Anastasia, and Dalia Said Mostafa, 'Popular Protest Music and the Egyptian Revolution', *Popular Music and Society* 37 (2014), 638–59.

Vighi, Fabio, and Heiko Feldner, *Žižek: Beyond Foucault* (Basingstoke, 2007).

Vinthagen, Stellan, and Anna Johansson, '"Everyday Resistance: Exploration of a Concept and Its Theories', *Resistance Studies Magazine* 1 (2013), 1–46.

Volcler, Juliette, *Extremely Loud: Sound as a Weapon*, trans. Carol Volk (New York, 2013).

Weiner, Marc A., *Richard Wagner and the Anti-Semitic Imagination* (Lincoln, NE, 1995).

Werbner, Pnina, Martin Webb, and Kathryn Spellman-Poots (eds.), *The Political Aesthetics of Global Protest: The Arab Spring and Beyond* (Edinburgh, 2014).

Williams, Raymond, *Culture and Materialism: Selected Essays* (London, 2005).

 Keywords: A Vocabulary of Culture and Society (London, 1983).

Žižek, Slavoj, *First as Tragedy, Then as Farce* (London, 2009).

In Defence of Lost Causes (London, 2008).
Living in the End Times (London, 2011)
(ed.), *Mapping Ideology* (London, 1994).
The Ticklish Subject: The Absent Centre of Political Ontology (London, 1999).
The Universal Exception, ed. Rex Butler and Scott Stephens (London, 2006).
Violence: Six Sideways Reflections (New York, 2008).

Index

absolute music, 35, 71, 77, 95

absolutism, 113

acclamation, politics of, 121

   and contemporary politics, 123–6

   and royal ceremonies, 119–22

activism

   academic, 199

   contemporary art as, 35, 63

Adamson, John, 118

Adorno, Theodor W., 25, 33, 84, 93–4, 97–101, 105, 163

   and the avant-garde, 99, 165

   and the culture industry, 99–100

   and negation, 164–6

   'On the Social Situation of Music', 70, 88–92, 98–9

aesthetic regime, 82–3

aestheticization of politics, 29, 179–80

aesthetics, politics of, 29, 92

   vs aesthetics of politics, 29–30, 32

affect, 18–22, 133

affirmation, 94, 99, 111, 116–17, 164, *See also* ideology

Afghanistan, 49–50

Afrobeat, 141

Agamben, Giorgio, 119, 121, 123, 125, 179

agency, 23–8, 34, 90, 147, 161

   vs structure, 17, 59, 65, 68, 73, 75

Agharta (band), 191, 195

Ahmadinejad, Mahmoud, 49

Alan Parsons Project, 126

Albarn, Damon, 51

Alexander I, tsar of Russia, 113, 116–17

alienation, 179, 197

   of labour, 17, 81, 167, 170

allegory, political, 147–8, 151, 153

Allende, Salvador, 48

Alternative für Deutschland (AfD), 196

Althusser, Louis, 16, 73, 101–4, 225

Amenta, Conrad, 144

anarchism, 4, 53, 61, 155

Anderson, Benedict, 121

Andropov, Yurii, 49

Angelow, Jürgen, 115

antagonism, 9–10, 199

anti-capitalism, 4, 53, 187–8

anti-globalization movement, 45, 128, 187, 192

anti-Semitism, 105, 189, 191

anti-war movement, 138

Arab Spring, 48, 62–4

Arendt, Hannah, 40

Argentina, 13

Arische Kämpfe (band), 189

Arisches Blut (band), 188

Aristotle, 6, 179

art

   autonomous vs political, 29, 33–5, 83–4, 86, 152

   end of, 83

   engaged, 34

   free vs applied, 34, 87, 109

   vs non-art, 34

   service, 34, 84

Attali, Jacques, 42–3, 78–81

Australia, 45

Austria, 113, 116

autonomous activism, 187

autonomy

   of art, 25, 29, 31, 71, 74, 76, 84, 99, 179

   of the individual, 7, 18, 31

avant-garde

   contemporary, 36, 162

   historical, 54, 90

Averill, Gage, 13

Bach, Johann Sebastian, 117

Badiou, Alain, 11–12, 17, 35

Baez, Joan, 144

Baily, John, 49

Bakunin, Michael, 155

Bal, Mieke, 28, 34

Bali, 118

Balibar, Étienne, 96, 106, 173, 177

bare life, 6, 179

Barnes, Julian, 158

Barrett, Michèle, 38, 60